PAUL ROBESON: THE GREAT FORERUNNER

Paul Robeson:

THE GREAT FORERUNNER

The Editors of *Freedomways*

ILLUSTRATED WITH PHOTOGRAPHS

DODD, MEAD & COMPANY, NEW YORK

Copyright © 1965, 1971, 1973, 1975, 1976, 1978
by Freedomways Associates, Inc.

Printed in the United States of America

1 2 3 4 5 6 7 8 9 10

Library of Congress Cataloging in Publication Data

Main entry under title:

Paul Robeson, the great forerunner.

   Bibliography: p.
   Includes index
   1. Robeson, Paul, 1898–1976—Addresses, essays,
lectures. 2. Afro-Americans—Biography—Addresses,
essays, lectures. I. Freedomways.
E185.97.R6475   790.2′092′4 [B]   78-7917
ISBN 0-396-07545-2

Oppression has kept us on the bottom rungs of the ladder, and even with the removal of all barriers, we will still have a long way to climb in order to catch up with the general standard of living. But the equal *place* to which we aspire cannot be reached without the equal *rights* we demand, and so the winning of those rights is not a maximum fulfillment but a minimum necessity, and we cannot settle for less.

—Paul Robeson in
Here I Stand

Contents

TRIBUTES IN PROSE

Photographs follow page 212.

PART I

THE GREAT
FORERUNNER

Paul Robeson: Black Warrior

BY PAUL ROBESON, JR.

At the end of his life my father lived in retirement, and his health did not permit him to resume his public life in any way. This, to some degree, obscured the fact that the ruling class of America and the media it controls continued their longstanding policy of trying to make Paul Robeson an "un-person." Not only had a web of lies and falsifications been institutionalized, but his entire record of achivement had been all but eradicated in the United States. This process had been so thorough that most people, including the vast majority of those involved in Black Studies programs, did not even know that the facts about Paul Robeson had been removed from available reference material.

The purpose of this curtain of silence was to keep the young from knowing and to discourage those who did know from saying.

The historical record clearly and indisputably shows three essential things: first, my father's achievements in several different fields were extraordinary taken individually; taken all together they were unprecedented. Second, he challenged the racism of this country to its foundation and linked the liberation struggles of black people in America to those of all oppressed peoples everywhere. In the Black Warrior tradition Paul Robeson told it like it was—told it for the whole world to hear. Third, he withstood the full weight of a massive campaign by the government and the mass media of the white establishment to silence him.

It is vital to mention my father's achievements because they have been so deliberately hidden from view. He won a scholarship to Rutgers University, which he attended from 1915 to 1919 during one of the most racist periods of modern U.S. history, and was one of just two black students on campus throughout his four years. He won Phi Beta Kappa honors in his *junior* year, was valedictorian of his graduating class and a debating champion, and won thirteen varsity letters in four sports. (He won election to the Cap and Skull Honorary Society, but, ironically, was not welcome to travel with the Glee Club because of the social events that followed its performances.)

He was also one of the greatest football players of all time. My father was named by Walter Camp, the most famous of All-America team selectors, as first team All-American end for two years—1917 and 1918. (He was also named on *all* the "consensus" All-America teams.) In choosing Robeson in 1917, Walter Camp said: *"There never has been a more serviceable end, both in attack and defense, than Robeson."* [1] My father stood 6'3" tall, weighed 217 pounds and was very fast. He was a great pass receiver and a great offensive blocker who was moved to tackle in short-yardage situations. On defense he was considered to be the best middle linebacker of his era.[2]

In spite of these credentials, my father was the *only* two-time Walter Camp All-American who is *not* in the College Football Hall of Fame. Not only that, the Hall of Fame is located at Rutgers, and Paul Robeson was the *first* Rutgers player to win All-America honors. It is also a fact that the book *College Football,* published in 1950 by Murray and Co. and labeled "the most complete record compiled on college football," listed a *ten-man* All-America team for 1918, the only ten-man team in All-America history. The missing man was an end named Paul Robeson. Those who run the Hall of Fame have excluded Robeson from it because they uphold the shameful tradition of the most reactionary segment of the U.S. ruling class.

Most Americans do not know that Paul Robeson was the leading concert singer in the world for most of the 1930s and 1940s and that his singing career spanned thirty-five years from 1925 through 1960, winning him unprecedented worldwide popularity. My father began his singing career with a concert in New York in 1925. It was historic because it was the first concert ever given that consisted solely of Negro music. Together with Lawrence Brown, his accompanist and a great musician in his own right, my father went on to bring the Negro spiritual as an art form to a foremost position on the concert stages of the world. Of that first concert the music critic of the *New York World* wrote:

All those who listened last night to the first concert in this country made up entirely of Negro music . . . may have been present at a turning point, one of those thin points of time in which a star is born and not yet visible—the first appearance of this folk wealth to be made without deference or apology. Paul Robeson's voice is difficult to describe. It is a voice in which deep bells ring. . . .

The New York Times critic wrote:

His Negro Spirituals have the ring of the revivalist, they hold in them a world of religious experience; it is their cry from the depths, this universal humanism, that touches the heart. . . . Mr. Robeson's gift is to make them tell in every line, and that not by any outward stress, but by an overwhelming inward conviction. Sung by one man, they voiced the sorrow and hopes of a people.

Thirty-three years later, a noted English music commentator, Benny Green, said:

. . . Running like a fine thread through the texture of the times is Paul Robeson's incomparable voice. . . . I accept all over again the immutability of Robeson as a great artist, and am reminded that the late Alexander Woollcott's comparison of Robeson with the redwood trees of California was particularly appropriate. . . . It is apparent to us all . . . that Robeson is one of the archetypal artists of the 20th Century. He is one of those all too rare people who can, through some miraculous alchemy of the spirit, reach out, and within the scope of a single gesture or phrase, touch the hearts of both the galleryites looking for a good time and the intellectuals probing for The Message. When he sings I hear the unsullied expression of the human spirit.

In short, if *anyone* were to list the ten greatest concert singers of the twentieth century, Paul Robeson would *have* to be among them. But go to any major bookstore or library and pick out any book on concert singers published after 1949, and you will find an amazing thing. Either Paul Robeson's name is not in the index at all, or you will find it once. If you look up the page, he is either mentioned in passing in one sentence with a lot of other names, or he is referred to in a footnote. This is true even in books written by or about Negroes, which are widely used in Black Studies programs. For instance, the book *Famous Negro Music Makers* by

Langston Hughes does not even list my father's name in the index!

Let us move on to the theatre. My father starred in over ten major plays in the U.S. and in England. They included the role of Crown in *Porgy and Bess*; a sensational success singing "Ol' Man River" in the musical *Show Boat;* and three plays by Eugene O'Neill: *All God's Chillun, The Hairy Ape,* and *The Emperor Jones.* His performance in the last-named play was considered to be a classic one by American, English and German drama critics. His crowning achievement in the theatre was his portrayal of Othello in the 1943-44 Broadway production. It was *the definitive* Othello of the modern theatre. It ran for 296 performances to set an all-time record for *any* Shakespearean play on Broadway (almost *double* the previous record of 158 performances). He received the Donaldson Award for the best acting performance in 1944, and the Gold Medal for the best diction in American theatre presented by the American Academy of Arts and Sciences. (Since the creation of the latter award in 1924 only nine people had received it.)

This was unprecedented for a black actor in those times. But, once more, any reference book published after 1949 has only the barest mention of Paul Robeson's acting career. For instance, Brooks Atkinson's book *Broadway,* supposedly a history of American theatre in the twentieth century, has only one sentence on Paul Robeson stating that his 1943-44 Othello was poorly acted— period. A similar book says only that my father played Othello in 1943-44 and was "overshadowed by Jose Ferrer's Iago." The daily and Sunday *New York Times* reviewed Moses Gunn's Othello and discussed other black actors who had played the role. Nowhere was Paul Robeson's name mentioned, although he played Othello with great success at the famous Savoy Theatre in London in 1930, and at the Shakespeare Memorial Theatre in Stratford-on-Avon, England, in 1959, in addition to the record Broadway run.

As I write this, I am looking at an inscription to my father which O'Neill wrote in a book of his plays:

> In gratitude to Paul Robeson in whose interpretation of "Brutus Jones" I have found the most complete satisfaction an

author can get—that of seeing his creation born into flesh and blood!

Again with gratitude and friendship,

Eugene O'Neill, July '25.

But if you refer to the books on the theatre used in Black Studies courses you will find the usual pattern of omission.

Then there are all the films in which my father starred. In 1924 he acted in *Body and Soul* produced by a black filmmaker named Oscar Micheaux for black audiences. In 1930 he starred in an experimental film titled *Borderline* which was far beyond its time in both film technique and its portrayal of black people. Then, from 1932 through 1939 he starred in eight major movies in England and the U.S.—most unusual for a black film actor in any times. Once again, you will look in vain for most of this information even in books about Negro film actors. You will also *not* find the important fact that in 1939 Paul Robeson retired from the film industry while at the peak of his career and denounced Hollywood. He said:

I thought I could do something for the Negro race in films— show the truth about them and about other people too. I used to do my part and go away feeling satisfied—thought everything was O.K. Well it wasn't. The industry is not prepared to permit me to portray the life or express the living interests, hopes and aspirations of the struggling people from whom I come. . . . You bet they will never let me play a part in a film in which a Negro is on top.

Today, most newsreel and film footage on Paul Robeson in these United States has vanished—it has been confiscated. Most of the newsreel footage which is available has had the sound track erased from it. Because the sight of Paul Robeson is so impressive, it is certainly no accident that television has always been the medium that imposed the most ironclad ban on him.

It is also not generally known that my father continued to develop the talent for scholarship that he demonstrated in college. He mastered more than twenty languages and taught himself not only to speak but also to write Chinese. He was always studying something wherever he went; whatever he was doing he had some books with him. Paul Robeson will go down in history as, among other things, one of the most intelligent personalities of this century. It is precisely this intelligence and knowledge that led him to be so far ahead of his time—a man with a great mind to go with a great heart.

Let us now deal with the reasons for this conspiracy of silence and distortion.

First my father refused to let his extraordinary success be used to explain away the oppression of millions of black Americans. More that that—he used his success and his immense prestige and talents as weapons in an all-out struggle against that oppression. He said:

> The artist must elect to fight for Freedom or for Slavery. I have made my choice.

Second, he *acted* on those convictions. He put his career, and at times his very life, on the line. In 1946 Paul Robeson led a delegation of the "American Crusade to End Lynching" to see President Truman to demand that he sponsor antilynch legislation. When Truman refused to do so my father told him flatly that if the federal government did not stop lynching, then *Negroes themselves* would stop them. He also said that the temper of the Negro people, and especially of Negro World War II veterans, had so changed that:

> . . . if they keep on being murdered by lynchers, there will be several national emergencies which will require federal intervention.

On another occasion a reporter asked my father if he thought Negroes should be patient and turn the other cheek when they were brutalized. My father replied:

> If someone hit me on one cheek, I'd try to tear his head off before he could hit me on the other one.

In Paris in 1949, at the height of the "Cold War," he challenged the idea that black men should fight a war to oppress others on behalf of their own oppressors. His exact words were:

> It is unthinkable that American Negroes could go to war on behalf of those who have oppressed them for generations against the Soviet Union which in one generation has raised our people to full human dignity.

It is important to note that the "establishment" led by the government itself (national, state and local) branded Paul Robeson "enemy No. 1" and declared open season on him. The racist, right-wing and "patriotic" organizations were openly encouraged to go after him. An executive order was read to my father at the Canadian border when he tried to enter Canada for a concert. That order forbade him to set foot outside the continental United States on penalty of five years in prison and a five thousand dollar fine. It added that U.S. border personnel had been instructed to apprehend him by *any means necessary* if he tried to cross any border—an obvious threat that he might be *shot* if he tried to leave the United States.

In 1947, at a hearing of the House Committee on Un-American Activities, a congressman from California asked a star anti-Communist witness how he identified Communists. The witness replied that among the surest criteria for identifying someone as a Communist were applauding at a Paul Robeson concert, or owning a Paul Robeson recording. The record shows that the witness was Adolphe Menjou—a prominent film actor; the congressman was none other than Richard Milhous Nixon.

The so-called "Peekskill riots" were a direct result of a nationwide campaign by the government and the mass media against Paul Robeson, specifically because of his Paris statement. The "riot" was in fact a *police riot,* because two thousand state and local police officers who were assigned to "keep order" joined the rioters in attacking those who came peacefully to attend a Paul Robeson concert. After that concert halls and public meeting halls were closed to him, and any organization that sponsored a Paul Robeson appearance was threatened. At a civil liberties meeting at Madison Square Garden in 1949 my father gave a clear answer to the campaign against his right to speak out:

> Let us be clear about this—we stand in the very forefront of this struggle by reason of the fact that the most powerful enemies of progressive mankind are closest to us. . . . These so-called defenders of the American way of life haunt the homes of every decent thinking intellectual—they tell us what to read, what to discover, and they have descended to corrupting every part of our constitutional system—the executive, the legislative, and now the judicial—to

serve their dirty anti-democratic and anti-humanistic ends. . . . It's about time we in America caught on. We chiefly are being hurt. We are the only ones hysterical, and the more hysterical we get, the more freedoms we lose. Yes, reaction is dangerous, deadly dangerous, but it's panting for breath. It's time we came to our senses and stepped into it, not away from it; forward, not backward; for we could deliver decisive after decisive blow. . . .

Paul Robeson continued to sing and speak in spite of all the repression. He said: "I will not retreat one thousandth part of one inch." He survived because some very courageous trade unionists and white radicals stood with him and, most important, because the rank-and-file people in black communities all over the country decided that Paul Robeson was not going to be obliterated by "the Man." And they protected him—bringing along plenty of "the means necessary" when it was called for.

My father's passport was revoked in 1950 and it was not reinstated until 1958—eight years later—after a long worldwide campaign and a Supreme Court ruling. It is very significant that the State Department's brief in the case said the following:

> . . . Furthermore even if the complaint had alleged . . . that the passport was cancelled solely because of the applicant's recognized status as spokesman for large sections of Negro Americans, we submit that this would not amount to an abuse of discretion in view of the appellant's frank admission that he has been for years extremely active politically on behalf of the colonial people of Africa. . . .

In commenting on this, my father said in his book, *Here I Stand:*

> Yes, I have been active for African freedom for many years, and I will never cease that activity no matter what the State Department or anybody else thinks about it. This is my right—as a Negro, as an American, as a man!

In 1958 my father won his passport and went abroad to fulfill concert, television and theatre engagements all over Europe, and in Australia and New Zealand. He returned home in 1963 in poor health and then retired. But the same media who were responsible for the conspiracy of silence about Paul Robeson sought to spread falsehoods about him. All of them spread the colossal falsehood that my father was a bitter, tragic figure who had changed his mind about his political stands. Nothing could be further from the truth. In 1964 my father issued a press release in which he said:

> The power of Negro action of which I wrote in my book *Here I Stand* in 1958 has changed from an idea to reality. . . . The concept of mass militancy, or mass *action,* is no longer deemed "too radical" in Negro life.
>
> The idea that Black Americans should see that the fight for a "Free World" begins at home—a shocking idea when expressed in Paris in 1949—is no longer challenged in our communities. The "Hot Summer" of struggle for equal rights has replaced the "Cold War" abroad as the concern of our people. . . .

The books on Paul Robeson available in the U.S. are full of misinformation and distortion. *Paul Robeson: The American Othello,* by Edwin P. Hoyt, presents a totally false image of my father as a man. It reminds me of William Styron's *Confessions of Nat Turner*—a white liberal's distortion of the personality and motivation of a black radical. The biggest misstatements of fact in Hoyt's book are his assertions that my father did not think for himself, that he was "politically naive," and that he was used by others because of his lack of understanding. This is absurd. The fact is that intellectual giants the world over respected Paul Robeson's sharp mind and great insight. They liked to talk philosophy and politics with him and were interested in what he had to say and what he thought.

Hoyt says:

> Paul was not led quickly into the arms of the Communist Party. It was the Marxist unions and the Marxist organizations that wooed him. There were equal opportunity groups where Negroes were welcomed as full members, such as the United Auto Workers Union, but these unions did not make the fuss over Paul that the Communist-dominated unions did. From the Communist point of view this was simple good sense: Paul represented the Negro race. . . . Capturing him, the Communists would, they thought, develop the entree into Negro life in America that they had always sought and always failed to obtain.
>
> So the Communists set to work to convert Paul Robeson to their views, and their adherence to the USSR.

Now this is sheer invention by Hoyt, as the following quote of Paul Robeson's clearly demonstrates (*Here I Stand,* pp. 46-48):

> My views concerning the Soviet Union and my warm feelings of friendship for the peoples of that land, and the friendly sentiments which they have often expressed toward me, have been pictured as something quite sinister by Washington officials and other spokesmen for the dominant white group in our country. It has been alleged that I am part of some kind of "international conspiracy."
>
> The truth is: I am not and never have been involved in any international conspiracy or any other kind, and do not know anyone who is. It should be plain to everybody—and especially to Negroes—that if the government officials had a shred of evidence to back up that charge, you can bet your last dollar that they would have tried to put me under their jail! But they have no such evidence, because that charge is a lie. . . .
>
> . . . In 1946, at a legislative hearing in California, I testified under oath that I was not a member of the Communist Party, but since that I have refused to give testimony or to sign affidavits as to that fact. There is no mystery involved in this refusal. . . . I have made it a matter of principle, as many others have done, to refuse to comply with any demand of legislative committees or departmental officials that infringes upon the Constitutional rights of all Americans. . . .
>
> . . . In the wide acquaintanceships that I have had over the years I have never hesitated to associate with people who hold non-conformist or radical views, and this has been true since my earliest days in the American theatre where I first met people who challenged the traditional order of things. And so today, Benjamin J. Davis is a dear friend of mine and I have always been pleased to say so; and he has been for many years a leader of the Communist Party of this country.

It is also noteworthy that *The New York Times* review of Hoyt's book said (Nov. 11, 1967):

> . . . After his [Robeson's] tour-de-force interpretation of Othello . . . there followed . . . his long exile in the Soviet Union. . . .

Here is another *big* lie—Paul Robeson could hardly have exiled himself to the Soviet Union, since the U.S. government canceled his passport from 1950 to 1958 so he couldn't travel *anywhere!* It is quite true that during his first visit to the Soviet Union my father said:

> Here for the first time in my life I walk in full human dignity. You can imagine what that means to me as a Negro.

But in answer to American critics who suggested that because he has praised Russia he should leave the United States and live in Russia he said:

> My father was a slave, and my people died to build this country, and I am going to stay and have a piece of it just like you. And no fascist-minded people will drive me from it. Is that clear?

It also happens to be a fact that Robeson visited the USSR a number of times but never lived there. His headquarters and home in Europe were always in London.

The Crisis of the Negro Intellectual, by Harold Cruse, devotes a chapter to Paul Robeson. I shall discuss two points in this chapter in some detail because the book is used in so many Black Studies courses, because the chapter is so full of outright falsehoods and distortions, and because it aids and abets the white establishment in hiding the facts about my father from today's black youth.

First, Cruse states (p. 286):

> . . . Robeson's active career embraced the 1920's, 1930's and the 1940's. . . . Something happened during those three decades that has to explain why Robeson failed during the crucial 1950's and was, therefore, unable to personify a real link with the new Negro movement of the 1960's. . . .

There is a monstrous omission here—no mention even of the fact that from 1949 to 1958 the establishment went all out to obliterate Paul Robeson, let alone the reasons why it did so. On the bottom of page 290 there is a footnote that says:

> August, 1949 was also the month of the disastrous anti-communist riots at Peekskill, New York, where Paul Robeson held open-air concerts. . . .

Even in his footnote, Cruse fails to mention the fact that the "riots" were not merely anti-Communist. They were specifically anti-Black, not just in the slogans that were used but in the vicious beatings of any black person who was even seen in the vicinity of the concert grounds. He also fails to mention the *specifically fascist* slogans of the rioters; their vicious anti-Semitic epithets, their explicit support of Hitler's anti-Semitism and anti-Communism, and their slogan "Wake up America" which was reminiscent of the Nazi slogan of the thirties—"Germany awake." That is a lot to leave out, even from a footnote. Further on, Cruse says (p. 288):

> There was involved in Robeson's career a unique problem in the dualism of illusion and reality. The reality was that Robeson was fundamentally an integrationist for whom the ideology of the political leftwing became a rationale for racial integration. This integration had to be both national and international . . . essentially all those leftwing ingredients of the American melting pot gambit carried over onto the international scene. . . .

In his book *Here I Stand* (pp. 56-57), he spoke directly to this point; it is noteworthy that Cruse chose not to quote Paul Robeson's own words on this subject published seven years earlier:

> . . . I learned that the essential character of a nation is determined not by the upper classes, but by the common people, and that the common people of all nations are truly brothers in the great family of mankind. . . . And even as I grew to feel more Negro in spirit, or African as I put it then, I also came to feel a sense of oneness with the white working people whom I came to know and love.
>
> This belief in the oneness of humankind, about which I have often spoken in concerts and elsewhere, has existed within me side by side with my deep attachment to the cause of my own race. Some people have seen a contradiction in this duality. . . . I do not think, however, that my sentiments are contradictory . . . I learned that there truly is a kinship among us all, a basis for mutual respect and brotherly love.

At the same time, in speaking of the criteria for Negro political leadership he said (*Here I Stand*, p. 111):

> Dedication to the Negro people's welfare is one side of a coin: the other side is *independence*. Effective Negro leadership must rely upon and be responsive to no other control than the will of their people. We have allies—important allies—among our white fellow-citizens, and we must ever seek to draw them closer to us

and to gain many more. But the Negro people's movement must be led by Negroes, not only in terms of title and position but in reality. Good advice is good no matter what the source and help is needed and appreciated from wherever it comes, but Negro action cannot be decisive if the advisers and helpers hold the guiding reins. For no matter how well-meaning other groups may be, the fact is our interests are secondary at best with them.

The unique and most important thing about my father was his personality—the man himself. C. L. R. James, in an article in *Black World* (November, 1970), wrote:

> To have spent half an hour in his company or to have 10 minutes alone with him was something that you remembered for days, and if I had to sum up his personality in one word, or rather two, I would say it was the combination of immense power and great gentleness.

It was this amazing quality of naturally embodying such seemingly contradictory traits that made it possible for my father to establish such intimate communication with audiences under conditions ranging from a living room to a football stadium. It enabled him to express overwhelming emotion and great compassion, while at other times he was capable of careful and objective analysis. He always weighed important matters, examined them from all angles, tested his ground, and took his time before pursuing a certain course. But once he made up his mind and was ready to move, he did so with enormous energy and total commitment. He could speak nonstop with an almost hypnotic force, and yet he could be a thoughtful listener, sometimes sitting attentively for hours with just an occasional searching question. He could respond with utmost spontaneity and yet at other times impose on himself the utmost self-discipline and reserve. He could be impatient and irritable, and yet draw upon a seemingly infinite reserve of patience when it was really necessary.

My father's approach to politics had a very personal style too. He was certainly *political*, but he never was, nor would he allow himself to become, a politician. He would never run for office nor be a political leader of a movement. He never considered himself in these roles—in fact he believed that accepting them would violate his own personal integrity, and that is something he never did under any circumstances. It is therefore simply academic to argue whether he could have or should have attempted to play either one of these roles at one time or another. They were not "his thing." He resolved the conflict between *artist* and *politician* quite simply—he was *always* an artist and *never* a politician.

My father was one of the very few people who always cast light and warmth on those near to him—never a shadow. It is because of his personal qualities that one had to *see* and hear him in order to appreciate him in his full dimension.

The sight and sound of this black warrior in his prime was truly something no one would ever forget.

Paul Robeson: His Political Legacy to the Twentieth-Century Gladiator

BY HARRY EDWARDS

It was not until the late 1960s and the revolts in both the domestic and international sports arenas that black athletes achieved even limited amelioration of their condition as twentieth-century gladiators in the service of capitalistic America. But long before the mass boycotts, demonstrations and strikes by Afro-American athletes in defense of fundamental principles, political ideas and cultural integrity, long before the courageous stands of Tommie Smith and John Carlos, long before Muhammad Ali, long before even the legendary Jackie Robinson, *there stood Paul Robeson.*

Born the youngest child of an escaped slave later turned minister, Paul Robeson very early in life internalized one of his father's ruling passions—the conviction that personal integrity was inseparable from the quest for maximum human fulfillment; that its very essence was a relentless struggle for the highest and richest development of one's full potential. In the autobiographical prologue to his political manifesto, entitled *Here I Stand,* Robeson discusses in detail the childhood and adolescent milieus within which the major role-themes of his life took root. However, here, the only direct mention of his early sports career informs us of a recurrent and perhaps prophetic observation:

> . . . The cheers of my fellow students as I played fullback on the football team—"Let Paul carry the ball! Yay—Paul"—seemed to curdle the very soul of Dr. Ackerman . . . [my] high school principal. . . .

The character of this, apparently Robeson's most deeply imprinted perceptual experience as a black athlete at an integrated high school, was prophetic on two counts. First it foretold the situation later to confront him personally as an athlete in the

17

much more competitive and then still largely segregated world of major collegiate sports. Second, the adolescent Robeson had discerned in his sports experience an irreconcilable dilemma permeating the whole of American life: to wit, how could white America continue its professed commitment to democracy through the competitive process while simultaneously holding fast to its racist presumptions of innate black spiritual, intellectual and physical inferiority in the face of mounting evidence to the contrary. Confronted with the undeniable equality—indeed, if not superiority—of performance by Afro-Americans such as Paul Robeson and others, it was perhaps inevitable that the more incorrigible racists in white America would resort to the irrational in their efforts to defend warped tradition against those Blacks who had the unmitigated temerity to excel in the integrated competitive situation.

Robeson was only the third Afro-American to attend Rutgers since its founding in 1766, and the only Black at the school in 1915. When he entered the college, the football team was already training at nearby Eatontown in preparation for a game with Princeton. Coach George Foster Sanford had already received word of Robeson's presence on campus and had some ideas of his boundless athletic potential. He had also received word, however, that if Robeson came to Eatontown to join the team, at least half of the thirty-man squad had pledged to rebel and go home "rather than play with a Negro." Not until the Rutgers team had been humbled by a ten to zero defeat at the hands of Princeton was Robeson allowed to join the squad.

Ralph White, a member of that 1915 Rutgers football team, later recalled that Coach Sanford had gathered the team together to inform them in advance that "a Negro was coming out for football." Their reaction: "Send him out—we'll kill him." And by all available accounts, they did not fail to kill him for lack of effort. For there were those on the team who were determined that Robeson, by whatever measures necessary, should be taught "his place," that the arrogance, the effrontery of a black man presuming even to compete as an equal among whites—much less portending to make a pivotal contribution toward improving the team—should not go unchallenged and unpunished.

Robeson subsequently recalled:

> On my first day of scrimmage, they set about making sure that
> I would not get on their team. One boy slugged me in the face and
> smashed my nose—an injury that has been a trouble to me as a
> singer ever since. And then as I was down, flat on my back, another
> boy got me with his knee. He just came over and dropped his knee
> into my upper body, dislocating my right shoulder.
>
> At the age of seventeen, that was tough going—a broken nose,
> a dislocated shoulder, a split lip, two swollen eyes and plenty of
> other cuts and bruises.

As a result of his injuries, Robeson was consigned to bed for a
week and a half. By the end of that period he was more determined than ever to play football at Rutgers; and his antagonists
on the team were seemingly just as determined that he would not.

Robeson's second scrimmage was a duplicate of the first, characterized as it was by surreptitious brutality and shameless un-
sportsmanlike conduct on the part of his white teammates.

The all-white varsity offensive team massed its plays against
Robeson's defensive line position, but he continued to make
tackle after tackle. Then on one play Robeson reports.

> I made a tackle and was on the ground, my right hand ex-
> tended beyond the pile-up and palm down. . . . A boy came over
> and stepped down hard on my hand. He meant to break the bones.
> The bones held, but the cleats of his shoes took every single one
> of the finger-nails off of my right hand.
>
> The next play again came right at my defensive end position;
> the whole backfield came at me. In rage, I swept out my arms . . .
> [and the] interference just seemed to fall down. Then there was
> only the ball carrier; I wanted to kill him . . . I actually had him
> up above my head . . . I was going to smash him so hard to the
> ground that . . . he'd break right in two.

It was at *that* moment that Paul Robeson made the first-team
varsity at Rutgers. The same coach who had stood silent as Robeson was being physically brutalized by his white teammates yelled
the first thing that came to his mind the moment the tables turned;
and what he yelled was, *"Robey, YOU'RE ON THE VARSITY!"*

The white challenges to the legitimacy of Robeson's participation did not end, however, either that season or with the lessons

taught his own teammates. He faced the racist behavior each time the Rutgers squad faced an opponent. Typical of such confrontations was one that occurred when Rutgers played West Virginia during the 1917 football season.

The West Virginia coach had requested that Sanford remove Robeson from the Rutgers lineup because, the coach is reported to have stated, "You know, some of my boys are from the South and they won't stand for a black man in there." Sanford refused and Rutgers played the favored West Virginia team with Robeson starting on both offense and defense.

By half-time, Robeson had so devastated both the offensive and defensive squads of the West Virginia team that its coach asserted,

> Any player who can take the beating that Robeson has taken from you, giving as good as he's gotten and without squealing, is not Black. *He's a white man!* Now go back out there and play like hell—and give him a break.

After the game, the West Virginia coach observed, "Why that colored boy's legs were so gashed and bruised that the skin peeled off when he removed his stockings."

It was inconceivable to a mind steeped in the racist ideology of white supremacy that a black man could perform as did Robeson in competition with and against whites. Thus, Robeson was simply defined as a *black* white man!

On road trips with his team, Rutgers' star football player lived in segregated lodging facilities and was compelled frequently to take his meals on the team bus. But Paul Robeson persevered. He saw himself as a *forerunner,* as a representative.

After that first scrimmage, he recalled,

> I didn't know whether I could take any more. . . . But my father . . . had impressed upon me that when I was out on a football field or in a classroom or anywhere else, I wasn't just there on my own. I was the representative of a lot of Negro boys who wanted to play football, who wanted to go to college; and as their representative, I had to show that I could take whatever they handed out. . . . This was part of our struggle. . . .

Paul Robeson, then, saw as a major component of his athletic role a representational responsibility. White America also came to view Robeson as a representative of Afro-Americans, but within a context that contrasted significantly with Robeson's own visions of his mission.

We must remember that between 1917 and the years subsequent to Robeson's matriculation at Rutgers, the Western world in general and the United States in particular came increasingly to be embroiled in a worldwide ideological struggle with Communist doctrine in its national political form. Because of the injustice permeating the situation of black people in this country, they were considered prime targets for Communist conversion by both domestic and foreign parties to the ideological struggle. In response to any such potentiality, America's establishment media launched, by the mid-1920s, a "Negroes-never-had-it-so-good-any-where-else-on-this-earth" campaign, a campaign that continued through the "Cold War" years of the 1950s and early 1960s and that continues today just beneath the rhetoric of China-Soviet-American "Détente" and "Peace Through Strength."

One major tactic in the U.S. effort to engender a rabid black anti-Communism was—and largely still is—to point up "successful Blacks" as evidence of the fruition of the American promise for all "who struggle for success regardless of race, creed, or color." Hence, a Paul Robeson who had excelled not *because of* but rather *despite* an unconscionably unjust and racist America, was now called upon to concur in a grotesque and deceitful hypocrisy. Thus the *Targum,* the Rutgers University newspaper and an organ whose files clearly documented the burden Robeson was by racist tradition compelled to bear over an extremely arduous road, carried an editorial following Robeson's graduation which stated in part:

> Individuals occasionally complain that there is no equality for members of the colored race in the United States. It is true that what is generally known as social equality has not been granted by the majority of whites. . . . But one fact which deserves consideration, and is too frequently neglected, is that equality does exist . . . for those colored men and women who struggle for success.
>
> Look at Paul Robeson, former All-American football player and one of four men tapped for the senior honor society when he was an undergraduate at Rutgers.

What other nation has a record of encouraging Negro achievement even remotely comparable to the record of the United States?

This is something to be emphasized through the length and
breadth of the land.

For when dictators of red radicalism and Black reaction really
concentrate on splitting America internally, they will no doubt
start by making fancy promises to the colored people—telling them
that they have been oppressed. . . .

And so before Robeson had reached his late twenties, the issue
between him and establishment America was already clearly
joined. While prevailing authority insisted upon a definition of
the black condition that validated the ideological *ideals* of American society, Paul Robeson had, by his eighteenth birthday, already determined that in the case of black people, the struggle
for success was not to be waged within bounds of anything even
approaching those ideals.

Following his matriculation at Rutgers, Robeson's eminence
grew and expanded into realms beyond athletics. The two-time
Walter Camp All-America football player and Phi Beta Kappa
Scholar achieved worldwide fame as actor, singer and orator. But
even as his fame grew and the capitalism-communism ideological
struggle intensified, there was no abatement of the racist humilia-
tions suffered by this great man.

During the years 1930 to 1950, Robeson increasingly spoke out
against injustice whatever its guise, and against domestic racism
in particular. As early as 1943, Robeson had led a delegation to
the office of baseball commissioner Kenesaw Landis and demanded
the removal of the color ban from baseball. In 1949, he had personally backed a move to prevent discrimination against black
athletes in areas where segregation was practiced. He publicly
worked for and later applauded an announcement by the president of Rutgers and its athletic director to the effect that no
future games would be scheduled or played by Rutgers against
any school not guaranteeing equal access to hotel accommodations
by all athletes regardless of their color.

Along with becoming increasingly more militant and outspoken about issues of racial injustice, Robeson had also developed some controversial opinions in the realm of international

political relations. Meanwhile, in every aspect of his career he found that doors previously open were now closed, and the sports institution too went about the sordid business of erasing all traces of Paul Robeson's brilliant athletic record from its annals. At least one football publication listed only a ten-man All-American team for 1918, rather than print Robeson's name. The Football Hall of Fame took a similar tack in failing to list him among its "Immortals" of the gridiron. Jimmie McDowell, the shrine's executive director at that time, explained, ". . . We take into account citizenship as well as accomplishments on the field." To this day, Paul Robeson still has not been inducted into the College Football Hall of Fame, *a fact made all the more shameful given that the shrine is located at Robeson's alma mater, Rutgers University!*

To its credit, the Black Athletes' Hall of Fame in April, 1976 did induct Paul Robeson, posthumously, into its shrine. In the past black officialdom, too, has largely avoided any association whatever with this great fighter for human dignity in general and black freedom in particular, and many so-called black "leaders" in the past were openly critical of his efforts and advocacies.

In the 1970s an understanding of Robeson's life is perhaps more crucial than at any other time in our history. And in no instance is this understanding more urgent than in the case of the athlete in general and the black athlete in particular.

While there has been change in the circumstances of the Afro-American—change achieved through unprecedented struggle and sacrifice—it has largely reflected alterations in *process,* not reorganization in the *structure* of power relationships in America. So, even though Blacks in sport no longer routinely encounter the obstacles to athletic participation experienced by Robeson, there exist informal quotas on black participation and "understood" proscriptions against Blacks holding certain jobs.

The black athlete thus came to be cast before the black masses as "proof positive" that if only black people were competitive, disciplined, and so forth they too could achieve high socioeconomic status and mobility—a lie the gravity of which is matched only by its insidious implication: to wit, that 85 to 90 per cent of the black people in America remain in the lower echelons of this society because that is where they, on the strength of their capabilities, contributions and efforts, legitimately belong. The black athlete, then, becomes an appointed spokesman for black people, a "Negro leader," and a "credit to his race."

It would be both unproductive and unrealistic to advocate that black athletes cease participating in sport. But increasingly they must become cognizant of the potential impact—and therefore the special burden of responsibility—emergent from the inherent exploitability of the athletic role. Without such an awareness and a willingness to shoulder the consequent obligations, they function merely as twentieth-century gladiators in the service of establishment capitalist America, perpetuating its hypocrisies, legitimating its lies, accessories to its oppressive traditions. Paul Robeson, then, through his exemplary life, has left the athletes of today and all time an indelible legacy, epitomized by his stalwart refusal to place a price tag on personal integrity, service and human dignity, his insistence upon confronting lies with truths no matter how powerful the liar, and his unflinching conviction that the only viable alternative to freedom is committed and all-encompassing struggle—because it is only through struggle that freedom is achieved.

The black athlete is in a unique position because of the relation between sport, ideology, and social control. With the Third World increasingly gaining its liberation, and with fundamental structures collapsing at home, there is little wonder that, given its tack of depriving the lower classes to ameliorate the pressures on the upper classes, the U.S. establishment is making the black athlete more visible than ever. While college attendance for Blacks and the poor overall is down, the recruitment of athletes, black athletes in particular, is actually up.

Thus it is not enough for black athletes as athletes in general simply to sit still and refuse to support establishment domestic positions and global policies. They must strive to do much more. The achievement of full human potential means to serve the interests of humanity. So the athlete today must be more than just a gladiator. He must openly and staunchly stand up for the development of a new vision, a new reality. Like other black people, he must become actually involved in carving out a place for that new vision and that new society. This, then, is the legacy of Paul Robeson.

Paul Robeson was not simply an extraordinarily gifted intellect, but a man of great passions as well. In his athletic career—as in all other sectors of his life—he never lost sight of the fact, that intellectuality devoid of passion results in technocratic sterility, while passion divorced from intellectuality inevitably leads to chaos. Therefore, any portrayal of the man and the significance of his deeds that did not encompass both would be to separate the shadow from the act, to emphasize the words while ignoring what is being said.

Paul Robeson on the English Stage *

BY MARIE SETON

Something happened in Drury Lane Theatre on the night when *Show Boat* opened there in April 1928. Leaving their five-month-old son Pauli in the care of Essie's mother, Mrs. Goode, the Robesons had sailed again for England for Paul to appear as Joe the Riverman in Jerome Kern's musical of Edna Ferber's book. Robeson sang "Ol' Man River" and everything else in *Show Boat* was forgotten by both audience and critic. His was the voice of a man speaking in the midst of a puppet-show. The audience did not realise that what moved them was the fusion point where real experience is transmuted into art.

As the weeks passed and more and more people went to see *Show Boat,* the impact of Robeson was like a chain reaction. The first to "discover" him were the smart Mayfair set who went in search of the latest sensations and inaugurated new fashions, but soon the county people who came up to London for the "season" were telling their friends to go to Drury Lane. Then the elderly, frowsty people who go to matinees began talking about Robeson's voice. Soon the "intelligentsia" of Bloomsbury and Chelsea, who seldom deigned to go to musical comedies, were discussing him. At last, young people from Clapham and Tooting could be heard talking about him on the tops of buses and on the Underground. Like many other Londoners, I went to see *Show Boat* shortly after it opened. I remembered Robeson's name from reviews I had read of *The Emperor Jones,* but I had not seen the O'Neill play.

When the curtain rose, *Show Boat* began to unfold according to the traditional mechanics of romantic musical plays. Only the

* From *Paul Robeson* by Marie Seton. London: Denis Dobson Co. Ltd., 1958.

26

setting was different—a steamboat plying the Mississippi River. Jerome Kern's musical was pleasant and tuneful; but twenty-four hours after leaving the theatre the romance based on Edna Ferber's story faded from one's memory. It was surprising that there seemed to be no dramatic build-up for the entrance of this new star, Paul Robeson.

The scene shifted from the steamboat to the wharf. Suddenly one realised that Joe the Riverman was Robeson, the silent figure endlessly toting bales of cotton across the stage—a black man with greyed hair moving about like a walk-on, an extra—in life the man who is overlooked because his role is to work and serve. Suddenly Joe, the riverman, filled the whole theatre with his presence. Paul Robeson began to speak in song. He sang about the flowing Mississippi, and the pain of the black man whose life is like the eternal river rolling towards the open vastness of the ocean:

> . . . Tote that barge and lift that bale,
> You get a little drunk,
> And you lands in jail.
> I gets weary and sick of tryin',
> I'm scared of livin' and feared of dyin'. . . .

The expression on Robeson's face was not that of an actor. "I'm scared of livin' and feared of dyin'. . . ."

The pathos of Robeson's voice called up images of slaves and overseers with whips. How had a man with such a history risen?

Sitting next to me was a middle-aged lady with a dry, yellowing face and the refined, dowdy clothes characteristic of certain English people who have repressed all strong feelings beneath a monotone of conformity. A child sat by her side. There was nothing beautiful or free in either the child or the ageing woman, except the pleasure in their eyes as they listened to Paul Robeson. Their entranced expression seemed reflected in face after face up to the dim balcony. It proclaimed that Robeson, so classically African with broad-flaring nostrils, full lips and dark skin, expressed something they felt most deeply. They clapped wildly.

A most startling quality appeared in Robeson as he accepted the applause. He stood as if it were his naked spirit which was receiving the response of the audience. He was visibly touched and yet remote. He seemed to have no greed for applause and he appeared to be a man stripped bare of mannerisms.

The story of romance on a showboat plying the Mississippi suddenly moved into the foreground and Joe, the son of slaves, went back to toting bales of cotton. I have never forgotten the bend of Paul Robeson's back. It was full of strength, yet it expressed a sorrow which seemed to know no end.

The response of London audiences to Paul Robeson was so phenomenal that Sir Alfred Butt, the manager of Drury Lane, embarked upon the experiment of sponsoring Sunday afternoon concerts at the theatre. Lawrence Brown was in Paris when *Show Boat* opened, and Robeson asked him to come over to London for three concerts.

These recitals are probably the only example of an actor appearing in a musical comedy being a solo concert artist in the theatre where he was playing nightly. The announcement of the concerts brought a rush of people to buy tickets.

"The English have taste and like naturalness and straightforwardness," said Lawrence Brown. "Their sense of fair play made them wholeheartedly recognise Paul's great talent."

Yet Robeson's fame in London exerted no influence upon the social attitude of Americans. The American Embassy deliberately ignored the presence of Paul and Eslanda Robeson, even though Robeson soon became probably the most admired and respected American in London. No invitation to the American Ambassador's yearly Fourth of July party in 1928, or in subsequent years, was sent to Robeson and his wife, even though every leading white American in England was invited.

Most English folk would have been astonished had they known that the American Embassy ignored the Robesons because they were Negroes. The London Press quite frequently mentioned the receptions at which Robeson had sung and the parties which he and his wife attended. Mrs. Robeson's clothes were described in the society columns along with the clothes of her fellow guests—peeresses and society women—who, as everybody knew, considered themselves to be the most aristocratic society in the world. For a while, Paul Robeson became the "lion" of London society.

"It was interesting," said Robeson, "but when I come to think of it now, I wonder why Lord Beaverbrook—the staunchest of imperialists—asked me to sing at a reception he gave. Was he anxious to find out what I thought? Anyway, the next time he gave a party, Essie and I were invited as guests. I remember it, because it ended with our sitting with a group all night after H. G. Wells had just walked up to me and begun to ask me a lot of questions."

At first, Robeson met person after person and went from house to house with no preconceived ideas. He was soaking up new and sharply contrasting impressions.

"Sometimes I met people I couldn't quite understand. I met William Rothenstein of the Tate Gallery. Then his wife asked me to tea. I went. Lady Rothenstein and her daughter, Rothenstein and his son—they were somehow so prim. I'd never met people quite like the Rothensteins before—you know what I mean? I didn't quite understand their primness—and yet they were kind and pleasant and I enjoyed myself.

"On sunny days I loved to sit—no, lie on the earth—try to press it to my bosom. Many times later I felt gay and joyous as I lay in the gentle breeze on the downs of Rottingdean, near Eastbourne. How I loved the English countryside. How understandable the lovely poetry flowing from it. How comprehensible the lovely music, the wistfully gay tunes; the gentle lilt of let us say:

> Over the mountains and over the hills,
> Under the fountains and under the rills,
> Under floods that are deepest which Neptune obey,
> Over rocks that are steepest,
> Love will find out the way.

"And how right that for so many of these songs, Roger Quilter provided the settings."

Lawrence Brown, who had made friends with Roger Quilter in the early 'twenties, took Robeson to Quilter's house. "Quilter was quiet, gentle, easy—so very English," Robeson remembered. "Larry and he found they had much in common. For me, in his work and in his person, Quilter was the essence of the finest of this tradition."

Interest in *Show Boat* did not wane and it ran on through the autumn and winter of 1928.

Paul and Essie Robeson decided to stay on in England even after *Show Boat* closed. Essie took a house in Hampstead overlooking the Heath and sent for her mother and the baby, Pauli. For the next few years, Mrs. Goode made herself mainly responsible for the rearing and well-being of her grandchild.

Within six months, Londoners read of Robeson moving in circles where they had seldom if ever heard of an actor moving before: among those who were authorities on the British Empire, its economics and politics, and among the leading members of the Labour Party, who were the traditional opponents of British imperialism.

On November 17th, 1928, a small group of Labour M.P.'s invited Robeson to lunch at the House of Commons, probably the first actor to be thus honoured.

He found himself sitting next to Ramsay MacDonald, the former Prime Minister, who talked to him earnestly about the future of the British colonies. This was, of course, the reason why Paul Robeson had been invited to lunch and why he found that he had something in common with the Labour Party people. After the lunch, Robeson was escorted, with all the formality accorded guests, into the Distinguished Strangers' Gallery.

Never in his life had he seen anything quite as distinctive in national character as the House of Commons: the Prime Minister, Stanley Baldwin, standing four-square for an unchanging status quo, and echoing in politics the concept of the "white man's burden."

But as Robeson's eye roved around the great panelled hall where the members ruled and wrangled over the Empire which still wielded the greatest power in the world, he caught sight of a man who looked most singularly un-English and, indeed, unlike any European. The man had rather wide-spaced eyes and his skin was so dark an ivory tone that it verged on brown. This was the man who some ten years later became Paul Robeson's friend and landlord.

When tea-time came, the stormy James Maxton with the Svengali hair, and the diminutive Ellen Wilkinson, who only reached a little above Robeson's waist, took him to the tea-room. He learned from them that the constituents of the Borough of Battersea, just across the Thames, had returned the unusually dark M.P. to his seat in the Commons. He was Saklatvala, an Indian by birth and a Communist by conviction. As Robeson later learned, Saklatvala would probably be languishing in a British prison if he were in India.

As Robeson said many years later: "My whole social and political development was in England and I became as much a part of English life as I now am of American.

"But odd as it may sound, that lunch with the Labour M.P.s at the House of Commons was not important to me at the time.

"I accepted the invitation," he explained, "but I didn't know anything about Socialism. I didn't realise that Socialism was something most people did know something about until one day I went to lunch with Larry's friend, Miss Douglas, and met Bernard Shaw."

Miss Douglas was an elderly lady with a deep appreciation of music. She had met and encouraged Lawrence Brown while he was living and studying in London in 1920.

"She liked to hear me sing and she was so kind," Paul Robeson continued. "I remember the lunch at Miss Douglas's house where I met Shaw. Sitting on the other side of him was Mrs. Calvin Coolidge, the wife of President Coolidge. She talked loudly, aggressively, and she was crude in her reactions to Shaw when he expounded on Socialism. It was the first exposition I ever heard. I was so struck by the difference between Mrs. Coolidge and Miss Douglas—but when Shaw asked me what I thought of Socialism, I hadn't anything to say. I'd never really thought about Socialism."

With the arrival of spring, 1929, Paul Robeson and Lawrence Brown went on a European tour. They stayed for several days in Vienna and gave their first concert in the blue-and-gold baroque Musikvereinsaal on April 10th. The hall was crowded to the roof.

The critic, Siegfried Geyer, who Robeson later said had understood his musical expression better than any other European critic, wrote in *Die Stunde* on April 11th, 1929:

> People wanted to see a Negro—they wanted to see how a Negro sings; and they suddenly found themselves assisting at an important artistic event. The cheap sensation did not materialise; what did materialise was a sensation of a different order. . . . A singer who embodies the hunted feeling of a tortured creature, the tragedy of the coloured man in the midst of a white society which credits itself with a character corresponding to the colour of its skin. . . .

> In "Water Boy," a genuine folk-song, with an almost joyous background, Robeson revealed more of the true personality of his race than half a dozen learned writings and discourses. "I Don't Feel No Ways Tired" was the crowning achievement of the man's creative fancy—a tempestuous climax in the prophetic words which foretell happier days to come and wing their way to a heavenly city with jubilant Hallelujahs; a hymn to a new and freer outlook on the world, to which Paul Robeson's deep notes do homage.

Robeson was deeply stirred when people, whose language he could not speak, grasped his hands as if, as if . . . . He was possessed with a desire to understand other languages, and he began to study German.

"I knew nothing about the conditions, or the politics of Europe at that time," said Robeson. "The poverty of the Viennese people was brought home to me in a way I've never forgotten. After the concert, a young man came to speak to me. He had a great deal of knowledge about music, but he said he had no money and couldn't have come to the concert at all had someone not given him a ticket. He asked me to come to his home. He was very interesting and I went to see him the next day. I've never forgotten the poverty in which he lived with his mother. Nor the shock it gave me to find her a very cultured woman. I couldn't understand people like that living in such poverty. I knew they were Jewish, but at the time, I didn't understand the position of the Jewish people in Europe."

The next concert was in Prague at Smetana Hall. In Czechoslovakia something happened which was quite unique in the experience of the Robesons.

Essie Robeson later described it: "We were astonished and gratified to find, on arriving in Prague, a formal, official and deeply cordial note of welcome from the American Minister to Czechoslovakia—a Mr. Einstein, by the way!

"Mr. Einstein and his staff attended our concert, entertained us at supper at the Legation, and invited the interesting and distinguished people of Prague to meet us, his fellow countrymen. His treatment of us was charming and considerate, with no hint whatever of patronage. He could not have been kinder to the President. I remember being driven from Smetana Hall, where the concert was held, to the Legation in the official car with its tiny American flag flying from the hood."

From Czechoslovakia they went to Budapest, where the *Pesti Kurir* declared that Robeson's "interpretations reminded one of the great Italian masters." It was here that Robeson discovered that Hungarian folk-songs, of both Slavonic and Gipsy origin, had an affinity with Negro music. The Hungarians, too, felt this affinity. He had noticed the same relationship between his people's music and that of the Czechs and Slovaks. It delighted and puzzled him. At that time, Robeson did not understand why there should be any similarity between the expression of the Negro people and the people of Central Europe.

Meanwhile, the tall screens flanking the main entrance of the Albert Hall in London announced PAUL ROBESON. The concert, scheduled for April 28th, 1929, was Robeson's first appearance there.

Since the opening of *Show Boat* in April 1928, Paul Robeson was the most discussed singer in London and the hall was crowded. The audience, composed mainly of those who regularly made a habit of going to the Albert Hall on Sundays, sat reading the programme as they waited for the concert to commence. I went because I remembered Paul Robeson's singing in *Show Boat*. I, too, sat and read the words of the songs printed in the programme. Many of them were couched in Biblical phrases yet they were in a new idiom.

The contrast between his appearance on the stage in *Show Boat* and here in white tie and tails was startling. His stiff white shirt against his walnut-coloured skin seemed to stress the strength and regularity of his features. His presence filled the hall, yet he stood reverently, as if dedicated to the thing he was about to do. He turned towards Lawrence Brown, who struck the first notes.

His songs were a new world of music and his style of singing in a new category. Every word was distinct and yet, at first, the words might have been in another language. The tones of Robeson's voice reaching out to the audience were most curiously like those of Chaliapin, yet not exactly. Some tones were so deep that they suggested the elemental sound of thunder; others were strangely clear, high, sweet and gentle.

The first Spiritual which came wholly alive to me was "Sometimes I Feel Like a Motherless Child, a long ways from home. . . ." The wistfulness of the words and the melody seemed to rise to an expression of the universal. There was something almost painful about this massive man with strong, forceful features speaking in song with such infinitely tender and sorrowful yearning.

As he waited to begin his second group of songs, Robeson stood with his head in sharp profile. The pride emanating from his head suggested that of a warrior. But there was no cruelty in his face. It was humane and bafflingly quiet.

Robeson's success in London led to his first provincial tour. Lionel Powell became his manager and he gave a concert in Blackpool. He also sang in Birmingham, Torquay, Brighton, Eastbourne, Folkestone, Margate, Hastings, Southsea and Douglas.

"Very early I had the idea of singing in the summer at the spas and seaside resorts," Robeson said. "It seemed to me a way to reach the British public. Even though this was not the usual tour for a singer, I wanted to try it. I offered to sing on a percentage basis to prove my point. That is how I began to build up an audience."

James Agate had commented after the Ambassadors' production of *The Emperor Jones* in 1925 that Robeson "should give

us his Othello." Finally, Robeson had agreed to appear with
Maurice Browne in *Othello*, but he wanted sufficient time to
study and perfect his pronunciation of the English of Shakespeare. For this reason, *Othello* could not be produced until the
spring of 1930.

In the meantime, on September 8th, 1929, Paul Robeson
signed a long-term concert contract with the American impre-
sario, F. C. Coppicus, who had managed the tours of Caruso,
Chaliapin, Rosa Ponselle, Jeritza and other major singers in the
United States. Shortly before Robeson left London for his first
American tour under the management of Coppicus, an incident
took place which shocked the British public when it became
known to them through the Press. Lady Colefax, who was in the
habit of giving parties for musicians and actors either at her
house or in restaurants, invited Paul and Essie Robeson to a
party in their honour at the Savoy Hotel. When they arrived
they were refused admittance to the Grill Room. Such a thing
had never happened to them in London before. Apparently, the
management of the Savoy Hotel, which was popular with American tourists, had capitulated to the demands of white American
patrons and refused to permit coloured people the use of the
hotel. England is not America, and this affront to the Robesons
became a public scandal.

Africans and West Indians—British subjects—came to the support of Robeson. They called a meeting on October 22nd, invited the Press, and read a letter from Robeson giving details of
what had happened. London newspapers gave prominence to the
story and the Savoy's management was shamed into saying that
the affair could not be traced. But still the matter was not permitted to die.

On October 27th the "colour bar" became a political issue.
The Labour M.P., James Marley—later Lord Marley—announced
that he would raise the matter in the House of Commons. Ramsay MacDonald, who was again Prime Minister, now showed less
concern for the human dignity of coloured people than he had
the year before when, out of office, he had entertained Robeson,
along with other Labour M.P.s at lunch at the House of Com-

mons. Said MacDonald: "It is not in accordance with our British hotel practice, but I cannot think of any way in which the Government can intervene."

"When Miss Douglas heard of this," said Paul Robeson, "she was so shocked that she telegraphed to Ramsay MacDonald insisting that he must do something. I've always remembered this because Miss Douglas's act represented to me the decency in British people."

A great many other people felt exactly as Miss Douglas. The Society of Friends (Quakers) called a conference and set up a joint Negro-white council to rally public opinion against racial discrimination. Lord Beaverbrook's *Evening Standard* published an article by Richard Hughes, author of *High Wind in Jamaica,* proposing that some unbiased person should visit London's leading hotels and ask the management to state whether or not they intended to refuse admittance to Negroes in the future. Paul Robeson's bad treatment had started a stir.

The replies of hotel proprietors were interesting. The manager of the Mayfair remarked, "as in the past, I shall rely solely on my own judgment." "I think," said the director of the Park Lane, "it is not right for people to take exception to the presence of coloured men in a hotel. It would be bad manners. We have always entertained coloured men." Both Claridge's and the Berkeley said that Negroes would not be refused admittance; while the manager of the Ritz replied that "if the Negro was a gentleman it would be unfair to refuse him. We have never done so."

The general attitude was against discrimination. Most people said without a second's hesitation that discrimination was "disgraceful" and "unjust," and that a person should be judged according to his own merit.

When it was announced that Robeson was to appear as Othello, there was lively discussion about it. No Negro actor had played Othello in England since the 1860s. The discussion was divided on what manner of man Shakespeare intended—an Arab or a Negro. Even those people who favoured the idea that Moors were Arabs were seemingly more favourable than antagonistic to the proposal that Paul Robeson should play the role. Some people had misgivings about an actor who was predominantly a singer playing Othello; but if there was any anti-racial angle, it was minor and mute.

Following his concert tour in America in the autumn and winter of 1929 Robeson returned to London. Again he appeared before an audience of 4,000 people at the Albert Hall. At the end of March, he went to Berlin to act *The Emperor Jones* at Reinhardt's Deutsches Kuenstler Theater for a week at the special invitation of Robert Kline: a German theatre presented for the first time an American play in English.

Robeson continued his intensive study, not only of *Othello,* but also of the English of Shakespeare's time. He read works on phonetics and listened to records in order to improve his already remarkable enunciation as a singer. Since he recognised that an American accent would clash with the accents of an English cast —he and Maurice Browne were the only Americans—he further studied English pronunciation by using the Furness variorum of *Othello,* where the text was printed in old English. Thus, Robeson learned by the archaic spelling of *chaunce* and *demaunde* how to pronounce "chance" and "demand" with an English accent.

His attitude to the play was a far cry from that of the usual star actor. He explained his views to a reporter for *The New York Times,* May 18th, 1930: "I have read virtually everything of Shakespeare. . . . Now that I know the English people and really understand what their country means to them, now that I am in touch with the English spirit, I feel I can play *Othello.* It is the same with music. People ask me why I do not sing Schubert and Brahms. Perhaps I shall one day, but not before I have lived in Germany.

"I have played various parts in America, but I always cared more for my singing. Now I want to act. Shakespeare amazes me. His psychology is uncannily true all the time. In taking Othello I find the lines come to life at every point. I feel the play is so modern, for the problem is the problem of my own people. It is a tragedy of racial conflict, a tragedy of honour rather than of jealousy. Shakespeare presents a noble figure, a man of singleness of purpose and simplicity, with a mind as direct as a straight line. He is important to the State but the fact that he is a Moor

incites the envy of little-minded people. Desdemona loves him,
he marries her, but the seed of suspicion is sown. The fact that
he is an alien among white people makes his mind work more
quickly. He feels dishonour more deeply. His colour heightens
the tragedy."

Robeson, indeed, understood Othello as no white actor could,
and he was going to play him "as a man whose tragedy lay in
the fact that he was sooty black." Thirteen years later when
Robeson played the role again, his understanding was still more
profound.

Sometime before, he had come to know Sir Frank Benson, the
dean of Shakespearean actors. "Some friends of his had a place
in the country and used to ask me down for weekends. Benson
and I would take long walks together. I'd listen to him talk about
Shakespeare and the tradition of Shakespearean actors. I learned
to appreciate other actors' performances and I felt I knew the
English theatre from listening to Benson: but still I couldn't ap-
ply to myself what he said. I never could grasp what was meant
by 'thinking one's role'."

Probably no first night in the London theatre caused greater
interest and speculation than that of the Robeson *Othello,* which
opened at the Savoy on May 19th, 1930. The young actress, Peggy
Ashcroft, played Desdemona; Sybil Thorndike played Emilia,
and Maurice Browne, Iago.

The settings were more modernistic than those generally seen
in a London production of Shakespeare, and Ellen van Volken-
berg, in her direction, tended to sacrifice the text to pageantry.

Years later, Robeson told me: "The strong point of the Savoy
production was the movement. At that time, I thought of Othello
as moving like a panther. I went to the Zoo to study the movement of the panther." No remark by Robeson better betrays his
lack of dramatic self-appraisal: his natural walk resembles that
of the panther and this was the movement he wanted to convey
as Othello!

Notwithstanding flaws in the Savoy production, at the end of
the first performance there were twenty curtain calls. Paul Robeson had swept away all doubts of his ability to act Shakespeare's

noble Moor. There were cries of "Robeson! Robeson! Speech! Speech!"

At last he stepped forward. "I took the part of Othello with much fear. Now I am so happy," he said.

He had fulfilled the expectations of Mrs. Pat Campbell who, it will be remembered, had encouraged him to play *Othello* when his intention was to become a lawyer.

The acclaim of the critics varied according to their individual point of view. The *Morning Post* reviewer said:

> There has been no Othello on our stage, certainly for forty years, to compare with his dignity, simplicity and true passion. . . . In general from an elocutionary point of view, one only wishes some of our actors could take example from his rolling and natural response to the rhythm and beauty of Shakespeare's verse.

The Savoy Theatre production created a stir in America, and on June 9th, 1930, Robeson broadcast for the first time to his native land through the British Broadcasting Corporation. In his talk, which was carried in America by the Columbia Broadcasting System, he explained how the daughter of Ira Aldridge, the internationally famous nineteenth-century Negro actor, had helped him to prepare his interpretation.

He said: "In Shakespeare's time, I feel, there was no great distinction between the Moor and the brown or black. . . . In Shakespeare's own time and throughout the Restoration, notably by Garrick, the part was played as a black man. This was not changed until the time of Edmund Kean, about the middle of the nineteenth century, when he (Othello) became brown. I feel that had to do with the fact that at that time Africa was the slave centre of the world and people wanted to forget the ancient glory of the Ethiopians. . . ."

Robeson concluded by saying that he was "positive that in the enlightened sections of the United States there can be only one question: Is this a worthy interpretation of one of the great plays of all times? I sincerely trust that I shall see you in October."

But due to the pressure of race prejudice the production in New York did not take place in 1930. Not until thirteen years later did Paul Robeson step on to the New York stage in the role of Othello.

It was shortly after *Othello* opened at the Savoy Theatre that I first met Paul Robeson. A mutual friend took me to meet him following a matinee. I was beginning to write dramatic criticisms and I thought that something about Robeson's interpretation of Othello would interest the readers of the magazine to which I was contributing special pieces.

To a budding dramatic critic, who had spent a couple of years as an actress surrounded by actors who strove to project "personality" and generally loved to talk about themselves and their performances, Paul Robeson afforded such a surprise that my first personal impression of him has never faded. His immediate impact was that of a man who, while polite, had no inclination to talk, least of all about himself.

I told him that I had seen *Othello* several times before and that I liked his performance, but my words called forth no conventional response. He did not smile and say as most actors receiving praise, "I'm so glad you liked me!"

"I tried to do the best I could," he answered, slowly.

He sat down and lapsed into silence, looking at his hands which I noticed were more expressive off the stage than on. He sat as if considering something. His reflection in the mirror of his dressing-table made a striking impression: the rich brocaded doublet—red shot through with a black thread—was in contrast to the sombre, earnest expression on his face.

He was not the dramatic figure he appeared to be on the stage a few minutes before; nor the impressive figure on the platform of the Albert Hall; nor the moving figure of Joe in *Show Boat*. The Paul Robeson who sat looking at his hands was a man removed from everything generally associated with the well-known actor. He seemed to belong to an entirely different world. I wondered how he could possibly have found his way into the theatre.

I asked him how he had gone about preparing his interpretation of Othello. He answered briefly that he had studied the play in order to attune his performance to those of his fellow actors. But he said nothing about his own performance, nor what his specific role in the theatre was. He said nothing about his ambitions. It seemed he did not want to talk about himself.

The few things he said were spoken in a gravely musical

voice. No actor I had met was as aloof, though not in an arrogant way. It was as if something beyond *Othello* and the theatre was occupying his mind. We shook hands and said good-bye.

I went to see Sybil Thorndike, who was playing Emilia. I thought that she could tell me something about Robeson. She said he was a wonderful person—the nicest man she had ever acted with—and that everyone in the cast of *Othello* felt the same way about him: but still she could not explain precisely what it was about Paul Robeson which caused everybody in the Savoy Theatre to like and respect him.

After this first meeting with Robeson I felt there was nothing concrete I could write about him. Years later, he explained his reticence to me: "I didn't know anything about the art of acting, so I didn't know what to say when anybody asked me about my performance. If you had asked me about the play, or about Shakespeare's period, then I could have talked because I had read everything I could lay my hands on."

Sometime after our first meeting, I accidentally met Paul Robeson again. He was walking with his wife, Eslanda, in a street off Shaftesbury Avenue. Not until his wife and I were about to bump into each other, did he stop, saying, "Aren't you . . . ?" He stopped, dug my name out from his memory and introduced me to Essie, whose positive and vivid personality was in the sharpest contrast to his own much more subdued one.

By the end of 1930, Paul Robeson's whole career was detailed in the British *Who's Who* for 1931. No mention, however, was made of him in the American *Who's Who*. Lawrence Brown later observed: "I would say that the audiences in England, and abroad, were always more friendly and enthusiastic than in America."

Following *Othello,* Robeson, emerging from a history of oppression, poverty and struggle, and a world of suffering unrealised by the British people, stood before them as a great artist who had scaled to a spur of a high mountain. Of necessity his fame presented him with many subtle problems for he was a man who not only felt a need to preserve the inner core of his being but one to whom material success and acclaim were singularly unessential. The banal and superficial disturbed him and he could take nothing for granted.

He felt that he understood the British people and felt himself to be part of the English scene. Each month, the easy, personal tempo of life had seeped deeper into his consciousness. As the country became more and more a part of him, he felt a new kind of individualism asserting itself within him, one that seemed to have no race or nationality; a consciousness neither black nor white but of the world.

"Paul always had a bigness," said Lawrence Brown. "There was nothing petty in him, and he cut through the mass of details and arrived at a large understanding." Larry made a circle with his two hands, as if suggesting the globe.

All his life, Robeson had felt himself rooted as a member of the Negro race. Now, quite suddenly, he felt both Negro and something else. For the first time he became truly aware of himself as an individual artist who had his own life to live irrespective of whether he was black or white, American or something else. He thought he would never live in America again.

In the eyes of artistic Londoners a seal was put upon Paul Robeson's individuality when Jacob Epstein sculpted his head. Epstein was already recognised as a great portrait sculptor, and his stone and wood carving bore a profound mark of African sculptural influence. Epstein's finished head of Robeson revealed Robeson as he felt rather than as he actually looked at the time: the head of a man of uncertain age tilted upwards with eyes seeking something in the distance—the face of Robeson as he would look when he was older and the character of his face had become more distinct and his features stamped with his life's experience. Epstein portrayed Paul Robeson in his early thirties as a man dominated by the spirit rather than the flesh. The portrait might have borne the title "Negro Moses." Robeson was in truth searching.

Soon after *Othello* closed, Paul Robeson cabled Lawrence Brown, who was in New York, asking him to return to London. On arrival, Brown learned that a new experimental programme was to be presented at the Savoy Theatre for eight performances in September.

The first half of the programme was to consist of the first and last scenes of *The Emperor Jones;* while the second half was to be devoted to Negro Spirituals with one innovation—a song by Beethoven. Robeson thus combined his career of actor and singer into a single programme.

Following the Savoy performances, Robeson and Brown went on tour with this unusual programme. They played a week in such cities as Manchester, Liverpool, Bradford and Cardiff, Glasgow and Edinburgh. The tour lasted for three months and introduced Robeson to many towns in the simultaneous role of actor and singer. "But," said Lawrence Brown, "it was as a singer that Paul captivated the provincial audiences."

At this time, and for several years, Robeson's thoughts and experiences were not clear cut. Of necessity, a whole area of his life remained a closed book to even his closest friends in England. They did not realise that each time Robeson and Brown went to their native land for concert tours, the mailed fist of racial prejudice came smashing against them, or that they moved in an oscillating atmosphere where public acclaim greeted them at every concert but where prejudice not only restricted them personally the next moment, but engulfed all the members of their race in conditions of discrimination and oppression. The character of racism in America was something that could not be explained to people abroad; it had to be experienced to be believed.

The scrapbook kept by Lawrence Brown recording their concert tours in England and the United States between 1929 and 1932, tells the story of Robeson's deepening mastery of his art and his increasing acclaim as an individual artist. But it reveals, too, why Robeson was constantly wondering about his ultimate role in the world and what should be his ultimate aim.

Under the exigencies of fame he discovered that he was incapable of betraying his heritage. Of his own volition he pushed aside those personal contacts which were in any way inimical to his pride of race.

Almost twenty years later, Robeson wrote an article for the readers of *Reynolds News* and told them what he had learned:

"I was made a fuss of by Mayfair. Then one day I heard one of your aristocrats talking to his chauffeur in much the same way as he would speak to his dog. I said to myself, 'Paul, that is how the southerner in the United States would speak to you.'

"That was how I realised that the fight of my Negro people in America and the fight of the oppressed workers everywhere was the same struggle."

"That incident made me very sad for a year," Robeson told me. "I sat home and read and wondered. If anything finally made class difference clear to me against the English background it was the general attitude towards servants and also the servants' acceptance of their status. In America Negroes are servants—but they hate their status and always hope to escape. I was attached to those friends—yet it was the chauffeur with whom I was concerned."

Paul Robeson, the great singer, did not strive to attain fame as a vocalist; nor did he aim at histrionic notoriety. Lawrence Brown said of him: "I don't know what to call him but a genius—though a unique genius. It seemed to me that if he strove in any direction, it was towards knowledge for its own sake. After the greatest ovations, Paul would go home and read or study language—an African dialect or Russian."

"I used to drop in to see the plays at the Embassy Theatre long before *Chillun*," said Paul Robeson. "Ronald Adam's policy interested me. It was a laboratory theatre similar to the Provincetown Playhouse in New York." The Embassy's choice of plays was a blending of the views of Ronald Adam, the manager who occasionally acted, and those of André van Gyseghem, the young director. Adam was particularly interested in plays involving important human problems; while van Gyseghem was concerned with plays which presented some social or political problem. Between the two, the fortnightly productions at the Embassy generally had something to convey in the realm of ideas.

In 1930 and 1931, when Robeson was dropping in to see the Embassy plays, neither Adam nor van Gyseghem knew that he visited the theatre. He never reserved seats, nor did he exert the actor's privilege and ask for complimentary tickets. Sometime during 1932, van Gyseghem told me that one of the plays he wanted Adam to present was O'Neill's *All God's Chillun Got Wings*.

"But it'll depend on whether we can get Paul Robeson," Van

explained. "The question is how can the Embassy pay the sort of salary he commands. Ronnie can't see Robeson playing at the Embassy for £10 a week! Still, I'm not going to give up hope. As you know, I'd like to do any play which attacks race prejudice."

The matter rested for several months. Then one day in the autumn of 1932, van Gyseghem was filled with triumph.

"Robeson's agreed to do *All God's Chillun*," he told me. "Flora Robson is to play Ella."

Later, Ronald Adam recounted how the production had been arranged. He had gone one evening to see the actor Sebastian Shaw, who lived with his wife, Angela Baddeley, in a basement flat near the Embassy Theatre. Paul Robeson was there.

"I had no discussion with Paul about it," Ronnie said. "I simply asked him if he'd be interested in doing a production of *Chillun* and he agreed there and then. It didn't seem to matter to him that we only paid £10 a week. He was interested in the effect of the play on an English audience. Flora agreed, for she has the same blazing sincerity about the theatre as Paul has. She has an enormous heart, belief in man and a great pity for the world's badness."

The production of *All God's Chillun Got Wings* was set for March 12th, 1933. Three weeks before rehearsals commenced, André van Gyseghem went with me on a hurried trip to Moscow in order to obtain the rights of the anti-Nazi play, *Professor Mamlock,* by the German dramatist, Friedrich Wolf, who had left Germany and was temporarily in Moscow, and to see Alexander Tairov's production of *All God's Chillun* at the Kamerny Theatre.

On our return journey, we stopped in Warsaw to see the first performance of *Professor Mamlock* with Alexander Granach at the Yiddish Theatre in the Warsaw ghetto. Hitler had become Chancellor of Germany. The Nazis had all but consolidated their grip on the country and they were already intensifying their policy of anti-Semitism. The continent was tense. I stayed in Berlin for a few days with the American correspondent, Fredrick Kuh, and his wife, while Van returned to London to start rehearsals with Flora Robson and Paul Robeson.

Many years later, van Gyseghem said: "Nearly all of us who

work in the theatre have one unforgettable experience, something
which at the time makes so profound an impression upon one as
to exert a permanent influence. Such an experience was mine during the production of *All God's Chillun*.

"Time and time again at rehearsals, directing Flora Robson
and Paul Robeson, I had the feeling of being on the edge of a
violent explosion; I had touched it off but the resulting conflagra-
tion was terrifying in its blazing intensity. I have seldom known
two performances fuse so perfectly; Miss Robson's emotional
power and the uncanny skill with which she stripped bare the
meagre soul of the wretched Ella was almost more than one could
bear at such close range.

"Such a technically superb performance found a perfect foil
in Robeson's utter sincerity—he *was* Jim, he had the facility for
making imagination visible; his magnificent voice seemed to vibrate with truth and to take command of his body until one was
blinded by naked suffering made solid and tangible. His giant
frame, his awkward, ungainly movements seemed to make his
tenderness and humility more moving, more truthful. He was,
instinctively, a great artist."

The production of *All God's Chillun* almost had to be cancelled when Eugene O'Neill's agent suddenly demanded that the
royalties be increased to 10 per cent and, further, that a down-
payment of $1,000 be paid for the rights.

The truth was that at the moment the Embassy didn't have a
penny with which to bless itself. To make matters worse, Ronald
Adam had gone to the South of France for a fortnight. Adam's
assistant, Eric Somers, who had charge of the theatre, went to
van Gyseghem at the end of a rehearsal and told him that the
play could not open because he knew of no way to raise the thousand dollars for Eugene O'Neill.

"Evidently, Paul must have heard what Eric said," Ronald
Adam told me. "Anyway, Paul saved the day. Within minutes of
Eric going back to the office, Paul walked in and asked 'Will this
help?' He handed Eric a cheque for £100. That's Paul Robeson!
He was dedicated to the production and—thank God—I gave him
a cheque on the first night."

Two days before *All God's Chillun* opened at the Embassy

Theatre, a seemingly quite unimportant thing took place: Fredrick Kuh's American news agency had just transferred him from Berlin to London. On the day of the Hitler "election" he was warned that the stormtroopers were coming to his flat to take him to a Brown House to "discipline" him because he had sent out the first story that the notorious Reichstag fire was an act of provocation. Arriving in London, Kuh needed "copy" to start his new assignment. He was a great admirer of Paul Robeson whom he had seen in *The Emperor Jones* in Berlin in 1930.

Kuh knew that Robeson's appearance in *All God's Chillun Got Wings* in London was a good story for America—the original production at the Provincetown Playhouse in 1924 having been an exceedingly controversial issue.

Kuh wanted to see a rehearsal of *All God's Chillun* and to interview Paul Robeson. Van Gyseghem had no objections and Freddy Kuh asked me to take him to the morning rehearsal. When there was a break for lunch I introduced Kuh to Robeson and the three of us went out to lunch.

As we went into L'Escargot in Soho Robeson's face brightened. For the first time I saw him smile as if he was delighted. "Why did not one ever bring me here before?" he asked.

I was surprised that a quiet and unostentatious French restaurant should so please him.

"In Soho, I feel completely at home," he continued. "There is refuge from that subtle prejudice that I feel among the 'aristocracy.'"

A short Italian waiter with hollowed cheeks made a dash towards us and, smiling up at Robeson, wanted to know where he would like to sit. Then the headwaiter made a great to-do and sat us down at the most central of the vacant tables as if we were a special decoration for the other patrons to gaze at.

Paul Robeson proved wretched "copy" for Freddy Kuh; he hardly said a word about himself. The conversation turned to Germany, and this was the reason a seemingly unimportant lunch was significant in Robeson's life.

From what he said it seemed that up till this moment he had paid little or no attention to international politics. Hitler and the rise of Fascism had lain beyond his ken. He was shocked to hear what Kuh and I had witnessed during the day of the so-called Hitler "election" when all semblance of democratic government was smashed by the Nazis' intimidation of the German voters.

"I didn't realise it was the end of democracy in Germany," Robeson said. "I didn't understand what was going on." It was hard for him to believe that Fredrick Kuh's wife, Renata, and I had spent the night of the "election," and the next night, waiting for the Nazis to knock on the door and ask for Freddy. Robeson looked bewildered when I told him that on my return to London I had found three of my German-Jewish student friends in my flat. They had only just escaped in time.

"I wish I didn't have to go back to rehearsal," Robeson said. "There are many things more important than the theatre."

Fredrick Kuh left for his office, but without much material for an interview with Robeson, with whom I drove back to the Embassy for the afternoon rehearsal.

The remote quality I had previously noticed in Robeson seemed to have disappeared. Evidently, he liked to talk about things outside the theatre.

"There's so much I've never studied," he said. "It's difficult for me to understand the things Kuh said."

On March 12th, 1933, when *All God's Chillun Got Wings* opened, people almost fought to get seats. The usual run of a fortnight was extended to three weeks and every performance was sold out, even the standing room.

It is interesting to contrast the reaction of the London critics with the reaction of the New York critics to the 1924 production at the Provincetown Playhouse. The contrast is most striking in the reaction to the characters of Jim and Ella.

The *Morning Post* critic, reviewing the play after its opening at the Embassy, said:

> In sheer emotional power there is most certainly nothing in London to compare with the acting of Mr. Paul Robeson as the Negro husband, and Miss Flora Robson as the white wife in this nightmare of Eugene O'Neill's. There are moments which do undoubtedly cut the heart out with their tragic irony.
>
> The play as a whole . . . remains something of an enigma. Ella having married Jim Harris, her coloured playmate, develops a

self-contradictory mania of passionate affection for him and a wild dread that her "inferiority complex" will be confirmed by his passing the entry-examination for the bar. . . .

The *New York Times* critic, writing after the opening at the Provincetown Playhouse in 1924, said:

> The hero of *All God's Chillun* is as admirable, honest and loyal as Uncle Tom. He is soundly ambitious, too, aspiring to be a lawyer. But he is as far as possible from being an idealisation. He is slow-witted and deeply impressed by a sense of inferiority of his position. He can scarcely graduate from school and fails miserably and repeatedly to pass his bar examination. . . . If one thought of Uncle Tom one also thought of Othello.

No American reviewer had made any mention of the reasons why O'Neill's Negro hero failed to pass the bar examination, which is the crux of the second half of the play. But the *Morning Post* critic explained:

> Almost with the same breath she (Ella) expresses tender devotion (for Jim), and yells "You dirty nigger!" She tries to stab him with a table knife, and keeps him awake at night so that he shall not be able to work. Through it all he maintains an agonised faith in their love. At the end he fails the examination. She is beside herself with joy. . . .

The *New York Times* critic, who was one of the few even to mention the character of Ella, dismisses her relationship to Jim in one sentence:

> The much discussed scene in which Ella kisses Jim's hand is a quite incredible mingling of genuine affection and demented fancy.
>
> Altogether a painful play in spite of its touches of fine sympathy.

American critics had to evade the content of O'Neill's play. They simply could not say, even if they thought it, that of the two human beings portrayed on the stage, the humanly superior one was the Negro man who in compassionate love tried to redeem the white girl he had loved as a child after she had been degraded by her own white world with its brutalised men who had failed to degrade the Negro characters into images of themselves.

The Cultural Philosophy of Paul Robeson

BY STERLING STUCKEY

"I suppose," Paul Robeson wrote in 1933, "I am the only black man in the world who does not want to be white." Whether Robeson exaggerated is not the point; the sentiment set him apart from most of his contemporaries and cut to the core of a major historical problem of black people, the desire of many to be shaped in the image of their oppressor. It has been that psychic aberration, a direct product of centuries of oppression at the hands of whites, that has militated, in concert with the very forces that produced it, against black people devising a more dynamic culture, that is, a more liberating way of life and a method of preserving it from generation to generation.

Though very few scholars are aware of it, few people in this country's history have taken as serious an interest in cultural questions as Robeson. The 1930s was the period of his most profound insights into the nature of the black past and present, the time of his deepest reflections on the state of world cultural groupings. His philosophy of culture was projected in that decade in a series of brilliant essays and in newspaper interviews. Robeson penetrated to the foundations of black culture, exposed the chief dangers of the culture of the larger society and accurately identified the essential ingredients of world cultures while calling for the synthesis that would save mankind.

Early in the decade, in one of his essays, Robeson identified important elements of character of the people who created black culture in America—"a people upon whom nature has bestowed, and in whom circumstances have developed, great emotional depth and spiritual intuition." The value dispensation of the Afro-American—especially as reflected in his religion and art—constitutes, Robeson contended, the only significant American culture since the inception of the country. More than any other single factor, however, a deep sense of inferiority, nurtured by white America, prevented large numbers of black people from being aware of the greatness of their culture.

Addressing himself to the question of the Negro's feelings of inadequacy, Robeson wrote that the sufferings undergone by the Negro had "left an indelible mark" on his soul, had caused him to become the victim of an inferiority complex that leads him to imitate white people.

> [It] has been drummed into him that the white man is the Salt of the Earth and the Lord of Creation, and as a perfectly natural result his ambition is to become as nearly like a white man as possible.

"I am convinced," the young scholar wrote, "that in this direction there is neither fulfillment nor peace for the Negro."

Robeson described the American Negro as that "tragic creature, a man without a nationality." Though he might claim to be American, to be French, to be British, *"You cannot assume a nationality as you would a new suit of clothes."* (Italics mine.) So wrote Robeson in 1934. With notable courage and insight, he pursued this line of investigation, remarking that the assumption of African nationality is "an extremely complicated matter, fraught with the greatest importance to me and some millions of coloured folk." The inferiority complex of large numbers of black people had helped complicate the matter. Such self-laceration was buttressed by the belief that they "had nothing whatever in common with the inhabitants of Africa"—a view that was reinforced by American educators who, with rare exceptions, carried in their heads grotesque but comforting stereotypes of African peoples and their history. Though Blacks in this country were a race without nationality, the effects of such a condition were, in Robeson's opinion, not immutable. But more than viewing Africa from afar would be required if the Negro were to secure some of the benefits of a nation in the absence of nationhood in the literal sense.

> In illustration of this take the parallel case of the Jews. They, like a vast proportion of Negroes, are a race without a nation; but, far from Palestine, they are indissolubly bound by their an-

cient religious practices—*which they recognize as such.* I emphasize
this in contradiction to the religious practices of the American
Negro, which, from the snake-worship practiced in the deep South
to the Christianity of the revival meeting, are patently survivals
of the earliest African religions, *and he does not recognize them
as such.* Their acknowledgement of *their common origin, species,
interest and attitudes binds Jew to Jew; a similar acknowledgement
will bind Negro to Negro.* (Last italics added.)

Robeson set himself the task of seeking, through "patient inquiry," to lay the foundations on which a new awareness of black
culture and tradition could be based. He would investigate a
great many questions regarding Africa and America and hoped,
by 1938, to have reached the peak of a campaign "to educate the
Negro to a consciousness of the greatness of his heritage."

His "patient inquiry" had doubtless begun some years before,
for he reported during the same year (1934) that he had already
"penetrated to the core of African culture when I began to study
the legendary traditions, folk songs and folklore of the West African Negro." Robeson's encounter with West Africa cultures, then,
was no mere academic exercise; he said it had been "like a homecoming" for him. He wanted to interpret the "unpolluted" African folk song, to do for it what he had done for the Spiritual, to
make it respected throughout the world; all of which, he hoped,
would make it easier for Blacks in America not only to appreciate
this aspect of their heritage but to play a role in exploring the
"uncharted musical material in that source." The researches of
Robeson into the folklore of West Africa were aided by his pro-
ficiency in several languages of the area, languages which, he
thought, had come easily to him "because their rhythm is the same
as that employed by the American Negro in speaking English."

Afro-Americans during the 1930s were often as dreadfully un-
informed about African languages as they were about other aspects
of African culture. Robeson's findings in this regard were for this
reason of special interest to these Blacks who thought, as many
did, that Africans communicated their ideas solely through gestures and sign language! Robeson concluded from his initial
studies of African languages that Swahili, for all its impurities, was
"constructed in the same way as that language which gave us the

wonder of Chinese poetry." (He would later become proficient in Chinese.) But he was not satisfied to point up such analogies, however thrilling they may have been to American Negroes of the thirties: "As a first step" in dispelling the "regrettable and abysmal ignorance of the value of its own heritage in the Negro race itself," he decided to launch a comparative study of the main language groups, Indo-European, African and Asian, "choosing two or three principal languages out of each, and indicate their comparative richness at a comparable stage of development."

> It may take five years to complete this work but I am convinced that the results will be adequate to form a concrete foundation for a movement to inspire confidence in the Negro in the value of his own past and future.

By 1935, Robeson was saying, in the context of a discussion of African and Asian ties, that "Negro students who wrestle vainly with Plato would find a spiritual father in Confucius or Lao-tze. . . ." His meaning on this point would become clearer as he, in later years, spelled out the salient cultural components of the East and West. Meanwhile, in addition to studying African linguistics and drawing conclusions which, though known to the few specialists in the field, were revelations to many, he had long since concluded that Blacks in this country were under quite substantial African influences (a position that he would retain, like almost all his cultural views of the thirties, for decades to come). The dances, songs and religion of the black man in America, he wrote, were the same as those of his "cousins" centuries removed in the depths of Africa, "whom he has never seen, of whose very existence he is only dimly aware." Robeson added that the American Negro's "peculiar sense of rhythm," his "rhythm-consciousness," as it were, "would stamp him indelibly as African."

Thus Robeson joined Du Bois and Woodson before him in affirming African "survivals," probing deeply into the specific, irreducible components of African influence, contending that the American Negro is too radically different in mental and emotional structures from the white man "ever to be more than a spurious and uneasy imitation of him. . . ." The emotive, intuitive and aesthetic qualities of the Afro-American not only linked him to the African homeland but to the West Indian Black as well. "The American and West Indian Negro," he argued, "worships the Christian God in his own particular way and makes him the object of his supreme artistic manifestation which is embodied in the Negro spiritual." He realized what few scholars knew at the time, that there was such a thing as black religion in the Caribbean and in the United States. As to what gives rise to the ties between people of African ancestry, Robeson ventured that "It would take a psycho-anthropologist to give it a name."

The achievement of Robeson's scholarship on African "survivals" is all the more evident when one takes into account the extreme backwardness of America's colleges and universities, of "higher" education, vis-à-vis Africa and her descendants in diaspora. When the decade of the thirties opened, even the most progressive and advanced white thinkers in America, scholars such as Franz Boaz and Ruth Benedict, had not realized the role Africa was playing in helping to fashion the black ethos in America. Advocates of the "culturally stripped" thesis, Boaz and Benedict were joined by the Chicago School of Sociology, which was an influential promoter of the "tangle of pathology" view of black culture. But unlike Boaz and Benedict, almost all the remaining intellectuals were unaware of the role of Africa in world history.

Apart from Melville Herskovits later in the decade, few indeed were the white scholars who were even close to understanding the continuing impact of Africa on Blacks in this country. While one might quarrel with certain particulars of Robeson's position on African influences on the black experience in America, with the extent to which, for example, he ascribes African attributes to our dance and song, his views here, though doubtless somewhat overstated, now appear to be, on balance, more persuasive than ever. Recent researches into comparative African and Afro-American dance and song styles, especially the work of Alan Lomax, in the main support Robeson's findings of more than thirty years ago. (When his thinking on African influences has been more thoroughly researched, there is reason to believe that he will move to the fore as perhaps the most significant contributor to Negritude theory to come out of America.)

Since the rehabilitation of Africa was central to his campaign to heighten the consciousness of American Negroes, he had to confront the fundamental issue of the nature of black African history while continuing his investigation into various aspects of contemporary African cultures. The schools of the West, especially in the United States, stressing African backwardness, made these concerns inescapable for Robeson. He asserted in fact that the younger generation of Negroes looks toward Africa and wants to know what is *there* to interest them; they want to know, he added, what Africa has to offer that the West cannot provide.

> At first glance the question seems unanswerable. He sees only the savagery, devil-worship, witch doctors, voodoo, ignorance, squalor, and darkness taught in American schools. *Where these exist, he is looking at the broken remnants of what was in its day a mighty thing; something which perhaps has not been destroyed but only driven underground, leaving ugly scars upon the earth's surface to mark the place of its ultimate reappearance.*" (Italics added.)

Still, much that was impressive was not hidden, certainly not from Robeson. In his writings, he called attention to the supreme artistry of West African sculpture, which had inspired leading European artists; hailed West African bronzes, which bore striking similarities to the finest examples of Javanese, Chinese and Mexican art; recognized the intricacies of African musical rhythms, which were far more complex than anything attained by a Western composer; stressed the flexibility and sophistication of African languages, which could convey subtleties of thought far beyond what was suspected by those unacquainted with African linguistics; and emphasized the rich spiritual heritage of Africa, which is also associated with the great civilizations of the East.

As comprehensive and painstaking as his inquiry was (he had learned east coast languages, including Swahili and the Bantu group, and proceeded to learn several West African languages), convincing black Americans that what they had been taught about Africa was false would very likely prove to be more difficult than persuading them that their people had made important cultural contributions while in America. Robeson intimated that the more privileged, the better "educated," young Blacks were less favorably disposed to revising their prejudices regarding their heritage than the great mass of older Blacks.

> I found a special eagerness among the younger and, I am sorry to say, the more intelligent Negroes, to dismiss the Spiritual as something beneath their new pride in their race. It is as if they wanted to put it behind them as something to be ashamed of—something that tied them to a past in which their forefathers were slaves.

Those Blacks who turned their backs on this folk music were, whether they realized it or not, contributing to their own destruction, for the Spirituals were, in Robeson's view, "the soul of the race made manifest." This position was integrally related to his deep concern about the black artist giving emphasis to the art "of other people in our Negro programs, magnificent and masterly though they may be." He felt that concessions to European music would lead to the "eventual obliteration of our own folk music, the musical idioms of our race . . . the finest expression and the loftiest we have to offer."

Robeson, realizing the potentially fatal consequences of the failure of sizable numbers of black intellectuals (and others) to appreciate their folk heritage, had posited in an interview in 1931 that if black musical groups did not "arise all over the land to cherish and develop our spirituals," Blacks would have to leave the country and "go to Africa, where we can develop independently and bring forth a new music based on our roots."

Robeson's interest in cultural independence for Blacks grew out of a deeply felt belief that the black man in America must be in a position "to set his own standards," which was "the pressing need." Urgent because American whites, generally closer than Blacks to Europeans in life styles, were dangerously, perhaps fatally entrapped by European dependence upon abstractions and hostility toward emotive and intuitive values.

In 1936, Robeson described a critical problem of the West, one with dire implications for the whole of mankind—"the cost of developing the kind of mind by which the discoveries of science were made has been one which now threatens the discoverer's very life." In fact, he argued, Western man appears to have gained greater powers of abstraction "at the expense of his creative faculties."

> But because one does not want to follow Western thought into this dilemma, one none the less recognizes the value of its achievements. One would not have the world discount them and retrogress in terror to a primitive state. It is simply that one recoils from the Western intellectual's idea that, having got himself on to this peak overhanging an abyss, he should want to drag all other people— on pain of being dubbed inferior if they refuse—up after him into the same precarious position.

"That, in a sentence," wrote Robeson, "is my case against Western values."

So it was simply that America was uncongenial to meaningful, creative living; the Western world as a whole seemed, short of very drastic changes, an unlikely place in which new forms of freedom, a new humanity, could develop. The West had gone astray as far back as the time of the Renaissance, if not before:

> A blind groping after Rationality resulted in an incalculable loss in pure Spirituality. Mankind placed a sudden dependence on that part of his mind that was brain, intellect, to the discountenance of that part that was sheer evolved instinct and intuition; we grasped at the shadow and lost the substance and now we are not altogether clear what the substance was.

Having identified the main weaknesses of the West, Robeson asserted that the person who embraced Western values completely would, in time, find his creative faculties stunted and warped, would become almost wholly dependent on external gratification. Becoming frustrated in this direction, neurotic symptoms develop, and it is borne in upon the victim that life is not worth living. In chronic cases he might seek to take his life. "This is a severe price," said Robeson, "to pay even for such achievements as those of Western science."

As one reads Robeson's brief against Western values, it is evident that he does not place great faith in the ability of Western man, left to his own devices, to halt his momentum and pull back from the precipice. He provides an index into the depth of the European disorder by drawing our attention to the fact that as abstract intellectualism became enthroned in Europe the artistic achievements of that section of the world declined steadily. He found in European art "an output of self-conscious, uninspired productions" which people of discriminating taste recognize as "lifeless imitations" rather than "the living pulsing thing." This malady was not confined to the small minority described as artists, "but unfortunately what shows amongst these is only a symptom of a sickness that to some extent is affecting almost every stratum of the Western world."

The relationship of the artist to society was of major concern to Robeson, and the position he took is but one more illustration of his special angle of vision: "The whole problem of living can never be understood until the world recognizes that artists are not a race apart." Artists, Robeson added, do not have potentialities unknown to large numbers of other human beings, for creativity means more than the ability to make music, to paint and to write. Each man has something of the artist in him; if this is uprooted "he becomes suicidal and dies." Robeson contended that, given the opportunities for creative development, very large numbers of people could contribute the sum of the artistic and spiritual achievements of a given society. He posited an organic tie between artist and society—a reciprocity of interests—that is distinctly non-Western.

Robeson remarked in 1936 that it has been a boon to the American Negro that he has managed, despite his presence in the white man's deadly spiritual world, and despite centuries of oppression, to retain a world view that is still largely non-Western, predicated on sensibilities similar to those of his African ancestors and to those people who live in cultures which place a higher priority on concrete symbols than upon abstractions:

> For it is not only the African Negro, and so-called primitive peoples, who think in concrete symbols—all the great civilizations of the East (with possibly the exception of India) have been built up by people with this type of mind. It is a mentality that has given us giants like Confucius, Mencius, and Lao-tze. More than likely it was this kind of thinking that gave us the understanding and wisdom of a person like Jesus Christ. It has given us the wonders of Central American architecture and Chinese art. It has, in fact,

given us the full flower of all the highest possibilities in man—with the single exception of applied science. That was left to a section of Western man to achieve and on that he bases his assertion of superiority.

The American Negro's great asset, then, is his "immense emotional capacity," though, Robeson added, emotive powers are at a discount in the West. His capacity for feeling, his intuitive and aesthetic gifts, with the proper guidance, might achieve wonders. His attainments in America to date, as impressive as they are in their own right, are merely sterile compared to what they might be in the future. Robeson thereby made it clear that Blacks should not glory in their gifts. Indeed he warned the American Black against "further isolating himself," pointing out that it was not only useful but necessary from a social and economic standpoint for the Negro to understand Western culture and ideas. He again placed science in perspective:

> Now I am not going to try to belittle the achievements of science. Only a fool would deny that the man who holds the secrets of those holds the key position in the world.

Robeson did not subscribe to the view that cultural traits are inherited in the genes. Conceding that many Blacks in America had become "pure intellectuals," he questioned whether they would allow themselves to proceed all the way down "this dangerous by-way when, without sacrificing the sound base in which they have their roots, they can avail themselves of the now-materialized triumphs of science and proceed to use them while retaining the vital creative side." This creative dimension, according to Robeson, had made possible the Afro-American's artistic and spiritual achievements. His description of the causes of the cultural strengths of Blacks may well be the best on record:

> Now, as to the most important part which . . . the Negro is qualified to play in the American scene, I would define it as "cultural," with emphasis upon the spiritual aspect of that culture. With the passing of the Indians, the Negroes are the most truly indigenous stock in North America. They have grown up with the country, becoming part of the soil itself. They have had a better chance than any other of the races which have come to America

to identify themselves with the atmosphere of the place, if only because they have been there much longer. They have been unhappy and badly treated, but they have retained (though they have not been allowed fully to express) their best and most characteristic qualities: a deep simplicity, a sense of mystery, a capacity for religious feeling, a spontaneous and entirely individual cheerfulness; and these have found expression in the only culture which Americans can point to as truly belonging to their country.

In fact, the young philosopher observed, the whole of American culture was deriving from black culture "those qualities which appeal most directly to the intelligent European who values a depth of native tradition in art." Despite the long period of repression that the black man's "cultural actualities" and "potentialities" have survived, "they can develop only with great difficulty in a hostile environment." The uncongenial hostile American environment constituted the "new Egypt" out of which Robeson wanted to lead his people "into a new promised land." That land, as we have seen, need not be Africa, provided Blacks would move en masse to gather together and build upon the foundation stones of their culture, the folk heritage which was an amalgam of African and American elements. But Blacks in this country would have a better chance of finding the new ground if they cultivated those qualities in their culture which tie them to the East and to Africa.* While the Negro "must take his technology from the West," Robeson observed, "instead of coming to the Sorbonne or Oxford, I would like to see Negro students go to Palestine and Peking." He added that he "would like to watch the flowering of their inherent qualities under sympathetic influences there."

A crucial objective of the cultural transformation would be that of a man mastering the emotional and intellectual dimensions of his personality. When he has learned "to be true to himself the Negro as much as any man" would contribute to the new cultural order. But Robeson, once again, had a special warning for Blacks: "unless the African Negro (including his far-flung collaterals) bestirs himself and comes to a realization of his potentialities and obligations there will be no culture for him to contribute." In

---

* It is especially notable that some of our leading jazz musicians have, over the past decade, turned increasingly to the East for artistic inspiration.

Robeson's terms, potentialities had to be developed into actualities that would tighten the bonds between Blacks, especially in America. Without moving closer to nationality, to making more effective use of the attributes of a nation, they could scarcely make the leap onto the international plane to help effect the needed cultural transformation. And nations contributing to the new cultural dispensation would be answering the demands of a world-necessity which would lead in time, Robeson hoped, "to the 'family of nations' ideal."

As essential as he felt the elements of nationalism to be, Robeson realized the limitations of the nation, that the "family of nations" ideal must become the eventual reality if mankind is to survive. He wanted, in the final analysis, to see a world striving for deep spiritual and cultural values that transcend "narrow national, racial, or religious boundaries." With the right encouragement, *that* impulse, he felt, could come from Blacks in America. Still, black people should share in the new world culture *as Africans*—a goal to be worked for, not willed.

A decade before the appearance of F. S. C. Northrop's important *The Meeting of East and West,* Robeson had systematized his thinking on the need for creative equilibrium between the spiritual and the material, between a life of *intuition and feeling* and one of *logical analysis.* In a word, he had called for a synthesis of the cultures of the East and West.

When Robeson turned to America he saw the worst qualities of Europe in magnified form. Having devoted years of research and reflection to identifying life styles peculiar to people on the major continents of the world, he placed white America in this broad cultural setting and found her wanting. Apart from technology (which because of its capitalistic guidance was not being used humanely), Robeson saw very little of value in white America.

> The modern white American is a member of the lowest form of civilization in the world today. My problem is not to counteract his prejudice against the Negro . . . that does not matter. What I have set myself to do is to educate my brother the Negro to believe in himself. . . . We are a great race, greater in tradition and culture than the American race. Why should we copy something that is inferior.

Black liberation in such a country would not be achieved through the NAACP's emphasis on racial cooperation. Many Afro-Americans, he argued, would have to fight and die for their freedom. "Our freedom is going to cost so many lives," he remarked, "that we mustn't talk about the Scottsboro case as one of sacrifice." He continued: "When we talk of freedom we don't discuss lives." His realization that, given the objective conditions, black people might have to resort to violence before achieving their freedom was by no means the only, or even the most significant, example of his prophetic insight. With awesome precision he predicted that if Negroes persisted in efforts "to be like the white man within the next generation they will destroy themselves." Developments over the past thirty years make it eminently clear that this instance of cultural analysis and prognostication is of a very high order indeed.

Robeson said that he would, as part of his effort to convince "my poor people that their culture traces back to . . . great civilizations," make films, produce plays, sing chants and prayers. He also expressed a desire "to play the great black emperor Menelik." Again reflecting on the black man's feelings of inferiority he said that he would "do anything to convince my people that they are great."

> Meanwhile in my music, my plays, my films I want to carry always this central idea: to be African. Multitudes of men have died for less worthy ideas; it is even more eminently worth living for.

This is not the place for attempting to determine precisely the extent to which Robeson helped his people realize their greatness. Yet it is possible to draw certain conclusions on the basis of what we now know about the man during the thirties. If he had not convinced, through his incredible array of gifts, the majority of his people of the greatness of Africa, he had by 1938 shown scores of thousands of them what genius is possible for one of African ancestry. Black people could look at his example and not find another in the entire world to equal it for wide-ranging brilliance. If the race pride of some was heightened by his achievements as singer and actor in the thirties, then he brought them that much closer to believing in the possibility of the greatness of the African past, of an African return to greatness.

Had more black people read his essays and interviews of the period, his influence would have been greater still, for he would then have illumined, for them, various aspects of their culture and heritage in America and on the African continent. But since his essays and interviews contain the theoretical basis for the unity which must be built, the political implications of his scholarship, as his cultural philosophy becomes more widely known, should be perceived before long by relatively large numbers of black people.

Though we need to know more about Robeson's scholarship, we already know that his command of African linguistics, art history, folklore and music appears to have been incomparable. Moreover, the degree to which he had, by the thirties, grasped the fundamental dynamics of world cultural groupings is especially worth pondering. This expansive knowledge, coupled with his own deep and multifaceted involvement in the arts, provided an extraordinary background for analyzing and understanding the vital components of black and white culture in America. His writings on culture, incontestably "nationalistic" in many respects, finally went beyond nationalism when he posited the preconditions for the world cultural revolution—the proper balancing of the emotional and rational, under some form of socialism, in order to avert the plunge over the precipice into the abyss of chaos and death; in order to give new, more creative life to the whole of mankind. The quest for nationality, to state the matter differently, was for Robeson a prerequisite for Blacks in this country having something of truly lasting worth to offer to the world community.

On the basis of what is now known about Robeson's scholarship, it seems not unreasonable to advance the view that he has easily earned a place high on that select list of major commentators on American culture, a list that includes W. E. B. Du Bois, Sterling Brown, Constance Rourke, F. S. C. Northrop, Ralph Ellison and Melville Herskovits. Before long, it should not be possible to conduct a serious discussion of black culture or to relate American culture to the main value systems of the world, without giving respectful attention to the cultural philosophy of Robeson. There is much irony here, for his most enduring and profound influence, despite all of the efforts to silence the man and to blot his example from our minds, will very likely be a result of his heretofore largely unknown intellectual achievements.

I wish to express my gratitude to Mr. Lamont Yeakey for invaluable assistance in the preparation of this paper—*Sterling Stuckey*.

The Culture of the Negro *

Critics have often reproached me for not becoming an opera star and never attempting to give recitals of German and Italian songs as every accomplished singer is supposed to do. I am not an artist in the sense in which they want me to be an artist and of which they could approve. I have no desire to interpret the vocal genius of half a dozen cultures which are really alien to me. I have a far more important task to perform.

When I first suggested singing Negro spirituals for English audiences, a few years ago, I was laughed at. How could these utterly simple, almost savage songs interest the most sophisticated audience in the world? I was asked. And yet I have found response amongst this very audience to the simple, direct emotional appeal of Negro spirituals. These songs are to Negro culture what the works of the great poets are to English culture: they are the soul of the race made manifest. No matter in what part of the world you may find him, the Negro has retained his direct emotional response to outside stimuli; he is constantly aware of an external power which guides his destiny. The white man has made a fetish of intellect and worships the God of thought; the Negro feels rather than thinks, experiences emotions directly rather than interprets them by roundabout and devious abstractions, and apprehends the outside world by means of intuitive perception instead of through a carefully built up system of logical analysis. No wonder that the Negro is an intensely religious creature and that his artistic and cultural capacities find expression in the glorification of some deity in song. It does not matter who the deity is. The American and West Indian Negro worships the Christian God in his

---

* An excerpt from an article in the London *Spectator*, June 15, 1934.

65

own particular way and makes him the object of his supreme manifestation which is embodied in the Negro spiritual. But, what of the African Negro? What is the object of his strong religious sense, and how does his artistic spirit manifest itself? These are the questions I have set myself to answer.

As a first step I went to the London School of Oriental Languages and, quite haphazardly, began by studying the East Coast languages, Swahili and the Bantu group which form a sort of Lingua Franca of the East Coast of Africa. I found in these languages a pure Negro foundation, dating from an ancient culture, but intermingled with many Arabic and Hamitic impurities. From them I passed on to the West Coast Negro languages and immediately found a kinship of rhythm and intonation with the Negro-English dialect which I had heard spoken around me as a child. It was to me like a homecoming, and I felt that I had penetrated to the core of African culture when I began to study the legendary traditions, folk song and folklore of the West African Negro. I hope to be able to interpret this original and unpolluted Negro folk song to the Western world and I am convinced that there lies a wealth of uncharted musical material in that source which I hope, one day, will evoke the response in English and American audiences which my Negro spirituals have done; but for me this is only one aspect of my discovery.

It is astonishing and, to me, fascinating to find a flexibility and subtlety in a language like Swahili, sufficient to convey the teachings of Confucius, for example, and it is my ambition to make an effort to guide the Negro race by means of its own peculiar qualities to a higher degree of perfection along the line of its natural development. Though it is a commonplace to anthropologists these qualities and attainments of Negro languages are entirely unknown to the general public of the Western world and, astonishingly enough, even to the Negroes themselves. I have met Negroes in the United States who believed that the African Negro communicated his thoughts solely by means of gestures, that, in fact, he was practically incapable of speech and merely used sign language!

It is my first concern to dispel this regrettable and abysmal ignorance of the value of its own heritage in the Negro race itself. As a first step in this direction I intend to make a comparative study of the main language groups: Indo-European, Asiatic and African, choosing two or three principal languages out of each group, and indicate their comparable stage of development. It may take me five years to complete this work, but I am convinced that the results will be adequate to form a concrete foundation for a movement to inspire confidence in the Negro in the value of his own past and future.

Time to Break the Silence Surrounding Paul Robeson?

BY LOFTEN MITCHELL

When I was a boy in Harlem during the 1920s, his name was on the lips of all my neighbors and friends. They spoke glowingly of this big, handsome, intelligent, brave man who "took nothing off nobody." He was even then a man among men.

From fellow Harlemites I heard the story of his appearance in Eugene O'Neill's play, *All God's Chillun Got Wings,* at the Provincetown Playhouse in Greenwich Village in 1924. This work, dealing with a black lawyer marrying a white woman, was published by the *American Mercury* prior to production. Yellow journalism flared. The press wondered if there would be a race riot at the play's opening. But there was no race riot. Paul Robeson very calmly walked on that stage and gave a remarkable performance.

Later, too, he performed the lead in O'Neill's *Emperor Jones,* on both stage and screen. He made a number of films in England and a Hollywood film version of *Show Boat.* But Robeson voiced discontentment and in 1939 he virtually retired from films, saying, "I thought I could do something for the Negro race in films, show the truth about them and other people, too. I used to do my part and go away feeling satisfied, thought everything was O.K. Well, it wasn't. The industry was not prepared to permit me to portray the life or express the living interest, hopes and aspirations of the struggling people from whom I come. You bet they will never let me play a part in a film in which a Negro is on top."

I remember this statement quite vividly. It had a profound influence on many theatre people who simply did not believe Hollywood would ever deal in depth with black America. To this very day, Robeson's statement makes sense for, despite the employment of black actors and black stars by the movie industry in these times, the work being offered is, by and large, "pop" stuff, superficially "relevant," perpetuating a new stereotype of the anti-everybody black man.

When Robeson left the movies, he continued with his concert career, ably accompanied by that great musician, Lawrence Brown. And Robeson was among the greatest and most successful concert singers of the twentieth century. Reviews by the music critics for *The New York World* and *The New York Times* document this repetitiously. And Benny Green, the noted English music commentator, had this to say of Robeson: "When he sings I hear the unsullied expression of the human spirit."

While Robeson was winning one accolade after another, he continued to do exactly what his enemies disliked: he never accepted his success at the expense of the suffering of his people. Personal success was not enough for him. He demanded success, liberation, freedom, for all mankind. This demand was contagious in terms of the Black Experience. Its influence was pervasive. In the literary field we see its influence in men like Langston Hughes not wanting to be the Negro writer but working assiduously to promote other black writers. We see it in Dick Campbell of the Rose McClendon Players (in the 1830s) and Abram Hill of the American Negro Theater (in the 1940s) struggling to produce plays by black writers. In short, Robeson was one of those who brought selflessness and brotherhood to fellow black men and women.

An example of this was during the 1930s when he rallied to the support of the Harlem Suitcase Theater. This group, founded by Langston Hughes and Hilary Phillips, produced Hughes's play *Don't You Want to Be Free?* in a loft at 317 West 125th Street, above the site of Frank's Restaurant. The leading role was played by Robert Earl Jones, father of James Earl Jones. Albert Grant, who later directed several of my plays and who is now a lawyer, succeeded Jones in the leading role when the latter joined the cast of a Katherine Cornell Broadway-bound vehicle. Robeson gave the Harlem Suitcase Theater enough of a fellowship for them to employ the brilliant Thomas Richardson to work with the group as artistic director on a full-time basis. Richardson, now deceased, had an enviable record of working with community theater groups and he promptly brought to the Suitcase such talented people as Owen Dodson, Canada Lee and other professionals.

Four years were to elapse before I saw Paul Robeson again. When I saw him then he was starring on Broadway in *Othello,* which featured Uta Hagen and José Ferrer. This work, presented during the 1943-44 Broadway season, was the definitive Othello of the modern theatre. It ran for 296 performances, an all-time record for any Shakespearean play on Broadway. Robeson won the Donaldson Award for the best acting performance in 1944 and the Gold Medal Award for the best diction in the American theater. This latter award, presented by the American Academy of Arts and Sciences, had been won by only nine people since its inception in 1924. There is another feature about Robeson's Othello and it goes unmentioned. He was one of the few actors who performed Othello's epileptic fits on stage, and he was brilliant.

What happened to Robeson as a result of his Othello was a prelude to the terror he later met and the curtain of silence that has been drawn around him.

The absolute inconsistency of the American press played a major role in Robeson's Othello experience. Critics at first sang praises of his performance. One prominent columnist lauded Robeson's performance, but uttered the hope that the great star would be cautious in terms of political activities. What the columnist said, in effect, was: "America has done well by you, black Paul Robeson, but you should sing its praises and not remind it that your black brothers are in chains."

The curtain of silence had begun to descend. The reasons for this curtain of silence, for the present-day question "Who is Paul Robeson?" are too obvious to mention. For one thing, Robeson refused to allow his success to obliterate the sufferings of other black Americans. Instead he used his prestige and talents as weapons in the struggle for freedom.

Second, he acted on his convictions. The racist, right-wing establishment, led by governmental forces, now launched a powerful offensive against this black man who did not "know his place."

This amazing man, this great intellect, this magnificent genius with his overwhelming love of humanity was a devastating challenge to a society built on hypocrisy, greed and profit-seeking at the expense of common humanity. A curtain of silence had to be brought down on him. He had to be kept off TV, maligned and omitted from the history books. Perhaps if we begin to lift the curtain of silence surrounding the accomplishments of Paul Robeson, we may begin to walk down the road toward nationhood and equality.

Paul Robeson in Film: An Iconoclast's Quest for a Role

BY ANATOL I. SCHLOSSER

The story of Paul Robeson as an actor in motion pictures is the story of a quest; a quest for roles in which he could portray the culture and the humanness of his people. The story is one of struggle to maintain his dignity as a Negro* and his integrity as a Negro artist. To reach these objectives he had to overcome an American film industry that perpetuated a racial stereotype of the Negro, and a British film industry that promulgated a colonial vision of Africa.

The history of the Negro in American performing arts up to World War I was the history of the development of the stereotyped Negro on the stage and screen. The advent of the Great War, the subsequent increased integration of the Negro into the American social fabric, and the attempts on the part of some white playwrights to utilize Negro themes, did not appreciably alter the general manner of presentation of Negro characters and themes. It was into this racial and artistic reality that Paul Robeson embarked on his career as an actor on the stage and in motion pictures.

Not long after Robeson's public acclaim for his Provincetown Playhouse productions of *The Emperor Jones* and *All God's Chillun Got Wings,* Hollywood, still in its infancy, began to cast an eye on the popular Negro artist. With the introduction of "talkies," rumors appeared that he was to appear with an "all coloured cast" in a film to be directed by Cecil B. DeMille.[1] The British film industry also looked in Robeson's direction, but

---

* The term "Negro" was one that was used by Paul Robeson in almost all of his writings. In terms of style and in an attempt to be in keeping with Robeson's point of view, I use the same term.

unlike its American counterpart, it was "windy of all 'black subjects'" and insisted on "a strong supporting white cast for a Robeson story."[2] The honor of affording Robeson his cinematic debut fell to film maker Kenneth Macpherson, with *Borderline,* an experimental film shot neither in Hollywood nor the Pinewood Studios, but in Switzerland. *Borderline* attracted little public notice; however, it was important for two reasons: it was "an attempt—the first made by film—to treat the Negro as a sensitive and intelligent being,"[3] and it served to "stimulate one's natural desire to see and hear Paul Robeson in a first rate talkie."[4] This natural desire was soon satisfied by his appearance in the film version of his earlier stage success, Eugene O'Neill's *The Emperor Jones.*

The entire production was housed and shot in a studio on Long Island. One of the major reasons for not shooting on location was the impossibility of filming any major part of the story in the South. In the agreement between the producers and Robeson it was stipulated that his services were to be "rendered by him at any place within the United States of America . . . excepting only such portions of the United States of America as may be south of a line along the Mason-Dixon Line from the Atlantic to the Pacific coasts. . . ."[5]

From the beginning of his film career, Robeson insisted that his dignity as a Negro remain inviolate. What he did in this film contract he was to do in many other instances. A stipulation such as this, even though potentially costly to him and to those working with him, was a means of his insuring that he would not be placed in a situation where he would not be accorded full and equal treatment as a human being.

O'Neill was not interested in having anyone but Robeson play the part of Jones.[6] On his part, Robeson admired the concept of Brutus Jones and considered it a "masterpiece," adding that "O'Neill sounded the very depths of Jones' soul— . . . without a false note in the characterization."[7] O'Neill was proven correct in his choice, for the film was greeted by a daily press that was mostly favorably disposed toward the film and its star. Giving it a rating of three and a half stars, the *Daily News* wrote that "Robeson is probably the only person of this day who is suited in every way to bring 'Emperor Jones' to the screen, and it is another victory for him." [8] However, there is some irony in the fact that what Robeson saw as admirable in the film and part, the Negro press found most objectionable. *The Amsterdam News* rebelled against the use of the word "nigger" finding its use in the film a "shame" and a disgrace," [9] while the *Philadelphia Tribune* editorialized that it found not "one redeeming feature" [10] in the film.

The star was silent on this criticism, perhaps because his thoughts on the role were already a matter of public record. Eight years earlier, when he played the role in front of a London audience he described what he wanted them to see:

> When my . . . audiences watch me play the Emperor Jones, the role of a bad Negro who captures and tyrannizes over the primitives of a tropic isle they see a modern Negro roll up the centuries and reveal primeval man. . . . One does not need a very long racial memory to lose oneself in such a part. . . . As I act, civilization falls away from me. My plight becomes real, the horrors terrible facts. I feel the terror of the slave mart, the degradation of the man bought and sold into slavery. Well, I am the son of an emancipated slave and the stories of my old father are his own. He is emerging from centuries of oppression and prejudice.[11]

In spite of the artistic acclaim garnered by the film and Robeson's own vision of the part, the Negro community saw it as a perpetuation of a stereotype.

Although he was enthusiastic about the technical aspects of the cinema, Robeson faced the problem of finding suitable stories and roles. He believed that the film industry could be used to break the stereotype Negro usually portrayed and to present the Negro as a human being. However, he was fearful of Hollywood, because it could "only visualize the plantation type of Negro—the Negro of 'Poor Old Joe' and 'Swanee Ribber.' " [12] He hoped that after the British film companies had seen *The Emperor Jones* they would see the potential in the number of stories that could be filmed starring a Negro—films that could use an African setting.[13] Among the characters in which Robeson saw potential were the Negro Emperors Menelik and Chaka;

and Rider Haggard's Zulu King, Umbopa, from *King Solomon's Mines.* [14]

The next film in Robeson's career was *Sanders of the River,* one that long plagued him and which was described by his friend, anthropologist Nancy Cunard, as "pure Nordic bunk." [15] Her observation was made out of hindsight and Robeson entered the film with the best of intentions. In the light of his interest in the Negro, Africa, and African culture, it is understandable that he would have been attracted to a film about Africa, especially one including many scenes of dance and song. It was to have been an opportunity for him to bring his African heritage to the eyes of Europe and America. The film, as originally construed, was not only designed to bring African culture to the screen, but also to establish a more dignified image of the Negro,[16] one that would be far removed from the old stereotypes. Under these conditions, the film offered Robeson "the part of his life." [17] He was originally "alight with enthusiasm over the project," [18] and embarked on the film with high hopes; but, as flattering as some of the reviews were, a favorable one such as the following was bound to cause some uneasiness in Robeson's mind: "Bosambo's doglike devotion to Sanders and trust in the magic of the King's law are portrayed by Mr. Robeson with something which transcends mere acting." [19] Something had happened to the film during the editing process. "Bosambo's doglike devotion" was not Robeson's intent, but it was the result.

Robeson found himself in a quandary:

> To expect the Negro artist to reject every role with which he is not ideologically in agreement, is to expect the Negro artist, under our present scheme of things, to give up his work entirely—unless of course he is to confine himself solely to the left theatre.[20]

In spite of this defense, the rapidly maturing artist rejected other offers from the same producer. Within a year, Robeson was less defensive and admitted that the attacks against him for the role were "correct." [21] During that year his view of the world and art expanded; his art and his politics were coming closer together. He would make no more *Sanders.* It became a film which he considered to be a "turning point in [his] public career." [22] Thirteen years later, the film was still on his mind, and he added, "I commited [sic] a faux pas which, when reviewed in retrospect, convinced me that I had failed to weigh the problems of 150,000,000 native Africans. . . . I did it all in the name of art. . . . I hate the picture." [23]

Robeson claimed that the film was changed during the editing and the imperialist stamp imprinted at that time. He was out of the country when the editing took place, crossing Europe on the way to the Soviet Union, where, for him, many changes were to take place. Passing through Germany he encountered the overt racism of Fascist storm troopers, a shock after spending years in England where he had been treated with respect and had met minimal prejudice. However, it was during his visit with Sergei Eisenstein, the Soviet film director, that his view of the world was radically altered. Before he left Moscow he told Eisenstein:

> I hesitated to come, I listened to what everybody had to say, but I didn't think this would be any different from any other place. But—maybe you'll understand—I feel like a human being for the first time since I grew up. Here I am not a Negro but a human being. . . . Here, for the first time in my life I walk in full human dignity.[24]

This new found human dignity was not only for himself. On a larger scale, Robeson saw that what was possible for the "so called" backward peoples of the Soviet Union was also possible for the people of Africa. He discovered a system which was able to bring people to full human economic and cultural dignity in less than three decades.[25] After this experience one can only imagine the upset and distress the artist must have felt upon viewing the final version of Sanders of the River.

A quick trip across the Atlantic, back to the United States, brought Robeson to Hollywood for the filming of Show Boat, in which he was to recreate his stage character of Joe and sing "Ol' Man River," the song that had become synonymous with his name. The script was padded, extra characters added, but the story line remained the same, as did the character of Joe. The film was a predictable success, the popular press lamenting Robeson's "insignificant part." [26] Most of the papers raved about

Robeson's singing, but once again, there were a few members of the Negro press who saw beyond the opulence of the film and the melodious voice. The unkindest cut came from the *California News* which wrote that Robeson "did a better job of portraying the Negro man as a shiftless moron than he did as a weak-kneed Prince in 'Sanders of the River.' " [27] Perhaps a bit harsh, considering Robeson's public admission of sorrow and rejection of *Sanders,* but nonetheless true in the sense that the role was not worthy of the rapidly maturing, more politically aware Robeson. It was to England that the star turned to continue his quest for the right film.

The Song of Freedom, his next venture, has been romantically, but not accurately referred to as "cinematically autobiographical." [28] The film concerns itself with Zinga, a singing dockworker who discovers that he is heir to the throne of an African tribe and goes to Africa to help his people. It was a motion picture that sent film crews scurrying across the Dark Continent to return with exotic footage.

This film reflected two aspects of Robeson's thinking. Socially, the film portrayed the ideas he expressed when writing his article "Primitives" [29] in which he described the union of Western and Eastern cultures. Zinga almost speaks for Robeson when he states, "I already have plans in my mind to bring western culture to this culture—to combine the two—to give them rein and hope and strength." [30] Artistically, both for the Negro and for the film industry, Robeson considered this film a step forward. As described by film historian Peter Noble, it provided an "antidote" to the Hollywood stereotype of the Negro.[31] Robeson himself wrote that "*The Song of Freedom* is the first film to give a true picture of many aspects of the life of a colored man in the west . . . this film shows him as a real man, with problems to be solved, difficulties to overcome." [32] While most Negro dockworkers are not descended from African royalty, the film does portray a commonplace work situation. Robeson's Negro worker is considered only as one of the men, with nothing special attached to his color. He must maintain relationships with his fellow workers as an individual and not as a Negro.

At a pre-release press conference for the film, the actor noted that protests from the Negro press and Negro organizations often greeted his new productions. Yet he held fast to his belief that he had a better chance of portraying the Negro in a positive manner in England than in Hollywood, which would attempt to make him another Stepin Fetchit.[33] "I want to disillusion the world of the idea that the Negro is either a stupid fellow, as the Hollywood superfilms show him, or a superstitious savage under the spell of witch doctors."[34] He later added, "In America the colour question is too acute, and prejudice is rampant. A serious Negro artist stands very little chance there."[35]

Although *The Song of Freedom* represented an advance in the portrayal of the Negro on the screen, the role was still inadequate for Robeson's talent. One writer astutely saw the basis of the problem: ". . . the trouble lies in the unimaginative commercialization of the screen, the insistence that a black man is not box office unless he be either an Uncle Tom or a dealer in hot rhythms."[36] He suggested that producers forget that Robeson is a Negro and let him simply portray "normal human beings in their mingled baseness and nobility, their greed and cruelty and sacrifice of self. . . ."[37] Certainly these were Robeson's sentiments; however, the "commercialization of the screen" made it difficult to find material which would meet the writer's and Robeson's ideals.

The next opportunity he had for achieving these ideals was with a script that he had long thought appropriate for him, *King Solomon's Mines* and the part of Umbopa. Emotionally, Umbopa bears a slight resemblance to Zinga, also a dispossessed king. A man who, when he sees the King Solomon Mountains, has a "look on his face of a man who has found the promised land."[38] Robeson, like Umbopa and Zinga, was looking for a spiritual homeland and found it in Africa.

He was eager for this role, for he claimed to be tired of stories that were written for him or around him. He was pleased that in this film there was a "definite part taken out of a book" for him.[39] Although he was reported to be pleased with the role, he urged changes in the script where it tended to perpetuate the film stereotype of the bloodthirsty savage.

The film received tepid reviews and was described as a

"thriller guaranteed to delight the youngsters." [40] From the stand-point of his progress in film making, the best comment came from the *Pittsburgh Courier* which found that "the fact that it didn't reek with the imperialistic theory of British superiority . . . is a big improvement." [41]

It was in his next film, *Big Fella,* in the role of Banjo, that Robeson found a role which gave him greater scope for his acting than his previous British pictures, and those who saw the film agreed. The trade journal *Kinematograph* applauded the role, which gave Robeson the opportunity to use his "tremendous histrionic ability." [42] At last Robeson had appeared in a story which did not touch on Africa or Negroes *per se*.[43] "Robeson is dressed for this one. . . . And for once, to his own delight, he is not playing a half-naked African chief." [44] A letter from the author to the director lends some insight into the pitfalls Robeson wished to avoid in the character of Banjo, pitfalls the authors sought to eliminate: ". . . we propose to make it clear in the dialogue that he does work for his living, mainly by doing odd jobs around the docks, and that the police know him as a steady, trustworthy sort of fellow." [45] The authors were aware of Robeson's thinking about the nature of the roles he had previously portrayed, the roles he sought, and how he wished to portray the image of the Negro on the screen. It was with this in mind that they changed the name of the film from *Banjo* to *Big Fella.* They wrote that *Banjo* "might lead the audience to expect a sort of 'Uncle Sambo' of the cotton plantations." [46] Apparently, it never occurred to anyone to change the name of the character for the same reason.

Nowhere in the film did the hero appear to suffer because of his color; like Zinga in *The Song of Freedom,* he was admired for his physical strength and character. Both men survived in an integrated society, the docks, and had to maintain relationships on an individual basis. These men were so strong, physically and spiritually, that there now developed the new possibility of portraying the Negro as superhuman. Neither of these roles was carried to such an extreme, but the pendulum of the stereotype, through them, was swinging in the other direction.

It was with anticipation that film buffs and Robeson fans

waited to see what his next film would bring. Unfortunately, the artistic expectations that were raised with *Big Fella* were not to be realized. *Jericho* was another African spectacle, with thousands of feet of scenic film of the African desert. It was regarded as a "praiseworthy but only moderately successful attempt." [47] The story of a Negro soldier befriending his white officer and helping him during the war in Europe and later in Africa, was a "disappointment." [48] Once again there was the familiar complaint, that "Surely a better story than that could have been invented to show Paul Robeson singing lustily in the African desert. . . ." [49]

In spite of the negative criticism of the film on the basis of its art, Robeson saw it as a positive advance in terms of his ideology. There were two parts to the character of Jericho that appealed to the artist. The first half involved the dehumanizing effects of the military and war; the second, the spiritual regeneration of the Negro who finds a home in Africa. Robeson thought that the role of Jericho was the best part he had played to date, and a long step away from the Negro caricature.[50] He was not alone in this belief. The usually critical Negro press wrote that "Mr. Robeson redeems himself . . . those who have been longing for this type of screen drama which will enable them to hold their heads in pride need look no further. . . ." [51]

In spite of his increasing success, Robeson announced his intention of retiring from commercial entertainment. The film industry had been too slow in finding vehicles suitable for his artistry and philosophy. The journal *Truth* sounded part of the basis of the problem: "It should not be beyond the powers of the film industry to give him a more suitable background. . . . And perhaps if someone were to offer him a serious Negro subject, a cross between *Othello* and *Emperor Jones*. . . ." [52]

This rupture with the film industry was long in coming. Robeson had previously expressed unhappiness about specific roles and the general direction in which the film industry appeared to be going, both in finding parts for him and in the nature of the portrayal of the Negro on the screen. Robeson's new roles represented a departure from the stereotype that the industry traditionally presented to the public, but the advance was not rapid enough. He had accepted roles offered to him and rose to the rank of star in the hope that when he achieved stardom he could "insist upon the type of roles he wanted." [53]

Reflecting on the situation, he wrote, "I thought I could do something for the Negro race in the films; show the truth about them—and about other people too. I used to do my part and go away feeling satisfied. Thought everything was O.K. Well, it wasn't." [54] The actor discovered that the industry was not prepared to permit him to "portray the life or express the living interests, hopes and aspirations of the struggling people from whom I come. . . . Any Negro who achieves success automatically becomes a representative of his people, and as such bears an added responsibility. . . ." [55] As a result of this situation, he announced that he was "no longer" willing to be identified with an "organization that entirely ignores the many dynamic forces at work in the world today." [56] As Robeson's artistic and political thought grew and developed, he began to see his predicament not as a personal one, but as one endemic to the entire industry:

> One realizes that the film also is the medium through which to express the creative abilities of the masses. That is what folk culture means at this time. The genius of the Negro people lies close to the mass roots. When the screen is prepared to show the people of the United States as PEOPLE getting away from love intrigues and from preoccupations with individualistic futility and, instead, focusing on the struggles and aspirations of the Negro masses for freedom, for liberty, and for the right to live a democratic life—when the film does that, it will clearly reflect the struggles and aspirations also of the whole American people. . . . [57]

In spite of his pronouncements and public discontent with the film industry, Robeson continued to receive offers from both American and British companies. He was forced to reject them because they wanted him to appear as, what he described as, a "savage doing that absurd tomahawk-throwing, spear-brandishing act." [58] He announced that he would return only if there were a "subject so worthwhile that he could not disregard it." [59]

For almost two years Robeson continued to refuse roles from major companies. Then he announced that he was going to appear in a film being produced by a small independent film company, in which he would "depict the Negro as he really is—not the caricature he is always represented to be on the screen." [60] David Goliath, hero of *Proud Valley*, was that worthwhile role for which Robeson had been waiting. Ealing Studios had found the script that met Robeson's specifications.

Proud Valley was a film about the Welsh miners in Blaendy and the difficult conditions under which they worked and lived; a film about David Goliath, a drifter who is befriended by a miner and taken into his home. Goliath in turn befriends the family and ultimately gives his life for his miner friends. The film, shot during the early part of World War II, received only mildly favorable reviews, suffering from comparison to *The Stars Look Down*, another recent film dealing with the life of the miners. However, the importance of the film was best summed up by *The Afro-American:*

> Hollywood should take note, for Hollywood has never produced a picture in which a colored actor or actress has been cast as Robeson is cast in "Proud Valley," which is Hollywood's loss, and more important, a loss to millions of moviegoers who have been waiting to see a colored man cast as a man. . . . The part he plays in shaping lives, loves and working opportunities in a little, poverty-stricken mining town—his smile, his pat on the back, his ability to take hardships—this is Robeson's real justification for being the picture's leading role.[61]

In theme and character this role was the best that Robeson had found or was ever to find. The role represented a culmination of his social and artistic thought. As one critic phrased it, "there is no colour bar in Blaendy; they are all black men in the pit." [62]

His quest for the right story and role continued. He returned to the United States and for three years refused offers from Broadway and Hollywood, stating: "I'm sorry, too, selfishly, but this resentment in my people goes deep. I can't let them down by doing the things they hate." [63] After waiting he decided to attempt a rapprochement with the American film industry and accepted a role in Twentieth Century Fox's *Tales of Manhattan*.

The film consisted of six stories connected through the travels of a dress coat. Each episode was studded with some of the biggest stars in Hollywood, which alone guaranteed long lines at the box office. The odyssey of the fancy dress coat began as the result of a bullet hole and finally concluded as it was jettisoned out of an airplane, its pockets stuffed with $43,000 of stolen money. The coat and the money fell on the land of a Negro sharecropper, Paul Robeson, and his wife, Ethel Waters. The money was divided among the members of the community and the film ended with a chorus of "Glory Day," sung by Robeson and the Hall Johnson Choir.

The film was a setback for Robeson, criticized by both white and Negro press for the picture he presented of the Negro as an "ignorant, child-like, tuneful creature. . . ." [64] However, one defending voice was that of Dan Burley, critic for the *New York Amsterdam News*, who saw it as Robeson did, as a powerful indictment of the absentee landlord and the sharecropping system. The portrayal, Burley thought, was legitimate, because such conditions of poverty and its attendant ignorance and superstition are actual. He concluded that "It is to be doubted that the producers themselves were aware of the excellent job of subtle slapping of America's caste system which they accomplished in *Tales of Manhattan*." [65]

The subtlety was apparently not lost in the South. It was reported that Southern distributors and exhibitors levelled criticism at the film because it ended with a Negro sequence and with Paul Robeson's uttering of "communistic" sentiments.[66] Archer Winston, critic for the *New York Post*, also commented on these sentiments, stating that it was "most interesting to hear Robeson demanding a tractor with his share of the money, suggesting that land be bought with it and a communal effort against poverty be made. These must have been the lines that persuaded him to take this role." [67]

His concluding speech and the real-life situation of abject poverty were indeed what had attracted Robeson to this role, although after completing the film he is quoted as saying, "I wouldn't blame any Negro for picketing this film." [68] He went on to say that "when I first read the script I told them it was silly," but he hoped that he could change it during the filming.[69] Robeson was disappointed because of his failure to effect any change in this film, and Hollywood's attitude. "Hollywood," he wrote, "says you can't make the Negro in any other role because it won't be box office in the South. The South wants its Negroes in the old style." [70] For him, the film was an unsuccessful attempt to reach some understanding with the Hollywood filmmakers. He decided that he was through with them until the industry "found some other way to portray the Negro besides the usual 'plantation hallelujah' shouters." [71]

His disenchantment with the industry prevented him from ever appearing in another film; however, he did lend his voice to two independently made films. He was the narrator in *Native Land,* a film which concerned itself with "brutal violations of the American Bill of Rights." [72] This film caught the attention of Congressman Martin Dies, Chairman of the Un-American Activities Committee, who charged that the film was Communist-inspired.[73] *Song of the Rivers* was the last film. It concerned itself with the working peoples of the world who toiled along the banks of the four great rivers of the world: the Mississippi, the Ganges, the Nile and the Volga. Robeson sang the lyrics written by Bertolt Brecht, which were set to music by Shostakovich. It was a film fitting to be his last. It represented the acme of his political and artistic development. Starting with his base and roots deep in his background and identity as a Negro, Robeson was able to grow ever upwards to link his spirit with peoples of other races and all exploited peoples. Through his understanding of the suffering of his people, he was able to reach out and embrace all others who toiled and suffered.

Artistically, in film, Robeson faced many of the problems that confronted him in the theatre, but the problems were intensified and more difficult to surmount, and have not yet been fully overcome. Film is a medium which, by its very nature and manner of presentation, reaches a larger audience than theatre. Lower admission prices than those for theatre also account for its greater popularity as a form of entertainment. Writing in 1930, James Weldon Johnson noted that:

> moving pictures are not made for one theatre or one city or even one section of the country; they are made to suit everybody as nearly as possible; so they are built on the greatest common denominator of public opinion and public sentiment. In no moving

picture then, has any Negro screen actor been permitted to portray as high a type as had been portrayed on the stage.[74]

It was in the midst of such conditions that Robeson was to work during his film career. Taking a great leap forward with *The Emperor Jones,* he took a giant step backward with *Sanders of the River.* It was a failure and remained a source of shame for him. Ironically, it was as a result of this film that he became "box office" in Europe, so that he became independent of Hollywood and was in a position to try to dictate the sort of role he wanted.[75] The slow but steady growth in his following films seemed to attest to this, for each showed a marked growth in the portrayal of the Negro on the screen. In his last four commercial films, Robeson appeared for the most part fully clothed, which in itself was an advance from the roles that used his physique as a salable commodity. In most of his films, Robeson appeared as a Negro star in mixed casts, playing opposite leading white actors, except in *Proud Valley,* where he was the only Negro—the star, with an all-white cast—in a major film production. In each of his later films, his characters possessed the material out of which standard celluloid heroes were made: bravery, brawn, intellect, sensitivity, good humor, loyalty, and at times, even a love interest with a loyal, devoted, and good woman.

But these were British films, which did not attract large audiences in the United States; Negro or white. Given the realities of racial prejudice, one could understand why the "common denominator" of the white audiences would not be attracted to a character of the dimensions portrayed by Robeson. But what kept the Negro audience away; the same audience that would crowd a hall to hear him sing? Herb Golden, writing for the showbusiness journal, *Variety,* offered a possible explanation for the lack of Negro as well as white interest, ". . . out is any mixing of Negroes and whites in a film. A picture costing $100,000 was made in England with Paul Robeson and an otherwise okay cast. It grossed virtually nothing among Negro audiences in this country." [76] Was it that neither side wished to cross the color bar?

Robeson as an actor in theatre and film was confronted with the choice that faced all Negro performers. Is the choice to play a role that one considers less than worthy a private or a public one? For years the Negro performer was content to get any role, much less a starring one. But somewhere along the way, Robeson, and many other artists, came to understand that the choice involved a responsibility to himself, not only as an artist, but to himself as a Negro, and to his people. Robeson made the choice, one that helped him grow as a person, as an artist, and one that helped his people. Claude McKay best sums up the importance of Robeson as an actor and the importance of his quest:

> As an *artiste* he has increased the dignity of and the respect for the Negro. . . . Robeson is hailed as a pathfinder by the large body of young educated Negroes. He is one of them. They see in him the iconoclast, breaking down the old traditions. . . .[77]

Paul Robeson's Mission in Music

BY ANATOL I. SCHLOSSER

In Paul Robeson's tripartite world of performance—theatre, film and music—music was the one in which he discovered that he could best realize his personal ambitions and political vision. In his native ante-bellum New Jersey, he was schooled in the ways of white America and his place as a Negro. It became apparent to him that in spite of a scholarship to and a degree from Rutgers University, in spite of being named an All-American football star, in spite of a law degree from Columbia University, the barriers of racial prejudice would stand between him and his ability to fulfill himself in his then chosen field of law. He turned to the stage, where he found that "whether singing or acting, race and color prejudices are forgotten. Art is one form against which such barriers do not stand." [1]

In the concert field he could command a more select audience than the one which attended the theatre and cinema. He could exercise more control over the content of a recital than over a play or a film script. He could dictate the cities and halls in which his concerts were held. Robeson also realized quite early in his acting career that "you can easily exhaust dramatic roles that a negro [sic] can choose from, but . . . there is no end to the songs he can sing [if] he has the voice." [2] For him, song was more closely linked to his people than acting. He noted that "the artist, as an actor, is a bit more removed from direct contact with his source than the singer. . . ." [3] He regarded his music as a medium to be used to educate, to convince: "When I stand up before an audience I know that somehow a power is given me to convince—as Walt Whitman says: By my presence. I long to convince the whites, of course, but my people more than all—that it is worth while being a Negro, that the Negro has something great to say." [4]

Almost from the very beginning, he spoke of a public, socially oriented aspect of his singing. "I want to sing," he stated, "to show people the beauty of Negro folk songs and work songs." [5] The "people" included his own, because "many of them have felt that the old spirituals were not in keeping with the aspirations of the modern Negro." [6] He believed that "the distinctive gift the Negro has made to America has not been from the brilliantly successful colored men and women . . . it is from the most humble of our people that the music now recognized as of abiding beauty has emanated." [7] This music was to him "unquestionably, a body of genuine folk music equally as genuine as English, Russian, German or French. . . . They are peculiar to America, and they have evolved out of a tradition of slavery. . . ." [8]

Robeson became a man with a mission: a mission to bring to light a true picture of the Negro. It was through song that he believed he could best serve them. ". . . to interpret the Negro soul through Negro song—that is what I've come to regard as my purpose in life." [9]

His years in England and contact with many Africans there increased his interest in his ancestral roots in Africa. He wrote numerous articles concerning the social condition of the American Negro and the American Negro's relationship to Africa. He also extended this thinking to music. When speaking of the spirituals, he did not refer only to their Biblical thematic origins, but also to their African melodic origins. "I think," he wrote of the spirituals, "they have definite connections with Central Africa, whence the natives were carried into slavery in America. It was under the lash of the whip that they developed their musical gifts and the Bible gave them a background for their spirituals." [10]

It was during these same years in England that much of Robeson's artistic and political maturity took place. There he developed a greater consciousness of his political self as a Negro and the relationship of the conditions of the American Negro to the conditions of the African, the European Jew and the Russian serf. He then expanded his thinking from a racial line, into one of class consciousness. His "whole social and political development was in England," [11] but always at the base of his thinking would be his consciousness of being a "black man." [12]

In 1934, Robeson and his wife went to the Soviet Union. Stopping over in Berlin, they met the new German order in the form of a group of Storm Troopers who hurled racial epithets at them. The years of personal tranquility in England had not prepared them for this and his reaction was quite strong: "I never understood what Fascism was before. I'll fight it wherever I find it from now on." [13] It was in the Soviet Union that he discovered the ideological weapons to use in that fight. He was impressed with what he saw there, especially the lack of prejudice.

These were the years when he discovered and spoke of the basis of his affinity for the music of other peoples:

> The songs of the peasant are nearest to my heart, no matter what the nation may be. . . . In my Negro heart lies buried the memory of centuries of oppression. The peasants are my kindred, and I do believe that there is a spiritual community among the peasants all over the world. . . .[14]

Robeson began to expand his repertoire. Moving rapidly away from, but always maintaining, a base of Negro spirituals and work songs, he included the folk songs of other peoples. "This is a permanent departure," he announced during an interview. "Folk songs are the music of basic realities, the spontaneous expression by the people for the people of elemental emotions. . . . Negro songs, Russian, Hebrew, and Slavonic folk songs, all have a deep, underlying affinity." [15]

He increasingly lent his talents to anti-fascist organizations. Even his regular concert tours were affected by his growing militant position. His "Ol' Man River," usually a much demanded encore, became a song with "more verve, less sepulchral resignation, than formerly. . . ." [16] At a rally in support of democratic Spain, Robeson changed the words of the song from "I'm tired of livin', and feared of dyin'" to "I must keep on strugglin' until I'm dyin'." [17] Even his Negro slave songs took on new meaning. "Strike the cold shackles from my leg," he sang with feeling, and the audience, sensing that he was singing of Spain, cheered again and again.[18] To his spirituals he added more militant interpretations: ". . . when he tells 'Ole Pharaoh to let my people go,' his eyebrows lower to a scowl which might well be aimed at a dictator. . . ." [19] "His voice," it was written, "is more and more becoming the voice of the soil and the voice of the people. . . ." [20] To reach more of the people, he lowered the price of admission to the stalls.

Robeson's agent worried about the effect that his political appearances and the new price scale would have on his box office.[21] But the ominous predictions of his agent did not materialize. The singer's popularity not only did not decline, but increased. His political activities appeared to have had no effect on his appeal, and coupled with his lowering of the admission price to his concerts perhaps aided in maintaining if not increasing his popularity.

Whereas in England Robeson's mixture of song and politics did not affect his career, there appeared some adverse criticism in his native land. Objections were raised regarding his inclusion of songs for "propaganda reasons," [22] with such objections causing a postponement of his appearance on a nationally broadcast radio program.[23] These faint rumblings against Robeson and his politics would, after the war, become thunderous and attempt to drown him out. None of this deterred the singer from his mission; he continued in his efforts on the part of the oppressed peoples, giving freely of his time and voice.

During the years of his country's involvement in the war, Robeson brought his talents to bear in support of the war effort, by both what he sang and where he sang. "When he sang 'Ballad for Americans,' there was a tenseness of patriotic fervor that swept through the spacious hall because the song was the song of these people. . . ." [24] He sang and spoke at meetings—many at no fee— for war relief groups, war bond drives, unions and factory workers. At the Apex Smelting Company, the largest aluminum smelter in the Chicago area, he gave a concert designed as a "stimulus to greater production and effort. . . ." [25] In a short talk to the workers he emphasized the need for victory and its relationship to the Negro people and to labor. His efforts did not cease with the termination of hostilities. In spite of his fatigue and need for rest,[26] the close of the war brought Robeson to Europe via a USO-sponsored camp show. His work on behalf of the American and Allied effort received recognition from numerous governmental officials and agencies. However, his recognized patriotism was soon forgotten by those who acclaimed him for it.

The postwar, cold war years saw the beginning of the freeze that would try to put the militant Negro into artistic cold storage. Letters arrived at his manager's office complaining of Robeson using his concerts as a "medium for Communist propaganda." [27] The letters objected to his including Russian songs in the concert. To free his voice from the constraints of commercial concerts and this type of attempt to pressure him, Robeson announced that he was going to retire from concert work and devote his talents to trade unions, colleges, and "gatherings where I can sing what I please." [28] The reaction to this announcement was swift. Concert halls across the country closed their doors to him. This did not stop him. He went to the churches of his own people. In spite of the growing opposition to his political songs, the audiences came to hear him.

In Paris, in 1949, Robeson attended a Peace Conference and made what became his renowned "passing remark": [at a meeting] "It is unthinkable that American Negroes would go to war on behalf of those who had oppressed us for generations . . . against a country [the Soviet Union] which in one generation has raised our people to full human dignity of mankind." [29] Interpreted as a treasonous statement, it brought about a further ideological alienation between Robeson and the bulk of the white community and part of the Negro community. It was this reaction to his unswerving militancy that occasioned the infamous Peekskill riots, and increased the difficulties in finding public concert halls.

The following years were to be ones of exile from regular concert halls and auditoriums: an artistic exile in his own land. The State Department's refusal to grant him a passport prevented him from seeking an audience abroad. An economic boycott was waged against him. His records were withdrawn from the shops. Robeson, however, was determined to sing. Denied entry into Canada, he sang to an estimated crowd of 40,000 listeners at the Peace Arch Park on the United States-Canada border.[30] He sang across the Atlantic via telephone to a group of Welsh miners. He also found his audiences in the churches. The son of the minister returned to the churches to sing, in the place of its origin, the music of his people. "My appearances in the churches, small and large, mean a great deal to me. In those churches I appear before the core of our nation." [31]

This period of curtailed activity and almost total media blackout slowly drew to an end. The tempo of his concertizing increased and he began once again to sing in public halls, to packed houses and cheering audiences. Asked if he would resume his concert career under regular auspices, the unbowed, still determined Robeson replied, "I don't know that I ever will. . . . My labors in the future will remain the same as they have in the past. They will be based on my whole experience . . . in the worldwide struggle of working people against their oppressors." [32] Robeson could not change. He added to his recitals part of the vocal finale of Beethoven's Ninth Symphony, including the line "All men are brothers." [33] "All my life," the singer said, "I have been fighting to prove that ALL men are brothers. I am still fighting to prove it. And I intend to continue fighting to prove it the rest of my life." [34]

His first Carnegie Hall concert in more than a decade was held in 1958. Sold out two weeks in advance, he was greeted by a capacity audience and standing ovation. He immediately established his old rapport with an audience from which he had been estranged for eleven years. Again it was not his speeches, but his songs that spoke for him. The Robeson mission was heard in the lines "March beside me, O my brothers, all for one and one for all," which was "not exactly an accurate translation of Schiller's text." [35] Singing the ballad of "Joe Hill," applause greeted the lines, "It takes more than guns to kill a man, says Joe—I never dies." [36] The audience "hung breathlessly" to the emotion of the words, "A house I live in . . . the people I meet, all races, all religions, that's America to me. . . ." [37] Indeed, Robeson had not changed.

In that same year Robeson was granted his passport, and he departed on a long overdue tour of Europe, Australia and New Zealand. While abroad he was asked why he kept his American citizenship. The singer who had given years of his life, art, time, money and talents to a nation that in part rejected him and attempted to imprison his voice, responded to that question: "Because I have a right to it, through the sweat, toil, and blood that were taken from my people." After five and a half years abroad, earning the acclaim of all who heard him, Paul Robeson, American citizen, son of an escaped slave, man with a mission, returned to his native land to rest.

Paul Robeson: Great Friend of the Soviet People

BY SLAVA TYNES

"Pavel Vasilyevich," that is how Paul Robeson, the great American actor and singer, asked to be called after the Russian manner when he visited the Soviet Union. In this way he stressed that in the USSR he had found not only close friends, but also a land of socialism for which he went on fighting so bravely at home, in the United States of America.

Paul Robeson made his first acquaintance with Soviet people in America in 1931. The year following his triumphant performance of Othello on the stage of the Savoy Theatre in London he returned home for a short time and having entered one of the Harlem nightclubs encountered two white men there. One of them was Eduard Tisse, a well-known Soviet cameramen. The other man was Sergei Eisenstein, his fellow-countryman and a world-famous film director. Robeson was pleasantly struck by their simple manner, friendliness and sincerity. They found common ground very soon and in a few days the chance acquaintance turned into real creative friendship.

Since then Paul Robeson started taking an interest in the life of the Soviet state. Three years later he took part in a session of the League of Colored Peoples in London where he spoke about how important it was to preserve and develop the culture of the African peoples. The majority of the speakers of the League larded their speeches with liberal phrases concerning the quest for ways that in the distant future would bring about an equality of people belonging to different races and having skins of different colors. However, one speech evoked some serious thoughts in Paul Robeson. A docker from the Thames, addressing the participants of the meeting, very convincingly said that there was no need to rack one's brains in search of "future ways" when there was the example of the Russians who were already solving national problems. Russia, the docker said, was performing a great deed, one had only to go there and see for oneself. It seemed to Robeson that the speaker was addressing him in particular and telling him that the road to Africa lay through socialism.

There was yet another person in London who prompted Robeson to make a trip to Soviet Russia. This was sixty-year-old Hewlett Johnson, the Dean of Canterbury Cathedral. Johnson said that an economic order that depreciated the achievements of science, an order that intensified the contrasts between luxury and poverty and extended the abyss between the classes, was doomed. According to Hewlett Johnson, everything that he had heard concerning the program of the Russians beginning with 1917 aroused his admiration. He believed that the country would cope with the tasks that had proved beyond the powers of all the ancient and modern states. The plans of the Russians were worth careful study.

The letter which Paul received from Moscow from Sergei Eisenstein, in which the film director invited his new American friend to visit him, put an end to the actor's hesitations. Some time later a report appeared in the press saying that Paul Robeson had announced his decision to visit the land of his forefathers. The way to Africa lay for him via Moscow.

At present it is difficult to describe all those feelings and emotions that Paul Robeson experienced and expressed when he arrived in the Soviet Union for the first time in 1934. A famous actor and singer, a man of great will power who had made his talent serve the struggle for the assertion of the human dignity of black Americans in spite of all the racist threats, arrived in a world completely unknown to him before.

Later Paul recollected that at the time he did not understand the meaning of the events taking place in Russia. The only thing that he, according to his own acknowledgment, understood from the very first moments of his stay in the Soviet Union was that in this country he had found much that he had been seeking for all his life.

In Moscow, Paul Robeson felt the friendly regard not only of Sergei Eisenstein and Eduard Tisse who had invited him. The citizens of the Soviet capital, smiling cheerfully, greeted him in the streets, often stopped him and asked him to tell them about life in America. The warm feelings of the Muscovites and of all the Soviet people whom Robeson met in the country could not help evoking in him an idea of the contrast in the attitudes toward him in the Soviet Union and the United States. Only in the Soviet Union, said Robeson, had he felt himself a real human being. And that is why later he took every opportunity of visiting the USSR again and again.

In the Soviet Union Paul Robeson realized that the liking and respect the Soviet people revealed toward him were explained not merely by politeness and hospitality to a foreigner, but by the international spirit of the Soviet people based on the sympathy and support of the just struggle of the peoples for freedom against all kinds of oppression. And listening to the "Song About Motherland" by Soviet composer Isaac Dunaevsky to the words of poet Lebedyev-Kumach, Paul joyfully repeated the words: "There are neither any black, nor colored people for us." Later, at home, he exclaimed with anger that he could not wait any longer, that Soviet Uzbeks, Turkmens and Kazakhs. had long become equals with their Russian brothers, and this was something to think about!

The acquaintance with the life of Soviet people greatly influenced the formation of Paul Robeson's political views, the development of his class consciousness and the molding of a convinced champion of freedom for his black fellow-countrymen. Communism stopped being something vague for him. Studying the life of the society whose friend he had become, Robeson saw that the ideas of the great philosophers of Marxism had brought freedom and equality to the life of Soviet people. As Paul himself said, it was here that he had found the right way of struggle for the equality of the nations.

In 1936 a fascist mutiny took place in Spain. At meetings held all over the country Soviet people condemned the aggression directed at overthrowing the government of the Popular Front and the establishment of a militarist dictatorship in Spain. At this time Paul Robeson was in the Soviet Union. He saw millions of people saying a resolute "No!" to fascism. He saw young girls and men volunteering to go to Spain to help the Spanish people. He saw internationalism in action. And he understood then that Soviet people followed the principle: it is not enough to love peace, it is necessary to fight for it; it is not enough to sympathize with someone's grief, it is necessary to help to create happiness. And Paul Robeson did his bit—he added thousands of rubles he had earned at the concerts he had given in the Soviet Union to the millions of rubles gathered in the USSR to help Spain in her struggle against fascism. This was his contribution to the cause of struggle for universal peace.

The example of Soviet people inspired Robeson and prompted him to think of many things with great seriousness. And again he visited Moscow, which he called "a university of real life." Robeson came to Moscow in 1937 and 1938. Once he spent almost a year at the Soviet capital. Another time only a few days. He flew over especially to see the New Year in with his Soviet friends. During these visits he derived strength and confidence in his struggle for the equal rights of his fellow-countrymen. That is why the achievements of Soviet people have always been so dear to him.

Once, saying goodbye to his Soviet friends, Paul Robeson said that he was leaving the Soviet Union in a state of elevation, as if he had grown wings that would carry him on to an even more intensive struggle for peace. At home in the USA, making a trip about the country and speaking at different meetings, he told his listeners about his stay in the Soviet Union where they were building a new life and fighting for peace. He called upon his fellow-countrymen to struggle against the preparations for a new war.

When Paul Robeson arrived in Spain in 1938, prompted by a feeling of solidarity with all the antifascists who, arms in hand, defended the republic in the country, he learned Russian songs from the Soviet soldiers of the international brigades. In the trenches of Spain Robeson observed the great friendship of the peoples and he wanted to sing about it. It was there, under the Spanish sky, that Paul Robeson's powerful bass, the voice of a singer and fighter, for the first time sang in Russian the Soviet song "Wide Is My Native Land." His voice came over the Spanish fields covered with the ashes of war, drowning the bursting of fascist bombs and shells, the whining of the bullets and the sound of diving aircraft. "I know no other land where man can breathe so freely . . ." he sang.

After Spain Paul Robeson returned to the USA. But he was a changed man. Now he was not merely a singer, but a convinced political champion. The defeat of the Spanish Republic had not broken him down. On the contrary, his voice became louder and more confident. He disclosed to the American people the truth about fascism and its plans of charging a mortal blow on the young Soviet state and all freedom-loving mankind.

This is how Paul Robeson's friendship with the Soviet people started, a friendship born in the joint struggle for peace and the triumph of justice. Now arriving in the Soviet Union Paul Robeson was not merely a visitor, but a great friend of the Soviet people. And when he spoke about the Soviet Union, he spoke of something very dear to him. Answering the anti-Soviet statements made in the United States Paul Robeson boldly announced that he regarded any insult directed against the Soviet Union as an insult to himself.

When in 1941 the fascist Hitlerite hordes encroached upon the borders of the USSR without declaring war, Paul Robeson directed all his activities at rendering all possible help to his Soviet friends. He spoke at meetings, calling upon Americans to take their place in the first ranks of the struggle against fascism. He told thousands of listeners that the defense of the USSR was a matter that concerned all progressive humanity and all honest Americans.

With all his heart and thoughts Paul Robeson was near Moscow and Stalingrad, near Kursk, on the fields of the great battles in which the fascist army was being defeated. Together with the Russians, the Ukrainians, the Uzbeks and other Soviet peoples he rejoiced in the victories over fascism. On the album of his records "Songs of Free Men" there were inscribed words of love for the land of the Soviets.

In 1945 Paul Robeson shared the joy of the Soviet people in the final victory over fascism. However, soon this joy was clouded by the enemies of the Soviet Union in the USA who were launching a new anti-Soviet campaign. And again Paul Robeson was in the first ranks of the fighters for peace. At the First World Congress of Peace champions held in Paris in April, 1949 he said: "We do not want to fight against the Soviet Union. . . . We stand for peace and friendship with all the nations, with Soviet Russia and the People's Republics. . . . Black people throughout the world will never fight against the Soviet Union, they will do everything in their power to defend the country which in the course of one generation has done away with the age-old backwardness of the national minorities inhabiting it." (Retranslated from the Russian.)

After the Congress was over, Paul Robeson visited Moscow again. He was welcomed as a dear and old friend here. His concerts in the Soviet capital turned into powerful demonstrations for peace of the indefatigable singer and tribune. The American singer and the multinational Soviet public were brought together by their common struggle, common feelings and thoughts.

And every time when Paul Robeson came to the USSR again paragraphs appeared in the Soviet press with warm words addressed to the dear and welcomed friend. Every time he was embraced by the Soviet people who greatly respect and admire his unbending heroic character, who are proud of him, who hold him up as an example for their children and have written books about him in order to commemorate for the generations to come the image of this extremely humane man. Paul Robeson has become a character in some plays by Soviet playwrights, while a mountain summit in the western Tyran-Shan and Trans-Ili Ala-Tau mountains in Central Asia has been named after him.

Paul Robeson is very near and dear to Soviet people.

Our Beloved Pauli

BY OLLIE HARRINGTON

The Bronx street where I grew up must have been the world's puniest black ghetto, one block long, and only half of it at that. On the other side of the street were the pungent Sheffield Farms stables whose sleek tenants in their warm stalls were the envy of every shivering black kid on the block. Our hopes were aimed low: a chunk of cardboard to plug the holes in our shoe soles, a bit of fat meat swimming in gravy and on Sunday, if God's mood was up to it, chicken. Our dreams, or at least my dreams, were more daring. Visions of Miss Murray made into fine hash by the wheels of a locomotive, in slow motion and color. She was the teacher who lasciviously licked her thin lips each time she told our class that all black kids belonged in the trash baskets. How our little white classmates giggled under the psychedelic kick of these first trips on racism. Another joyous dream, awake or asleep, was the howling death of Duffy, that blue-uniformed menace who lurked in the alley next to Belsky's candy store, hungry nightstick twirling on leather thong. Duffy's stick had already put Melvin Toles into bed. He was only nine, but paralysis would keep him there for life. We didn't realize it then, probably because the jack-leg preacher over at Thessalonia Baptist had explained that Melvin was only "kind'a sprained by the Law." Each Fourth of July Duffy's fat buttocks pranced along the Grand Concourse in the Veterans of Foreign Wars parade. Duffy always carried the Stars and Stripes.

Mornings, dry or wet, a tiny flock of black mothers stumbled in arthritic disorder over to Grant Avenue where they numbly waited for the penny-pinching white ladies who would hire them for ten hours. The menfolk trudged across the New York Central tracks to Schrimer's umbrella factory or to the ice-plant. Shame-faced they underbid each other for a day's work. The surplus floated back to some day-long card game or sat in squalid flats staring out of the vapor-glazed window panes.

Saturday nights the air seemed to vibrate. "Sportin' folks" clamored into the inevitable rent party where they stomped and rubbed bellies before settin' down to a heap of heavily tabascoed chitlins washed down with tub-fresh gin. Kids along the block lay awake waiting for the explosion of shouting, cussing, screaming and shattering glass. Often after these happenings Reverend Passley, the barber-bricklayer-undertaker (and, some said, root man) had work to do in the part-time mortuary behind the barbershop. The good Reverend had only one oration which began with: "We so confused and upset all the time that we got to lash out at one another. . . ." Unfortunately the folks often lashed out with a straight razor and this inhibited the Reverend's talents considerably. Which is probably why, it was widely whispered, he preferred the ice-pick which left the deceased looking more natural.

Our sources of inspiration were meager. There was Ray Mitchel the "genius" who could "put just about anything together and make a radio out of it." But to be that "deep" called for schooling and such "fool notions" were throttled at birth by the high-minded dedications of Duffy and Miss Murray. One other possible goal was fuzzily sketched by Mr. Sweet Reuban, who not only owned the corner poolroom but also a most formidable pile of gold on constant display in the open showcase of his upper and lower gums. Sweet Reuban would tip back his pearl-grey, exposing a magnificent head of conked locks and pronounce, "You little 'niggers' will never git nowhere workin' wif your hands and sweatin' all over the damn place. You ever heard of a president sweatin'?" With that he would reach into his vest pocket for the famous gold toothpick and gently dig around the nuggets with little sucking noises. But by then the predatory eyes of the oracle were focused on some other world and we knew that we'd been dismissed.

The kids disappeared one by one into the fog of other black slums. All except Biffo, our beloved jester. Biffo found his golden hoard—all $17.50 of it—in a night-shuttered tailor shop. The widowed Polish woman who owned the shop lay in a pool of her own blood the next morning. Biffo's gravelly laugh floated up from the dark cellars and vestibules along the block for several nights. In these hastily commandeered love bowers Biffo squandered his fortune, converted into chocolate-covered nut bars, on giggling, squealing teenage girls. Duffy followed the candied spoor and pounced, delivering Biffo to the plainclothesmen and eventually the electric chair at Sing Sing. We climbed the rickety tenement stairs to the flat of Biffo's work-gnarled father, drawn by whispered rumors of horrible burns on Biffo's skull. But he lay in a sealed coffin and we quietly crept out, leaving the huge black father rocking wordlessly over an oilcloth-covered kitchen table.

My hopeless world was smashed by Meyer Fischer. Every morning at five Meyer and his wife Blanche rolled in the heavy ten-gallon milk containers, then tugged and swiveled the bulky bread baskets to open their unheated grocery store. They were, and always would be poor Jews because they couldn't resist mumbled pleas for credit which was rarely repaid. Many afternoons I sat on a meal sack while Meyer, clasping and unclasping his blue-veined hands, his tiny mouth puffing vapor in the freezing cold store, told me of black poets, teachers, black doctors. One day he told me of an unbelievable black man named Paul Robeson. He told me of this black man who was not as good as white men. He had to be, and he was, ten times better. Meyer's piercing eyes refused to release my unbelieving stare. They willed me to think that perhaps there was such a black man! And if there was it would mean that we were not trash and dirt—even though black. It was a soul-splitting thought. It was a blowtorch burning out the foundations of existence. I, along with every child and adult on the block, was cruelly maimed by everything I'd ever seen, or heard, or even tasted. We knew that we were a tiny lepers' island surrounded by the "land of the free and the home of the brave." Even the church steeple "crosstown" had its backside turned in our faces. The red-faced butcher, who could barely speak English, kept a special pile of offal for his "nigger trade." If there were ever a Nobel Prize for the vivisection of living, breathing black kids Miss Murray should have had it. Duffy the Law was tearing out palpitating black hearts long before Dr. Barnard left the diaper stage. And when we thought of Duffy we thought of the Stars and Stripes. We were "niggers" and we'd been so magnificently brainwashed in what that meant that the only art, the only poetry in our little "nigger" hearts was:

> A chicken aint nothin' but a bird
> A nigger aint nothin' but a turd.

The caterpillar, covered with grey-green, undulating hairs, hides its slimy ugliness inside a cocoon. When the season arrives some magic in nature opens the prison and a completely new creature emerges to rest on a leaf in God's air. Gently it folds and unfolds its breathlessly beautiful wings in the strength-building sunlight. Black children carrying their "niggerness" like lead weights on anxiety-tensed shoulders can experience this same metamorphosis. It's happening all around us. On my single-street ghetto it happened when Meyer Fischer first told me of Paul Robeson.

Five years later my "wings" had lifted me out of the tiny Bronx ghetto and set me down in a real people-sized one—Harlem. The rest of America was being cruelly ravaged by the depression but Harlem only giggled over the sounds of self-pity which the wind carried from across the Central Park lake. "Baby, if you crave to see some real, honest-to-goodness depression, come to Harlem, the Home of Happy Feet," giggled the wits on "the turf." I discovered that I wasn't any more hungry learning to draw and paint at the National Academy of Design than I would be huddled up in my room. Anyway it was free and the academy rooms were warm. At night bunches of us milled around the sidewalk outside the Idle-Wyle or the Big Apple. Downtown they were still mournfully talking about the good, solid white folks who had walked into space from Wall Street's many windows. Uptown we were talking about Paul Robeson, who was singing songs that gripped some inner fibres in us that had been dozing. And he was saying things that widened black eyes and sharpened black ears, things that sounded elusively familiar. But there were a few cats in the crowd who somehow managed to own one Brooks Brothers suit. They sported frat pins (jimcrow frats) and pretended to read the finan-

cial section of *The New York Times* which they'd found on the
floor of some Lenox Ave. IRT local. "That damn Robeson," they
grumbled, "gon' make the big white folks mad, you just wait and
see." They were right. Robeson did make the big white folks mad.
But when his voice boomed, "I hear America singing," he blew
flame in the souls of black folk, and a hell of a lot of white folks
too, where dim embers had barely glowed since the days of reconstruction.

One blustery night the space between the bar and the lunch
counter at the "Harlem Moon" rocked and reeled in the heat of
another "Robeson debate." Hopeless fear, cynicism and outraged
frustration quickly drew the lines between "Uncle Tom niggers"
and "goddamn red niggers." A flat-footed, sad-eyed waiter from
New Haven said to me, "Son, them students up there got so much
money they don't know what to do. They requires an awful lot of
service. Now if you can get together enough for one semester you
can hustle your way through." It was a long story but I got there.
One of the waiters in the Chi Psi house where I was installed as
head—and only—dishwasher asked me, "How in the hell did a
little-assed 'nigger' like you get to come to Yale?" All I could answer was, "I guess it was Paul Robeson." "What," he gasped, "you
know Paul Robeson?" I lifted a tray of steaming glasses out of the
suds and said, "Nope. Just know of him."

My first real job was as art editor of the *People's Voice*. Adam
Powell, Charlie Buchanan and Ben Davis published that great
sheet and one day Adam called me into his office. "Ollie," he said,
"there's someone I want you to meet." A beaming giant of a man
left his chair, thumped me on the back with a hand as powerful
as John Henry's sledgehammer and boomed, "Feller, I just wanted
you to know that those cartoons of yours are great." Of course it
was Paul Robeson. I can't remember doing much more than gulp-
ing. What can one say to a mountain? But it was the beginning
of a treasured friendship.

Paul walked into that ramshackle Harlem newspaper office one
afternoon with Ilya Ehrenburg, one of the world's great writers.
With them came a tiny slip of a woman, the captain of a Soviet
ship that had been torpedoed and sunk in a convoy. Robeson
spoke to the staff. Ehrenburg spoke and thanked all Americans,

in the name of the Soviet Union, for the weapons the Red Army was putting to such good use against Hitler's killer hordes. And he made it clear that this deep gratitude included all the people of Harlem. The little ship's captain—I believe her name was Valentina—spoke no English but she beamed as if she'd lived in Harlem all her life. Later we discovered that she'd lost all her clothing at sea. In two days a bespectacled black tailor on 126th Street had made her a uniform and overcoat that must have been the pride of the Soviet merchant fleet. MADE IN HARLEM and joyfully paid for by everyone on the staff, from editor to telephone receptionist.

There are many other treasured snapshots engraved in my mind. Paul, a great one for a session of "talkin' and signifyin'," sitting astride an ancient-looking desk in the miniature-sized office of his publication *Freedom*. Again I was contributing cartoonist and fascinated spectator. Paul was holding forth on the wizardry of old Josh Gibson, Satchel Paige and other black ballplayers jimcrowed out of what was euphemistically called the national pastime. Listening were editors Lou Burnham and George Murphy, with Lou exploding every now and then with a characteristic, "Amen, Amen!" Behind the desk sat a diminutive secretary whose lovely brown face was illuminated with a serenity that seemed curiously out of place in a loft on 125th Street. "One day," said Paul, "our boys are going to bust right into the Yankee Stadium dugout and teach 'em the fine points of the game." The little secretary's eyes twinkled and she asked, "Mister Robeson, shall I make a note to get a committee together this afternoon?" Paul stopped in mid-sentence and then "fell out." Lou dissolved into a laughter-shaken mass on a pile of newspapers, and George, always cool, sat shaking his head. The secretary who was there gently growing her wings was Lorraine Hansberry.

There are many other memories. A huge sea of black folk silently filling Seventh Avenue as far as one could see. It was Ben Davis's last campaign for a seat on the City Council and it was night, drizzling. Ben had lost, with the help of the cops who somehow managed an epidemic of polling booth breakdowns that day. But the crowds waited patiently outside Ben's election headquarters in the Theresa Hotel. One of those thoroughly reliable Harlem rumors had it that Paul would sing. "Naw," said someone, "his man lost so what he gon' sing for?" An old church sister just smiled and said, " 'Cause he said he would." And then there was Robeson and the heart-filling voice singing, "What is America to me."

Not very long ago I was invited by the satirical *Krokodile* to see the Soviet Union. In Tashkent I sat on a park bench where I could drink in the breathtaking oriental beauty of the opera house. I was thinking of coming back the next day with my sketch pad when a little Uzbek girl came to me holding out a flower. Her oval face was so lovely, even with the tooth missing from in front. Of course I couldn't understand what she was saying but Yuri, my interpreter, explained, "She asks if you are Paul Robeson?" Her mother appeared and suddenly it seemed there were hundreds of Uzbek children with their mothers, all carrying hastily picked flowers. I was terribly flustered but I managed to explain that I wasn't Paul Robeson but that he was my friend. And then one Uzbek mother, proud of her English said, "Here, he is our beloved Pauli."

American Negroes in the War *

BY PAUL ROBESON

World War II has been repeatedly and eloquently described as a war in the interest of the common man, the little man—a people's war of liberation. Americans who have not known through personal experience the meaning of fascist oppression may be prone to think of such characterizations of the war as only fine rhetorical and idealistic expressions.

But the Chinese, the Ethiopians, the Russians and all the peoples of Europe upon whom the axis forces have heaped murder and destruction know full well what it is they are fighting for. *They* understand—in their hearts and in every conscious moment of their existence—what a people's war of liberation means.

I was in Spain when the loyalist forces, alone and singlehanded, were struggling to liberate their country from the rising power of fascist tyranny. I saw there what the fight against fascism was. I saw it in the eyes of little children and women, and in the eyes of the soldiers, the Spaniards and their volunteer allies, the noble International Brigade, which I am proud to say included some American Negroes.

Other people, however, besides the direct victims of axis aggression also have a genuine awareness of the democratic significance of the present conflict. Their awareness is born of their yearning for freedom from an oppression that has predated fascism, and their confidence that they have a stake in the victory of the forces of democracy.

The American Negro has such an outlook. It dates from the fascist invasion of Ethiopia in 1935. Since then, the parallel between his own interests and those of oppressed peoples abroad has

---

* Speech at the Twelfth Annual *Herald Tribune* Forum, November 16, 1943.

been impressed upon him daily as he struggles against the forces that bar him from full citizenship, from full participation in American life.

The disseminators and supporters of racial discrimination and antagonism are to the Negro, and are, *in fact,* first cousins if not brothers of the Nazis. They speak the same language of the "master race" and practice, or attempt to practice, the same tyranny over minority peoples.

There are three things in American life which today arouse the bitterest resentment among black Americans and at the same time represent the greatest handicap upon his full participation in the national war effort. First is their economic insecurity, which they know to be the result of continuing discrimination in employment even now, coupled with other forms of economic exploitation and social discrimination in urban communities such as Harlem.

Second is the segregation and inferior status assigned to Negroes in the armed forces, and their complete exclusion from most of the women's auxiliary services. Added to this are the insults and acts of physical violence nurtured by the segregation policy, which have been inflicted upon them in many of the camps and camp communities, even in areas that, before the coming of the army camps, had been free from racial prejudice. This is a shameful condition. Several appeals have been made to the president, from whites as well as Negroes, urging him to issue an executive order against racial discrimination and segregation in the armed services. Such an order is as essential to the morale and fighting spirit of our war machine as to the morale and productive capacity of our industrial machine.

Third is the poll tax system of the South, which operates to maintain undemocratic elements in places of authority not only below the Mason-Dixon line but in our national life as a whole.

And yet there are some who deplore the Negro's present-day struggle for democracy and equality as *endangering* national unity and our war effort. They point to the trouble (so they say) that the FEPC has stirred up in the South, and to the disgraceful race riots—*insurrections* or *pogroms* would be more accurate—in Detroit and other industrial centers which resulted (so they say) from Negro militancy.

Such people are looking at the world upside down or hind-parts forward. They believe the wagon is pushing the horse. They are the people who believe Hitler's lie that Nazism and Fascism were and are necessary in order to save the world from Communism.

Today's militant protest of the Negro people, as illustrated in the recent election of a Negro communist to New York's City Council and the general trend of the Negro vote toward acceptable candidates rather than party labels—this militant protest represents the development of a clearer understanding among Negroes of their goals, their allies and their enemies. Negroes know that their rights can only be achieved in an America that has realized *all* its democratic ideals.

A few days ago Americans honored the Soviet Union on the occasion of the tenth anniversary of the establishment of friendly diplomatic relations between that great nation and ours. We honored the heroic fight which the people of that nation have made against Hitler's erstwhile invincible legions. Two years ago, many Americans, like Hitler, expected the Soviet Union to crumble under the treacherous blitz attack. Now Americans are beginning to know something of the great power of the Russian people—a power born of unity, of legally enforced equality, of opportunity for all the many millions within its borders, regardless of race, creed, nationality or sex. No other nation on earth has achieved such a thing. And no other nation has stated with such explicitness its war aims: "abolition of racial exclusiveness; equality of nations and integrity of their territories; the right of every nation to arrange its affairs as it wishes."

The United States and Great Britain must learn the true meaning and application of democracy to minority and colonial peoples from their Soviet ally. Upon these three great powers rests the primary responsibility, accepted by them jointly in the recent Moscow Conference decisions, of turning military victory into enduring peace and security for all peoples. America and Britain must prove to the world that they are in truth waging a people's war of liberation, or they must face the shame and scorn of the world.

Let Americans remember the words of their commander-in-chief, President Roosevelt, spoken on the second anniversary of the signing of the Atlantic Charter: "We are determined that we shall gain total victory over our enemies, and we recognize the fact that our enemies are not only Germany, Italy, and Japan: they are all the forces of oppression, intolerance, insecurity and injustice which have impeded the forward march of civilization."

A Rock in a Weary Lan'

Paul Robeson's Leadership and "The Movement" in the Decade Before Montgomery

BY J. H. O'DELL

A panoramic view of the United States of America at the end of the Second World War and the decade that follows (1945-55) points up the surfacing of a number of political and social contradictions of such a magnitude as to leave their indelible mark on the present period in our national history.

The development of the Freedom Movement of black Americans *since* Montgomery, Alabama, is much better known to the average movement activist and citizen of our country. However, it is impossible to understand in any comprehensive way the journey we have traveled "from Montgomery to Memphis" without dealing with the events of that critical decade *before* the dawn that was Montgomery. For it was in that ten-year period that the die was cast. The confluence of our Freedom Movement with the mighty tidal wave of liberation from colonialism engendered by the peoples of Africa, Asia and Latin America, and the role of the U.S. government as the chief defender of the old dying colonial regimes became an objective law of development of American society. It is a functional operative process, the final outcome of which is still being determined in today's struggles.

Growth of the Freedom Movement and Changes in Its Class Composition

By the time the Second World War had ended, it was the industrial working class of the black community whose organizational strength was making the most profound impact on the outlook and style of the Freedom Movement. Drawing upon the accumulated experiences of the Depression years, in which hundreds of thousands of black workers had helped to build a militant trade union organization (CIO), their influence in the larger Freedom Movement was now on the rise. The battering ram for beginning to break down the economically profitable corporate-sponsored tradition of racial prejudice and racist practice was these class organizations of industrial workers. Our movement for equal rights and freedom had shifted sharply to the left during the Depression years. The direction of this shift was away from the nationalist-separatist trend of the 1920s, as represented by the Garvey movement, to the class struggle organizing trend in such unorganized heavy industries as steel, packinghouse, longshore and auto. Black and white workers got together, and that was power.

Other long-established and respected organizations of the Freedom Movement, such as the NAACP, Urban League and local groups like the Booker T. Washington Trade Association, continued to play a constructive role but one of secondary importance. These traditional organizations represented the indigenous black middle class and the intellectual spokesmen drawn from this class. The real power, the real dynamism of the Freedom Movement in this period centered in the bold, energetic, "together" movement created by the working class. That movement was not dominated by the George Meanys of the day. It was the heart of the general movement for social change in our country which had emerged and come to maturity during President Roosevelt's New Deal and Paul Robeson as artist, citizen and freedom fighter identified with this.

Another far-reaching and significant change affecting the general features of our Freedom Movement in this period was the growth in the number of NAACP chapters in the small towns and rural areas of the South. The big cities, like Atlanta, New Orleans and Memphis, had for years developed strong NAACP chapters. Now with the close of World War II, a pattern of chapter organization had spread to places like Monk's Corner, South Carolina.

Robeson had returned to America, the land of his birth, in 1939 after more than a decade of active participation in the cultural life and social movements in Europe. A highly successful concert and acting career on the European stage and an important body of experience gained from being involved with various antifascist movements had prepared him well to make a unique contribution to the struggles developing here.

Above all, the world scene was beginning to undergo profound political changes as millions of people broke away from world capitalism's long-established system of colonialism and became politically independent. Under the leadership of Mahatma Gandhi and Jawaharlal Nehru, the Indian National movement reestablished India's political independence from Britain in 1947, and the following year Burma took the same path. A general uprising of the Indonesian people which lasted for three years (1946-1949) ended centuries of Dutch political rule, while the Democratic Republic of Vietnam declared its independence from France and went on to fight for that independence under the revolutionary leadership of the venerable Ho Chi Minh. This Asian drama reached a crescendo of achievement in 1949 with the victory of the Chinese people over the feudal landlords and foreign rule resulting in the establishment of the Chinese People's Republic. With more than a billion people in Asia now on the road to social emancipation, freedom from colonial slavery would inevitably spread to the African continent as well.

"No Honor Among Thieves"

Confronted with these massive developments on a world scale, combined with the devastation that World War II had produced in Europe, the old European colonial powers were in bad shape. Britain's currency was devalued from $4.85 to $2.85; the British electorate dismissed Churchill, the wartime leader, in favor of a Labour Government. France and Italy now had huge left-wing political parties opposed to capitalism, well rooted in the trade union movement and capable of pulling up to 40 per cent of the vote in any election, and with Britain unable to increase its rate of investment in South Africa, the right-wing Afrikaner government was beckoning to United States corporations to fill the gap.

The U.S. empire builders whom President Roosevelt had earlier characterized as the "economic royalists" then embarked upon a course of action which the American people are still paying for. Their strategy consisted of two concurrent parts. First, breaking up the New Deal coalition which was still intact and scattering it before it began to be influenced by the revolutionary currents developing in the world. Secondly, launching a concerted drive to take over their colonial markets and sources of raw material from the faltering European powers. In the course of this, they hoped to reverse the anticolonial struggle.

The Four Freedoms which President Roosevelt had committed the U.S. to pursue as a goal of foreign policy were now scrapped, while the rhetoric was retained. The Biblical ideal which they embodied, that "the meek shall inherit the earth," was now translated to mean that General Motors, Standard Oil and the Chase National Bank would attempt to inherit the earth.

Central to the succcess of this overall strategy was the need to intimidate and brutalize the Negro community, thereby "putting them back in their place." A national Administration made up of southern segregationists was now in power headed by Truman of Missouri as President, James F. Byrnes of South Carolina as Secretary of State and Tom Clark of Texas as Attorney General. A wave of mob violence and lynchings was unleashed in the South in Columbia, Tennessee; Monroe, Georgia; and elsewhere. It was the old terror formula which had been used following the First World War and was now being revived.

Into this turbulent milieu, a milieu so full of hope for the oppressed and so full of dangers that our aspirations for freedom would be drowned by the counterrevolution, stepped Paul Robeson.

Huge in physical stature, eloquent and fearless in his castigation of the racist American-way-of-life, always communicating a quality of integrity and devotion to our struggle by putting his immense prestige and achievements on the line for freedom, and being sufficiently black in skin color to satisfy the psychological need our community had to identify, Robeson emerged as the prototype of a folk hero. The outreach of his cultural achievements included having mastered the languages and music of many peoples. This gave *us* as a people a special link, through him, to an understanding with the peoples of Africa, Asia and the growing socialist world community in that critical period in world history. Then too, Paul knew as personal acquaintances many of the newly emerging leaders of Africa and Asia whom he had met while living abroad.

At any rate, the issues were joined. The New Deal was over as power sections of American big business interests moved boldly to push the country to the right. Robeson understood this political fact of life and its implications for the people of our country perhaps better than any other black leader with a popular following. By comparison, most spokesmen for the Negro community did not clearly discern the sharp shifts taking place in the country and were honestly still caught up in the euphoria created by the New Deal. Others were just plain opportunistically "playing it safe" and leaving themselves open to the illusions being reinforced by Truman's skillful demagogy, pretending to be a "civil rights President."

Because of his almost legendary record as a black athlete and his role as a militant spokesman, Robeson was immensely popular among the youth, particularly on the college campuses in the South. He was particularly close through his association with the Southern Negro Youth Congress (SNYC), the organization which, in a historical sense, was a forerunner of the Student Nonviolent Coordinating Committee (SNCC). Paul was an inspiration to the many youthful freedom fighters who got their earliest experiences in the struggle as members of SNYC.[1] Robeson once told a group of us who were members of the Miami Chapter of the Southern Negro Youth Congress and had gone out to meet him at the airport upon his return from a concert tour in Panama, "I wouldn't believe these boys were playing so rough if I wasn't looking at them." That was early spring, 1947. Later that year, he canceled a series of eighty concerts in the Scandinavian countries and an anticipated fee of $100,000 rather than appear under the auspices of a Scandinavian newspaper which had editorially endorsed the NATO[2] alliance. "I will not appear in concert under the auspices of any organization which supports NATO," he declared, "because the guns of NATO are ultimately pointed at the African people struggling for their independence." Anyone who seriously doubts the correctness of that political judgment made nearly a quarter of a century ago need only to answer the question, where indeed does Portugal get its guns to shoot down the freedom fighters in Mozambique, Angola and Portuguese Guinea today?

Events moved swiftly apace. Winston Churchill, long a spokesman of the Conservative political school of British imperialism, was invited over to speak in Fulton, Missouri, as President Truman's guest. On this occasion, Churchill laid down the "cold war" line, positing that the Soviet Union, which had suffered thirty million casualties during the Second World War and had an area of its country as large as the distance between Chicago and New York City destroyed, was now the main enemy of the so-called "free world."

The "Iron Curtain" which Churchill declared had descended over Europe camouflaged the fact that indeed an Iron Curtain of repression was being lowered over the civil rights and liberties of the American people. An all-sided attack on the New Deal coalition and against all dissent was now unfolded by the Truman administration over the course of a very few years. As had been the case in Hitler's Germany, first the leadership of the Communist party was jailed under the charge that they were "conspiring to teach and advocate the overthrow of the government by force and violence." This charge originated as one of the provisions of a piece of legislation passed in 1940 called the Smith Act whose author was Congressman Howard Smith, a segregationist from Virginia. In fact, the Smith Act had been slipped through Congress as a rider to an *oleomargarine bill.*

The jailing of the leaders of the Communist party then set the stage for the next moves by the federal government. Every organization in Negro life which was attacking segregation *per se* was put on the "subversive list" by Attorney General Tom Clark. The National Negro Congress, a civil rights protest organization of the forties, which had submitted a petition to the United Nations seeking UN support for our cause in 1946, was one such organization. Then there was the United Negro and Allied Veterans Association, made up mostly of World War II vets who refused to join the Jim Crow American Legion Posts. There was the Council on African Affairs, whose co-chairmen were Paul Robeson and Dr. Du Bois and whose activities involved publishing a news letter and organizing public support for various struggles on the African continent. And of course the Southern Negro Youth Congress, whose activities were a thorn in the side of the monolithic southern segregationist clique. These and many other organizations were declared to be "Communist fronts" by the government, while state and local politicians quickly picked up the signal. A virtual dragnet of arrests, blacklistings and firings followed. The range of attacks victimized screenwriters and actors in Hollywood, teachers in the public schools and professors in colleges, and clergymen like some of the leaders of the Methodist Federation for Social Action. Many seamen and longshoremen were denied the right to work by Coast Guard "screening" programs. Foreign-born residents of many years, who had not been allowed to become naturalized U.S. citizens because of their trade union or civil liberties activities, were now being deported by the government on the grounds that they were not citizens, but "undesirable aliens." The once militant CIO was split and a number of unions representing nearly a million members were expelled from the body on the unfounded charges of being "Communist dominated." The kind of hysteria generated among the public reached such proportions that even the Cincinnati Reds baseball team, for a time, changed their name to *Redlegs*. Such was the state of the American public mind in those glorious days of Truman's "Fair Deal" administration. Out of this later grew the era popularly referred to as McCarthyism. The animal had turned on itself as McCarthy charged members of the Truman administration as being Communists or "soft on communism."

Despite the carefully calculated atmosphere of repression, the movement found the strength to fight back, and this spirit of fighting back took many forms of organization and initiative. A mass mobilization in Washington, D.C., demanding that Congress pass a fair employment practices bill, took place in 1946 with Paul Robeson the central figure. There is a famous picture, taken on that occasion of Paul standing in the midst of this huge crowd in front of the White House, and the policeman with his hand on his pistol holster telling him that he may not go in to see President Truman. Two years later were the presidential elections and the history-making campaign conducted by Henry Wallace's Progressive party. Robeson accepted the vice chairmanship of the Progressive party and for several months in 1948 set aside all of his concerts so as to give full time to that election campaign. One of the most significant features of the activities of the Progressive party was its impact on the South.

A group of us in New Orleans had formed a *Seamen for Wallace Committee,* and worked with the larger Progressive party movement in Louisiana to get the party on the ballot. Paul came down in the early summer to give a fund-raising concert and 1,500 people came out to the concert at the old Coliseum. Robeson sang some of the songs for which he was most famous, performed excerpts from *Othello,* and spoke of the program of the Progressive party and why he had made the choice to become involved in it. The audience was completely unsegregated. Everything else in New Orleans was segregated but not the Coliseum that day, for Robeson never accommodated the Jim Crow laws at his concerts in the South. The lasting impact of the Progressive party was the initiative and vehicle it provided for a number of pioneering efforts by black citizens running for public office. Larkin Marshall ran for the United States Senate from Savannah, Georgia, on the Progressive party ticket. Mrs. Sonora Lawson was a candidate for Congress from Richmond, Virginia. Professor Rudolph Moses of Dillard University was a candidate for secretary of state in Louisiana, and there were many others. None of these was elected, however, but it must be kept in mind that this was only four years after the Supreme Court decision outlawing the Democratic party's white primary. These Progressive party candidates, therefore, were an announcement to the nation that the black community in the South was returning to the political arena in the most serious way since reconstruction. These pioneering black candidates were the forerunners of the now more than 2,200 black elected officials in the South today. One of the main posters circulated by the Progressive party campaign had the picture of a black child; the top of the poster quoted from a statistic of the period and said, "A black child born on the same day in the same city as a white child is destined to die 10 years earlier." Then at the bottom of the poster was the slogan, "We are fighting for those 10 extra years!" Henry Wallace's southern tour that autumn before the election electrified and inspired the campaign nationally. It is also of note that of the several cities Wallace visited, only in Shreveport, Louisiana, did he meet any mob violence. It was also in the course of this election campaign that the vice presidential candidate of the Progressive party, Senator Glenn Taylor of Idaho, was arrested by Police Commissioner "Bull" Connor in Birmingham. Senator Taylor was charged with violating the "Jim Crow" laws by refusing to enter a designated door of a church where a convention of the Southern Negro Youth Congress was being held. The white candidates who ran on the Progressive party ticket were mostly southerners also. They too demonstrated courage and there was a small body of white supporters who remained firm in freedom's cause as some had during the Abolitionist Movement a century earlier. The finest expression of these was to be found among the dedicated leadership and staff of the Southern Conference Educational Fund (SCEF), who were an indispensable part of the Freedom Movement.

Meanwhile, the NAACP was continuing to do some brilliant and effective legal work in the courts in the area of challenging the inferior conditions in the public schools in the South. Between 1945 and 1949, the NAACP in Atlanta filed a series of court suits asking the United States District Court to "issue a permanent injunction restraining the Board of Education from denying Negro school children in the city of Atlanta equal education opportunity and advantages as white children." The NAACP was attacking in these suits the real inequality present in the separate-but-equal formula. The underlying idea being that if there must be separate segregated schools for black and white children, they must be made equal in all respects. These and other suits were filed under the Equal Protection clause of the Fourteenth Amendment.

In Richmond, Virginia, in 1948 a leading NAACP official, Lester Banks, actually led some black students to the "for white only" King George High School and demanded admission. The superintendent of the area met him at the door and told him such a thing was "unthinkable."

The general struggle for Fair Employment Practices (FEP) legislation was being duplicated at the state level, especially in the North at this time. One of the byproducts of this effort was the opening up of baseball to black athletes. Robeson's prestige as a pioneering sports hero came in good stead as he participated frequently in mass picket lines in front of the offices of the baseball club owners in various cities. The hiring of Jackie Robinson by the Brooklyn Dodgers was a direct outgrowth of both the mass action and the passage of FEP legislation in New York. This effort at forcing the major league ball clubs to stop discriminating against black athletes was of very significant long-term importance in the general struggle against racism, for this is the period in which television was introduced as a popular mass medium and the impact of the visual presence of talented black athletes on the baseball field certainly makes its impact on the American public mind.

The voter registration thrust in the South was also a vital element in the fight-back movement against reaction. Under Strom Thurmond of South Carolina, the extreme right wing of the Democratic party in the South split the party over the civil rights issue and put forward its own Dixiecrat candidates in the 1948 presidential election.

Our answer as a Freedom Movement was to accelerate the effort to increase the black vote which at that time was little over a quarter million registered voters. Some of the voter registration drives organized during this period became a model of organization. The Negro Suffrage Movement leaped ahead after the '48 elections, painfully but deliberately, and there were over three million black voters on the registration rolls in the South.

The general climate of government-promoted repression reached a frenzied pitch at Peekskill, New York, a conservative upstate town, the weekend of Labor Day, 1949. A week earlier, Paul Robeson's concert had been broken up by a racist mob and some of the concert-goers beaten. Robeson was an honorary member of our union, the National Maritime Union, by a vote of the membership. Like many other people, we on the New York waterfront were determined to do anything necessary to guarantee that Paul could have a concert anywhere without a lynch mob threatening his safety. This attack upon him at Peekskill represented, to us, Mississippi moving to New York. Anyway, there was a massive mobilization all over New York City for the Labor Day concert the following week. Plans were well laid for a peaceful concert if it was possible to have one, but other contingencies were taken care of also. The mobs were made up of American Legionnaires, Catholic war veterans, some Jewish war veterans, aided and abetted by the New York state troopers. A lot of us felt that the position of the Jewish War Veterans was indeed paradoxical since the mobs were calling the concert-goers "kikes" and "Communist niggerlovers." Some of these "patriots" even waved swastikas behind the backs of nonchalant state troopers. Anyway, good planning resulted in the afternoon concert on that beautiful day going well. More than 25,000 people came by every conceivable means of transportation to that concert in an open field in Peekskill. The highways leading to Peekskill were jammed with bus loads of people from Harlem and elsewhere who never got to the picnic grounds because of the traffic congestion. The trouble came at the end of the concert which had lasted all afternoon. As dusk was approaching and the automobiles were leaving the picnic ground, they were pelted with rocks, windshields were broken, people suffered from broken glass. Further down the highway, some cars were overturned by roving mobs, and of course none of this was interfered with by the state troopers. Paul Robeson had been able to hold his concert that day, and thousands of people had demonstrated by their presence a willingness to uphold freedom of speech in general and the right of this great artist to perform in particular. Nevertheless, the violence we confronted at the end of that day confirmed the fact that the hysteria in the country was still very much with us, aided and abetted by the government itself.

Peekskill will long be remembered, because once again Paul Robeson became the focus of the defense of civil liberties and at the same time, the focus of the attack upon civil liberties as the policy of repression was being escalated.

By 1950 the contest between human rights and a growing native American fascism in our country had reached a critical point. Robeson's passport had been lifted by the government. The denial of his right to travel was an attempt to silence him. However, this was to become indicative of a more general pattern as the passports of other prominent black leaders were taken as well. Mrs. Charlotta Bass, publisher of *The California Eagle* in Los Angeles, a black newspaper, and Mrs. Theresa Robinson of the women's division of the Elks, one of our largest fraternal organizations, were cases in point. Senator Joe McCarthy was now riding high with his illegal investigating committee. The NAACP was beginning to show signs of buckling under to the McCarthy hysteria. Its Boston Convention that year was somewhat hysterical with its anti-Communist resolutions. Up North the extradition of black men back to chain gangs in Mississippi, South Carolina, Georgia and elsewhere in the South by "liberal" governors was becoming rapidly a pattern of intimidation reminiscent of the Fugitive Slave Law of the last century. John Foster Dulles, a Republican and a member of the Wall Street investment firm, Dillon-Reade, had become a special advisor to President Truman. With five million unemployed, the Korean War began in June.

This event became the excuse and occasion for stepping up a deluge of jingoistic and national chauvinist propaganda. A rash of Confederate flags, the flag of slavery and the slave-holders, became everywhere in evidence. It was flown from the masts of battleships and over the court houses in many southern states. The policy of staffing the national government with southern segregationists was extended as Millard F. Caldwell of Florida became the head of Civil Defense. In New Orleans the Jim Crow city buses were painted red, white and blue in an attempt to whip up a fervor of "patriotism" while the Confederate flag flew over the courthouse and the city jail.

More than 7,000 people, mostly sharecroppers, were dispossessed from their homes in Ellenton, South Carolina, to make way for a new H-bomb project on the Savannah River. The following year began with Dr. W. E. B. Du Bois being arrested as (to quote the government) "an agent of a foreign principal," and the year ended with the bombing of the home of Mr. and Mrs. Harry T. Moore in Miami, Florida, on Christmas night. This couple were NAACP leaders of the voter registration drive in that area and both were killed in the bombing.

However, business was good. General Motors opened its new twenty-million-dollar plant in Port Elizabeth, South Africa; the South African government received an eighty-million-dollar loan in return for American corporations to have "purchase rights to great quantities of uranium." General Lucius Clay, a director of the Newmont Mining Corporation, was able to report nine million dollars in profits for his company over a three-year period on a seven-million-dollar investment in Southwest Africa, a country which was at that time under trusteeship to the South African government.

Keeping the Movement Moving

The challenges which the Korean adventure posed, the hypocrisy and racist arrogance which accompanied it and the general economic conditions of the black community as still the last hired and first fired shaped the program around which the Freedom Movement had to mobilize. And to mobilize meant to prevent McCarthyism from fragmenting the movement, thereby rendering it impotent.

A newspaper was needed—a black newspaper—which spoke clearly to the issues and would itself be an organizer. To serve this need, Paul Robeson founded the paper *Freedom,* with Louis E. Burnham as editor-in-chief. Paul had known Lou Burnham over many years for he had been one of the leading organizers of the Southern Negro Youth Congress with its headquarters in Birmingham. For the next five years, *Freedom* played a major role in bringing clarity out of confusion even though publishing under difficult circumstances.

The summer of '51 saw the city of Chicago serve as host to a Mid-Century Conference on Peace and Jobs. This meeting brought together some 2,500 delegates from around the country who had been active in developing the antiwar movement as well as civil rights workers and trade unionists. The purpose of the meeting essentially was to set a different direction for the nation, away from the developing of a war economy and toward a peacetime economy that would address itself to the growing problems of adequate housing, medical care, etc.

Paul Robeson, as might be expected, was invited to give the keynote address at this Mid-Century meeting. In October of that year, the founding convention of the National Negro Labor Council was held in Cincinnati. Here were black trade unionists from packinghouse, steel, the canneries, longshore, electrical manufacturing, auto. They came from both coasts and the South. Some white unionists were also present. Their aim was to mobilize their power within the trade union movement on the issue of jobs, upgrading and more representation in official positions. Ferdinand Smith, formerly the general secretary of the National Maritime Union, William Hood, president of the big Ford Local 600 of the United Auto Workers, and Asbury Howard, of the Mine-Mill Union in Bessemer, Alabama, an international vice president of the union for the southern region, were among the outstanding leaders of this organization. The main thrust of this important founding convention was the launching of a nation-wide petition campaign directed to Congress for the passage of national fair employment practice legislation. In addition certain companies were selected as targets to focus on job discrimination, among them American Airlines, Sears Roebuck and the Statler Hotels. Picket lines, boycotts and of course negotiations were the techniques used. Paul was invited to give the keynote address to this founding convention as well.

Together with William Marshall, the actor, Paul headed the Performing Artists' division of the National Negro Labor Committee (NNLC). This latter responsibility served to underscore Robeson's continuing interest in the performing arts and in the struggles black artists were initiating to end discrimination in television and on the stage. The leading organization in this effort was known as the Committee for the Negro in the Arts (CNA), in which two rising young stars were very active, Harry Belafonte and Sidney Poitier.

Paul also gave of his time and moral support to the Domestic Workers' Union in Harlem. Some 70 per cent of the Negro women workers in New York State were either in domestic work or farm labor, such were the limited job opportunities faced at that time. The average working day for them was thirteen hours. The Domestic Workers' Union was attempting to organize the workers for securing an eight-hour day and higher pay.

The wide range of offensive and defensive struggles undertaken by organized black workers in the early fifties is demonstrated by two examples. The Norfolk Movement in Virginia was organized around the issue of securing jobs for Negro workers above the janitor level at the new Ford plant which had recently been built there. The company which had just secured a thirty-one-million-dollar "defense" contract had hired some 2,000 workers which included only ten Negro workers and these were confined to janitors and car washers.

This of course is the classic discrimination pattern that American industry has traditionally followed. We had the same problem with Lockheed Aircraft in Atlanta a decade later, and our taxes were to go in part to bail Lockheed out of its financial crisis.

The Mine Mill Union among the ore workers in Alabama had to fight off a raid by the combined forces of the Ku Klux Klan and the United Steel Workers, who were attempting to break up this union. This was a bitter battle which covered several months, and in one encounter, Maurice Travis, one of the white brothers, lost an eye. The raiding policies which many unions with large black membership faced in this period were indicative of how far the once militant CIO had deteriorated in regards to its working-class ethics. "AN INJURY TO ONE IS AN INJURY TO ALL," the founding motto of the militant CIO was no longer adhered to as a matter of principle by the top bureaucrats in the union structure. It had been replaced by anti-Communism, the policy dictated by the industrialists.

An additional struggle front of the movement was opened up in this period by Dr. Mary Church Terrell, one of the greatest women activists in this century. It was in the early fifties after being a long-time Women's Rights Movement activist that Dr.

Terrell, in her late eighties, began a campaign of organizing nonviolent mass demonstrations against segregation in the nation's capital. In doing so, she seized hold of one of the great moral contradictions of this society, the existence of the racist system of segregation in the very capital of the nation whose leaders were so loudly proclaiming their "leadership of the free world." Washington, D.C., at that time was just like any other city in Georgia, but the movement led by this courageous black woman won important victories.

While Paul Robeson's mass support base in the Freedom Movement centered among the trade unionists and sections of the church-going population in the big cities, the government's arrest of Dr. Du Bois increased the concern and active involvement of the black middle class. Up to that point this class in Negro life and its spokesmen had stayed clear of Paul, at least in terms of *public* support. The fact of the matter is that Robeson's uncompromising militancy had loosened up some concessions for them that they were not about to put in jeopardy. The few niggardly handouts the rulers of the system were permitting looked like "manna from heaven." So, with few notable exceptions, they kept quiet or dissociated themselves from what the press was interpreting as Robeson's public position. However, when "the man" put handcuffs on Dr. Du Bois, even the most reticent among them said "this time the government has gone too far." Black college presidents and deans joined with the editors of student campus newspapers and other campus organizations demanding the government stop its persecution of Dr. Du Bois. Objectively this broadened the base of participation and strengthened the Freedom Movement significantly.

"Like a Tree Standing by the Water . . ."

Paul Robeson's deep involvement in the many facets of the Freedom Movement throughout this period also served to enhance his growing international prestige. Despite passport restrictions, invitations from people and organizations around the world continued to come to him urging that he visit their country for concerts and speaking engagements. Invitations came from youth organizations and peace groups in Calcutta and Bombay, from Jamaica in the West Indies where two years earlier he had sung to 75,000 people, from the executive board of the Mine Workers Union in Scotland and many other parts of the world. One invitation was accepted from Canada and on Sunday, May 18, 1952, Paul Robeson gave a concert under the Peace Arch on the Canadian border out on the West Coast. However, he could not step foot across the border without being in violation of an Executive Order issued by President Truman forbidding him to leave the United States and instructing border guards to apprehend him if he tried to do so. Forty thousand people assembled on the other side of the Canadian border to hear that concert.

These invitations from abroad were a form of pressure on the government for they demonstrated an international interest in the situation here in the United States at that time. Consequently, the State Department heads during both the Truman and Eisenhower administrations proposed that Robeson could get his passport back if he would sign an affidavit agreeing that he would only *sing* but not *speak* abroad. What was being proposed was that he give up his right to freedom of speech as a citizen in order to be able to exercise the right to work at his chosen profession. Of course Paul Robeson rejected this. Like a tree standing by the water, he would not be moved.

Any serious review of the movement, its life and thought in the decade under consideration inevitably points to Paul Robeson as the central rallying figure of the Freedom Movement in one of the darkest hours of our national existence on this continent. As such, his place in the long history of struggle by Afro-Americans is massive and secure.

Of his many contributions, none was of greater long-term significance than the knowledge he brought concerning the multimillions of the world who were breaking the bonds of colonialism. In speech and in concert, Paul always brought the message that the peoples of the Soviet Union and China were our friends, brothers and sisters like those of the African continent, and that understanding their aspirations was to understand better our own condition. Underlying this perception was the basic idea that it is an illusion to try to separate domestic and foreign policy.

Robeson understood that there was to be no real "democracy" at home while the U.S. was militarily about the business of crushing freedom abroad in the name of "anti-Communism."

By the long-standing rules of the American tradition, a "nigger," even one with a Phi Beta Kappa key, wasn't supposed to know anything about U.S. foreign policy, much less be critical of it. And, we must admit, a lot of black folk, mentally conditioned as a consequence of segregation, had such low self-esteem they believed that also. Our movement finally turned the corner on this question with the outbreak of the U.S. military intervention in Vietnam, as Dr. Martin Luther King, Jr., articulated the moral outrage of the black community and called attention to the fact that our aspirations for an end to poverty were being shot down on the battlefields of Vietnam.

This simply means that never again will the racist decision-makers of America be able to launch one of their murderous crusades and have the benefit of the silent acquiescence of American Negro leadership, so anxious to be "accepted" by the Big White Folks. This mentality is over with forever. In the tradition of internationalism pioneered by Frederick Douglass, Bishop Henry McNeal Turner of the AME Church and W. E. B. Du Bois, Paul Robeson made a singularly valuable contribution to our achieving, as a people, a new level of political maturity.

Contemporary writers and publishers of Black History texts and social studies materials who leave brother Paul out of the story are not writing *our* history. Let us be abundantly clear on that point. Nor was he just a singer and actor deserving a few lines of passing reference as some of the "better" Black Studies materials would have us believe.

This enormously talented and dedicated freedom fighter was the central rallying figure and charismatic personality of the movement during a certain period. This is a role and responsibility only a mere handful of giant personalities in our history have successfully fulfilled. We are reminded that following Robeson that role was filled by Dr. Martin Luther King, Jr. It is a role which has been invested with honor, sacrifice and the highest integrity. So it is not to be dismissed or rendered inconsequential by falsifiers who claim to be writing history.

A Negro spiritual, that musical art form which he did so much to make widely known and appreciated throughout the world, perhaps best describes Paul Robeson's significance for the Freedom Movement in the decade before the Montgomery bus protest. He was, in the words of that ancestral song, "A Rock in a Weary Lan'."

Paul Robeson at Peekskill

BY CHARLES H. WRIGHT

Few people had heard of Peekskill, N.Y., before 1949. Two dramatic events which occurred on August 27 and September 4 of that year attracted worldwide attention to this Hudson Valley hamlet, and its name, henceforth, became synonymous with mob violence.

Paul Robeson was the star of the Peekskill performance. Having been there before, he knew the scene well. Now, however, time and circumstances were fused in an explosive mix that would make his 1949 appearances memorable. Subsequent events suggest that Peekskill bears the same relationship to the Civil Rights Movement as Fort Sumter does to the Civil War.

In retrospect, it can be postulated that Robeson began a collision course with the United States establishment as early as 1934. En route to the Soviet Union for the first time in December of 1934, he was racially abused and threatened by Nazi storm troopers outside the Berlin railroad station. Here began his eternal war against fascism. He crossed the Russian border a few hours later, and the Russian people, by contrast, welcomed him with open arms. Thus was born his abiding friendship with the peoples of the Soviet Union. These two events changed the course of Robeson's life. He paid dearly for both of them.

Opinions differ as to when the Peekskill confrontation became inevitable. Marie Seton, author of *Paul Robeson,* is certain that the die was cast in 1947 when Robeson included the song "Joe Hill" in his concert at the University of Utah. Never before, in this area, had anyone dared sing this lament to the ill-fated labor organizer, Joseph Hillstrom, whose death before a Utah firing squad had caused an international crisis earlier in the century. Robeson must have known that there were "copper bosses" in the audience. His plaintive rendition of the song disturbed the uneasy consciences of many listeners. After a stunned period of silence, some of the audience clapped loudly. Others clinched their fists. Nothing seemed to go well for Robeson thereafter.

His concert series began to crumble almost immediately. Peoria, Ill., and Albany, N.Y., led the way. When all of the returns were in, more than eighty concerts were cancelled. Public pressure forced Albany officials to relent but not before anti-Robeson forces surfaced among Catholic students in New York City and veterans' organizations in Peekskill, N.Y.

Prior to 1947, Robeson was the national champion of the rights of the working man. Nearly a dozen unions had honored him with life memberships. He appeared regularly as guest artist at their national conventions, marched in their picket lines and gave benefit concerts to support their causes. Cold War politics, a way of life in the late forties, and a compliant judiciary changed Robeson's relationship with most of organized labor appreciably. Implementation of President Harry Truman's anti-Communist foreign policy and the passage of such labor legislation as the Taft-Hartley law forced labor organizations to make difficult decisions in 1947. They either had to support a foreign policy of "Communist containment" and expel those radicals who had been so vital to their earlier organizing drives, or suffer suppression, suspension and possible destruction. This new look in labor made Robeson's brand of militant unionism unfashionable. He was no longer welcome in the halls of the conformist unions. Some groups even attempted to withdraw his life memberships. Only the "renegade" unions had the audacity to invite Robeson to their meetings in the late forties and the early fifties.

Robeson's support of the Progressive party in 1948 aroused the enmity of the power brokers in the Democratic party. Michael Quill, president of the Transport Workers' Union, expressed some of the prevailing sentiment of the period. He blamed Robeson and the progressives for the loss of New York State to the Republicans in 1948. Speaking before the National Convention of the National Maritime Union in 1949, Quill predicted that Robeson might run for the U.S. Senate from New York. Such unpopular

activity plus his public challenge to President Truman to support antipoll tax and antilynch legislation isolated Robeson from
the Democratic party.

Aside from his unpopular political stands, Robeson engaged in
other activities that increased his enemies exponentially. In 1947,
he responded to a plea from black workers in Winston-Salem,
N.C., who were striking the R. J. Reynolds Tobacco Co. He
boosted their morale and raised money for their support. Some
time later, a Russian radio broadcast carried an interview with
Robeson in which he criticized the poor working conditions for
black workers in the tobacco industry. Local officials, already dis-
pleased with Robeson's interference in their internal affairs, seized
this opportunity to discredit Robeson and undermine the strike
effort. Not only was the union effort defeated, but the R. J. Reynolds Co. remains unorganized to this day.

Also in 1948, Robeson went to Hawaii in support of the Longshoremen's and Warehousemen's Union, the parent union of the
sugar cane and pineapple workers. The "Big Five" took a dim
view of Robeson's presence. He was accused of aiding the Communists, and threats were hurled at him from many quarters.

The rift between the United Public Workers (UPW) and their
parent, the Congress of Industrial Organizations (CIO), was widened when the UPW sent Robeson into the Panama Canal Zone
in 1947 in support of the Silver-roll workers. Government officials
were resentful of and embarrassed by Robeson's public criticisms
of the vicious racist practices against their nonwhite employees
in the Canal Zone.

Pressure Mounts

The arrival of the fateful year of 1949 found Robeson under
heavy pressure from the business community, the government and
some segments of the labor force. With his recording contracts
canceled, under constant surveillance by the government, barred
from all radio and other public appearances of similar nature
which reduced his income to only a fraction of what it had been,
Robeson went abroad in February of 1949. In Europe and England
he sang to sell-out audiences. Although his tour was a financial

success and bolstered his ego, it was a disaster for his public image back home and his future as an American citizen.

Robeson compounded his problems by announcing from England that he would, upon his return, testify in support of the Communist leaders then on trial at the Foley Square courthouse in New York City. Hard on the heels of that bombshell, he appeared in Paris at the World Peace Congress, organized by the partisans of peace.

Robeson criticized the racist practice of the U.S. government and found little to choose between it and the fascist government of Nazi Germany. He labeled President Truman's Point Four Program for colonial development as a "new form of slavery," especially for Africans. His one statement that caused an international furor was :

> It is unthinkable that American Negroes could go to war on behalf of those who have oppressed them for generations, against the Soviet Union, which in one generation has raised our people to full human dignity.[1]

Although *The New York Times* quoted Robeson accurately and in full, secondary waves of editorial comment quoted Robeson as saying, "American Negroes would never fight against Russia."

Revulsion against Robeson reached new heights in the States. The architects of our foreign policy, only a year away from the Korean War, concluded that they had to do something about Robeson once and for all. A frantic federal officialdom summoned an impressive list of black leaders to Washington to discredit Robeson and assure them that the black populace would fight to preserve the system. The black leaders, for the most part, told the uneasy politicians what they wanted to hear.

Robeson arrived home from Europe on June 16, 1949. Included in the welcoming party were twenty uniformed policemen, a sign of things to come. A few days later, Robeson spoke to a tense, overflow crowd at the Rockland Palace, New York City. Word had spread through Harlem that "Big" Paul was mad. The rank-and-file black workers, uninfluenced by high-level politics and name-calling, came in droves to welcome their hero home and hear him tell off his enemies. They were not disappointed. Throwing caution to the winds, the fury of Robeson's attacks spared no one. His sharpest blasts, however, were directed toward those Blacks who had tried to discredit him. When the storm subsided, Robeson had few friends in high places anywhere in this country. Henceforth, his major support would come from the political left and the apolitical black masses, who continued to follow him despite vilification and intimidation.

Now as never before the federal government began to close in on Robeson and the left-wing organizations with which he was identified. The State Department of the Executive Branch, both houses of the Legislative Branch and a sympathetic Judicial Branch of the government were mobilized to secure national conformity with our anti-Communist foreign policy. Robeson was cited by the House Un-American Activities Committee more than 200 times. Called before the committee several times, he denied under oath that he was a Communist, the first time he was asked. Afterwards, he vowed never to answer that question again, believing that such questions about a man's political beliefs were unconstitutional.

Violence at Peekskill

Thus, the storm clouds hung low and were heavily charged when the Harlem Chapter of the Civil Rights Congress announced, late in July, that Robeson would give a benefit concert for them on August 27, 1949, in Peekskill. Representatives of Peoples Artists Inc. rented the Lakelands Acre Public Grounds for the affair. Immediately, members of the Peekskill Junior Chamber of Commerce condemned the concert and called for group action to discourage it. The sponsors were undeterred. Apparently, they had forgotten that it was the Peekskill Post of the American Legion that had attacked Robeson in Albany two years before. They had also issued a protest against Robeson's Peekskill concert in 1948. Even then the local press had warned against another concert.

As the date of the concert approached, the smoldering coals of anti-Robeson sentiment were fanned into flame by the actions of some members of Peekskill's Veterans of Foreign Wars, the Jewish War Veterans, the Catholic War Veterans and the Junior Chamber of Commerce. The local press and radio were used to keep the issue alive. Several groups in Peekskill and New York City warned local and state officials of the threat of violence. The anti-Robeson forces attempted to get an injunction against the concert, but they failed. Local groups tried to dissuade the veterans' groups from a showdown. They also failed. Governor Dewey was preoccupied with weightier matters, and he turned the problem over to subordinates. In the absence of any strong, meaningful preventive measures, violence became a reality.

Adding to the dangerous drift of political polarization, the attorney general listed the Civil Rights Congress as a Communist-front organization and listed Robeson as one of its chief supporters. Public disclosures in Peekskill indicated that Peoples Artists, Inc. had been labeled a "red front" organization by a loyalty group in California. The timing of these two reports was perfect for the anti-Robesonites. It gave them a *cause célèbre* and crowned their effort with a halo of patriotism.

The veterans' forces and their allies scheduled a parade in the vicinity of the concert site to coincide with the time of the concert. Many in military uniform carried sticks and rocks of varying sizes. They appeared to be on the best of terms with the local law enforcement officers. When concert-goers arrived they found the roads leading to the picnic grounds blocked by legionnaires. The majority were turned around and forced to run a gantlet of rocks and anti-Jewish, anti-Black, anti-Communist epithets as they fled the scene. A few less forunate persons did reach the concert area. Attacked from all sides, the men locked arms to form a protective circle around their women and children. The attackers, frustrated by this defensive maneuver, reduced the stage to splinter wood, shredded the sheet music and set them to the torch. Eventually, the hapless group escaped from their attackers and fled in disorder.

Robeson never reached the picnic grounds, which was just as well. Unaware of the rising tide of hatred that was flooding the concert area, he arrived at the Peekskill railway station alone. He was met by a woman and two children, ages ten and twelve. She hustled him into her car and smuggled him out of sight before he was recognized.

Robeson's son, Paul Jr., did not make it either. His wife fell ill just before the departure time, and he elected to remain with his bride of two and one-half months. This was just as well, also. The automobile in which he was scheduled to ride was damaged by flying missiles.

The Peekskill forces were jubilant over the success of their military expedition. They congratulated themselves on providing an excellent example to the nation of how to deal with "domestic Communists."

Undaunted, a mass meeting was held in Harlem a few days later. Robeson vowed to return to Peekskill as soon as possible. The crowd responded with a standing ovation of approval and support. This Harlem decision galvanized the Peekskill protagonists into a fury of resistance against a second invasion into their territory. One of their first moves was to make sure that the picnic grounds would not be available again. Peoples Artists Inc. rented the former Hollow Brook Country Club, now a meadow, from Stephen Szego for Sunday, September 4, 1949. This meadow is located in Cortlandt, just outside of Peekskill. Apparently, some of the local citizens looked with displeasure upon Szego's actions. Shortly after signing his agreement with Peoples Artists Inc., several shots were fired at his home. Later, there were four separate attempts to burn down his house. When he tried to collect for the fire damages, his insurance contract was cancelled.

Peace-loving citizens of Peekskill and environs again called upon Governor Dewey to insure the safety of the visitors to their vicinity. Representative Vito Marcantonio and Paul Robeson called on the governor to fire all officials who were responsible for the violence the week before. Governor Dewey held emergency sessions with his law enforcement officers and deployed 904 men to garrison the concert site and the surrounding area. He assured the public that his men had the situation well in hand.

Favorable weather made September 4th an ideal day for the fifty-mile drive from New York City to Peekskill. Thousands took advantage of the opportunity. The anti-Robeson forces were more numerous, better disciplined and more heavily armed than before. Making use of their military experience, the veterans allowed the visitors to enter the meadow with nothing more damaging hurled at them than sullen glances and racial epithets. Once the crowd was assembled, the opposition closed certain exit routes, forcing egress along prearranged corridors. Arrayed against this external force were 2,500 Robesonites who volunteered to form a wall to protect Robeson and the audience of 25,000. The majority of these men were trade unionists from such unions as the Furriers, United Electrical, Clothing Workers and the Newspaper Guild.

Soon after the concert got underway, Robeson arrived escorted by a detail of alert, unsmiling workers. He sang with his back against a tree, flanked by a formidable phalanx of muscle and grim determination. Robeson opened his portion of the concert with a chanson and "Go Down Moses" and ended with "Ol' Man River." His security guards enclosed him in a protective cocoon as he left the area. Only someone with a strong suicidal bent would have attempted a direct assault at that time. The "Honor Guard" delivered Robeson back to New York intact, but his automobile was damaged by a hail of stones.

The concert ended soon after Robeson's departure, around 3:30 P.M. Violence erupted as the concert-goers tried to leave the meadow. Forced to pass along the preplanned routes, they were jeered and attacked from both sides with sticks and flying objects of great variety. The newspapers reported that 145 people were injured and hundreds of cars were damaged, some totally. Many of the injured criticized the police for inaction; others accused them of complicity in the violence. The former charge proved to be unfounded, for the law enforcement officers were quite busy writing speeding tickets for those victims who tried to flee the area. Those who did not get away were ticketed for driving with broken windshields. Subsequent news photographs of the event supported the latter charge of complicity. At its height, the violence covered a ten-square-mile area and extended as far south as Yonkers. The spreading tentacles of disorder enveloped innocent people who had no idea of what was happening. One such group, returning from a visit to the shrine of Franklin D. Roosevelt at Hyde Park, sustained injury and was delayed for several hours.

The world press reported the details of the Peekskill violence in blazing headlines. Opinion from abroad was, for the most part, critical of the lax law enforcement and the mob action. They praised the efforts of the law-abiding citizens of Peekskill who did what they could to avert disaster and, failing that, deplored the inhumanity of their fellow citizens.

Domestic opinion was sharply divided. It was not surprising that under the circumstances the majority were sympathetic to the anti-Robeson forces. Robeson was described as a dupe of the Communists to foment disunity at a time when "our national security is at stake." The liberal and left-wing press, including the newssheets of the noncompliant labor unions, supported Robeson and compared the violence of Peekskill with the Nazi onslaught in Europe. This group demanded that Governor Dewey order a full-scale investigation by a special grand jury.

Many trade unionists suffered physical injury and property damage in the Peekskill melee. A giant stone was thrown through the windshield of the car of Irving Potash, an official of the Furriers Union. He suffered the loss of sight in one eye, damage to the other, a fractured skull and crushing injury to the nose and cheek bones. Despite his injury, Potash joined labor officials from the United Electrical and other unions in streetcorner protests in downtown Manhattan. They called upon Attorney General Howard McGrath to prosecute those who had caused the Peekskill riots. Members of the Newspaper Guild of New York called upon Governor Dewey to launch a full investigation of the violence and to remove all of the state and local officials responsible for it.

On September 20, 1949, 300 people boarded a train in New York City for Albany, the capital, to express their outrage directly to the governor. A special detail of armed guards insured the safety of the train as it passed through Peekskill. Albany police restrained a crowd of nearly 5,000 who lined the sidewalks as the delegation marched to the capital. Aside from a few tomatoes and eggs, which missed their marks, there was no violence in Albany. As a matter of fact, there was very little action of any kind. Instead of the governor, the group was received by Lawrence Walsh, the noncommittal assistant counsel to the governor. He listened attentively, promised little and sent them on their way.

Eighty-three victims of the Peekskill disorder filed suit against Westchester County officials for property damages totaling $20,345, charging official negligence. Several attempts were made to have the charges dismissed. They eventually succeeded, and the federal court dropped all charges against all defendants.

Robeson and writer Howard Fast, along with twenty-six plaintiffs, filed a civil suit for $2,020,000 against Westchester County and two veterans' groups in September of 1949. The case was in litigation until January 23, 1952, when the federal court again dismissed all charges against all defendants. Neither the investigations nor the court actions yielded any significant relief for the petitioners.

In the wake of the civil disorder, the Peekskill community became alive with rumors. Szego reported that the threat of a fascist takeover was causing many people to consider moving out of the Peekskill area. Another rumor had it that the insurance rates against property damage would be increased substantially. On September 27, a Peekskill merchants' group announced the cancellation of their Jan Peek celebration, honoring the founders of the city. They considered it unwise to hold public assemblies at that time. Many other social and civic activities were cancelled or postponed.

Robeson Continues the Crusade

The Robeson group, on the other hand, scheduled appearances for Robeson in many cities across the country. The tour became a vehicle for him to continue his unpopular crusade for peace and a nonmilitary rapprochement (détente) with world Communism, despite the growing threat of war in Korea.

When the tour schedule was published, veterans' groups in New Haven, Pittsburgh, Chicago and other cities urged that the meetings be cancelled. When they failed to effect cancellation, the groups forbade their members to attend any of Robeson's appearances.

Robeson's Detroit appearance occurred on October 9, 1949. Nearly 50,000 people jammed the area of Forest and Hastings Streets, overflowing the Forest Club and forcing the diversion of traffic for three blocks in all directions. One thousand police kept watch over the crowd from the windows and roofs of adjacent buildings, as well as at ground level. Secret service and FBI men infiltrated the crowd, keeping records for future use. Members of the establishment, Black and white, were prominently absent.

Reverend Charles Hill, one of Detroit's most fearless freedom fighters, had the cooperation of many rank-and-file trade unionists in completing the arrangements for Robeson's appearance. They provided Robeson with a tight security guard during his stay and established their own surveillance network to find, report and deal with any signs of violence against Robeson. Detroit's officials breathed a sigh of great relief when he left the city without mishap.

The Peekskill affair accelerated many events that were already in progress and made many others possible that seemed only probable before. The activities of the nonconformist trade unions in Peekskill widened the split within the CIO. Both the purse and power of the investigative committees of the House and Senate were increased in the name of national security. Senator Joseph R. McCarthy (D-Wisconsin) was already testing the anti-Communist line with which he would strangle the nation with brief and terrifying success. Freedom was threatened on all sides by a proliferation of federal, state and local legislation of dubious constitutionality.

This national conflict and controversy nearly drowned out Robeson's own statement on Peekskill. Under the heading "My Answer," he gave his position and issued a plea and a prophecy:

> . . . I am well equipped, now, although I have not always been so, to make the supreme fight for my people and all other underprivileged masses, wherever they may be. Here, I speak of those bereft of uncompromising, courageous leadership that cannot be intimidated and cannot be swerved from its purpose of bringing true freedom to those who follow it.
>
> . . . This thing burns in me, and it is not my nature or inclination to be scared off.
>
> . . . They revile me; they scandalize me and try to holler me down on all sides. That's all right. It's okay. Let them continue. My voice topped the blare of the Legion's bands and the hoots of hired hoodlums who tried to break up my concert for the Harlem

Division of the Civil Rights Congress. It will be heard above the screams of the intolerant.

My weapons are peaceful; for it is only by peace that peace can be attained. The Song of Freedom must prevail.

Robeson's position paper enraged his enemies more than ever, and spurred them on to more imaginative acts of violence against him. His prophecy and plea, out of tune with the times, were ignored.

Peekskill's first anniversary was more than two months away when the United States military forces entered the Korean phase of our Southeast Asian misadventure that would eventually waste millions of lives, trillions of dollars and accelerate our headlong plunge into financial and moral bankruptcy. Before a year had elapsed, the disruptive fissure within the CIO became an unbridgeable chasm, as the latter-day saints, then in power, began to exorcise the militant demons of the left. Guardians of the status quo in Birmingham, Bogalusa and Selma were instructed and encouraged by the permissiveness of Peekskill. They bided their time and kept their powder dry.

In less than a year, Robeson's passport was cancelled by a punitive State Department. Denied the opportunity to make a living at home and unable to travel abroad, he was sentenced to a slow death by economic strangulation and political repression. Robeson, as usual, would not cooperate with his enemies. Not only did he refuse to die, he lived to see all of his unpopular causes become a part of the everyday American way of life.

Despite the vindications of time and circumstance, Robeson remains a prophet without honor in his own land. One of the most glaring evidences of this dishonor is Robeson's absence from the College Football's Hall of Fame. He is the only two-time All-American so ignored. A reversal of this decision, long overdue, could signal the start of a timely revaluation of this controversial American and, perhaps, a change in his outrageous fortune.

Paul Robeson's Impact on History

BY DARLENE CLARK HINE

Paul Robeson used the collective experience of black Americans and his own unique individual experiences as a black man in America to construct a lens through which he viewed and interpreted world events. In 1950, Paul Robeson was placed under "house arrest" in his own country with the revocation of his passport. By 1950, his name had become synonymous with protest against the continued subjugation of colonial people throughout the world. Because of this, he was ostracized. His biographies were banned from library shelves, his recordings were withdrawn from record stores. Theatre halls across America closed their doors. Robeson's earnings shrank from approximately $104,000 a year to a little over $6,000. Paul Robeson, in short, became a nonperson. A generation of young Blacks "knew his name not."

From 1950 to 1958, Paul Robeson fought against the combined might of the United States government and the business community to retrieve his passport. In so doing, he challenged the power of the State Department to decide whether or not individuals should be permitted to travel abroad. While the essential constitutional issue involved focused on the right to travel, the case was complicated by Robeson's political views and his commitment to the liberation of the colonial peoples of Africa, Asia and Latin America. His "crime" was his speaking and singing for the cause of freedom—not just for black Americans, but for all oppressed peoples. This was the basic reason for white America's blind and heedless fear. To understand fully Robeson's two-pronged struggle for the right to travel and his role in the liberation struggles of colonial peoples, it is necessary to review the decade of the 1940s. Such an examination will increase our appreciation of Robeson's impact on history and his legacy to black and white Americans.

The principal event which the State Department used to take away Robeson's right to travel was the statement Robeson made in 1949 in Paris at the World Peace Congress. In this statement Robeson said that President Truman's Four Point program for colonial development meant a new slavery. As demonstrated in Africa the program was an invasion by the former secretary of state, Edward Stettinius and "his millions." Robeson added, "It is unthinkable that American Negroes could go to war on behalf of those who have oppressed them for generations against the Soviet Union, which in one generation has raised our people to full human dignity." [1]

A young black historian, Lamont Yeakey, in an incisive analysis of the implications of Robeson's words and activities and the response of the United States government, asserted that "the fact that he [Robeson] made seemingly irrefutable analogy between the plight of his people here and those of the Third World abroad alarmed the government. His comparison between those who exploited and oppressed colonial peoples in the Third World and the structure of that dominance, and those who oppressed Blacks in this country through institutional racism was simply too much for the white political and economic establishment to bear. Robeson made sense, not only to those government officials and opponents of democracy in America, but he made sense to the hundreds of thousands who heard him." [2] Throughout the 1940s Robeson fought the twin evils of international and domestic racism and "linked the struggle of black America with the struggles of black Africa, brown India, yellow Asia, and the Blacks of Brazil and Haiti and the peons of Mexico and South America." [3]

Robeson's words shocked white America, but they were not new. He spoke out of the revolutionary black tradition of people such as David Walker, Henry Highland Garnet, H. Ford Douglass and Bishop Turner. As historian Sterling Stuckey points out, David Walker in 1829 said that Blacks could not fight in earnest for a country that did not accord them their rights. Henry Highland Garnet argued in 1841 that if the government should attempt to arm black men in the North to send them to Kentucky to put out a slave rebellion, Blacks would never go for that. In 1868 in the Georgia State Legislature Bishop Turner proclaimed that he would not fight to protect the flag of either Georgia or America until those flags began to protect American citizens who were Black.[4] Superimposed on this revolutionary tradition out of which Robeson spoke and acted were the alienation, anger and frustration born of his concerted efforts to help America and the Allies defeat Hitler's Nazism during the Second World War.

The World War II years were a rude awakening for most black Americans, particularly for Paul Robeson. Concerning these years, James Baldwin wrote: "The treatment accorded the Negro during the Second World War marks . . . a turning point in the Negro's relation to America. To put it briefly, and somewhat too simply, a certain hope died, a certain respect for white America faded." [5] Robeson pondered: "What difference is there between the Master Race idea of Hitler and the White Supremacy Creed of Eastland? Who can convince the European peoples that the burning cross of the white-robed Klan is different from the *swastika* of the Brownshirts?" [6]

World War II unveiled the hypocrisy and paradox in fighting against an enemy preaching a master race ideology while at the same time upholding racial segregation and white supremacy. During the war years, thousands of Blacks fought and died in a rigidly segregated army. While the marines and air corps excluded Blacks entirely, the navy allowed them to join an all-black messman's branch. The black press continually criticized the United States for its reluctance to end segregation in the armed forces, for its discrimination in employment and for its disfranchisement via the poll tax. As the black press increased its protests, increased efforts were made to censure the black press. Individuals within the federal government pressured the White House and the Justice Department to indict some black editors for sedition and interference with the war effort. As one historian of the period illustrates:

> One of the most widely publicized attacks on the Negro press was made by the southern white liberal, Virginius Dabney, editor of the *Richmond Times Dispatch*. He charged that "extremist"

Negro newspapers and Negro leaders were "demanding an overnight revolution in race relations," and as a consequence they were "stirring up interracial hate." Dabney concluded his indictment by warning that "it is a foregone conclusion that if an attempt is made forcibly to abolish segregation throughout the South, violence and bloodshed will result." [7]

The democratic ideology of the Second World War forced Blacks to reexamine their position in American society. During the postwar years, Robeson and others such as the great black scholar Dr. W. E. B. Du Bois stimulated an awareness of America's counterrevolutionary posture. From 1945 to 1949 millions of people in Asia, Africa and Latin America attempted to throw off the shackles of colonialism. Under the leadership of Mahatma Gandhi and Jawaharlal Nehru, the Indian National Movement reestablished India's political independence from Britain in 1947. In a three-year struggle, 1946 to 1949, the Indonesian people successfully ended centuries of Dutch rule. Ho Chi Minh, whom Robeson dubbed "the Toussant L'Ouverture of Indo-China," led the Vietnamese in their fight for independence against France.[8] In 1949 the Chinese people won out over the feudal landlords and foreign rule and established the Chinese People's Republic.[9]

Paul Robeson clearly understood the American influence on the difficulties these nationalists confronted. In an address before the National Labor Conference for Negro Rights in Chicago on June 10, 1950, Paul stated that "our nation has become the first enemy of freedom and the chief tyrant of the mid-century world." He elaborated:

How well and how bitterly do we recall that soon after Roosevelt died, American arms were being shipped to the Dutch—not for the protection of the Four Freedoms, not to advance the claims of liberty—but for the suppression of the brave Indonesian patriots in their fight for Independence.

That was in 1946, and today—four years later—we have the announcement of another program of arms shipments to destroy a movement for colonial independence—this time arms for the French imperialists to use against the brave Vietnamese patriots in what the French progressive masses call the "dirty war" in Indo-China.[10]

In 1954 Robeson again spoke on the subject of Vietnam.

Now, when France wants to call it quits, Eisenhower, Nixon and Dulles are insisting that Vietnam must be re-conquered and held in colonial chains. "The Vietnamese lack the ability to govern themselves," says Vice President Nixon.

Vast quantities of U.S. bombers, tanks and guns have been sent against Ho Chi Minh and his freedom-fighters; and now we are told that soon it may be "advisable" to send American GI's into Indo-China in order that the tin, rubber and tungsten of Southeast Asia be kept by the "free world"—meaning white Imperialism.[11]

Paul Robeson reiterated the question that revealed his continued adherence to the position he articulated in 1949 concerning Blacks fighting for a country that oppressed them. "What business did a black lad from Mississippi or Georgia share-cropping farm have in Asia shooting down the yellow or brown son of an impoverished rice-farmer?" [12] Dr. Martin Luther King was to ask the same question in 1967 and 1968.

Robeson saw an America that had only recently become visible to most other citizens. Columnist Jack Anderson wrote: "The heirs of George Washington and Thomas Jefferson actively have aided and abetted the rise of military dictatorships in the Western hemisphere. In a few short years, Latin America has become largely a martial Pax Americana, with the pentagon as its Vatican." In 1963 four Latin American nations—El Salvador, Honduras, Nicaragua and Paraguay—were ruled by military dictators. By 1973 these four were joined by the military dictatorships of Brazil (1964), Panama (1968), Bolivia (1969), Ecuador (1972), Chile and Uruguay (1973) and more recently Argentina. Over a period of thirty years the Pentagon squandered two billion dollars' worth of hardware and training on the military establishments of Latin America. Murder, torture, imprisonment and poverty are the lot of the poor masses in these countries. Robeson foresaw this trend and waged a tremendous struggle against it. Ironically, Anderson noted, "The military governments of Latin America have turned in desperation not to Washington but to Havana." [13]

Robeson spoke out on behalf of all colonial peoples, but those occupying a special place in his heart were the Africans. In 1941 he joined in the founding of the Council on African Affairs which called attention to the vital economic and political role Africa would play in the postwar world. In considering Africa's potential economic clout, Robeson observed that four thousand tons of uranium ore were extracted yearly from the Belgian Congo (now Zaire), which was the main source of the United States supply. Africa, Robeson noted, provided more than half the world's gold and chrome, 80 per cent of its cobalt, 90 per cent of its palm kernals, one-fifth of its manganese and tin, one-third of its sisal fiber and 60 per cent of its cocoa.[14]

In the political realm, Robeson stressed the inseparability of African liberation from imperialist overlords and the black American's struggles against American exploitation and oppression. Robeson wrote, "the free peoples of the free colored nations are our natural friends: their growing strength is also ours." [15] In a 1957 address before the United Nations, the Minister of Justice of Ghana, Ako Adjei, underscored Robeson's heartfelt convictions:

> Ghana has a special responsibility and obligation towards all African peoples or peoples of African descent throughout the world who are struggling to free themselves from foreign rule, or even who, by the mere reason of their color, are denied the enjoyment of very elementary civil and political rights which the Constitutions of their own states guarantee to all citizens. I should like to request all Members of the United Nations to take note that the new State of Ghana is concerned with the freedom of all African peoples and also with the treatment that is meted out to all peoples of African descent, wherever they may be in any part of the world. . . .[16]

There is a direct correlation between Robeson's passport revocation and his involvement in liberation struggles and his leadership in the Council of African Affairs. When Secretary of State Dean Acheson revoked Robeson's passport in 1950, he explained that Robeson's travel abroad "would be contrary to the best interests of the United States." [17] Robeson immediately sought redress through the courts and in February, 1952 the Court of Appeals upheld the denial of his passport. The State Department's brief is quite revealing:

. . . Furthermore, even if the complaint had alleged, which it does not, that the passport was cancelled solely because of the applicant's recognized status as spokesman for large sections of Negro Americans, we submit that this would not amount to an abuse of discretion in view of appellant's frank admission that he has been for years extremely active politically in behalf of independence of the colonial people of Africa.[18]

Robeson reapplied for a passport in 1953, 1954, 1955 and 1956. To reclaim his passport "became the central factor in his life"; for as he wrote, "From the days of chattel slavery until today, the concept of *travel* has been inseparably linked in the minds of our people with concept of *Freedom*." Drawing upon the nineteenth-century black struggle for freedom and that of his own father who escaped from slavery via the underground railroad, Robeson persisted in the struggle for the right to travel. He says in his autobiography:

> From the very beginning of Negro history in our land, Negroes have asserted their right to freedom of movement. Some of the runaway slaves went to foreign countries not to secure their own freedom but to gain liberation for their kinsmen in chains. The good work they did abroad lives on in our own time, for that pressure which comes today from Europe in our behalf is in part a precious heritage from those early Negro sojourners for freedom who crossed the sea to champion the rights of black men in America.[19]

During the seven years of litigation, the State Department's and the court's rationales for denying travel privileges to Robeson went from the sublime to the ridiculous. Initially the courts held that the American citizen does not have a right to travel abroad; travel is a privilege granted at the convenience of the government. Later the court ruled that the State Department had the right to restrict the travel of any American citizen in the national interest. And finally it held that Robeson had failed to exhaust administrative remedies open to him. He had, for example, declined to execute an affidavit concerning past or present membership in the Communist party. To have signed such an affidavit would have amounted to acquiescence to extortion.[20]

By 1958 the international pressures on the American government to release Paul Robeson had become enormous. Peoples, leaders and statesmen in India, China, and the Soviet Union and Africa agitated for Robeson's freedom. As one biographer correctly posits, "The detention of Paul Robeson within the national limits of the United States during these years was the single most costly act America might have taken in terms of propaganda to the colored peoples of the world." [21]

Because of this international pressure, the Supreme Court of the United States in 1958 ruled upon two cases that contested the Secretary of State's arbitrary authority to revoke passports. The decision in those cases had a direct bearing on Robeson's petitions, which were again locked into the legal machinery. In the five-to-four decision in the *Rockwell Kent* v. *John Foster Dulles* case, Justice Douglas ruled that the Secretary of State did not have the authority to withhold a passport because of an individual's political views. To make the issuance of a passport contingent upon the filing of an affidavit as to his membership in the Communist party was to deny a constitutional right (not privilege) without the due process of law of the Fifth Amendment.[22] Paul Robeson received his passport in June, 1958 and by July, 1958 he was in Europe.[23]

The striking and invaluable legacy Robeson left to black and white America—and thus his impact on history—is a dual one. One side of the legacy was the lesson derived from his individual struggle for freedom, which was embodied in his pursuit of the passport and the right to travel. This one aspect of his life clearly reveals the extent to which white government officials were willing to go in order to nullify the Constitution and suspend the rights of American citizens who strayed from the beaten path of exploitation of the masses for the private gain of a few. Robeson's activities and statements in behalf of liberation for all oppressed peoples and his analysis of the role the American government plays in the perpetration and continuation of national and international oppression of colored people throughout the world comprise the other side of his legacy. From him we can learn, develop and sharpen our own commitment and resolve to participate in and support the collective international struggle for peace and freedom.

Robeson's *Here I Stand:*
The Book They Could Not Ban *

BY LLOYD L. BROWN

"Let's see by a show of hands—how many of you have read Paul
Robeson's book, *Here I Stand?*"

The question was directed by Dizzy Gillespie to a large audience that attended a tribute to Robeson sponsored in New York
by Local 1199, Drug and Hospital Union. The noted jazz musician, who was one of the many star performers on the program,
shook his head reproachfully when only a few hands were raised.
"Now that is one book," he said, "that all of you really ought
to read."

But where would they find it? Written and published under
the conditions of Robeson's total banishment within this country, his book has been out of print for a decade. When *Here I
Stand* appeared on February 14, 1958, the "Big White Folks,"
whom Robeson had defiantly challenged in its pages, made a
concerted effort to boycott the book and thus silence his voice
in print as they had silenced him in all other mass media.

In one area the boycott achieved a near-total success: with
one insignificant exception, *no white commercial newspaper or
magazine in the entire country so much as mentioned Robeson's
book.* Leading papers in the field of literary coverage, like *The
New York Times* and the *Herald-Tribune,* not only did not review it; they refused even to include its name in their lists of
"books out today."

Recently, when this writer asked the *Times* about the matter,
the Sunday Editor, Daniel Schwarz, wrote in reply: "We have

---

* This article by Lloyd L. Brown is based on his preface to the new edition of
Here I Stand, published in September 1971, by Beacon Press, Boston, Mass.

tried to find some record of what happened to Paul Robeson's book, 'Here I Stand,' but our files do not go that far back. . . . I am told that Paul Robeson's book doesn't appear in the listings of the Book Review Digest, so apparently it was not only The Times Book Review which decided not to review the book. I just want to assure you that we carefully consider every book we receive and I am certain that any book by Paul Robeson would not have been rejected for review if in the judgment of the editors it merited attention."

However, even if one could imagine that every one of the editors of the entire American white press, individually and without pressure, came to the same judgment that Robeson's book did not merit attention, there exists an overwhelming fact to prove that their unanimity was not a miraculous coincidence. That fact is this: *in two other areas, which were beyond the control of the boycotters, many editors came to an altogether different judgment.*

One of these areas was the world beyond the U.S. borders that Robeson was forbidden to cross. Although *Here I Stand* was addressed primarily to black Americans, reviewers in all the many lands where the book was republished found that it *did* merit attention. Nor was this judgment limited to the Soviet Union and other socialist countries where Robeson had long been a legendary hero. Unlike the liberal *Times* in New York, the Tory *Times* in London reviewed the book (August 14, 1958). Noting that "Robeson is a single-minded crusader, his mission is to secure equal social and political rights for the American Negro," the London reviewer went on to say that his book "commands attention because he is a great artist, because he is accused of Communism, and because, by refusing him a passport for many years, the American government promoted him to the status of a political martyr."

Another striking example of that different judgment was the widespread attention that the Japanese edition of *Here I Stand* received. In a note accompanying a batch of laudatory reviews printed in Japan's leading papers, the translator, Akira Iwasaki, reported to Robeson's U.S. publisher: "The book got a very good critical appraisal. It was more than I expected, since the 'bourgeois' newspapers and magazines here usually omit to mention the works of progressive artists. But they were impressed by the personal integrity of Mr. Robeson."

In India, the mass-circulation tabloid, *Blitz,* published (April 5, 1958) a four-page illustrated supplement which, under the headline "Black Voice of God," was devoted entirely to Robeson's book. The editor felt that the book not only merited attention but called for action as well. "We must take Robeson's slogan, THE TIME IS NOW," he wrote, "and arrange mass demonstrations to show that we completely and solidly support the cause of the American Negro."

However, far more significant than the response abroad was the response in the second large area where the anti-Robeson ban was broken—in the black communities of America. The breakthrough began in Harlem where Othello Associates, an independent Negro publishing company, brought out Robeson's book. (It might be noted that among the many meaningful misstatements in Edwin P. Hoyt's biography of Robeson was that author's assertion that *Here I Stand* was published abroad by a white publisher. The fact is, the British edition Hoyt cites, and all the other foreign editions, were produced by arrangement with the black U.S. publisher.)

What followed the publication of Robeson's book was a development altogether unprecedented in the period of McCarthyite repression: an important section of the Afro-American press moved with speed and energy to publicize and promote the sale of a book that expressed the ideas of a man considered by the dominant class to be Enemy Number One. The fact that the Negro editors were well aware of the source of the anti-Robeson ban was indicated by a Chicago *Crusader* editorial (March 8, 1958) that referred scornfully to certain "other Negro editors [who], scared that Washington might send the F.B.I. to check on them, took to their heels whenever the name of Robeson was mentioned."

The Baltimore *Afro-American* (with editions in several other cities) took the lead in the widespread defiance of the ban. As soon as *Here I Stand* was off the press, the *Afro* began its forceful campaign to get a hearing for it. That effort started with an editorial (February 22, 1958) that hailed Robeson's "remarkable book," and announced that the *Afro's* magazine section would serialize several of its chapters. Then came the five-part series, starting with the March 15 issue, which also featured a notable review of *Here I Stand* by Saunders Redding. (Later, in his annual year-end roundup for the paper, on January 10, 1959, Redding listed Robeson's book among the ten works that "impressed this reviewer most strongly in 1958.")

The *Afro* followed up (May 3) with a second editorial, titled "The Paul Robeson Story," that deservedly took "some pardonable pride" in the fact that the first printing of *Here I Stand* was sold out in the first six weeks. The editorial noted that Robeson had chosen a "different technique from that of more orthodox leaders," and justified the paper's support of him by asserting: "In fighting slavery, John Brown and Frederick Douglass resorted to different methods, but they were both on the same side."

The late Carl Murphy, who as the *Afro-American's* president directed this campaign, was joined by the parallel efforts made by another leading black journalist, P. L. Prattis, then chief editor of the Pittsburgh *Courier*. The fact that the influential *Courier* was a close second to the *Afro* in defying the ban against Robeson was largely due to the integrity of Prattis, who, along with Murphy, had earlier dared to condemn the frame-up of Dr. Du Bois when few others would do so.

The main front-page headline in the *Courier* of February 22, 1958, was: "PAUL ROBESON STATES HIS CASE," and the cover story of its magazine section of that date dramatized the news that Robeson had written an important book. Though the *Courier* published no review of the book (probably a friendly act, since the book editor was the arch-conservative George S. Schuyler), Prattis devoted his column (March 29, 1958) to a discussion of *Here I Stand*. His paper printed numerous news stories about the successful campaign to sell the book, as well as many enthusiastic letters from Robeson's readers.

The only negative review of *Here I Stand* that this writer knows about appeared in the March, 1958, issue of the NAACP's magazine, *The Crisis,* and was written by its editor, James W. Ivy. The book was deemed to be "disorderly and confusing" and its author was described as a man whom "Negroes . . . never regarded as a leader," and who "imagines his misfortunes to stem, not from his own bungling, but from the persecution of 'the white folks on top.' " (The founding editor of *The Crisis* and eminent historian, W. E. B. Du Bois, evidently shared Robeson's alleged delusion, since he said at the time: "The persecution of Paul Robeson by the government . . . has been one of the most contemptible happenings in modern history." *Autobiography of W. E. B. Du Bois*, p. 396.)

An opposite view to that of *The Crisis* on Robeson's persecution and his status as a leader was given by the Chicago *Crusader*, which devoted most of its editorial page (March 8, 1958) to a lengthy statement titled "Paul Robeson: A Man." Welcoming his book, the editorial said: "We have thought all along that the great singer, athlete and lawyer, as well as freedom fighter, has been persecuted because he wouldn't bow down to the white folks." On the subject of his leadership, the *Crusader* asserted: "Paul Robeson has been one of the mightiest of all Negro voices raised against world oppression of people based on race, color, nationality and religion. He is known wherever there are people as a champion of the rights of man."

The editorial had more to say on that subject: "There are times in our struggle for full equality when stalwart men like Robeson, carved in the heroic mould of Cudjo, Fred Douglass, Jack Johnson, Dr. Ossian Sweet of Detroit, and Oscar DePriest of Chicago, are needed for the physical example. This is the kind of leadership that Paul Robeson lives and sings about that will get Negroes off their knees where they are being executed daily before the firing squad of racial prejudice, discrimination, Jim Crow and anti-Negro terrorism, onto their own two legs on which they must stand like men and fight this thing out toe to toe. White folks are scared of this type of leadership. They feared it in Edward H. Wright in Chicago, Wright Cuney in Texas and Ben Davis in Georgia. They were enraged at Jack Johnson who could look a white man in the eye in such a way as to make him cringe. In Paul Robeson they have met their match again."

Not all reviewers could be that outspoken, and in some cases they quoted at length Robeson's most militant statements without making any comment. In one case, the reviewer (Buddy Lonesome in the St. Louis *Argus*, April 25, 1958) quoted various paragraphs from Chapter 4 ("The Time Is Now"), and Chapter 5 ("The Power of Negro Action"), which he saw as "particularly pertinent." Then he came to a key point in the latter chapter where he felt that Robeson had gone too far. However, in stating his disagreement, the reviewer strongly hinted that he had in fact got the message:

"He [the author] gives an example of a Negro family huddling in their newly purchased home while a mob of howling bigots mills around the house. Robeson then candidly asks, 'Where are the other Negroes?' There I differ with him, for it certainly wouldn't be right for Negroes to rush to arms, thereby creating another mob, to still the howls of the indignant white bigots. But then I remember the indulgent smirks of Americans around the country when Indians in Lumbee, N.C., grabbed rifles to rout a klavern of white-sheeted ku kluxers, and I pause for deep reflection."

The most analytical assessment of Robeson's ideas on the black liberation struggle that appeared in the Negro press was the review in the Los Angeles *Herald-Dispatch* (May 8, 1958). The reviewer, William C. Taylor, focused attention on Chapter 5, which, he said, "by itself makes this book a 'must' on every reading list." He noted that, "While strongly advocating unity of Negro and white, Robeson warns of a 'rising resentment against the control of our affairs by white people, regardless of whether that domination is expressed by the blunt orders of political bosses or more discreetly by the *advice* of white liberals which must be heeded or else.' "

Along with his insistence that the liberation movement must be led by an independent black leadership, Robeson had stressed that another quality was also needed: "To live in freedom one must be prepared to die to achieve it. . . . He who is not prepared to face the trials of battle will never lead to a triumph." (*Here I Stand*, pp. 110-11.) To the Los Angeles reviewer Robeson's ideas on this subject were "right down the alley," and he quoted the following passage on page 110 as being especially meaningful: "The primary quality that Negro leadership must possess, as I see it, is *a single-minded dedication to their people's welfare* . . . for the true leader all else must be subordinated to the interests of those whom he is leading." (Emphasis in original.)

In addition to much of the black press, the left-wing newspapers and magazines of the country also considered that Robeson's book merited attention. Among the reviewing publications in this area and their respective writers were: *National Guardian*, Cedric Belfrage (3/10/58); *New World Review*, Louis E. Burnham (May, '58); *Mainstream*, Shirley Graham (March, '58); and *The Worker*, Phillip Bonosky (5/4/58). The principal Marxist response to *Here I Stand* appeared in *Political Affairs* (April, 1958, pp. 1–8). The reviewer was the late Benjamin J. Davis, a noted black militant, Communist party leader, and son of the Ben Davis of Georgia whose leadership was praised in the above-quoted Chicago *Crusader*.

Davis asserted that with the publication of *Here I Stand* "a new dimension is added to the massive array of Robeson's contributions to the goal of human dignity," and he described the book as "beautifully, simply and movingly written, bold in conception, sound in content, broad in approach." Noting that there was a "conspiracy of muteness on the part of the monopoly press" regarding the book, Davis said that the reason for the boycott was that Robeson's book "brings forward a people's program of action which, if seized upon by the Negro people and their allies, could not fail to have the most profound positive effects upon the present struggles of the Negro for dignity and full citizenship."

The Marxist reviewer discussed one aspect of the author's stand that had been skipped over by the nonleft reviewers, namely, that "Robeson makes no bones about his friendship with the Soviet Union" and the other socialist countries. He quoted the passage where Robeson wrote of "my deep conviction that for all mankind a socialist society represents an advance to a higher stage of life—that it is a form of society which is economically, socially, culturally, and ethically superior to a system based upon production for private profit."

Perhaps the core of Davis's assessment was this: "Communists, in particular," he wrote, "should learn from the opinion of others, especially those outside their ranks, who, like Robeson, are participants in, fighters for, and students of the struggle for a better life. . . . A strong partisan of socialism, he, nevertheless, recognizes that the attainment of the Negro's full citizenship is a massive struggle requiring the unity of people of diverse views and parties on a common program of action. . . . Robeson's book introduces into the market place of ideas the basic question of how one who believes in the principles of scientific socialism can project a program broader and more effective than any yet advanced on the American scene by any people's leader."

In concluding this survey of the response to *Here I Stand,* a few words from the present writer may be in order. I am grateful that I had the opportunity to serve as Robeson's collaborator in the writing of *Here I Stand,* and to be one of the "Othello Associates" who published the book despite the ban. It has been gratifying to see that many of Robeson's militant ideas have been taken up by today's liberation movement, and that many young people are finding their way along paths blazed by this great man of whom most of them have never heard.

Unfortunately, however, when young people do hear of him they usually hear only the testimony of his enemies. For example, students are often directed to Harold Cruse's *The Crisis of the Negro Intellectual,* with its thoroughly false treatment of Robeson. Cruse's book contains many of the big lies being told to make young black militants scorn a man they would honor if they knew the truth. For instance, on page 297 Cruse writes: "As I have pointed out, the Negro actor-performer-singer has always developed an ambivalent communion (or none at all) with the Negro creative artist—upon whom the interpreters seldom depend for their artistic accomplishments or financial status." Incredibly, the prime—indeed the *only*—example Cruse gives to illustrate his dubious generalization is—Paul Robeson!

On the other hand, students have not been directed to the primary source, Robeson himself, where they would learn the truth (which Cruse knows but conceals from them), as in this passage from *Here I Stand:* "Early in my professional musical career I had the great good fortune to become associated with Lawrence Brown, an extraordinarily gifted Negro composer and

arranger, and over the years this association grew into a successful partnership and personal friendship. It was this musician who
clarified my instinctive feeling that the simple, beautiful songs
of my childhood, heard every Sunday in church and every day
at home and in the community—the great poetic song-sermons
of the Negro preacher and the congregation, the work songs and
blues of my father's folk from the plantation of North Carolina—
should also become important concert material. Lawrence Brown,
who also knew and played the folk music of other peoples, as well
as the great classics of Western song literature (many of which
are based on folk themes), was firm in his conviction that our
music—Negro music of African and American derivation—was
in the tradition of the world's great folk music. *And so for my
first five years as a singer my repertoire consisted entirely of my
people's songs."* (p. 57, emphasis added.)

Any honest appraisal would show that Robeson's internationalism, his all-embracing humanism, developed *through* his deep
communion with the Afro-American heritage. Indeed, twenty
years ago the present writer, arguing that the Negro creative
writer could best reach the goal of universality by basing his work
on the cultural heritage of his own people, cited Robeson as a
living example of that achievement. I wrote: "A giant figure in
our country exemplifies this concept in another field of the arts—
Paul Robeson. Here is a man who is the foremost people's artist
of America and a world artist. He sings the songs of the peoples
of the world in the languages of those peoples and touches their
hearts; they call him brother, son. And what is the primary source
of his universal art? His people. His art is great for it has a great
foundation—the rich national culture and psychology of the Negro people: sorrow song and jubilee, work song and dance song."
(*Masses & Mainstream,* April, 1951, p. 54.)

In the face of Cruse's falsification, some lines of an old, familiar song from the black-culture repertoire of Robeson come
to mind:

You call that a brother? No! No! Scandalize my name.

It may be expected, however, that the inquiring minds of the
new generation will break through to the truth. Inevitably, like
a mountain peak that becomes visible as the mist is blown away,

the towering figure of Paul Robeson will emerge as the thick
white fog of lies and slanders is dispelled. Then he will be recognized and honored here in his homeland, as he is throughout the
world, as Robeson the Great Forerunner.

The Power of Negro Action

From Here I Stand

BY PAUL ROBESON

"How long, O Lord, how long?"—that ancient cry of the oppressed is often voiced these days in editorials in the Negro newspapers whose pages are filled with word-and-picture reports of outrages against our people. A photograph of a Negro being kicked by a white mobster brings the vicious blow crashing against the breast of the reader, and there are all the other horrible pictures—burning cross, beaten minister, bombed school, threatened children, mutilated man, imprisoned mother, barricaded family—which show what is going on.

How long? The answer is: *As long as we permit it.* I say that Negro action can be decisive. I say that we ourselves have the power to end the terror and to win for ourselves peace and security throughout the land. The recognition of this fact will bring new vigor, boldness and determination in planning our program of action and new militancy in winning its goals.

The denials and doubts about this idea—the second part of the challenge which confronts us today—are even more evident than those I noted in regard to the first. The diehard racists who shout "Never!" to equal rights, and the gradualists who mumble "Not now," are quite convinced that the Negro is powerless to bring about a different decision. Unfortunately, it is also true that to a large extent the Negro people do not know their own strength and do not see how they can achieve the goals they so urgently desire. The basis for this widespread view is obvious. We are a minority, a tenth of the population of our country. In all the terms in which power is reckoned in America—economic wealth, political office, social privilege—we are in a weak position; and from this the conclusion is drawn that the Negro can do little or nothing to compel a change.

It must be seen, however, that this is not a case of a minority pitting itself against a majority. If it were, if we wanted to gain something for ourselves by taking it away from the more powerful majority, the effort would plainly be hopeless. But that is not the case with our demand. Affirming that we are indeed created equal, we seek the equal rights to which we are entitled under the law. The granting of our demand would not lessen the democratic rights of the white people: on the contrary, it would enormously strengthen the base of democracy for all Americans. We ask for nothing that is not ours by right, and herein lies the great moral power of our demand. It is the admitted *rightness* of our claim which has earned for us the moral support of the majority of white Americans.

The granting of our demand for first-class citizenship, on a par with all others, would not in itself put us in a position of equality. Oppression has kept us on the bottom rungs of the ladder, and even with the removal of all barriers we will still have a long way to climb in order to catch up with the general standard of living. But the equal *place* to which we aspire cannot be reached without the equal *rights* we demand, and so the winning of those rights is not a maximum fulfillment but a minimum necessity and we cannot settle for less. Our viewpoint on this matter is not a minority opinion in our country. Though the most rabid champions of "white superiority" are unwilling to test their belief by giving the Negro an equal opportunity, I believe that most white Americans are fair-minded enough to concede that we should be given that chance.

The moral support of the American majority is largely passive today, but what must be recognized—and here we see the decisive power of Negro action—is this:

Wherever and whenever we, the Negro people, claim our lawful rights with all of the earnestness, dignity and determination that we can demonstrate, the moral support of the American people will become an active force on our side.

The most important part of the Little Rock story was not what Governor Faubus and the local mobs did, nor was it what

President Eisenhower was moved to do: the important thing was that nine Negro youngsters, backed by their parents, the Negro community and its leadership, resolved to claim their right to attend Central High School. The magnificent courage and dignity these young people displayed in making that claim won the admiration of the American public. Their *action* did more to win the sympathy and support of democratic-minded white people than all the speeches about "tolerance" that have ever been made.

Little Rock was but one of the first skirmishes in the battle to end Jim Crow Schools; much greater tests of our determination will soon be at hand. The desegregation of public education is as yet only in the first stages and the hard core of resistance has not been met. But there is no turning back, and the necessity to prepare ourselves for the struggles that lie ahead is urgent.

I have pointed to the sources of strength that exist at home and abroad. What power do we ourselves have?

We have the power of numbers, the power of organization, and the power of spirit. Let me explain what I mean.

Sixteen million people are a force to be reckoned with, and indeed there are many nations in the UN whose numbers are less. No longer can it be said that the Negro question is a sectional matter: the continuing exodus from the South has spread the Negro community to all parts of the land and has concentrated large numbers in places which are economically and politically the most important in the nation. In recent years much has been written about the strategic position of Negro voters in such pivotal states as New York, Ohio, Pennsylvania, Michigan, Illinois and California, but generally it can be said that the power of our numbers is not seen or acted upon. Let us consider this concept in connection with something that is apparent to all.

Very often these days we see photographs in the newspapers and magazines of a Negro family—the husband, wife, their children—huddled together in their newly purchased or rented home, while outside hundreds of Negro-haters have gathered to throw stones, to howl filthy abuse, to threaten murder and arson; and there may or may not be some policemen at the scene. But something is missing from this picture that ought to be there, and its absence gives rise to a nagging question that cannot be stilled: *Where are the other Negroes?* Where are the hundreds and thousands of other Negroes in that town who ought to be there protecting their own? The *power of numbers* that is missing from the scene would change the whole picture as nothing else could. It is one thing to terrorize a helpless few, but the forces of race hate that brazenly whoop and holler when the odds are a thousand to one are infinitely less bold when the odds are otherwise.

I am not suggesting, of course, that the Negro people should take law enforcement into their own hands. But we have the right and, above all, we have the duty, to bring the strength and support of our entire community to defend the lives and property of each individual family. Indeed, the law itself will move a hundred times quicker whenever it is apparent that the power of our numbers has been called forth. The time has come for the great Negro communities throughout the land—Chicago, Detroit, New York, Birmingham and all the rest—to demonstrate that they will no longer tolerate mob violence against one of their own. In listing the inalienable rights of man, Thomas Jefferson put *life* before *liberty, and the pursuit of happiness;* and it must be clear that for Negro Americans today the issue of *personal security* must be put first, and resolved first, before all other matters are attended to. When the Negro is told that he must "stay in his place," there is always the implicit threat that unless he does so mob violence will be used against him. Hence, as I see it, nothing is more important than to establish the fact that we will no longer suffer the use of mobs against us. Let the Negro people of but a single city respond in an all-out manner at the first sign of a mob—in mass demonstrations, by going on strike, by organizing boycotts—and the lesson will be taught in one bold stroke to people everywhere.

It was an excellent idea to call for a Prayer Pilgrimage for Freedom to assemble in Washington on May 17, 1957, the third anniversary of the Supreme Court decision, and the thousands who gathered there were inspired with a sense of solidarity and were deeply stirred by the speeches that were made. In terms of dignity and discipline the gathering was a matter for great pride.

But there was at the same time a sense of disappointment at the size of the rally which did not, as a national mobilization, truly reflect the power of our numbers. Various charges were later made in the press, and heatedly denied, that important elements of leadership had "dragged their feet" in the preparations, but no constructive purpose would be served by going into those arguments here. The point I wish to make is this: when we call for such a mobilization again (and it ought to be done before another three years passes), we must go all-out to rally not tens of thousands but hundreds of thousands in a demonstration that will show we really mean business. And we should do more than listen to speeches and then go quietly home. Our spokesmen should go to the White House and to Congress and, backed by the massed power of our people, present our demands for action. Then they should come back to the assembled people to tell them what "the man" said, so that the people can decide whether they are satisfied or not and what to do about it.

The time for pussyfooting is long gone. If someone or other fears that some politician might be "embarrassed" by being confronted by such a delegation, or is concerned lest such action seem too bold—well, let that timid soul just step aside, for there are many in our ranks who will readily go in to "talk turkey" with any or all of the top men in government. We must get it into our heads—and into every leader's head—that we are not asking "favors" of the Big White Folks when, for example, we insist that the full power of the Executive be used to protect the right of Negroes to register and vote in the South. And when we really turn out for such a demand the answer can only be yes.

The *power of organization,* through which the power of numbers is expressed, is another great strength of the Negro people. Few other areas of American life are as intensively organized as is the Negro community. Some people say that we have far too many organizations—too many different churches and denominations, too many fraternal societies, clubs and associations—but that is what we have and there is no use deploring it. What is important is to recognize a meaningful fact which is so often denied: Negroes can and do band together and they have accomplished remarkable works through their collective efforts. "The trouble with our folks"—how often you have heard it (or perhaps said it yourself)—"is that we just won't get together"; but the plain truth is that we just about do more joining and affiliating than anybody else. "Our folks are just not ready to make financial sacrifices for a good cause," we hear, and yet we see that all over the country congregations of a few hundred poor people contribute and collect thousands of dollars year in and year out for the purposes that inspire them.

The Negro communities *are* organized and that condition is not made less significant by the fact that our people have formed a great number of organizations to meet their needs and desires. Organizations like the NAACP, which has won many splendid victories in the courts for our rights and has done much other notable work, deserve a much greater membership and financial support than is now the case. Yet it is clear that to exert fully our power of organization we must bring together, for united action, all of the many organizations which now encompass the masses of our people. The great struggle and victory in Montgomery, Alabama, against Jim Crow buses proved beyond all doubt that the various existing organizations of the Negro community can be effectively united for a common purpose. Of course the factor of leadership, which I shall discuss later in this chapter, is a key point, but what I wish to emphasize here is that the *organizational base* for successful struggle exists in all other communities no less than in Montgomery. And who, in the face of the brilliant organization of every practical detail that was devised and carried through by our people in Montgomery, can still assert that Negroes do not have the capacity for effective collective action? What other mass movement in our country was better planned and carried out?

The central role that was played in Montgomery by the churches and their pastors highlights the fact that the Negro church, which has played such a notable part in our history, is still the strongest base of our power of organization. This is true not only because of the large numbers who comprise the congregations, but because our churches are, in the main, independent *Negro* organizations. The churches and other groups of similar independent character—fraternal orders, women's clubs and so forth—will increasingly take the lead because they are closer to the Negro rank-and-file, more responsive to their needs, and less subject to control by forces outside the Negro community.

Here let me point to a large group among this rank-and-file which is potentially the most powerful and effective force in our community—the two million Negro men and women who are members of organized labor. We are a working people and the pay-envelope of the Negro worker is the measure of our general welfare and progress. Government statistics on average earnings show that for every dollar that the white worker is paid the Negro worker gets only 53 cents; and that the average Negro family has a yearly income of $2,410, compared with an average of $4,339 per year for white families. Here, on the basic bread-and-butter level, is a crucial front in our fight for equality and here the Negro trade unionists are the main force to lead the way.

It must be seen, too, that in relation to our general struggle for civil rights the Negro trade unionists occupy a key position. They comprise a large part of the membership of our community organizations and at the same time they are the largest section of our people belonging to interracial organizations. Hence, the Negro trade union members are a strategic link, a living connection with the great masses of the common people of America who are our natural allies in the struggle for democracy and whose active support must be won for our side in this critical hour.

To our men and women of organized labor I would say: a twofold challenge confronts you. The Negro trade unionists must increasingly exert their influence in every aspect of our people's community life. No church, no fraternal, civic or social organization in our communities must be permitted to continue without the benefit of the knowledge and experience that you have gained through your struggles in the great American labor movement. You are called upon to provide the spirit, the determination, the organizational skill, the firm steel of unyielding militancy to the age-old strivings of our people for equality and freedom.

Secondly, on your shoulders there is the responsibility to rally the strength of the whole trade union movement, white and black, to the battle for liberation of our people. Though you are still largely unrepresented in the top levels of labor leadership, you must use your power of numbers to see to it that the leadership of the AFL-CIO, which has shown much concern for the so-called "crusade for freedom" abroad shall not continue to be silent and unmoving in our crusade for freedom *at home.* You must rally your white fellow workers to support full equality for Negro workers; for their right to work at any job; to receive equal pay for equal work; for an end to Jim Crow unions; for the election of qualified Negroes to positions of union leadership; for fair employment practices in every industry; for trade union educational programs to eliminate the notions of "white superiority" which the employers use to poison the minds of the white workers in order to pit them against you.

I have watched and participated in your militant struggles everywhere I have been these past years—in Chicago with the packinghouse workers; with the auto workers of Detroit; the seamen and longshoremen of the West Coast; the tobacco workers of North Carolina; the miners of Pittsburgh and West Virginia; the steel workers of Illinois, Pennsylvania, Indiana and Ohio; the furriers, clerks and garment workers of New York and Philadelphia; with workers in numerous other places throughout the land —and I feel sure that you will meet the challenge which confronts you today.

To all groups in Negro life I would say that the key to set into motion our power of organization is the concept of *coordinated action,* the bringing together of the many organizations which exist in order to plan and to carry out the common struggle. We know full well that it is not easy to do this. We are divided in many ways—in politics, in religious affiliations, in economic and social classes; and in addition to these group rivalries there are the obstacles of personal ambitions and jealousies of various leaders. But as I move among our people these days, from New York to California, I sense a growing impatience with petty ways of thinking and doing things. I see a rising resentment against control of our affairs by white people, regardless of whether that domination is expressed by the blunt orders of political bosses or more discreetly by the "advice" of white liberals which must be heeded or else. There is a rapidly growing awareness that despite all of our differences it is necessary that we become unified, and I think that the force of that idea will overcome all barriers. Coordinated action will not, of course, come all at once; it will develop in the grass-roots and spread from community to community. And the building of that unity is a task which each of us can undertake wherever we are.

A unified people requires a unified leadership, and let me make very clear what I mean by that. Recently the distinguished Negro journalist Carl T. Rowan, who had published in *Ebony* magazine an interview with me, was himself interviewed about that subject on a radio network program where he said: "It's Robeson's contention that the Negro people will never be free in this country until they speak more or less as one voice, and, very obviously, Robeson feels that that one voice should be something close to his voice."

Actually, that is *not* how I feel, and I would not want Mr. Rowan or anyone else to misunderstand my view of this matter. The one voice in which we should speak must be the expression of our entire people on the central issue which is all-important to every Negro—our right to be free and equal. On many other issues there are great differences among us, and hence it is not possible for any one person, or any group of people, to presume to speak for us all.

Far from making any such claim for myself, what I am advocating is in fact the opposite idea! I advocate a unity based upon our common viewpoint as Negroes, a nonpartisan unity, a unity in which we subordinate all that divides us, a unity which excludes no one, a unity in which no faction or group is permitted to impose its particular outlook on others. A unified leadership of a unified movement means that people of *all* political views—conservatives, liberals, and radicals—must be represented therein. Let there be but one requirement made without exception: that Negro leadership, and every man and woman in that leadership, place the interests of our people, and the struggle for those interests, above all else.

There is a need—an urgent need—for a national conference of Negro leadership, not of a handful but a broad representative gathering of leadership from all parts of the country, from all walks of life, from every viewpoint, to work out a *common program of action* for Negro Americans in the crisis of our times. Such a program does not exist today and without it we are a ship without a rudder; we can only flounder around on a day-to-day basis, trying to meet developments with patchwork solutions. We must chart a course to be followed in the stormy days that are here and in the greater storms that are on the way, a course that heads full square for freedom.

The need for a *central fund*, not only for legal purposes but for all the purposes of Negro coordinated action, has been expressed in various editorials in the press and elsewhere; and the national conference I speak of could meet this need. A central fund would be a "community chest" to help our struggles everywhere. Nonpartisan and not controlled by any single organization, this fund would be a national institution of our whole people, and a well-organized campaign to build it would meet with a generous response from Negro America. And more: such a fund would undoubtedly receive a great deal of support from white people who sympathize with our struggle.

If we must think boldly in terms of the power of numbers, we must likewise think big in terms of organizations. Our cause is the cause of all, and so our methods of reaching our goal must be such that all of our people can play a part. The full potential of the Negro people's power of organization must be achieved in every city and state throughout the land.

The *power of spirit* that our people have is intangible, but it is a great force that must be unleashed in the struggles of today. A spirit of steadfast determination, exaltation in the face of trials —it is the very soul of our people that has been formed through all the long and weary years of our march toward freedom. It is the deathless spirit of the great ones who have led our people in the past—Douglass, Tubman and all the others—and of the millions who kept "a-inching along." That spirit lives in our people's songs—in the sublime grandeur of "Deep River," in the driving power of "Jacob's Ladder," in the militancy of "Joshua Fit the Battle of Jericho," and in the poignant beauty of all our spirituals.

It lives in every Negro mother who wants her child "to grow

up and be somebody," as it lives in our common people everywhere who daily meet insult and outrage with quiet courage and
optimism. It is that spirit which gives that "something extra" to
our athletes, to our artists, to all who meet the challenge of public performance. It is the spirit of little James Gordon of Clay,
Kentucky, who, when asked by a reporter why he wanted to go
to school with white children, replied: "Why shouldn't I?"; and
it is the spirit of all the other little ones in the South who have
walked like mighty heroes through menacing mobs to go to
school. It is the spirit of the elderly woman of Montgomery who
explained her part in the bus boycott by saying: "When I rode in
the Jim Crow buses my body was riding but my soul was walking,
but now when my body is walking my soul is riding!"

Yes, that power of the spirit is the pride and glory of my people, and there is no human quality in all America that can sur-
pass it. It is a force only for good: there is no hatefulness about
it. It exalts the finest things of life—justice and equality, human
dignity and fulfillment. It is of the earth, deeply rooted, and it
reaches up to the highest skies and mankind's noblest aspirations.
It is time for this spirit to be evoked and exemplified in all we
do, for it is a force mightier than all our enemies and will triumph over all their evil ways.

For Negro action to be decisive—given the favorable opportunity which I have outlined in the previous chapter and the
sources of strength indicated above—still another factor is needed:
effective Negro leadership. In discussing this subject I shall not
engage in any personalities, nor is it my intention either to praise
or blame the individuals who today occupy top positions in our
ranks. Such critical appraisal must, of course, be made of their
leaders by the Negro people, and so I would like here to discuss
not this or that person but rather the *principles* of the question,
the standards for judgment, the character of leadership that is
called for today.

The term "leadership" has been used to express many different concepts, and many of these meanings have nothing to do
with what I am concerned with here. Individuals attain prominence for a wide variety of reasons, and often people who have
climbed up higher on the ladder are called leaders though they

make it plain that their sole interest is personal advancement and the more elevated they are above all other Negroes the better they like it. Then, too, it has been traditional for the dominant group of whites, in local communities and on a national scale as well, to designate certain individuals as "Negro leaders," regardless of how the Negro people feel about it; and the idea is that Negro leadership is something that white folks can bestow as a favor or take away as punishment.

The concept that I am talking about has nothing to do with matters of headline prominence, personal achievement or popularity with the powers-that-be. I am concerned, rather, with Negro leadership in the struggle for Negro rights. This includes those who are directly in charge of the organizations established for such purpose, and many others as well—the leaders of Negro churches, fraternal and civic organizations, elected representatives in government, trade union officials, and others whose action or inaction directly affects our common cause.

The primary quality that Negro leadership must possess, as I see it, *is a single-minded dedication to their people's welfare.* Any individual Negro, like any other person, may have many varied interests in life, but for the true leader all else must be subordinated to the interests of those whom he is leading. If today it can be said that the Negro people of the United States are lagging behind the progress being made by colored peoples in other lands, one basic cause for it has been that all too often Negro leadership here has lacked the selfless passion for their people's welfare that has characterized the leaders of the colonial liberation movements. Among us there is a general recognition— and a grudging acceptance—of the fact that some of our leaders are not only unwilling to make sacrifices but they must see some gain for themselves in whatever they do. A few crumbs for a few is too often hailed as "progress for the race." To live in freedom one must be prepared to die to achieve it, and while few if any of us are ever called upon to make that supreme sacrifice, no one can ignore the fact that in a difficult struggle those who are in the forefront may suffer cruel blows. He who is not prepared to face the trials of battle will never lead to a triumph. This spirit of dedication, as I have indicated, is abundantly present in the ranks of our people but progress will be slow until it is much more manifest in the character of leadership.

Dedication to the Negro people's welfare is one side of a coin: the other side is *independence*. Effective Negro leadership must rely upon and be responsive to no other control than the will of their people. We have allies—important allies—among our white fellow-citizens, and we must ever seek to draw them closer to us and to gain many more. But the Negro people's movement must be led by *Negroes,* not only in terms of title and position but in reality. Good advice is good no matter what the source and help is needed and appreciated from wherever it comes, but Negro action cannot be decisive if the advisers and helpers hold the guiding reins. For no matter how well-meaning other groups may be, the fact is our interests are secondary at best with them.

Today such outside controls are a factor in reducing the independence and effectiveness of Negro leadership. I do not have in mind the dwindling group of Uncle Toms who shamelessly serve even an Eastland; happily, they are no longer of much significance. I have in mind, rather, those practices of Negro leadership that are based upon the idea that it is white power rather than Negro power that must be relied upon. This concept has been traditional since Booker T. Washington, and it has been adhered to by many who otherwise reject all notions of white supremacy. Even Marcus Garvey, who rose to leadership of a nationalist mass movement in the 1920s and who urged that the Negro peoples of the world "go forward to the point of destiny as laid out by themselves," believed that white power was decisive. Indeed, no one has stated the idea more clearly than Garvey did in his essay "The Negro's Place in World Reorganization," in which he said:

> The white man of America has become the natural leader of the world. He, because of his exalted position, is called upon to help in all human efforts. From nations to individuals the appeal is made to him for aid in all things affecting humanity, so, naturally, there can be no great mass movement or change without first acquainting the leader on whose sympathy and advice the world moves.

Much has changed since those words were written, and I have no doubt that if Garvey were alive today he would recognize that the "white man of America" is no longer all-powerful and that the colored peoples of the world are moving quite independently of that "sympathy and advice."

In Booker Washington's day it was the ruling white man of the South whose sympathy was considered indispensable; today it is the liberal section of the dominant group in the North whose goodwill is said to be the hope for Negro progress. It is clear that many Negro leaders act or desist from acting because they base themselves on this idea. Rejecting the concept that "white is right" they embrace its essence by conceding that "might is right." To the extent that this idea is prevalent in its midst, Negro leadership lacks the quality of independence without which it cannot be effective.

Dedication and independence—these are the urgent needs. Other qualities of leadership exist in abundance: we have many highly trained men and women, experienced in law, in politics, in civic affairs; we have spokesmen of great eloquence, talented organizers, skilled negotiators. If I have stressed those qualities which are most needed on the national level, it is not from any lack of appreciation for much that is admirable. On the local level, especially, there are many examples of dedicated and independent leadership. Indeed, the effective use of Negro power—of numbers, of organization, of spirit—in Montgomery was the result of Negro leadership of the highest caliber. And the whole nation has witnessed the heroic dedication of many other leaders in the South, who, at the risk of their lives and all they hold dear, are leading their people's struggles. There are many from our ranks who ought to be elevated to national leadership because by their deeds they have fully demonstrated their right to be there.

We should broaden our conception of leadership and see to it that all sections of Negro life are represented on the highest levels. There must be room at the top for people from down below. I'm talking about the majority of our folks who work in factory and field: they bring with them that down-to-earth view which is the highest vision, and they can hammer and plow in

more ways than one. Yes, we need more of them in the leadership, and we need them in a hurry.

We need more of our women in the higher ranks, too, and
who should know better than the children of Harriet Tubman,
Sojourner Truth and Mary Church Terrell that our womenfolk
have often led the way. Negro womanhood today is giving us
many inspiring examples of steadfast devotion, cool courage under
fire, and brilliant generalship in our people's struggles; and here
is a major source for new strength and militancy in Negro leadership on every level.

But if there are those who ought to be raised to the top, there
are some others already there who should be retired. I have noted,
in another connection, that the Negro people are patient and
long-suffering—sometimes to a fault. The fault is often expressed
by permitting unworthy leaders to get away with almost anything.
It is as if once a man rises to leadership, his responsibility to his
people is no longer binding upon him.

But, in these critical days, we ought to become a little less
tolerant, a little more demanding that all Negro leaders "do
right." I have in mind, for example, the case of an important
Negro leader in a large Northern city, who, at the time when
mobs were barring the Negro children from high school in Little
Rock and beating up Negro newspapermen, got up before his
people and said: "We cannot meet this crisis by force against
force. Under no circumstances can Federal troops be used. This
would be a confession of our moral decadence, it would precipi-
tate a second Civil War—it would open the stopper and send democracy down the drain for at least our generation and maybe
forever." These words, so utterly devoid of any concern for his
people and lacking all regard for the truth, were hardly spoken
before the president sent in federal troops! No civil war was
started, democracy got a new lease on life, the mobs were dis-
persed, the Negro children were escorted to school, and for the
first time since 1876 the lawful force of the federal government
was called out against the lawless force of White Supremacy in
the South.

When, as in this case, a Negro leader vigorously opposes that
which he should be fighting for and makes it clear that some

other folks' interests are of more concern to him than his own people's—well, the so-called "politically wise" may say: "Oh, that's just politics—forget it." But the so-called "politically dumb" just can't see it that way. How can we be led by people who are not going our way?

There are others, honest men beyond all doubt and sincerely concerned with their people's welfare, who seem to feel that it is the duty of a leader to discourage Negro mass action. They think that best results can be achieved by the quiet negotiations they carry on. And so when something happens that arouses the masses of people, and when the people gather in righteous anger to demand that militant actions be started, such men believe it their duty to cool things off.

We saw this happen not long ago when from coast to coast there was a great upsurge of the people caused by the brutal lynching of young Emmett Till. At one of the mass protest meetings that was held, I heard one of our most important leaders address the gathering in words to this effect: "You are angry today, but you are not going to do anything about it. I know that you won't do anything. You clamor for a march on Mississippi but none of you will go. So let's stop talking about marching. Just pay a dollar to our organization and leave the rest to your leaders. If you want to do something yourself, let each of you go to your district Democratic leader and talk to him about it."

Well, what would a congregation think of their pastor if the best he could do was to tell them: "You are all a bunch of sinners, and nothing can make you do right. There is no good in you and I know it. So, brothers and sisters, just put your contributions on the collection plate, go home and leave your salvation to me."

No, a leader should encourage, not discourage; he should rally the people, not disperse them. A wet blanket can never be the banner of freedom.

Of course there must be negotiations made in behalf of our rights, but unless the negotiators are backed by an aroused and militant people, their earnest pleas will be of little avail. For Negro action to be effective—to be decisive, as I think it can be— it must be *mass* action. The power of the ballot can be useful only if the masses of voters are united on a common program;

obviously, if half the Negro people vote one way and the other half the opposite way, not much can be achieved. The individual votes are cast and counted, but the group power is cast away and discounted.

Mass action—in political life and elsewhere—is Negro power in motion; and it is the way to win.

An urgent task which faces us today is an all-out struggle to defeat the efforts of the white supremacists to suppress the NAACP in the South. As in South Africa, where the notorious "Suppression of Communism Act" is used to attack the liberation movement, the enemies of Negro freedom in our country have accused the NAACP of being a "subversive conspiracy" and the organization has been outlawed in Louisiana, Texas and Alabama, and legally restricted in Georgia, Virginia, South Carolina and Mississippi. City ordinances, as in Little Rock, are also used for this purpose.

The indifference with which various other organizations viewed the suppression in 1955 of the Council on African Affairs, which was falsely labeled a "Communist front," should not be repeated now by any group in the case of the NAACP. The Red-baiting charges against that organization are utterly untrue, as the makers of such charges know full well; and those elements in Negro leadership who have in the past resorted to Red-baiting as a "smart" tactic should realize that such methods serve no one but our people's worst enemies.

Throughout the South—in Little Rock, in Montgomery and elsewhere—the state and local leaders of the NAACP have set a heroic and inspiring example for Negro leadership everywhere. All of us—the Negro people of the entire country—must rally now to sustain and defend them.

In presenting these ideas on the power of Negro action, the sources of that power, and the character of leadership necessary to direct that power most effectively, I offer them for consideration and debate at this time when the challenge of events calls for clarity of vision and unity of action. No one, obviously, has all the answers, and the charting of our course must be done collectively. There must be a spirit of give and take, and clashing viewpoints must find a common ground. Partisan interests must be subordinated to Negro interests—by each of us. Somehow we must find the way to set aside all that divides us and come together, Negroes all. Our unity will strengthen our friends and win many more to our side; and our unity will weaken our foes who already can see the handwriting on the wall.

To be free—to walk the good American earth as equal citizens, to live without fear, to enjoy the fruits of our toil, to give our children every opportunity in life—that dream which we have held so long in our hearts is today the destiny that we hold in our hands.

A Distant Image: Paul Robeson
and Rutgers' Students Today

BY EUGENE H. ROBINSON

"Paul who?" the earnest young Black Panther asked with puzzled, weary bewilderment. It was late 1969 and the newest strugglers for a worldwide progressive society were being wiped out from one end of America to the other. Yet, true to the historical (and often antihistorical) life style of the New Left, black and white, if something or someone young hadn't experienced it NOW, it didn't matter.

So with Paul Robeson, a giant oak whom America attempted to cut down with McCarthyite axes in his prime for his progressive beliefs and radical actions. Professor Harold Weaver, director of the Rutgers College (New Brunswick) Afro-American Studies Program, has accurately estimated that at least 75 per cent of the black students at Rutgers don't know WHO Paul Robeson was or is.

With the numerous "special" programs in the New Brunswick area, black students number approximately 1,500 or 10 per cent of the total enrollment; so, perhaps 1,100 are not aware of Paul Robeson's accomplishments. The white student awareness is probably very, very significantly lower.

How, then, to write honestly under the suggested title for this essay, "Paul Robeson Inspires Rutgers' Students Today"? Answer: it can't be done.

Yet following the ancient and universal dictates of history, to unswervingly seek the truth of the happenings of the past, one can honestly write of black activists and their use of the *image* of Paul Robeson while decrying their lack of willingness to attempt to understand the historical-political meaning of the MAN.

History being also man's *interpretation* of the past, the reader should be informed that my active participation in many of the historical events which are being described and evaluated contributes all the good and bad aspects of "participant-observer historian" as opposed to the allegedly objective but perhaps less honest "armchair historian."

Rutgers College (New Brunswick area) of Rutgers University is featured because Paul Robeson attended the so-called "jewel of Rutgers," because events relating specifically to him were mainly centered there and because my personal-research knowledge evolves around there.

Although some black alumni have claimed the existence in the middle 1950s of a black fraternity at Rutgers College, it was not until May, 1960 (at the end of my freshman year) that eleven of us formed a civil rights organization at Rutgers, the Rutgers-Douglass NAACP. In the midst of the widespread sit-in movement, it was deemed a radical step but there was little or no connection, public or otherwise, with the great humane radical Robeson of Rutgers.

Here my knowledge is limited by hearsay because I spent from June, 1960 to June, 1963 in the United States Army. Yet occasional letters from former classmates and infrequent visits revealed no mention of the Robeson name. Very few individuals had broken through "the conspiracy of silence," as Paul Robeson, Jr. calls it.

Friends spoke of NAACP activities involving pickets and demonstrations over major issues such as the legal right to get scalped in a white barbershop. But no Paul Robeson.

From September, 1963 to June, 1965, a period which covered my sophomore and junior years of increasing NAACP activity, there were more pickets and boycotts and fierce five- and three-hour fights among NAACP members over the meaning of "integration." Still no Paul Robeson.

Of the Rutgers (and Douglass) school years of 1965-66 and 1966-67, I have little or no knowledge as I was working in "the real world" with no campus interests. There is little evidence, however, which suggests large-scale awareness of Robeson.

By the end of 1966, however, nationalism was in the air around Rutgers. "Black Power!" had become the cry heard, if reluctantly, around black communities throughout the nation. Black pride was slowly on the move generally and gallopingly increasing among black activists laying the foundation of the Black Liberation Movement. This, upon the bedrock of Malcolm, Garvey, Du Bois, Carmichael and H. Rap Brown.

The major significance here is that even the "Negro History" of near-meaningless nonpolitical goulash, of minute dates and events "FIRST EVER done by a Negro" would tend to make the New Black activists, if not black students at Rutgers, more aware of a man named Robeson.

In December, 1966 some fifteen Rutgers black students had attended a Black Students' Conference at Columbia University involving some 250 black students from approximately fifty predominantly white northeastern college-level institutions. It is not known whether Floyd McKissick, then CORE executive director, mentioned Paul Robeson in his keynote address.

It was highly possible because McKissick stressed at a Rutgers appearance in November, 1967 that Paul Robeson had always been one of his heroes and should be also for all politically conscious black people, particularly black students at Rutgers.

The known historical significance of the December meeting was that Rutgers black students came back inspired by McKissick's admonition to return to their communities and work for Black Power. So, they formed a Rutgers SAS, the Students' Afro-American Society, on February 15th with some twenty-five members out of the one hundred or so black students at Rutgers and fifty at Douglass College.

Seeking to maintain its previous campus hegemony, the Rutgers-Douglass NAACP held Negro History Week Festivities in February which featured Paul Robeson in a prominent manner. Unfortunately, the concentration was rather narrow, featuring only his campus and show business activities. The politically conscious words and deeds of the middle forties through sixties and the terrible personal-career retribution dealt out by the U.S. national (and thus international) white power structures were ignored.

The first concrete campus stand of SAS was also the first organized move by a black group to raise the American Iron Curtain, the deadly sinister "conspiracy of silence" around Paul Robeson at Rutgers and throughout the nation.

In April, 1967, SAS decided to back the *Press Club Weekly* in its attempt to get Paul Robeson nominated by Rutgers University officials for the Hall of Fame. The *Press Club Weekly,* an informal effort by journalism department majors at rivaling the traditional *Daily Targum,* was dismayed because Rutgers had not nominated Robeson for some years.

I volunteered and was dispatched by SAS to add our name as a sponsor to the *Press Club Weekly* campaign. After finally being convinced that we were an official organization whose character had been approved by the student council, *Press Club Weekly* added us to the list of sponsors.

The net result was that beginning in the fall of 1967 Rutgers resumed and has continued nominating Paul Robeson to the Hall of Fame. As yet, however, his name has not passed the regional level. The excuse given by the Hall of Fame, when pressed, is that due to Robeson's alleged "Communist sympathies" he does not pass the "citizenship" test of nomination to the Hall. This ignores completely his all-American thrust for social justice for all.

For the next year from April, 1967 to April, 1968 Robeson's name was still somewhat infrequently mentioned; at least little in-depth research was done on him. As the elected president of SAS from May, 1967 to April, 1968, I bore the brunt of that burden.

Yet in comparison to the years preceding, there was a significant increase in the mention of his name and use as an inspirational symbol. Robeson's name and sacrifice of personal gains "for the cause" were increasingly invoked by other SAS officers and myself in order to show that "studying" was not all black students should be about at Rutgers.

As mentioned previously, Floyd McKissick of CORE spoke at the Rutgers Gym before nearly 3,000 students in November, 1967. At the prespeech dinner, during the actual speech and afterwards at a reception for black students only, McKissick constantly mentioned how Paul Robeson had "made" Rutgers a national name and how he had "fought the good fight virtually alone" for several decades. Black students were noticeably moved.

On February 19, 1968, SAS held Martyrs Day Activities honoring Malcolm X and eleven other Blacks viciously attacked by racist white power structures for their progressive antioppression actions. Paul Robeson's name and activities were prominently mentioned in on-and-off-campus publicity. After two speakers at an evening dinner spoke on Malcolm X, I ended by speaking for five minutes on how Robeson had deliberately sacrificed for us and how we should likewise not be afraid to "lose our cool" in emotionally committing ourselves to the movement. The fifty black students seemed to be very much inspired by this account of Robeson's selflessness.

In March, 1968 when Muhammad Ali came to Rutgers, I introduced him on the theme of "profiles of courage" in Rutgers history. At that time I vigorously mentioned Paul Robeson's brave stands and the mention was enthusiastically applauded. It was not clear, however, if some who clapped were not moved by the vigor of presentation and yet ignorant of Robeson's multifold activities.

Like Blacks around the nation, black students at Rutgers were greatly upset by the assassination of Dr. King on Thursday, April 4, 1968.

That night a small group of black students met to plan "retaliation" by emulating the revolts or so-called "riots" which struck around the nation. The following morning at eleven o'clock over 100 Blacks marched on Old Queens, the administrative center of Rutgers College in New Brunswick. There they turned the Rutgers and United States flags upside down as a symbol of "international distress," handed a set of demands to President Mason Gross and marched two abreast through New Brunswick to Douglass College where the actions at Rutgers were repeated. Later, black students held a five-hour unity meeting.

Meetings were held on Saturday in emergency session with the student council and the following week with the board of governors. Among the dozen or so black demands was a major one that some prominent building be named after Paul Robeson.

I had resigned as SAS president in March after several weeks of political infighting over personality-policy differences with a fellow student who had been my chief lieutenant; yet the need for unity at such a critical moment had naturally drawn me back. Although no longer leading, I was an active supporter here of the new SAS leadership of Jerry Harris, Michael Jackson and Chuck Bowers.

At the student council meeting the legislators wisely passed all the demands by margins from 12-1-2 to 15-0-0. An emotional highlight occurred when I took strong exception to continual white liberal mentioning of Robeson as "the greatest *black* Rutgers graduate." I logically downgraded Ozzie Nelson and the owner of the 21 Club as allegedly "superior" to Robeson's stature, called Robeson "Rutgers greatest graduate" and asked, "Is Robeson to be a prophet without honor in his own country?" This evoked a massive clapping tribute to Robeson by the seventy-five Black students and perhaps some of the twenty white students present.

The first SAS meeting with the board of governors was the following week and came off very peacefully, perhaps too much so. They allotted us an hour of their regular meeting time and we took two. New and old SAS officers including Jerry Harris and Chuck Bowers of the new seven-man ruling board, former Vice President Elijah Miller and I spoke of the difficulties of being Black in an overwhelmingly white school.

The board, composed largely of literal "corporate liberals" (from numerous big business boards) was duly sympathetic and outwardly "touched" enough to suggest an emergency meeting in two weeks to deal just with "the Black Problem." In a blatant move at understanding-cooptation, they further offered us a "picnic" for us and them to feel better toward each other.

SAS knew their major objection would be to the Robeson demand because of Rutgers being a state university and the reputation of the state legislators for super anti-Communism.

Because I again volunteered and had most often spoken of Robeson in the sense of my history major, I was detailed to do in-depth research on Robeson.

So, I researched five books in which Robeson was mentioned prominently and some nine encyclopedias. Robeson's name was in only five of them—he had vanished like the wind. A nonexistent personality, whose career had spanned four decades in the public limelight.

Robeson was even missing from *Who's Who*—the American edition. According to Paul Robeson, Jr., this is the only *Who's Who* in the world without Robeson in it.

Having missed the second board of governors' meeting due to personal matters, I nevertheless passed on my research. The session seems to have been indeed a lively one.

At one point, Bruce Hubbard, Black Student Councilman, asked why Robeson's alleged "Communist sympathies" should disqualify him from having a building named after him. Especially since a very, very high Rutgers official—then present—had once admitted to having been a member of the Communist party, U.S.A.

The official is said to have merely murmured, "But I didn't ask to have a building named after me." Yet Mason Gross, president of Rutgers University, is alleged to have jumped straight up yelling, "Goddam dirt. Goddam dirt. You know it's goddam dirt, Bruce." Mistaking Bruce's tack for a new McCarthyism, Gross left the room angrily for fifteen minutes until his composure returned.

Meanwhile, the board of governors said it was highly impractical in terms of legislative sentiment to name a building after Robeson. They further claimed buildings were only named after past Rutgers' presidents. But, said SAS, was not the school named after a donor and not a president?

Bring us some tangible proof of student backing, said the board, and maybe we'll reconsider.

It was too late in the school year for a massive effort but September, '68 saw it begun.

SDS, sensing the rare possibility of a black-white coalition which might "pull the covers off" the board's alleged liberalism seemed to do most of the work. There were, however, some SAS volunteers.

Thirty-five hundred signatures were collected out of some 6,000 Rutgers students. But the board cagily said, how do we really know the majority of Rutgers students want the new student center named after Robeson?

And so student council put up a referendum. On the surface, things seemed to be going well. SDS was gathering student radical support and various liberals were rallying their constituencies. The idea was to *not* raise a ruckus which might stir the right wing, on and off campus, to action in a neo-McCarthyite way.

Then, on the day of the election, the *Daily Targum* came out with two heartbreakers.

Firstly, the *Daily Targum's* editorial thought naming a building after a nonpresident would open the flood-gates to special interest pleas. But they weren't against it—oh, no. They were just wondering. . . .

Secondly, they printed a letter which attacked the Robeson proposal by claiming Robeson had been "a known Communist."

The proposal failed by 200 votes out of 900 some. But a second election was called for by student council due to alleged interference by black pollsters with voters' activities.

With black and radical morale down low, a 700-vote turnout resulted in a solid loss by some 400 votes. Who was at fault?

The *Daily Targum* said most.

But I had sat on the first voting day with black campaign and SAS leaders and it seemed as if they—or should it be we, expected the proposal to fail. Because "whitey won't vote for a building to be named after a nigger." Also, "the board of governors wouldn't honor a positive vote anyway."

We had thought cynically of Robeson only as a "useful image" —not a MAN—to discard at will and it didn't seem to me that anyone had made sure the black vote got out. Especially the many nonpolitical Blacks.

The high point of student interest in Robeson had passed. There would be further mention of the name. But we had missed educating the general campus public, black and white, to Robeson's accomplishments, before or after the vote! A deal was made to keep SAS from joining SDS in protesting the lack of a student center "open door" community policy. Eventually, in the spring of 1969 a Paul Robeson Arts and Music Lounge was dedicated. President Gross came and got his picture taken afterwards but said nothing. The event was covered only by a picture and a caption in the *Daily Targum*. No written story, on or off campus. Black student participation in the lounge ceremonies was low although over half the audience was black.

In February of the 1969 semester I had written a *Daily Targum* column entitled "A Letter to Paul." At first intended as a blast at the school for ignoring Robeson, it was then shifted, to satire. But in writing it, I became angry at all of us—black activists, white liberals and radicals.

So, it ended up as a sardonic cutting edge on all of us. It portrayed, in a disillusioned style, a young student hoping Paul would be proud of us for having tried so hard. The irony was supposed to be that we failed so much because we didn't really give a damn—for the MAN—underneath.

Angry also at the image of Robeson, I had the student end by saying we, too, were "daylight nationalists and nighttime integrationists." Hadn't Paul always won? Even to keeping a militant spirit despite the destruction of his U.S. stage career? Why had *he* allowed us to fail?

But better yet, why had *we* not sought out the nuances of the man? And the implications of the kind of system behind the dastardly reactions against men of his, Richard Wright's and Du Bois's qualities?

In March, 1969 the Rutgers campus tottered on the brink of all-out physical rebellion. Black students were angry at the lack of fulfillment of the post-King demands.

Buildings were seized in Camden and Newark in a coordinated effort. Minds, hands, hearts and kerosene were ready to set the New Brunswick campus literally aflame.

Again, Robeson's name was mentioned as a flaming symbol. But, it was Malcolm, Carmichael and H. Rap Brown who were on the tongues of the "Now" generation before the crisis subsided.

In the next year, Robeson's name came to light in a minor and major way. But even the major way had muted impact, due to no fault of its own.

The minor way was that my "Black Thought in the Twentieth Century" class was so moved in Spring, 1970 by my recital of Robeson's accomplishments and sufferings that they voted to write and thank him personally so that he would know some Blacks still cared. But the April spring vacation and May final exams somehow insidiously crowded in together so that the deed was not done.

The major event was Sunday, April 5, 1970, when Alpha Phi Alpha, Robeson's old fraternity, held a rededication ceremony of the Paul Robeson Art and Music Lounge. By direct request, President Gross was present and even spoke. The Reverend Clinton A. Hoggard of New York City's African Methodist Episcopal Church spoke eloquently of personal dealings with Rutgers as a student around 1936 and as a personal friend of Robeson's. As a substitute speaker for Greg Stewart, I struck some emotional sparks within the predominantly black crowd by showing Paul Robeson as a symbol of today's black students (read black activists) of courage, excellence, and dedication. Paul Robeson, Jr. enthralled the group with his precise historical knowledge of his father's record as well as personal insights into the granite-like character of the man. President Mason W. Gross provided the historically important tone of Rutgers' partial atonement for abandonment of its most famous son in time of crisis. He said in part, "Paul Robeson was fifty years ahead of his time" and "we have yet to finish his important work." Still, most black students were not present, off at the wedding miles away of the popular black activist, Leon Greene.

I was so elated at this and the considerable on- and off-campus publicity that I wrote a *Daily Targum* column called "A Tale of Two Rutgersmen" showing how the separate Rutgers' "profiles in courage" of Robeson and Gross had now coincided. Later, some black girls reminded me of Gross's acts at that fateful board of governor's meeting long ago. So, I unfortunately did a drastic and even perhaps cynical rewrite in the *Black Voice* disparaging Gross's statements.

Not exactly a profile in courage.

So, finally, what of Paul Robeson's name today at Rutgers when perhaps 75 per cent of black students don't know who he was and is? When the black activists have graduated or are graduating who at least struggled narrowly for the Image (though not the Man unfortunately)?

White "hippies" use the lounge, not knowing or caring who Robeson is.

The *Black Voice* did print a summary of his life which was a little sketchy.

Some black students did force the Center Board to display again Al Hollingsworth's donated brilliant painting of Robeson in his many phases.

Live photos of Robeson's many-faceted careers hang with a brief chronology in a busy hall of the student center.

Professor Harold Weaver is assiduously working on a Paul Robeson biography.

Football coach John Bateman and President Gross in November, 1970 blasted the Hall of Fame in black (not white) newspapers for again denying Robeson's entry.

There is, thanks to Professor Weaver, a "Paul Robeson Independent Studies" part of the Rutgers College Afro-American Studies Program.

But more is needed.

What?

An annual event with nationwide, if not international publicity, which honors Robeson the Man in life, love, laughter, word and deed; this should be sponsored by SAS, Alpha Phi Alpha, black alumni and possibly *Freedomways*.

The same sponsors should raise funds for Paul Robeson Scholarships for black scholar-activists selected by leaders and members of Rutgers' black student organizations.

Then, and only then, can we say *fully,* as has been here said partially, that "Paul Robeson inspires Rutgers' students today."

Paul Robeson: The Artist as Activist and Social Thinker

BY JOHN HENRIK CLARKE

Paul Robeson was indeed more than an artist, activist and freedom fighter. The dimensions of his talent made him our Renaissance man. He was one of the first American artists, black or white, to realize that the role of the artist extends far beyond the stage and the concert hall. Early in his life he became conscious of the plight of his people, stubbornly surviving in a racist society. This was his window on the world. From this vantage point he saw how the plight of his people related to the rest of humanity. He realized that the artist had the power, and the responsibility, to change the society in which he lived. He learned that art and culture are weapons in a people's struggle to exist with dignity, and in peace. Life offered him many options and he never chose the easiest one. For most of his life he was a man walking against the wind. An understanding of his beginning and how he developed artistically and politically will reveal the nature of his mission and the importance of the legacy of participation in struggle that we have inherited from him.

He was born, April 9, 1898, at a time of great crisis for his people. When he died, January 23, 1976, his people were still in a crisis, partly of a different nature, and partly the same crisis that they faced in the closing years of the nineteenth century, when Paul Robeson was born. He was born three years after Booker T. Washington made his famous Atlanta Exposition address, 1895, and two years after the Supreme Court announced a decision in the Plessy versus Ferguson Case, whereby the concept of "separate but equal" facilities for black Americans became law. Of course the separateness never produced any equalness. The time and the decision did produce some of the problems to which Paul Robeson would address himself in later years.

His early years were strengthened by binding family ties. They were not easy years. He recalled those years and reflected on their meaning in the introductory issue of the newspaper *Freedom,* November 1950.

> My father was of slave origin. He reached as honorable a position as a Negro could under these circumstances, but soon after I was born he lost his church and poverty was my beginning. Relatives from my father's North Carolina family took me in, a motherless orphan, while my father went to new fields to begin again in a corner grocery store. I slept four in a bed, ate the nourishing greens and cornbread.

> Many times I stood on the very soil on which my father was a slave, where some of my cousins were sharecroppers and un-employed tobacco workers. I reflected upon the wealth bled from my near relatives alone, and of the very basic wealth of all this America beaten out of millions of Negro people, enslaved, freed, newly enslaved until this very day.

He made his professional debut at the Harlem YWCA in 1920 in a play, *Simon the Cyrenian,* by Redgely Torrence. The play was about an Ethiopian who steps out of a crowd to help a tired and haggard Jesus Christ carry his cross up Calvary Hill to be crucified. His role in this play was symbolic of his commit-ment to just causes and to oppressed people the world over, a dominant dimension of his life. He was not persecuted, denied a passport and attacked at Peekskill because he was a world fa-mous concert singer and activist.

In the years following the First World War, black Americans were discovering themselves, their culture and their history. Thousands of black soldiers had returned from the war in Eu-rope to face unemployment, bad housing and lynchings. The Universal Negro Improvement Association led by Marcus Gar-vey and the intellectual movement called the Harlem Literary Renaissance reached their respective highs during this period. The years of the nineteen-twenties were proving grounds for Paul Robeson's development as an artist and a responsible person.

Many of the roles that Paul Robeson played in America were repeated in the theatres of London. It has been reported his political ideas took shape after George Bernard Shaw introduced him to the concept of socialism in 1928. This may be partly true about his political ideas in a formal sense, though his social awareness started before this time. His first visit to the Soviet Union in 1934 had a more profound influence on the shaping of his political ideas and understanding. Later, he publicly expressed his belief in the principles of scientific socialism. It was his conviction that a socialist society represents an advance to a higher stage of life for all mankind. The rest of his life was a commitment to this conviction.

He spoke out against oppression wherever he saw it, and not just the oppression of his own people. He went to Spain during the civil war in that country and sang for the Republican troops and for the members of the International Brigades. This was part of a gathering of antifascist forces who were in battle against the army of General Franco, who was backed by Hitler and Mussolini. When Paul Robeson returned to the United States he expressed the belief that the war in Spain represented dangers to the world far beyond that country's borders.

"I saw the connection between the problems of all oppressed people and the necessity of the artist to participate fully," he said.

He opposed every form of racism in his own country—he was the first American artist to refuse to sing before a segregated audience. He spoke out against lynching, segregated theatres and eating places a generation before the beginning of what is referred to as the Black Revolution. He supported all organizations that he thought were working genuinely to improve the lot of his people and mankind.

In his book, *Robeson: Labor's Forgotten Champion* (Detroit, Mich.: Balamp Publishing, 1975), Dr. Charles H. Wright states that

> Robeson saw the struggle of the working classes of Spain in the same terms that he saw the struggles of the black man in the United States. He made this clear after he left Spain and embarked on a series of public appearances on behalf of the Republicans, both on the continent and in England. It was from the continent, probably the Spanish Embassy in Paris that he issued what became known as his Manifesto against Fascism.

The Manifesto reads as follows:

Every artist, every scientist must decide, now, where he stands. He has no alternative. There are no impartial observers.

Through the destruction, in certain countries, of man's literary heritage, through the propagation of false ideas of national and racial superiority, the artist, the scientist, the writer is challenged. This struggle invades the former cloistered halls of our universities and all her seats of learning.

The battlefront is everywhere. There is no sheltered rear. The artist elects to fight for freedom or slavery.

I have made my choice! I had no alternative!

The history of the era is characterized by the degradation of my people. Despoiled of their lands, their culture destroyed, they are denied equal opportunity of the law and deprived of their rightful place in the respect of their fellows.

Not through blind faith or through coercion, but conscious of my course, I take my place with you. I stand with you in unalterable support of the lawful government of Spain, duly and regularly chosen by its sons and daughters.

In January 1938 he visited Spain with his wife, Eslanda. Plans had already been made for him to sing to the troops in the International Brigades.

This was not his introduction to the international aspects of the fight against fascism. The Spanish Civil War started in June 1936; the Italian-Ethiopian War had started the year before. On December 20, 1937, Robeson had participated in a meeting on the Spanish Civil War at Albert Hall in London. This and other antifascist activity disenchanted the United States Department of State. This was probably the formal beginning of his harassment by that agency. This harassment would continue for another twenty years. In his writings and speeches, for most of the years of his active career, Paul Robeson was very explicit in explaining the motives and antecedents of his fight against every form of racism and oppression. At a Welcome Home Rally in Harlem, June 19, 1949, he restated his position and the nature of his commitment.

I have travelled many lands and I have sung and talked to many peoples. Wherever I appeared, whether in professional concert, at peace meetings, in the factories, at trade union gatherings, at the mining pits, assemblies of representative colonial students from all over the world, always the greeting came: "Take back our affection, our love, our strength to the Negro people and to the members of the progressive movement of America."

It is especially moving to be here in this particular auditorium in Harlem. Way back in 1918, I came here to this very hall from a football game at the Polo Grounds between Rutgers and Syracuse. There was a basketball game between St. Christopher and the Alphas. Later I played here for St. Christopher against the Alphas, against the Spartans, and the Brooklyn YMCA, time and time again. This was a home of mine. It is still my home.

I was then, through my athletics and my university record, trying to hold up the prestige of my people; trying in the only way I knew to ease the path for future Negro boys and girls. And I am still in there slugging, yes, at another level, and you can bet your life that I shall battle every step of the way until conditions around these corners change and conditions change for the Negro people all up and down this land.

The road has been long. The road has been hard. It began about as tough as I ever had it—in Princeton, New Jersey, a college town of Southern aristocrats, who from Revolutionary time transferred Georgia to New Jersey. My brothers couldn't go to high school in Princeton. They had to go to Trenton, ten miles away. That's right—Trenton, of the "Trenton Six." My brother or I could have been one of the "Trenton Six."

Almost every Negro in Princeton lived off the college and accepted the social status that went with it. We lived for all intents and purposes on a Southern plantation. And with no more dignity than that suggests—all the bowing and scraping to the drunken rich, all the vile names, all the Uncle Tomming to earn enough to lead miserable lives.

He could not see himself accepting any form of Jim Crow Americanism. He said in many ways he hated what America was, but he loved what it promised to be. He defended the stated higher ideals and potential of the United States while calling attention to the fact that the nation's promise to all of its people had not been kept. He said:

And I defied and I defy—any part of this insolent, dominating America, however powerful, to challenge my Americanism; because by word and deed I challenge this vicious system to the death.

Paul Robeson would not let his public acceptance as an actor and singer make him relax in comfort and forget the struggle for basic dignity still being waged by the rest of his people. On this point he said:

I refuse to let my personal success, as part of a fraction of one per cent of the Negro people, to explain away the injustices to fourteen million of my people; because with all the energy at my command, I fight for the right of the Negro people and other oppressed labor-driven Americans to have decent homes, decent jobs, and the dignity that belongs to every human being!

Somewhere in my childhood these feelings were planted. Perhaps when I resented being pushed off the sidewalk, when I saw my women being insulted, and especially when I saw my elder brother answer each insult with blows that sent would-be slave masters crashing to the stone sidewalks, even though jail was his constant reward. He never said it, but he told me day after day: "Listen to me, kid." (He loved me very dearly.) "Don't you ever take it, as long as you live."

In my opinion, the artistic and political growth of Paul Robeson had its greatest stimulation during the nineteen-thirties. Paul was always discovering something new in the human situation, and new dimensions in old things he already knew. He was, concurrently, both a student and a scholar, in pursuit of knowledge about the world's people and the conditions of their lives. Africa, its people and cultures, was of special interest to him. In a note, dated 1936, included in his *Selected Writings,* published by the Paul Robeson Archives, 1976, he makes this comment:

I am a singer and an actor. I am primarily an artist. Had I been born in Africa, I would have belonged, I hope, to that family which sings and chants the glories and legends of the tribe. I would have liked in my mature years to have been a wise elder, for I worship wisdom and knowledge of the ways of men.

His artistic strength was in his love for the history, songs and folk culture of his people. In this way he learned to respect the cultures of all people.

In an article published in the *Royal Screen Pictorial*, London, April 1935, he said:

I am a Negro. The origin of the Negro is African. It would, therefore, seem an easy matter for me to assume African nationality. . . . At present the younger generation of Negroes in America looks towards Africa and asks, "What is there to interest me? What of value has Africa to offer that the Western world cannot give me? . . ." Their acknowledgement of their common origin, species, interest and attitudes binds Jew to Jew; a similar acknowledgement will bind Negro to Negro. I realize that this will not be accomplished by viewing from afar the dark rites of the witch doctor. It may be accomplished, or at least furthered, by patient inquiry. To this end I am learning Swahili, Twi and other African dialects—which come easily to me because their rhythm is the same as that employed by the American Negro in speaking English; and when the time is ripe, I propose to investigate on the spot the possibilities of such a regeneration as I have outlined. Meanwhile, in my music, my plays, my films, I want to carry always this central idea—to be African. Multitudes of men have died for less worthy ideals; it is more eminently worth living for.

He now saw the logic in this culture struggle and realized, as never before, that culture was an instrument in a people's liberation, and the suppression of it was an instrument that was used in their enslavement. This point was brought forcefully home to him when the British Intelligence cautioned him about the political meaning of his activities. He knew now that the British claim that it would take one thousand years to prepare Africans for self-rule was a lie. The experience led him to conclude that

Yes, culture and politics were actually inseparable here as always. And it was an African who directed my interest in Africa to something he had noted in the Soviet Union. On a visit to that country he had travelled east and had seen the Yakuts, a people who had been classed as a "backwards race" by the Czars. He had been struck by the resemblance between the tribal life of the Yakuts and his own people of East Africa.

What would happen to a people like the Yakuts now that they were freed from colonial oppression and were a part of the construction of the new socialist society?

I saw for myself when I visited the Soviet Union how the Yakuts and the Uzbeks and all the other formerly oppressed nations were leaping ahead from tribalism to modern industrial economy, from illiteracy to the heights of knowledge. Their ancient culture blossoming in new and greater splendor. Their young men and women mastering the sciences and arts. A thousand years? No, less than 30!

During his London years, Paul Robeson was also involved with a number of Caribbean people and organizations. These were the years of the Italian-Ethiopian war, the self-imposed exile of Haile Selassie and Marcus Garvey, and the proliferation of African and Caribbean organizations, with London headquarters, demanding the improvements in their colonial status that eventually led to the independence explosion. In an article in the *National Guardian*, December 20, 1948, "Freedom in Their Own Land," Paul Robeson spoke of his impressions of the Caribbean people, after returning from a concert tour in Jamaica and Trinidad. He said:

I feel now as if I had drawn my first breath of fresh air in many years. Once before I felt like that. When I first entered the Soviet Union I said to myself, "I am a human being. I don't have to worry about my color."

In the West Indies I felt all that and something new besides. I felt that for the first time I could see what it will be like when Negroes are free in their own land. I felt something like what a Jew must feel when first he goes to Israel, what a Chinese must feel on entering areas of his country that now are free.

Certainly my people in the islands are poor. They are desperately poor. In Kingston, Jamaica, I saw many families living in shells of old automobiles, hollowed out and turned upside down. Many are unemployed. They are economically subjected to landholders—British, American and native.

But the people are on the road to freedom. I saw Negro professionals: artists, writers, scientists, scholars. And above all I saw Negro workers walking erect and proud.

Once I was driving in Jamaica. My road passed a school and as we came abreast of the building a great crowd of school children came running out to wave at me. I stopped, got out of my car to talk with them and sing to them. Those kids were wonderful. I have stopped at similar farms in our own deep South and I have talked to Negro children everywhere in our country. Here for the first time I could talk to children who did not have to look over their shoulders to see if a white man was watching them talk to me.

I think that this nearness to freedom, this being on the road and so near the goal, had a great deal to do with the way they received me. It was like nothing that has ever happened to me before. If I never hear another kind word again, what I received from my people in the West Indies will be enough for me.

They crowded around my car. For hours they waited to see me. Some might be embarrassed or afraid of such crowds of people pressing all around. I am not embarrassed or afraid in the presence of people.

I was not received as an opera singer is received by his people in Italy. I was not received as Joe Louis is received by our own people. These people saw in me not a singer, or not just a singer. They called to me: "Hello, Paul. We know you've been fighting for us."

In many ways his concert tours were educational tours. He had a similar experience in New Orleans on October 19, 1942, when he sang before a capacity audience of black and white men and women, seated without segregation, in the Booker T. Washington School auditorium. On this occasion he said:

I had never put a correct evaluation on the dignity and courage of my people of the deep South until I began to come south myself. I had read, of course, and folks had told me of strides made . . . but always I had discounted much of it, charged much of it to what some people would have us believe. Deep down, I think, I had imagined Negroes of the South beaten, subservient, cowed.

But I see them now courageous and possessors of a profound and instinctive dignity, a race that has come through its trials unbroken, a race of such magnificence of spirit that there exists no power on earth that could crush them. They will bend, but they will never break.

I find that I must come south again and again, again and yet again. It is only here that I achieve absolute and utter identity with my people. There is no question here of where I stand, no need to make a decision. The redcap in the station, the president of your college, the man in the street—they are all one with me, part of me. And I am proud of it, utterly proud of my people.

He reaffirmed his commitment to the black struggle in the South by adding:

We must come south to understand in their starkest presentation the common problems that beset us everywhere. We must breathe the smoke of battle. We must taste the bitterness, see the ugliness . . . we must expose ourselves unremittingly to the source of strength that makes the black South strong!

In spite of the years he and his family spent abroad, he was never estranged from his own people. In his book, *Here I Stand,* he explained this in essence when he said:

I am a Negro. The house I live in is in Harlem—this city within a city, Negro Metropolis of America. And now as I write of things that are urgent in my mind and heart, I feel the press of all that is around me here where I live, at home among my people.

In 1944, Paul Robeson was awarded the Spingarn Medal by the National Association for the Advancement of Colored People. Soon afterwards he took the lead in a course of actions more direct and radical than the NAACP. He led a delegation that demanded the end to racial bars in professional baseball. He called on President Truman to extend the civil rights of Blacks in the South. He became a founder and chairman of the Progressive Party which nominated former Vice President Henry A. Wallace in the 1948 presidential campaign.

In the years immediately following the Second World War, Paul Robeson called attention to the unfinished fight for the basic dignity of all people. The following excerpt is from a speech he made in Detroit, Michigan on the tenth anniversary of the National Negro Congress:

These are times of peril in the history of the Negro people and of the American nation.

Fresh from victorious battles, in which we soundly defeated the military forces of German, Italian and Japanese fascism, driving to oppress and enslave the peoples of the whole world, we are now faced with an even more sinister threat to the peace and security and freedom of all our peoples. This time the danger lies in the resurgent imperialist and pro-fascist forces of our own country, powerfully organized gentlemen of great wealth, who are determined now, to attempt what Hitler, Mussolini and Tojo tried to do and failed. AND THE ELECTED POLITICAL LEADERSHIP OF THE UNITED STATES IS SERVING AS THE SPEARHEAD OF THIS NEW DRIVE TOWARD IMPERIALIST WAR IN THE WORLD AND THE RUTHLESS DESTRUCTION OF OUR FREEDOM AND SECURITY HERE AT HOME.

I understand full well the meaning of these times for my country and my people. The triumph of imperialist reaction in America now would bring death and mass destruction to our own and all other countries of the world. It would engulf our hard-won democratic liberties in the onrush of native fascism. And it would push the Negro people backward into a modern and highly scientific form of oppression, far worse than our slave forefathers ever knew.

I also understand full well the important role which my people can and must play in helping to save America and the peoples of all the world from annihilation and enslavement. Precisely as Negro patriots helped turn back the redcoats at Bunker Hill, just as the struggles of over 200,000 Negro soldiers and four million slaves turned the tide of victory for the Union forces in the Civil War, just as the Negro people have thrown their power on the side of progress in every other great crisis in the history of our country—so now, we must mobilize our full strength, in firm unity with all the other progressive forces of our country and the world to set American imperialist reaction back on its heels.

His words, often exaggerated out of context, turned every right-wing extremist organization in America against him. Their anger reached a sad and destructive climax during two of his concerts in Peekskill, New York in the summer of 1949.

His interest in Africa, which had started early in his life, continued through his affiliations with The Council on African Affairs and the column that he wrote regularly for the newspaper *Freedom*.

In 1950 Paul Robeson's passport was revoked by the State Department, though he was not charged with any crime. President Truman had signed an executive order forbidding Paul Robeson to set foot outside the continental limits of the United States. "Committees To Restore Paul Robeson's Passport" were organized in the United States and in other countries around the world. The fight to restore his passport lasted eight years.

For Paul Robeson these were not lost or inactive years; and they were not years when he was forgotten or without appreciation, though, in some circles, his supporters "dwindled down to a precious few." He was fully involved, during these years, with the Council on African Affairs, *Freedom* newspaper, The American Labor Movement, The Peace Movement, and The National Council of American-Soviet Friendship.

From its inception in November 1950 to the last issue, July-August 1955, Paul Robeson wrote a regular column for the newspaper *Freedom*. After his passport was restored in 1958, he went to Europe for an extended concert tour. In 1963 he returned to the United States with his wife Eslanda, who died two years later. After her death he gave up his home in Harlem and moved to Philadelphia to spend his last years with his sister, Mrs. Marion Forsythe.

Next to W.E.B. Du Bois, Paul Robeson was the best example of an intellect who was active in his people's freedom struggle. Through this struggle both men committed themselves to improve the lot of all mankind. Paul Robeson's thoughts in this matter are summed up in the following quote from his book, *Here I Stand.*

> I learned that the essential character of a nation is determined not by the upper classes, but by the common people, and that the common people of all nations are truly brothers in the great family of mankind. . . . And even as I grew to feel more Negro in spirit, or African as I put it then, I also came to feel a sense of oneness with the white working people whom I came to know and love.
>
> This belief in the oneness of humankind, about which I have often spoken in concerts and elsewhere, has existed within me side by side with my deep attachment to the cause of my own race. Some people have seen a contradiction in this duality. . . . I do not think,

however, that my sentiments are contradictory. . . . I learned that there truly is a kinship among us all, a basis for mutual respect and brotherly love.

At the time of his death, January 23, 1976, a new generation was discovering Paul Robeson for the first time. An older generation was regretting that it had not made the best use of the strengths and hope that he had given to them. The writer, L. Clayton Jones, made this comment in the *Amsterdam News* after his death.

One watches with restrained anger as a nation of hypocrites grudgingly acknowledges the passing of a twentieth century phenomenon, Paul Robeson, All-American Athlete, Shakespearean Actor, Basso Profundo, Linguist, Scholar, Lawyer, Activist. He was all these things and more.

In December, 1977, an Ad Hoc Committee to End the Crimes Against Paul Robeson was formed to protest the inaccurate portrayal of Paul Robeson in a new play by Philip Hayes Dean. Their statement read, in part:

The essence of Paul Robeson is inseparable from his ideas—those most profoundly held artistic, philosophical and political principles which evolved from his early youth into the lifelong commitments for which he paid so dear and from which he never wavered down to his final public statement in 1975. In life, Paul Robeson sustained the greatest effort in the history of this nation to silence a single artist. He defied physical and psychological harassment and abuse without once retreating from these principles and the positions to which he dedicated his life. We believe that it is no less a continuation of the same crime to restore him, now that he is safely dead, to the pantheon of respectability on the terms of those who sought to destroy him.

Robeson is the archetype of the black American who uncompromisingly insists on total liberation. His example and his fate strike to the very heart of American racism.

For the nation to confront him honestly would mean that it confronts itself—to begin at last the process of reclamation of the national soul.

The Paul Robeson Archives: Legacy of Courage

BY HARRIET JACKSON SCARUPA

> "My father's immense power and great gentleness, his intense
> spiritual force and great intellect, his unbending courage and
> his deep compassion have left each one of us with special mem-
> ories that will always sustain us, for each was touched by him in
> a very special way."—Paul Robeson, Jr., at his father's funeral,
> January 27, 1976, Mother A.M.E. Zion Church, Harlem, New
> York.

These words were running through my mind on the way to speak
with Paul Robeson, Jr., about the Paul Robeson Archives, a
project to collect, preserve and catalogue the tremendous amount
of material about his father. Robeson's story—its triumphs and
its trials—is movingly documented in the Archives.

New York's Carnegie Hall played a special role in the Robeson story. It was there in 1958 that Robeson gave two jubilant
concerts after an eleven-year McCarthyism-imposed absence. It
was there that a host of celebrities and ordinary people came to
salute him on his seventy-fifth birthday in 1973 and posthumously last October at a benefit for the Archives. Both programs
were glowing testimonials to the effort waged by Paul Robeson,
Jr., and others to restore Paul Robeson to his rightful place in
American history.

The Archives, of course, are a key part of that effort. Appropriately, the project's office is located directly across the street
from Carnegie Hall. The office consists of three cramped, decid-
edly unchic rooms, crowded with boxes and file cabinets, with
the ever-present hum of an overworked copying machine in the
background. Dominating the space and seeming to give it an
aura of calm is a huge photograph of Paul Robeson when he
was about twenty-eight years old. There he stands, brimming

over with self-confidence, an engaging grin on that familiar broad-nosed face, eyes lit up with the pure joy of living, hands jauntily thrust into the pockets of a rather debonair three-piece suit.

With this photograph as a backdrop, Paul Robeson, Jr., speaks about the Archives and their significance. He is forty-nine, a thin, handsome man whose gray-flecked goatee doesn't quite seem to match either his boyish face or his manner. By profession he is a translator, drawing on his engineering background (he holds a degree in electrical engineering from Cornell) and his knowledge of Russian to translate technical journals into English.

But this is just one side of his life. When his father was alive, Paul Robeson, Jr., stood right beside him, helping him make records when recording studios barred their doors, organizing bodyguards to prevent violence-prone hecklers (like those at Peekskill) from disrupting concerts and serving as his father's spokesman when he became too ill to do it himself. Now that his father is dead, Robeson, Jr., carries on, devoting a great deal of his time to the Archives. In a sense he is passing on his father's gift to the world through the Archives.

At first he is reserved, almost wary, confining most of his remarks to facts about the Archives. But he soon warms to his subject and before long is speaking vigorously about what his father stood for. He exclaims, "His [Paul Robeson's] image was that of one who hit the man"—and he thrusts his fist into the air in the Black Power salute. "He was the image of total opposition to the status quo. It was that image the establishment was trying to cut down. It cannot deal with a black man who projects that type of image. He was the very opposite of the idea 'to get along, you go along,' the very opposite of 'let's do things gradually.' His point of view was 'Take it. Don't beg.' It was that image that got him into trouble."

When I ask about the view expressed in some quarters that his father was a "tragic figure" who had allowed political naiveté to destroy his career and had become disillusioned in his old age, Robeson, Jr., looks at me with exasperation.

"There's material right here that answers all that," he says, his hand sweeping over the files and boxes in the Archives. "As I said in the eulogy at my father's funeral, he never regretted the stands he took because he made his basic choice way back in 1937. He said then, 'The artist must elect to fight for freedom or for slavery. I have made my choice. I had no alternative.' In taking positions that were on a direct collision course with the system, he knew the price he might have to pay. He didn't expect to be around in the fifties. He was prepared for someone to blow him away. That his career was affected seemed mild compared to that.

"As for being disillusioned," he adds, again with exasperation, "look at my father's later statements. They're right here in the Archives. My God, look at the words he sent to the 1973 salute: 'I am the same Paul. . . . I must keep fighting until I'm dying.' [The last words are from "Ol' Man River," the song Robeson transformed into a worldwide battle cry against oppression.] Now if someone wants to say Paul Robeson was disillusioned after reading these kinds of things, he obviously has an axe to grind. There's nothing I can do about that. If I spent all my time answering all the comments, trying to clear up all the distortions, that would be all I could do.

"All I can do is direct people to what Robeson actually did and said and help put it in historical context," he observes. "I'm not on any big personal crusade, 'Look everybody. Look at what a great guy my father was.' When exposed to Paul Robeson, people will dig him. Let people become acquainted with him and they can do their own analysis. I try to stay away from that. I'm too close.

"But while I don't feel a need to crusade, I do feel strongly about breaking the curtain of silence around my father," he goes on. "That's one of the reasons we're trying so hard to get copies of all the documentary film about him that was confiscated during the McCarthy period. I do feel strongly about the fact that when Paul Robeson was under fire *The New York Times* wouldn't print one line about him and wouldn't even mention his book, *Here I Stand* [published simultaneously in Toronto, Canada: McClelland and Stewart, Ltd., 1958 and London: Dennis Dobson, Ltd., 1958], but when he died, it devoted columns of space to him [the obituary]. *The New York Times* is screaming about human rights today [in the case of the Russian dissidents], but why wasn't it screaming about human rights when it came to Paul Robeson? I do keep these kinds of contrasts in mind and I feel people should be aware of them. But I don't have to prove anything about my father. That's demeaning. I'm just making the material on him available."

That material consists of some 50,000 items: letters, speeches, press statements, articles, records, tapes, sheet music, scripts, posters, programs, awards, photographs, Robeson's own personal library, African artifacts and a few costumes. At least 90 per cent of it was owned by the Robeson family, the rest was acquired—and is still being acquired—from England, the Soviet Union and elsewhere.

"One of the reasons the Archives are so fascinating," Paul Robeson, Jr., said, "is that they show what a complex, multidimensional man my father was. There were so many Robesons."

There was, to begin with, Paul Robeson the son. A picture in the Archives shows the Reverend William Drew Robeson as a powerful, proud-looking black man with a hint of stubbornness about the jaw. He had escaped from slavery at the age of fifteen and throughout his life remained a man of solid principle. Robeson adored his father ("The glory of my boyhood years was my father," he wrote in *Here I Stand*) and took him as his role model. "Just as he [Reverend Robeson] had refused to remain a slave in his youth, so he disdained to be an Uncle Tom during his manhood," Robeson wrote. "From him we learned, and never doubted it, that the Negro was in every way the equal of the white man. And we fiercely resolved to prove it."

There was Paul Robeson, the actor. The Archives contain scores of photographs of Robeson as Othello, in addition to a pertinent 1930 interview in which he explained his interpretation of the role. "I feel the play is so modern," he said, "for the problem is the problem of my own people. It is a tragedy of racial conflict, a tragedy of honor, rather than of jealousy."

Included, also, are photographs of Robeson in the films in which he appeared—among them, *Showboat*, *Emperor Jones* and *Sanders of the River*. But there is also his heartfelt 1939 statement on why he would no longer work in Hollywood: "I thought I could do something for the Negro race in films—show the truth about them and about other people too. I used to do my part and go away feeling satisfied—thought everything was O.K. Well it wasn't. The industry is not prepared to permit me to portray the life and express the living interests, hopes and aspirations of the struggling people from whom I come. . . . They will never let me play a part in a film in which a Negro is on top."

Paul Robeson, Jr., believes the Archives' material refutes the perception, encouraged somewhat by his father himself, that Robeson was a "natural actor." "The Archives show he studied *Othello* for many years," he says. "We've found tapes on which he practiced *Othello* in three different languages—French, German and Russian. He did this not so he could perform them in these languages but to get from them different values that could be translated into English. Knowing this helps account for how he came about delivering some of his lines the way he did. In the courtship of Desdemona, for instance, he used French to help give the English a certain soft, lyrical quality."

There was Paul Robeson, the singer. Housed in the Archives is the original score of the eleven-minute choral work, "Ballad for Americans," written by John Latouche with music by Earl Robinson, which electrified the country when Robeson first sang it over CBS radio in 1939. This was no empty patriotic ditty. Robeson sang of how "man in a white skin can never be free / while his black brother is in slavery" and of how the greatness of America lies in its ordinary people, "the Etceteras and the And-so-forths, that do the work."

In light of Robeson's deep patriotism, what happened at Peekskill stands in painful irony. The Archives contain his tearful words after that shattering onslaught. "I will sing," he said, "whenever the people want to hear me. I sing of peace and freedom and of life."

Also included in the Archives are encomiums to his voice. Gwendolyn Brooks speaks of Robeson as the major, adult voice:

> Warning, in music-words
> devout and large,

that we are each other's
harvest:
we are each other's
business:
we are each other's
magnitude and bond.*

And there is the simple sentence of a London critic upon hearing Robeson for the first time: "He broke our hearts with beauty."

A look at Robeson's heavily annotated sheet music provides evidence that he was no more a "natural singer" than he was a "natural actor." "He spent an enormous amount of time picking out songs syllable by syllable, working them over so they would be easy to enunciate," Paul Robeson, Jr., explains. "With some songs, we've found three different versions, arranged in three different keys. He did this so he could pick the version he could get the most out of depending on the condition of his voice or the hall. If he was a 'natural singer,' he worked very hard to become that way."

There was Paul Robeson, the prophet. He foreshadowed the interests of black Americans in exploring their links with Africa. In a 1934 article in *The London Spectator* he wrote of how when he was studying some West Coast African languages, he "immediately found a kinship of rhythm and intonation with the Negro-English dialect which I heard spoken around me as a child. It was to me like a homecoming."

He anticipated the concept of black power. In his book, *Here I Stand,* he wrote, "The Negro people's movement must be led by Negroes, not only in terms of title and position but in reality. Good advice is good no matter what the source and help is needed and appreciated from wherever it comes, but Negro action cannot be decisive if the advisers and helpers hold the guiding reins."

He anticipated, too, the questions raised in the protest against the Vietnam War. In a 1953 article, he wrote: "No one has yet explained to my satisfaction what business a black lad from a

---

* From *Family Pictures.* Copyright © 1970 by Gwendolyn Brooks. Used by permission of Broadside Press.

Mississippi or Georgia sharecropping farm has in Asia shooting down the yellow or brown son of an impoverished rice-farmer."

He foresaw the necessity of détente with the Soviet Union: "At Paris, in 1949, I was convinced—and time has only served to deepen that conviction—that a war with the Soviet Union, a Third World War, was unthinkable for anybody who is not out of his mind."

There was, of course, Paul Robeson, the freedom fighter. The transcript of his testimony in 1956 before the House Un-American Activities Committee is in the Archives. "Why didn't you stay in Russia?" demanded one member of this inquisition. Robeson retorted, "Because my father was a slave, and my people died to build this country, and I am going to stay here and have a part of it just like you. And no fascist-minded people will drive me from it. Is that clear. . . ?

And there was Paul Robeson, the father. The Archives contain engaging photographs of Robeson and his wife Eslanda, a chemist, anthropologist and writer, as they proudly look down at their son. Which brings us full circle back to Paul Robeson, Jr.

For years, he was identified in the press as "Robeson's Soviet-trained son." The label amuses him. "I studied in the Soviet Union a grand total of one year and nine months," he points out. (The rest of his education took place in England, Canada and the United States.) "It was a good experience. I was with Russian schoolboys and I learned the language." Ironically, it was his knowledge of the language, courtesy of his so-called Soviet training, that enabled him to earn a comfortable living when he found there were no electrical engineering jobs to be had for a black man named Robeson—especially since he openly supported his father.

When I ask if he sees parallels between his own relationship with his father and his father's relationship with his father, Robeson, Jr., pauses thoughtfully for a moment, then says, "My father grew up with his father when he [the father] was an older man. He was twenty when his father died. My experience was different. I was closest to Dad from the time I was twelve on and in the most difficult years—the fifties. It was a much different relationship. But there was a similarity. He got his basic values from his father, which he passed on to me."

As he speaks, one can't help but think how the Robeson clan seems suffused with an uncommonly powerful strand of father-son love. For perhaps it is love, more than any other motivation, that explains why Paul Robeson, Jr., has persisted in waging his sometimes lonely battle to remove the cloud of nonpersonhood that surrounded his father so long. Some of the anonymity imposed by that cloud exists still. But it will soon be lifted. And the Archives will spur it along.

Since the Archives office opened in 1973 (it is organized as a nonprofit corporation and is financed by fund-raising affairs and grants from small foundations), about a dozen people have contributed time to copying and organizing the holdings. Among them are: Marilyn Robeson, Paul Robeson, Jr.'s, wife of twenty-eight years; and the two Robeson children, Susan, twenty-four, a filmmaker and photographer, and David, twenty-six, an electrical engineer like his father.

"We're aiming to make this massive amount of material accessible," Paul Robeson, Jr., explains. "That means going at it in a painstaking way, boiling it down, digesting it, arranging it so it can make sense. Once that's finished, probably by the end of the year, we'll turn all the material over to a major black educational institution and the function of this office will end. That institution will have the space to exhibit and store the collection so it can be used by people interested in writing books, doing films or just learning more about Paul Robeson."

Paul Robeson, Jr., and the Board of the Paul Robeson Archives are in advanced states of negotiations with the Moorland-Spingarn Research Center of Howard University for the purpose of donating the entire Paul Robeson and Eslanda Goode Robeson Collection to them. Placing the collection at the Moorland-Spingarn Research Center, a repository for a vast amount of material documenting the history and culture of black people throughout the world, will ensure that Robeson's remarkable achievements will assume their rightful place as a permanent part of this nation's historical record. Following the transfer of the collection to its permanent repository, the Robeson family will continue to ensure that copies of the materials will be made available to interested individuals, libraries and educational institutions throughout the world.

And so, the documents that tell the Paul Robeson story will soon be released to the world. Let them serve as a powerful reminder. A reminder that what happened to Paul Robeson because his views happened to offend the powers-that-be—what one writer termed that "attempt to blot from history a man's meaning"—must never happen again. Never again. Never.

The best explanation of Paul Robeson's views is undoubtedly his own book, *Here I Stand,* which Beacon Press reissued in 1971, while a handy compendium of views on Robeson is found in this volume.

Epilogue

"We're Moving!" *

BY PAUL ROBESON

While I must continue my temporary retirement from public life I am, of course, deeply involved with the great upsurge of our people. Like all of you, my heart has been filled with admiration for the many thousands of Negro freedom fighters and their white associates who are waging the battle for civil rights throughout the country and especially in the South. Along with the pride has been the great sorrow and righteous wrath we all shared when the evil forces of white supremacy brutally murdered the Birmingham children and some of our finest heroes, like Medgar Evers and the three young men in Mississippi.

For me there has also been the sorrow that I have felt on returning home and experiencing the loss of persons who for many long years were near and dear to me—my beloved older brother, Reverend Benjamin C. Robeson, who passed away while I was gone; and my long-time colleague and coworker, Dr. W. E. B. Du Bois, foremost statesman and scholar of our people, who died last year in Ghana. And now has come deep grief at the death of Benjamin J. Davis, a precious friend whose indomitable courage and dedication to the fight for freedom has always been a glowing inspiration for me.

Many thousands gone . . . but we, the living, are more firmly resolved: "No more driver's lash for me!" The dedicated lives of

---

* Statement by Paul Robeson, August 28, 1964.

(On the first anniversary of the historic March on Washington, Mr. Robeson issued a statement to the black press, from which the following is excerpted. Because of his illness, he issued no further statement to the press before he died.)

211

all who have fallen in our long uphill march shall be fulfilled, for truly "We *shall* overcome." The issue of *freedom now* for Negro Americans has become the main issue confronting this nation, and the peoples of the whole world are looking to see it finally resolved.

When I wrote in my book, *Here I Stand,* in 1958, that "The time is now," some people thought that perhaps my watch was fast (and maybe it was a little), but most of us seem to be running on the same time—now. The "power of Negro action," of which I then wrote, has changed from an idea to a reality that is manifesting itself throughout our land. The concept of mass militancy, of mass action, is no longer deemed "too radical" in Negro life.

The idea that black Americans should see that the fight for a "Free World" begins at home—a shocking idea when expressed in Paris in 1949—no longer is challenged in our communities. The "hot summer" of struggle for equal rights has replaced the "cold war" abroad as the concern of our people.

It is especially heartening to me to see the active and often heroic part that leading Negro artists—singers, actors, writers, comedians, musicians—are playing today in the freedom struggle. Today it is the Negro artist who does *not* speak out who is considered to be out of line; and even the white audiences have largely come around to accepting the fact that the Negro artist is— and has every right to be—quite "controversial."

Yes, it is good to see all these transformations. It is heartening also to see that despite all the differences in program and personalities among Negro leadership, the concept of a united front of all forces and viewpoints is gaining ground.

There is much—much more—that needs to be done, of course, before we can reach our goals. But if we cannot as yet sing: "Thank God Almighty, we're free at last," we surely can all sing together: "Thank God Almighty, we're *moving!*"

Paul Robeson in his sixties.

As a junior at Rutgers University.

At Rutgers University on the football field. (1919)

On a visit to London in 1923.

In Showboat, *Drury Lane Theatre, London.* (1928)

In Australia with factory workers. (1930s)

Paul and Eslanda Robeson in London. (1932)

With troops defending the Spanish Republic just beyond the front lines in the Madrid Barracks. (1937)

Set of King Solomon's Mines, *London. Paul and Eslanda Robeson with member of cast. (1938)*

With students at Bennett College, Greensboro, North Carolina, and accompanist Lawrence Brown. (1940s)

At the Southern Negro Youth Congress convention, Tuskegee Institute, Alabama. With him, Tuskegee students, and in foreground, Esther Jackson, now Managing Editor of Freedomways *magazine. (1942)*

Robeson with Dr. W.E.B. Du Bois and Congressman Vito Marcantonio. (1940s)

With Mayor Fiorello La Guardia at awards program for students. (1940)

*With Lawrence Brown,
friend and accompanist.
(1940s)*

*With singer-actress Lena
Horne. (1940s)*

Robeson singing at Peekskill concert. Around the artist are war veterans and concert-goers who acted as bodyguards. (1949)

Robeson singing national anthem with chorus of employees, Moore Dry Dock Company, Oakland, California. (September 20, 1942)

The Theatre Guild presents Paul Robeson in the Margaret Webster production of Othello *at the Shubert Theatre in New York. Uta Hagen is Desdemona. (1943)*

Robeson being greeted by famed composer W.C. Handy, "The Father of the Blues," at Robeson's forty-sixth birthday celebration in New York City. (April, 1944)

Robeson arrives at Southern Youth Legislature, Columbia, South Carolina. Greeted by President S.R. Higgins of Allen University and Esther Jackson, now of Freedomways *magazine. (October 17, 1946)*

Marion Anderson sings in a church in Harlem at a meeting sponsored by the Council on African Affairs. Attorney Hubert Delaney and Paul Robeson are seated in right rear. (About 1947)

With son Paul, Jr., at Welcome Home Rally held at Rockland Palace. (1949)

With Communist leaders Benjamin J. Davis, a member of the New York City Council (left), and Henry Winston (right), now National Chairman, U.S. Communist Party. At a reception in Harlem for defendants in the Smith Act trials. (1949)

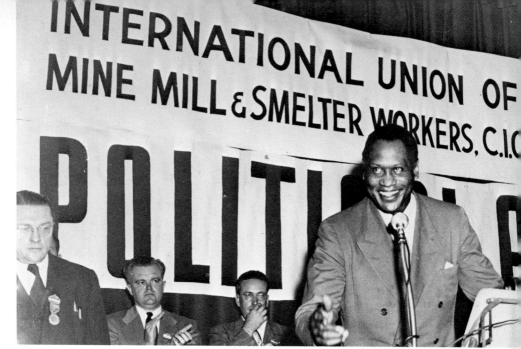

Paul Robeson acknowledges the tremendous ovation given him after introduction by President Reid Robinson (left) to the delegates at the 42nd Convention of the International Union of Mine, Mill and Smelter Workers.

Visiting with world heavyweight boxing champion, Joe Louis, at Louis's training camp.

With Alan Booth, his accompanist of the 1950s.

With actress Beah Richards and attorney William L. Patterson of the Civil Rights Congress. (1950s)

Robeson being welcomed in the streets of Harlem. (1950s)

At the International Peace Arch on the Canadian–U.S. border. (May 8, 1952)

Speaking at a church in Harlem. In the rear, Maude White Katz, community leader, and Dr. W. Alphaeus Hunton. (1950s)

Receiving honorary lifetime membership in the International Longshoremen's and Warehousemen's Union (ILWU) from President Harry Bridges. (1950s)

With leaders of the National Negro Labor Council. Left to right, Coleman A. Young, now Mayor of Detroit, Michigan; Robeson; William Hood, former President of Ford Local 600, United Automobile Workers; and William Marshall, actor. (1951)

Robeson greeting Dr. W. Alphaeus Hunton, Director of the Council on African Affairs, just after Hunton's release from prison for refusing to inform on contributors to the Civil Rights Congress bail fund. Left to right, Dr. Hunton, his wife Dorothy, Robeson, and Dr. W.E.B. Du Bois. (1951)

Singing at May Day celebration, New York City. (May 1, 1954)

Addressing a meeting of the Council on African Affairs in a Harlem church. (1955)

In the English production of Othello. Staged at Stratford-on-Avon, Shakespeare's birthplace, during the Quadricentennial celebration. (1959)

Robeson in demonstration in front of the White House for a Fair Employment Practices Commission. Leading the picketing, Louis E. Burnham, editor of Robeson's newspaper, Freedom.

In England, Spring 1960.

Paul Robeson talks to some workers at the Moscow Automated Gear Plant after the peace meeting at which he spoke and sang. (1960)

Speaking at ceremony awarding gold medals to Soviet peace movement winners.

Robeson welcomed in streets of Moscow during his visit following the successful campaign to restore his passport.

In concert at Yalta, USSR.

In Moscow, 1960.

Robeson greeted by Helene Weigel, leading actress of Germany and wife of Bertolt Brecht, the great playwright and anti-fascist artist. (Early 1960s)

Robeson greeted by children of the German Democratic Republic. (Early 1960s)

Berlin youth welcome Robeson.

With children of the Soviet Union at a summer camp on the Black Sea.

Singing at children's camp in the USSR.

Eslanda Robeson, Paul, and Nigerian leader Nnamdi Azikiwe at Nigerian Independence Celebration in London.

At reception preceding tribute by Freedomways *magazine at Americana Hotel, April, 1965.*

Head of Paul Robeson by Sir Jacob Epstein.

Paul and Eslanda Robeson at the Welcome Home Birthday Salute. With Freedomways staff and editors, J.H. O'Dell, Eslanda, John Henrik Clarke, Paul, Norma Rogers, Esther Jackson. (April, 1965)

At the Welcome Home Birthday Salute. Eslanda Robeson, Paul, and actress Diana Sands. (April, 1965)

Singing at Welcome Home Birthday Salute. (April, 1965)

Miscellaneous photographs of Robeson.

Photographs used by permission of The Paul Robeson Archives, the *Daily World*, Mrs. Dorothy Hunton, and *Freedomways* magazine.

PART II

SELECTIONS
FROM ROBESON'S
WRITINGS
AND SPEECHES

Negro-Labor Unity for Peace *

No meeting held in America at this mid-century turning point in world history holds more significant promise for the bright future for which humanity strives than this National Labor Conference for Negro Rights. For here are gathered together the basic forces— the Negro sons and daughters of labor and their white brothers and sisters—whose increasingly active intervention in national and world affairs is an essential requirement if we are to have a peaceful and democratic solution of the burning issues of our times.

Again we must recall the state of the world in which we live, and especially the America in which we live. Our history as Americans, black and white, has been a long battle, so often unsuccessful, for the most basic rights of citizenship, for the most simple standards of living, the avoidance of starvation—for survival.

I have been up and down the land time and again, thanks in the main to you trade unionists gathered here tonight. You helped to arouse American communities to give answer to Peekskill, to protect the right of freedom of speech and assembly. And I have seen and daily see the unemployment, the poverty, the plight of our children, our youth, the backbreaking labor of our women— and too long, too long have my people wept and mourned. We're tired of this denial of a decent existence. We demand some approximation of the American democracy we have helped to build.

Who Built This Land?

Who have been the guarantors of our historic democratic tradition of freedom and equality? Whose labor and whose life have produced the great cities, the industrial machine, the basic culture

---

* Excerpts from address to National Labor Conference for Negro Rights, Chicago, June 10, 1950.

and the creature comforts of which our "Voice of America" spokesmen so proudly boast?

It is well to remember that the America which we know has
risen out of the toil of the many millions who have come here
seeking freedom from all parts of the world:

The Irish and Scotch indentured servants who cleared the
forests, built the colonial homesteads and were part of the productive backbone of our early days.

The millions of German immigrants of the mid-nineteenth
century; the millions more from Eastern Europe whose sweat and
sacrifice in the steel mills, the coal mines and the factories made
possible the industrial revolution of the eighties and nineties; the
brave Jewish people from all parts of Europe and the world who
have so largely enriched our lives on this new continent; the workers from Mexico and from the East—Japan and the Philippines—
whose labor has helped make the West and Southwest a rich and
fruitful land.

*And, through it all, from the earliest days—before Columbus—
the Negro people, upon whose unpaid toil as slaves the basic
wealth of this nation was built!*

These are the forces that have made America great and preserved our democratic heritage.

They have arisen at each moment of crisis to play the decisive
role in our national affairs.

The Strength of the Negro People

In the Civil War, hundreds of thousands of Negro soldiers who
took arms in the Union cause won, not only their own freedom—
the freedom of the Negro people—but, by smashing the institution
of slave labor, provided the basis for the development of trade
unions of free working men in America.

And so, even today, as this National Labor Conference for
Negro Rights charts the course ahead for the whole Negro people
and their sincere allies, it sounds a warning to American bigotry
and reaction. For if fifteen million Negroes, led by their staunchest sons and daughters of labor, and joined by the white working

( )   class, say that there shall be no more Jim Crow in America, then there shall be no more Jim Crow!

If fifteen million Negroes in one voice demand an end to the jailing of the leaders of American progressive thought and culture and the leaders of the American working class, then their voice will be strong enough to empty the prisons of the victims of America's cold war.

If fifteen million Negroes are for peace, then there will be peace!

And behind these fifteen million are 180 million of our African brothers and sisters, sixty million of our kindred in the West Indies and Latin America—for whom, as for us, war and the Point Four program would mean a new imperialist slavery.

The Issues of Our Time

I know that you understand these problems—and especially the basic problem of peace. You have already outlined the issues in your sessions, and they are clear to liberty-loving men around the world.

Shall we have atom bomb and hydrogen bomb and rocketship and bacteriological war, or shall we have peace in the world; the hellish destruction of the men, women and children, of whole civilian populations, or the peaceful construction of the good life everywhere?

This for all men is the overriding issue of the day. From it all other questions flow. Its solution, one way or the other, will decide the fate of all other questions which concern the human family.

Shall we have fascist brute rule or democratic equality and friendship among peoples and nations; the triumphant enshrinement of the "master race" theories our soldiers died to destroy, or liberty and freedom for the American people and their colonial allies throughout the world?

And finally, shall we have increased wealth for the already bloated monopolies in the midst of rising hunger, poverty and disease for the world's poor; or shall the masses of toiling men and

women enjoy the wealth and comforts which their sweat and labor
produce?

American Imperialism vs. the Colonial World

Yes, these are the issues.

They will be resolved in our time—and you may be sure that
you have met not a moment too soon. Because in the five years
since V-J Day the American trusts and the government which they
control have taken their stand more and more openly on the side
of a cold war which they are desperately trying to heat up; on the
side of the fascist and kingly trash which they seek to restore to
power all over Europe and Asia; on the side of the princes of economic privilege whose every cent of unprecedented profits is
wrung out of the toil-broken bodies of the masses of men.

How well and how bitterly do we recall that soon after Roosevelt died, American arms were being shipped to the Dutch—not
for the protection of the Four Freedoms, not to advance the claims
of liberty—but for the suppression of the brave Indonesian patriots in their fight for independence.

That was in 1946, and today—four years later—we have the announcement of another program of arms shipments to destroy a
movement for colonial independence—this time arms for the
French imperialists to use against the brave Vietnamese patriots
in what the French progressive masses call the "dirty war" in Indo-
China.

These two acts of the Truman administration are significant
landmarks of our time!

They cry out to the world that our nation, born in a bloody
battle for freedom against imperialist tyranny, has itself become
the first enemy of freedom and the chief tyrant of the mid-century
world. They warn more than half the world's population who
people the vast continents of Asia and Africa that, until the course
of our foreign policy is changed, they can no longer look to the
U.S. government for help in their strenuous struggles for a new
and independent life.

And, to be sure, they have already averted their gaze from us.

In every subject land, in every dependent area, the hundreds of millions who strive for freedom have set their eyes upon a new star that rises in the east—they have chosen as the model for their conduct the brave people and stalwart leaders of the new People's Republic of China. And they say to our atom-toting politicians, "Send your guns and tanks and planes to our oppressors, if you will! We will be free in spite of you, if not with your help!"

Africa in World Affairs

What special meaning does this challenge of the colonial world have for American Negro workers and their allies?

We must not forget that each year 4,000 tons of uranium ore are extracted from the Belgian Congo—the main source of United States supply. And that Africa also provides more than half the world's gold and chrome, 80 per cent of its cobalt, 90 per cent of its palm kernels, one-fifth of its manganese and tin, one-third of its sisal fiber and 60 per cent of its cocoa—not to mention untold riches yet unexplored.

And with this wealth, Africa produces also an immeasurable portion of the world's human misery and degradation.

But the African peoples are moving rapidly to change their miserable conditions. And 180 million natives on that great continent are an important part of the colonial tidal wave that is washing upon the shores of history and breaking through the ramparts of imperialist rule everywhere.

The Congo skilled worker extracting copper and tin from the rich mines of the land of his fathers may one day be faced with the same materials in the shape of guns provided his Belgian rulers by the Truman administration under the Marshall Plan—but he is determined that the days of his virtual slave labor are numbered, and that the place for the Belgians to rule is in *Belgium* and *not in the Congo.*

And twenty-five million Nigerians—farmers, cattle raisers, miners, growers of half the world's cocoa—are determined that the land of *our* fathers (for the vast majority of American Negro slaves were brought here from Africa's West Coast) shall belong to their fathers' sons and not to the free-booters and British imperialists supported by American dollars.

And twelve South African workers now lie dead, shot in a peaceful demonstration by Malan's fascist-like police, as silent testimony to the fact that, for all their pass laws, for all their native compounds, for all their Hitler-inspired registration of natives and nonwhites, the little clique that rules South Africa is baying at the moon. For it is later than they think in the procession of history, and that rich land must one day soon return to the natives on whose backs the proud skyscrapers of the Johannesburg rich were built.

How are we to explain this new vigor of the African independence movements? What is it that shakes a continent from Morocco to the Cape and causes the old rulers to tremble?

The core of the African nationalist movements, the heart of the resistance to continued oppression, the guiding intelligence of the independence aspirations of the Africans are invariably the organizations of the workers of the continent. Trade unions have arisen all over Africa and, as everywhere in modern times, they are the backbone of the people's struggle.

And what is true of Africa is even more strikingly true in the West Indies, in Cuba, Brazil and the rest of Latin America where sixty million Negroes are building strong trade unions and demanding a new day.

The Tasks of Labor

Your tasks, then, are clear. The Negro trade unionists must increasingly exert their influence in every aspect of the life of the Negro community. No church, no fraternal, civic or social organization in our communities must be permitted to continue without the benefit of the knowledge and experience which you have gained through your struggles in the great American labor movement. You are called upon to provide the spirit, the determination, the organizational skill, the firm steel of unyielding militancy to the age-old strivings of the Negro people for equality and freedom.

On the shoulders of the Negro trade unionists there is the tremendous responsibility to rally the power of the whole trade union movement, white and black, to the battle for the liberation of our people, the future of our women and children. Anyone who fails in this does the Negro people a great disservice.

And to the white trade unionists present—a special challenge. You must fight in the ranks of labor for the full equality of your Negro brothers; for their right to work at any job; to receive equal pay for equal work; for an end to Jim Crow unions; for real fair employment practices within the unions as well as in all other phases of the national life; for the elimination of the rot of white supremacy notions which the employers use to poison the minds of the white workers in order to pit them against their staunchest allies, the Negro people—in short, for the unbreakable unity of the working people, black and white, without which there can be no free trade unions, no real prosperity, no constitutional rights, no peace for anybody, whatever the color of his skin. To accept Negro leadership of men and women and youth; to accept the fact that the Negro workers have become a part of the vanguard of the whole American working class. To fail the Negro people is to fail the whole American people.

I know that you who have come from all parts of the nation will meet this challenge. I have watched and participated in your militant struggles everywhere I have been these past years. Here in Chicago with the packinghouse workers; with auto workers of Detroit; the seamen and longshoremen of the West Coast; the tobacco workers of North Carolina; the miners of Pittsburgh and West Virginia; and the steel workers of Illinois, Indiana, Ohio, Michigan and Minnesota; the furriers, clerks and office workers of New York, Philadelphia and numerous other big cities and small towns throughout the land.

I have met you at the train stations and airports, extending the firm hand of friendship. You have packed the meetings which followed Peekskill to overflowing, thus giving the answer to the bigots and the warmakers. I know you well enough to know that, once the affairs of my people are in the hands of our working men and women, our day of freedom is not far off. I am proud as an artist to be one who comes from hearty Negro working people— and I know that you can call on me at any time—South, North, East or West—all my energy is at your call.

So—as you move forward, you do so in the best traditions of American democracy and in league with the hundreds of millions throughout the world whose problems are much the same as yours.

These are peoples of all faith, all lands, all colors and all political beliefs—united by the common thirst for freedom, security and peace.

Our American press and commentators and politicians would discourage these basic human aspirations because Communists adhere to them as well as others. Now I have seen the liberty-loving, peace-seeking partisans in many parts of the world. And though many of them are not, it is also true that many *are* Communists. They represent a new way of life in the world, a new way that has won the allegiance of almost half the world's population. In the last war they were the first to die in nation after nation. They were the heart of the underground antifascist movements and city after city in Europe displays monuments to their heroism. They need no apologies.

Mr. Truman calls upon us to save the so-called Western democracies from the "menace" of Communism.

But ask the Negro ministers in Birmingham whose homes were bombed by the Ku Klux Klan what is the greatest menace in their lives! Ask the Trenton Six and the Martinsville Seven! Ask Willie McGee, languishing in a Mississippi prison and doomed to die within the next month unless our angry voices save him. Ask Haywood Patterson, somewhere in America, a fugitive from Alabama barbarism for a crime he, nor any one of the Scottsboro boys, never committed. Ask the growing numbers of Negro unemployed in Chicago and Detroit. Ask the fearsome lines of relief clients in Harlem. Ask the weeping mother whose son is the latest victim of police brutality. Ask Maceo Snipes and Isaiah Nixon, killed by mobs in Georgia because they tried to exercise the constitutional right to vote. Ask any Negro worker receiving unequal pay for equal work, denied promotion despite his skill and because of his skin, still the last hired and the first fired. Ask fifteen million American Negroes, if you please, "What is the greatest menace in your life?" and they will answer in a thunderous voice, "Jim-Crow Justice! Mob Rule! Segregation! Job Discrimination!"—in short white supremacy and all its vile works.

The Battleground Is Here *

Officers and members of the Council—Friends:

It's good, so good, to be here—to enjoy once again the brother-hood and sisterhood of this great body of Negro working men and women, to share with you the dream of freedom, to plan with you for its achievement not in some distance but *now, today.*

I have been in many labor battles. It has seemed strange to some that, having attained some status and acclaim as an artist I should devote so much time and energy to the problems and struggles of working men and women.

To me, of course, it is not strange at all. I have simply tried never to forget the soil from which I spring.

Never to forget the rich but abused earth on the eastern coast of North Carolina where my father—not my grandfather—was a slave; and where today many of my cousins and relatives still live in poverty and second-class citizenship.

Never to forget the days of my youth—struggling to get through school, working in brickyards, in hotels, on docks and riverboats, battling prejudice and proscription—inspired and guided forward by the simple yet grand dignity of a father who was a real minister to the needs of his poor congregation in small New Jersey churches, and an example of human goodness.

No, I can never forget 300-odd years of slavery and half-free-dom; the long, weary and bitter years of degradation visited upon our mothers and sisters, the humiliation and Jim Crowing of a whole people. I will never forget that the ultimate freedom—and the immediate progress of my people rest on the sturdy backs and the unquenchable spirits of the coal miners, carpenters, railroad workers, clerks, domestic workers, bricklayers, sharecroppers, steel

---

* Excerpts from an address to the Annual Convention of the National Negro Labor Council, November 21, 1952, at Cleveland, Ohio.

and auto workers, cooks, stewards and longshoremen, tenant farmers and tobacco stemmers—the vast mass of Negro Americans from whom all talent and achievement rise in the first place.

If it were not for the stirrings and the militant struggles among these millions, a number of our so-called spokesmen with fancy jobs and appointments would never be where they are. And I happen to know that some of them will soon be looking around for something else to do. There's a change taking place in the country, you know. My advice to some of this "top brass" leadership of ours would be: *you'd better get back with the Folks—if it's not already too late.* I'm glad I never left them!

Yes, the faces and the tactics of the leaders may change every four years, or two, or one, but the people go on forever. The people—beaten down today, yet rising tomorrow; losing the road one minute but finding it the next; their eyes always fixed on a star of true brotherhood, equality and dignity—*the people* are the real guardians of our hopes and dreams.

That's why the mission of the Negro Labor Councils is an indispensable one. You have set yourself the task of organizing the will-to-freedom of the mass of our people—the workers in factory and farm—and hurling it against the walls of oppression. In this great program you deserve—and I know you will fight to win —the support and cooperation of all other sections of Negro life.

I was reading a book the other day in which the author used a phrase which has stuck in my memory. He said, "We are living in the rapids of history," and you and I know how right he is. You and I know that for millions all over this globe it's not going to be as long as it has been.

Yes, we are living "in the rapids of history" and a lot of folks are afraid of being dashed on the rocks. But not us!

No, not us—and not 200 million Africans who have let the world know that they are about to take back their native land and make it the world's garden spot, which it can be.

In Kenya Old John Bull has sent in his troops and tanks, and has said Mau Mau has got to go. But Jomo Kenyatta, the leader of Kenya African Union, with whom I sat many times in London, has answered back. He says, "Yes, someone has got to go, but in

Kenya it sure won't be six million black Kenyans. I think you know who'll be leaving—and soon."

And, in South Africa there'll be some changes made too. FREE-DOM is a hard-won thing. And, any time 7,000 Africans and Indians fill the jails of that unhappy land for sitting in "White Only" waiting rooms, for tearing down Jim-Crow signs like those which are seen everywhere in our South, you know those folks are ready for FREEDOM. They are willing to pay the price.

The struggle in Africa has a special meaning to the National Negro Labor Council and to every worker in this land, white as well as Negro. Today, it was announced that the new Secretary of Defense will be Charles E. Wilson, president of the General Motors Corporation. General Motors simply happens to be one of the biggest investors in South Africa, along with Standard Oil, Socony Vacuum, Kennecott Copper, the Ford Motor Company and other giant corporations.

You see, they are not satisfied with wringing the sweat and sometimes the blood out of ore miners in Alabama and Utah, auto workers in Detroit and Atlanta, oil workers in Texas and New Jersey. They want superduper profits at ten cents an hour wages, which they can get away with only if the British Empire, in one case, or the Malan Fascists, in another, can keep their iron heels on the black backs of our African brothers and sisters.

Now, I said more than three years ago that it would be unthinkable to me that Negro youth from the United States should go thousands of miles away to fight against their friends and on behalf of their enemies. You remember that a great howl was raised in the land. And I remember, only the other day, in the heat of the election campaign, that a group of Negro political figures pledged *in advance* that our people would be prepared to fight any war any time that the rulers of this nation should decide.

Well, I ask you again, should Negro youth take a gun in hand and join with British soldiers in shooting down the brave peoples of Kenya?

I talked just the other day with Professor Z. K. Mathews, of South Africa, a leader of the African National Congress, who is now in this country as a visiting professor at Union Theological Seminary in New York.

Professor Mathews's son is one of those arrested in Cape Town for his defiance of unjust laws. I ask you now, shall I send my son to South Africa to shoot down Professor Mathews's son on behalf of Charles E. Wilson's General Motors Corporation?

I say again, the proper battlefield for our youth and for all fighters for a decent life, is here; in Alabama, Mississippi and Georgia; is here, in Cleveland, Chicago and San Francisco; is in every city and at every whistle stop in this land where the walls of Jim Crow still stand and need somebody to tear them down.

Playing Catch-up *

For ninety years since Emancipation our people have been playing "catch-up" in American life. We have been battling for equality in education, health, housing and jobs.

And now, today, ninety years later, despite all the croaking about the great progress we're making, any Negro who's not looking for a second-string job on Eisenhower's "team" will tell you we've still got a long way to go.

How are we going to get there?

Will shooting down Chinese help us get our freedom? Will dropping some bombs on Vietnamese patriots who want to be free of French domination help American Negroes reach a plane of equality with their white fellow-citizens? And, most important, will a war in support of Malan in South Africa, or the British exploiters in Kenya, or the French in Tunisia place black Americans on the same footing with whites?

To ask the question is to answer it. No!

No one has yet explained to my satisfaction what business a black lad from a Mississippi or Georgia sharecropping farm has in Asia shooting down the yellow or brown son of an impoverished rice-farmer.

Mr. Eisenhower or Senator McCarthy would have us believe that this is necessary to "save" the so-called "free world" from "communism." But the man who keeps that Negro sharecropper from earning more than a few hundred dollars a year is not a Communist—it's the landlord. And the man who prevents his son from attending school with white children is not a Communist—it's Governor Talmadge or Governor Byrnes of the U.S. delegation to the United Nations.

I believe, and I urge upon this convention the belief, that any

---

* Speech, October, 1953, printed in *Freedom.*

Negro who carries his brains around with him and has not been bought and paid for must agree that it is time for fifteen million colored Americans to dissociate themselves from a foreign policy which is based on brandishing the atom bomb, setting up hundreds of air bases all over the world, and threatening colored peoples with death and destruction unless they humbly recognize the inalienable right of Anglo-Saxon Americans to sit on the top of the world.

Negroes, as I said, are still playing "catch-up." And with the kind of war that the atom-happy U.S. diplomats are planning we won't be catching up—we'll just be "catching," and relinquishing any hope for liberation and freedom.

I say that, even though Eisenhower is meeting at this very moment with Churchill in Bermuda, we will not, and must not support the British overlords in Kenya—we will fight to free Kenyatta! I say, even though Laniel of France is right there with Eisenhower and Churchill, we must not approve the squandering of billions of American taxpayers' money on the dirty war in Indo-China—we must insist that the French rule in France and leave the Vietnamese to govern themselves. And I trust that this convention will record that it is against the interests of Negro workers, the entire Negro people and the nation as a whole to pursue one step further the suicidal, blundering, threatening, war-minded foreign policy which is the hallmark of the administration. What Negroes need, and all America needs, is PEACE.

Ho Chi Minh Is Toussaint L'Ouverture
of Indo-China *

As I write these lines, the eyes of the world are on a country in-habited by twenty-three million brown-skinned people—a popula-tion one and a half times the number of Negroes in the U.S. In size that country is equal to the combined area of Mississippi, South Carolina and Alabama. It's a fertile land, rich in minerals; but all the wealth is taken away by the foreign rulers, and the people are poor.

I'm talking about Vietnam, and it seems to me that we Negroes have a special reason for understanding what's going on over there. Only recently, during Negro History Week, we recalled the heroic exploits of Toussaint L'Ouverture, who led the people of Haiti in a victorious rebellion against the French Empire.

Well, at the same time that the French were fighting to keep their hold on the black slaves of Haiti, they were sending an army around to the other side of the world to impose colonial slavery on the people of Indo-China. And ever since then the Indo-Chi-nese have been struggling to be free from French domination.

"My children, France comes to make us slaves. God gave us liberty; France has no right to take it away. Burn the cities, destroy the harvests, tear up the roads with cannon, poison the wells, show the white man the hell he comes to make!"

Those fiery words, addressed to his people by Toussaint L'Ouverture when Napoleon sent Le Clerc with an army of 30,000 men to reenslave Haiti, are echoed today by Ho Chi Minh, who is the Toussaint of Vietnam. Yes, and a French general called Le Clerc was also sent against Ho Chi Minh, but like the Blacks of Haiti, the plantation workers of Indo-China have proved uncon-querable.

---

* *Freedom*–March, 1954.

In 1946 France was forced to recognize the Republic of Vietnam, headed by Ho Chi Minh; but like the double-crossing Napoleon in the time of Toussaint, the French colonial masters returned with greater force to reenslave the people who had liberated themselves. The common people of France have come to hate
this struggle; they call it "the dirty war"; and their rulers have not
dared to draft Frenchmen for military service there.

"Who are the Vietminh?" said a French officer to a reporter
from the Associated Press. "Where are they? Who knows? They
are everywhere." And the reporter wrote:

> Ho Chi Minh's barefoot hordes infiltrate French-held territory at
> will in the guise of peasants, arms concealed under brown tunics.
> They have allies who hide them and feed them—allies who are not
> Communists but just people who hate the French, hate the for-
> eigner and want him to go.

Now, when France wants to call it quits, Eisenhower, Nixon
and Dulles are insisting that Vietnam must be reconquered and
held in colonial chains. "The Vietnamese lack the ability to govern themselves," says Vice President Nixon.

Vast quantities of U.S. bombers, tanks and guns have been
sent against Ho Chi Minh and his freedom-fighters; and now we
are told that soon it may be "advisable" to send American GI's
into Indo-China in order that the tin, rubber and tungsten of
Southeast Asia be kept by the "free world"—meaning White Imperialism.

The whole world cries out for peace; but Dulles insists that
the war must go on and threatens Asians again with atomic and
hydrogen bombs.

That's the picture, and I ask again: shall Negro sharecroppers
from Mississippi be sent to shoot down brown-skinned peasants in
Vietnam—to serve the interests of those who oppose Negro liberation at home and colonial freedom abroad?

What are our Negro leaders saying about this? They are all
too silent.

The true issues involved are well known, for only recently
The Crisis, official organ of the NAACP, published an article
filled with factual proof that the Vietnamese are fighting against

colonial oppression. The article shows that the charge of "Red Aggression" in Indo-China is a phony, and that the sympathies of our people belong with the side resisting imperialism.

Three years ago Mordecai Johnson, president of Howard University, said that "For over 100 years the French have been in Indo-China, dominating them politically, strangling them economically, and humiliating them in the land of their fathers. . . . And now it looks as though they can win, and as they are about to win their liberty, we rush up and say: 'What on earth are you all getting ready to do? . . . We are the free people of the world, we are your friends, we will send you leaders. . . .'

"And they look at us in amazement and they say: 'Brother, where have you been. Why if we'd known you was a-comin' we'd have baked a cake.' "

Today, more than ever, is the time for plain speaking.

Peace can be won if we demand it. The imperialists can be halted in their tracks. And as we think about Ho Chi Minh, the modern-day Toussaint L'Ouverture leading his people to freedom, let us remember well the warning words of a Negro spokesman, Charles Baylor, who wrote in the *Richmond Planet* a half-century ago:

"The American Negro cannot become the ally of imperialism without enslaving his own race."

PART III

TRIBUTES

TRIBUTES IN POETRY

Paul Robeson

BY GWENDOLYN BROOKS

That time
we all heard it,
cool and clear,
cutting across the hot grit of the day.
The major Voice.
The adult Voice
forgoing Rolling River,
forgoing tearful tale of bale and barge
and other symptoms of an old despond.
Warning, in music-words
devout and large,
that we are each other's
harvest:
we are each other's
business:
we are each other's
magnitude and bond.

For Paul Robeson

BY RICHARD DAVIDSON

Paul
I remember hearing you as a kid,
Back in Chicago in the long, turning summer of '48,
There you were singing your songs
And Henry Wallace running for president.
I remember growing up with those songs
And the bright, young girls with ribbons of peace in their hair,
And guitars on hills and the roaring belief in the magic of
The working class.
I grew older and there was Korea,
My friends from the same block crumbling their bones
In the basket of Mr. Truman's war.
I grew older and there was Julius and Ethel
Slaughtered by a ruling class who lives by slaughter.
We marched in Washington with placards for their release,
With your songs charging like an anthem in the spaces
Of our mind.
I grew older and you grew older
But the songs didn't cease and still have not.
We didn't win in '48 Paul,
But today more than half the world
Knows of you and listens to your music.
You were a pioneer and the small black child on a hundred and
Twenty-fifth street
Feels your magic pouring through his blood.
There is much to do today Paul,
And your songs live as the students
Storm the citadels of the phony seats of power.
Your songs live as we strike for peace,

As we strike for welfare,
As we strike for the better day of the better world.
Your songs live as Angela Davis fights for life
And as we remember Willie McGee and Martin Luther King.
We didn't win in forty-eight, Paul,
And today the road is beckoning,
The people are moving,
And in the silence of the clear stars of night,
Your hymn like a burning torch of freedom
Leading your people and my people and all people
To that better day
That better world
That better time.

The Lion in Daniel's Den

(for Paul Robeson, Sr.)

BY NIKKI GIOVANNI

on the road to damascus
to slay the christians
saul saw the light
and was blinded by that light
and looked into the Darkness
and embraced that Darkness
and saul arose from the great white way
saying "I Am Paul
who would slay you
but I saw the Darkness
and I am that Darkness"
then he raised his voice
singing red black and green songs
saying "I am the lion
in daniel's den
I am the lion thrown to slaughter"

do not fear the lion
for he is us
and we are all
in daniel's den

To Paul Robeson

BY NAZIM HIKMET

They don't let us sing our songs, Robeson,
Eagle singer, Negro brother,
They don't want us to sing our songs.

They are scared, Robeson,
Scared of the dawn and of seeing
Scared of hearing and touching.
They are scared of loving
The way our Ferhat* loved.
(Surely you too have a Ferhat, Robeson,
What is his name?)

They are scared of the seed, the earth
The running water and the memory of a friend's hand
Asking no discount, no commission, no interest
A hand which has never paused like a bird in their hands.

They are scared, Negro brother,
Our songs scare them, Robeson.

---

* A legendary Turkish lover, like Romeo or Tristan.

Suite of the Singing Mountain: For Paul Robeson (A Blues/Jazz Cantata)

BY ANTAR SUDAN KATARA MBERI

> Erect as the sun at high noon, you rise
> like a mountain

Sun and mountain, ray and stone:
your name forever dances
on the Pyramids pinnacles
with the precision of mountain goats,

Erect as the sun at high noon,
you rise like a mountain,
through the smog crouched in executive quarters.

You can never fall,
from the seasons grace,
not one thousandth part of an inch,
you can never fall
from us.

Your name is the gutteral chant
of the chanter chanting in the dawn,
the gutteral hymn spun out
in the autumn's threadlike whispering.

Your name is Mount Robeson,
the spring's nuptial rain,
the river's vast blood:
the Mississippi and the Don,
the Missouri and the river Niger,

the Shenandoah and the Volga,
the Hudson and the Yantzse,
the Ohio and the Thames,

You are the Blue and White Nile,
the Red and Black Seas, the Hocking
and the Zambesi,
flowing in song and strength
like the Gulf of Mejico,
through the rugged proletarian veins
                              of the earth.

Conch horn of assegai desire
trembling in the mountain's ferruginous throat,
your martial songs touch the lips
of the continents of young children,
our children, from Harlem to Tashkent to South
Africa to Ireland to Chile,
in every country, your seminal horn bellows
like a sea bull and drums the earth
with hooves of a volcano, erupting
and our children grow strong, erect
as the sun's zenith.

Your vows are the green suit
the grass and sea put on
with the dew's gaelic arrival.

Your deeds are the rare stones
fashioned by the oyster's proletarian heart:
                              the sun's
black kiss trapped in the pearl's breast.

You strike the stars and thunder
mounts its buffalo stallion, and armored
goes galloping heavily across cobblestones of clouds.

You throw back your mountainous head,

and your laughter lifts the night from the gutter,
and causes light to spill over like sperm.

You storm, your anger deeper than the memory
and the lightning dresses in yellow
carnations, and goes off following the rain.

Like sunshine breaking through clouds
you fling and fling and fling to the earth
your warmth and songs like apple seeds,
like nuptial rice, the naked kernels of corn,
and earth always gives back
flowers and petals
                    pure as a mother's pregnant dimensions.

You are the impregnable hour,
the second hand spinning out terrestrial time,
like the spider and the bee sewing the earth
into one web of honey.

And if I should suddenly begin weeping
tears of fire,
forgive me nothing,
for my heart breaks upon the temporal blade
of your unknown tombstone,
upon the blade of ashbone buried in the wind, in the earth,
the blade of grass and trees
that wears your name,
poised in defense of the future.

Go on Mount Robeson, go on
Himalayas, go on
Kilimanjaro, go on
Rockies, Andes, Alps, go on
Urals, go on
singing *Deep River*
          I want to cross over
          into camp ground.

for we've saved the highest place for you,
we've saved the lunar bird's solar lineage,
the planets turning eternally
beneath the universe's plow

for you

we've saved the molten metal,
the carnation and the ruby's red eye,
the emerald syllables of spring
that nature tutors the planet with

for you

we've saved the highest place
for you, for you
to go stepping like the rising sun
across mesa, mountain and plain, city and cave,
for you to go climbing the ancient stairs
of blood and stars.

Ode to Paul Robeson *

BY PABLO NERUDA

Once he did not exist.
But his voice was there, waiting.

Light parted from darkness,
day from night,
earth from the primal waters.

And the voice of Paul Robeson
was divided from the silence.

The darkness struggled to hold on.
Underneath roots were growing.
Blind plants fought to know the light.
The sun trembled.
The water was a dumb mouth.
Slowly the animals changed their shapes,
slowly adapting themselves to the wind
and to the rain.

Ever
since then
you have been the voice of man,
the song of the germinating earth,
the river and the movement of nature.

The cataract unleashed its endless thunder
upon your heart,
as if a river fell

---

* Translated by Jill Booty.

upon a rock,
and the rock sang
with the voice of all the silent
until all things, all people
lifted their blood to the light
in your voice,
and earth and sky, fire and darkness and water
rose up with your song.

But later
the earth was darkened again.
Fear, war,
pain
put out the green flame,
the fire of the rose.

And over the cities
a terrible dust fell,
the ashes of the slaughtered.
They went into the ovens
with numbers on their brows,
hairless,
men, women,
old, young,
gathered
in Poland, the Ukraine, Amsterdam, Prague.

Again
the cities grieved
and silence was great,
hard
as a tombstone
upon a living heart,
as a dead hand
on a child's voice.

Then
Paul Robeson,
you sang.

Again
over the earth was heard
the potent voice
of the water
over the fire;
the solemn, unhurried, raw, pure
voice of the earth
reminding us that we were still men,
that we shared the sorrow and the hope.
Your voice
set us apart from the crime.
Once more the light
parted
from the darkness.

Then
silence fell on Hiroshima.
Total silence.
Nothing
was left:
not one mistaken bird
to sing on an empty window,
not one mother with a wailing child,
not a single echo of a factory,
not a cry from a dying violin.
Nothing.
The silence of death fell from the sky.

And again,
father,
brother,
voice of man
in his resurrection,
in hope
resounding
from the depths,
Paul,
you sang.

Again
your river of a heart
was deeper,
was wider
than the silence.

It would be small praise
if I crowned you king
only of the Negro voice,
great only among your race,
among your beautiful flock
of music and ivory,
as though you only sang for the dark children
shackled by cruel masters.

No,
Paul Robeson,
you sang with Lincoln,
covering the sky with your holy voice,
not only for Negroes,
for the poor Negroes,
but for the poor,
whites,
Indians,
for all peoples.

You,
Paul Robeson,
were not silent
when Pedro or Juan
was put out into the street,
with his furniture,
in the rain.
Or when the fanatics of the millennium
sacrificed with fire
the double heart
of their fiery victims,
as when

in Chile
wheat grows on volcanic land.
You never stopped singing.
Man fell and you raised him up.
Sometimes
You were a subterranean river,
something
that bore
the merest glimmer of light
in the darkness,
the last sword
of dying honour,
the last wounded fork of lightning,
the inextinguishable thunder.

You,
Paul Robeson,
defend man's bread,
honour,
fight,
hope.
Light of man,
child of the sun,
our sun,
sun of the American suburb
and of the red snows
of the Andes:
you guard our light.

Sing,
comrade,
sing
brother of the earth,
sing,
good father of fire,
sing for us all,
for those who live by fishing,
by hammering nails with battered hammers,

spinning cruel threads of silk,
pounding paper pulp,
printing.
Sing for all those sleepless in prisons,
awake at midnight,
barely
human
beings,
trapped
between two tortures,
and for those who wrestle with the copper
twelve thousand feet up
in the barren solitude of the Andes.

Sing,
my friend,
never stop singing.
You broke the silence of the rivers
when they were dumb
because of the blood they carried.
Your voice speaks through them.
Sing:
your voice unites
many men who never knew each other.
Now,
far away
in the Urals,
and in the lost Patagonian snow,
you,
singing,
pass over darkness,
distance,
sea,
waste land;
and the young stoker,
and the wandering hunter,
and the cowboy alone with his guitar
all listen.

And in his forgotten prison in Venezuela,
Jesús Faría,
the noble, the luminous,
heard the calm thunder
of your song.

Because you sing,
they know that the sea exists
and that the sea sings.

They know that the sea is free, wide and full of flowers
as your voice, my brother.

The sun is ours. The earth will be ours.
Tower of the sea, you will go on singing.

To Paul Robeson

BY EDWARD ROYCE

No colonialist is safe!
Imbedded
In the hearts
of millions —
Your freedom calls,
The heart rending
anguish—
For the oppressed,
Reverberates
With the fury of a volcano.

Until They Have Stopped

(Dedicated to Paul Robeson, Sr.)

BY SARAH E. WRIGHT

Until they have stopped glutting me with slop from
    the kitchen's garbage to make fat profit of me like a hog,
Until they have stopped slitting my throat like the defenseless
    animal's in the near-Christmas time killing for the Christmas
    feast,
Until they stop the knife which in my tenderest years
    I had learned to anticipate,
Until they stop the bloodletting, the blood purging, and the
    Joyful shouts over the slaughter for the feast—
Exultantly saying in many ways: She has borne enough pigs
    that will grow up to be hogs for the next year's feast,
Until they have stopped, my Mother of Christ,
I will not desist from saying, "No!"

Until they have stopped standard-branding me
    on the television and radio
With the junk of how a real he-man is one who prefers the
    blondest, less-gray-hair type of woman,
One who sails a speedboat going umpteen too-many fast
    miles an hour,
While smoking a famous name brand cancer-producing cigarette;
And a real she-woman is one who adores the sexual sell—loves
    nothing better than running a home with brainless effortless-
    ness
While indulging herself in a profusion of useless commodities
    And purring like a little tiger kitten,
Until they have stopped, my earth, my people,
I will not desist from saying, "No!"

Until they have stopped filling my lungs with tear gas in
    Alabama, U.S.A.
And vomiting gas in Vietnam—knowing that to rob a person
    of will is to rob them of life,
Until they have stopped disgracing the languages of the
    peoples of this globe
By calling these murderous attacks "humane"—and out-and-out
    war "deterrent activity,"
Until they have stopped this assault to my natural intelligence,
I will not desist from saying, "No!"

"No!" to the would-be destroyers of my mother's milk,
Full of earth and determination and broken fingernails—
Hurting to the quick from digging and groveling and
Making this and that do when she knew by the standards of her
    Christ
Nothing else would do except
A more equitable distribution of the wealth of this earth.
Until they stop the necessity of millions of mothers
All over this earth from having to feed children on
Fairy tales as a substitute for food,
Until they stop! I will not desist from saying, "No!"
For no fairy tale will do when the belly bleeds
    from the claws of hunger.
No fancy hair sprays will do when the body is aging
Or frightened from economic illnesses unattended.
Nothing will do but another borning of humanity,
A clean new day free of degrading wars,
Against the working people of this earth—
A tomorrow lit by the suns of peace
And the stars of constructive human achievement.
Nothing will do except the coming of a time for love
For the spirit of Paul Robeson—for the hallowed spirit
Of the great man Robeson—nothing but a time for love.

TRIBUTES IN PROSE

By Edward J. Bloustein *

We are here to pay homage to a great American; a man who through his worldwide acclaim brought esteem to our nation and our university. Today, after a period of neglect by this university of which I am ashamed, we return to Paul Robeson some small portion of that great honor he brought to us.

A scholar, he graduated from Rutgers College as class valedictorian; Paul Robeson is a man of intellect. *An athlete,* he won twelve varsity letters and achieved All-American status twice; Paul Robeson provides a model of physical grace, strength and prowess. That prowess, it is my hope, will soon be recognized by membership in the Football Hall of Fame. *An artist,* he established himself as one of the greatest American singers and actors of this century; Paul Robeson is universally acclaimed for his professional preeminence. *A voice of his people,* he spoke and lived black pride before it became politically acceptable in the white community; Paul Robeson is a model of black political activism.

Were this the full measure of the man, it would be sufficient reason for us to honor him. But, Paul Robeson is even more than this. He transcended his time, his race and his own person to join that select group of souls who speak for all humanity. Let me quote briefly from his book *Here I Stand.*

> But I *do* care—and deeply—about the America of the common people whom I have met across the land . . . the working men and women whose picket-lines I've joined, auto workers, seamen, cooks and stewards, furriers, miners, steel workers; and the foreign-born, the various nationality groups, the Jewish people with whom I have been especially close; and the middle-class progressives, the people of the arts and sciences, the students—all of that America

---

* Speech at the dedication of the Paul Robeson Campus Center at Newark-Rutgers, April 9, 1972.

of which I sang in the *Ballad for Americans,* "the Etceteras and the And-so-forths, that do the work."

Thus, crowning all else, Paul Robeson is a great humanist, a man who helps to bring us all together, helps us, amid differences in which we can and should take great pride, to find, nourish and glory in our common humanity.

Now, therefore, with pleasure and pride and by virtue of the authority vested in me by the Board of Governors of Rutgers, the State University, I declare this building the Paul Robeson Campus Center to stand for all time in honor of a man for all time.

By Brigitte Bogelsack

When Paul Robeson stayed for some months in 1963 in the German Democratic Republic to take some medical treatment, many old friends visited him who had known him during the time of their emigration in England or in the United States when the Nazis were in power.

Paul Robeson was ill. His friends in the GDR recognized that the lifelong struggle against racism and oppression, the fight for peace, freedom and equal rights had nearly consumed his physical strength.

They decided, as it is not possible in an imperialist country to preserve and to care for the works of a humanist and in the socialist sense progressive personality, to establish a PAUL ROBESON ARCHIVES at the GERMAN ACADEMY OF THE ARTS in Berlin. In the spring of 1964 well-known personalities in the political, scientific and artistic life of the GDR formed a Paul Robeson Committee and in the autumn of 1965 the Paul Robeson Archives began its work with the written authorization of the Robeson family.

What is being collected in our Archives are not only testimonials to his high art as actor and singer, but proofs of his fight for human rights as well. Thus the Archives contain recordings, tapes, books and biographies, his addresses and articles, photographs and films, correspondence and documents, newspaper articles, which appeared in many countries about his art and his fight, radio and television appearances, posters, program notes.

The important materials made it possible to arrange an extensive exhibition on the occasion of his seventieth birthday in 1968. The purpose of this exhibition was to present Paul Robeson's political development and his work, as well as his activities in the field of art, and to pay homage to the significant relation between his personality and his life and the international fight for peace, for friendship with all people, and against racism and fascism. Beyond this immediate aim, we tried through this exhibition to evoke in the visitors a feeling of common purpose with those who still had to fight for peace, freedom and equal rights.

This exhibition is divided into different sections which follow each other, without interruption. It consists of photographs and texts.

I. THE TWENTIES

Well-known student athlete
Brief activity as lawyer
Concerts and plays in the USA and England
Move to England

II. THE THIRTIES

Othello in England
Encounter with fascism in Germany
Travels through the USSR, comparisons with the USA, Africa
Struggles of the workers in England
Civil War in Spain
Proud Valley (Movie about and with Welsh Miners)

III. WAR YEARS (1939-45)

Return to the USA
Antifascist and civil rights struggles
For friendship between the USA and USSR
Work with the trade unions
"Ballad for Americans," Cantata
Othello in the USA

IV. POSTWAR YEARS (1945-49)

Fights against anti-communism and racism
Concerts for trade unions in Panama and Hawaii
Electoral struggles for the Progressive party (1948)
First World-Peace Congress in Paris (1949)

V. 1950-61

Boycott against Paul Robeson (1950-58)
Struggle for the passport

Solidarity for Paul Robeson in the entire world

Music theory and language studies

Celebrations of the 60th birthday in more than 30 countries

Return of the passport

Touring Europe and Asia (1958-61)

Othello in England

VI. PAUL ROBESON IN THE GDR—1960

Festivity arranged by the ND-Press (ND = "Neues Deutschland"—New Germany)

"Star of Friendship Among People" presented by Walter Ulbricht

Dr. H. C. (Honorary Ph.D.) awarded by Humboldt University in Berlin

Corresponding Member of the German Academy of Fine Arts at Berlin

Medal of Peace of the GDR

VII. PAUL ROBESON'S LEGACY: A REALITY IN THE GDR

Sections of the Constitution of the GDR, with photographic illustration

Photomontage by Heartfield: "United in the Struggle against the Enemies of Peace"

The Paul Robeson Exhibition has been shown in several large cities of the GDR. Many thousands of interested visitors have seen it and have learned more about this great son of the American people, who inspired millions the world over with his art and his readiness to fight for the rights of man.

Enthusiasm greeted the Paul Robeson Exhibition in the Soviet Union in November, 1970. It was opened first in Tashkent, where many of the visitors of the exhibition remembered Paul Robeson's stay in their city in 1958. He participated at that time as an honored guest of the Afro-Asian Film Festival, and gave a concert in the Pachtakor Stadium. A cordial friendship united him with the many Uzbekian people, who since the establishment of Soviet power had transformed their Republic from a half-feudal into a highly industrialized country. By means of intelligent irrigation they had awakened a steppe plagued by hunger into blooming life, and cultivated and harvested their enormous tea and cotton plantations with efficient machinery which they had produced in their own Republic.

While we were opening the Paul Robeson Exhibition in Tashkent, there happened to be also a group of American tourists there at the same time. We lived in the same hotel. One evening we invited the Americans to visit this exhibition of the life and work of a famous American. There were some rather long faces when they saw in faraway Tashkent an exhibition about their compatriot, produced by the German Academy of Fine Arts in the GDR.

In April, 1971, the Paul Robeson Committee initiated and organized a major conference on the topic: "Paul Robeson and the Fight of the Working Class and of the Afro-Americans of the USA Against Imperialism." The appreciation of Paul Robeson as the outstanding artist and fighter for the liberation of his people was the main note of the symposium. He understood in a unique manner how to use his inspiring art as a weapon in the fight for human rights, and to win with it millions of people for this fight. Artist and fighter are inseparable in his person.

By Lloyd L. Brown

The tallest tree in our forest has fallen. Along with the countless persons here and around the world who mourn his loss, I think Nature herself must feel that with the passing of Paul Robeson something uniquely wonderful has departed from the earth. Surely Nature must have smiled to see the arrival on this planet of the seventh and last child born to Maria Louisa Robeson and the Reverend William Drew Robeson in Princeton, New Jersey, on April 9, 1898.

Over the years, that cosmic smile of pleasure glistened on a myriad of faces as audiences were touched by the human grandeur of this Afro-American who stood before them like Shakespeare's noblest Roman: "The elements so mix'd in him that Nature might stand up and say to all the world: *This was a man!*"

Then too, there always glinted on those faces the tears he evoked by his overwhelming compassion, for as a London critic noted after Paul's first concert there: "He broke our hearts with beauty." The smiles and the tears alternated like the lines of the spiritual—first, the joyful triumph of "No more auction block for me," and next, the illimitable sadness of the refrain, "Many thousands gone."

Here tonight, there is no need for me to recount the fabulous achievements of Paul Robeson. Now that he is gone the media are telling in vivid detail much of the Robeson story. Now it is fit to print that he had a "magnificent voice . . . it spoke in dramatic power and in passion; it spoke of gentleness and the warmth of humankind," and indeed, "the voice of Paul Robeson enriched the culture from which it grew and the lives of all who heard it."

How true that is. But what about the millions of young people who never had the chance to hear that voice or see the man in person, on TV or in the movies? A whole generation must be

263

startled to learn now that such a person actually existed in their lifetime—a modern-day black American with the manifold talents of a Renaissance man! I can hear those young people exclaim in wonder, "Out of sight!" as they read about his all-around genius as athlete, scholar, singer, actor, linguist and freedom fighter; and perhaps their inquiring minds will seek to learn why Paul Robeson was literally kept out of their sight and out of their textbooks for all these years.

As we assemble here to bid a last farewell to our dear friend, let me tell you about an earlier farewell that was given to him when he was only twenty-one. When Paul, who had first won fame as "Robeson of Rutgers," graduated from that college, the local newspaper reported that the leading citizens of New Brunswick gave him a banquet "to express their regrets at the departure of one so well-loved and respected." Following the speeches of the various dignitaries, the account noted that "Mr. Robeson in reply said he hoped his life work would be a memorial to his father's training, and that his work was not for his own self but that he might help the race to a higher life."

Though he then had no idea where such a selfless mission would lead him, it was inevitable that this well-loved young man whom the Establishment then and later honored would someday become a target of its wrath. For how can one help to raise his people from oppression without coming into conflict with those who are determined to hold them down?

By following his father's ethical precepts, by practicing the doctrine of the brotherhood of man—that "oneness of mankind" Paul always spoke about—he became an impassioned advocate of social justice, with a special concern for black liberation at home and for colonial liberation abroad. Thus, to promote the cause of African freedom he founded in 1937 the Council on African Affairs where he was later joined by men like Dr. W. E. B. Du Bois and Alphaeus Hunton. But since African liberation was then deemed to be "communistic"—a charge still made by the white fascist rulers of South Africa and their American backers—the Council on African Affairs was suppressed by the federal government in 1955.

I remember one day during that period when I was working

with Paul in the building next door to this church (that was his brother's parsonage where Paul was then living), he called to my attention a quotation from Frederick Douglass. Himself a son of a former slave, Robeson greatly admired the ex-slave Douglass, and in a voice so filled with passion that I sat there transfixed, he read to me these words of Douglass concerning the oppression of his people in this land:

> What man can look upon this state of things without resolving to cast his influence with the elements which are to come down in ten-fold thunder and dash this state of things to atoms.

Then, speaking very slowly for emphasis, Robeson added, "Well, that's *exactly* how *I* feel!"

And later in his book *Here I Stand* Robeson wrote:

> When we criticize the treatment of Negroes in America and tell our fellow citizens at home and the peoples abroad what is wrong with our country, each of us can say with Frederick Douglass: "In doing this, I shall feel myself discharging the duty of a true patriot; for he is a lover of his country who rebukes and does not excuse its sins."

You see, Paul Robeson considered himself and men like his imprisoned Communist friend, our former City Councilman Benjamin J. Davis, Jr., to be following the best traditions of our country.

Only the serious breakdown of his health could sideline Robeson from his dedicated efforts to make a better world; and that happened in 1965 when he was forced to retire from public life. He wanted to live in complete seclusion and so he consistently declined to be interviewed. Last fall when the pressure for such interviews grew stronger as a result of the developing rediscovery of him by some of the media, I asked Robeson how he would explain his decision to preserve his total privacy.

"People should understand," he said, "that when I could be active I went here, there and everywhere. What I wanted to do, I did. What I wanted to say, I said. And now that ill health has compelled my retirement I have decided to let the record speak for itself. As far as my basic outlook is concerned, everybody should know that I am the same Paul Robeson, and the viewpoint that I express in my book *Here I Stand* has never changed."

Quite naturally, Robeson keenly regretted the fact that while he was the same man in spirit, he could no longer "bear the burden in the heat of the day." A song bird who can no longer sing, an eagle who can no longer soar, a Joshua too weak for any more battles—of course, there was for him that kind of sadness.

Who can doubt that the man who went to Spain in the thirties to sing for the antifascist troops would in the sixties have gone to Vietnam to sing for their liberation army? Indeed, knowing Paul's genius for languages, we can be sure that he would have sung their freedom songs in the purest Vietnamese. And Africa—so dear to his heart for all these years—how he would have welcomed the chance to stand with the liberation movements there!

But despite those regrets, this you should know: during the years of his illness Paul Robeson felt safe and secure in the bosom of his family. While his son, Paul Jr., devotedly took care of his affairs, Paul lived with his sister, Marion, in Philadelphia. All of us who knew and loved Paul Robeson should rejoice in knowing that throughout his last years he was sustained and comforted by the loving devotion of Marion. Just as in his boyhood Paul grew up in the sheltering love of his father, during his declining years—thanks to that miracle of love named Marion—he was able to find once again "a home in that rock."

Bless you, dear Marion, and may you find solace in knowing that though countless thousands admired and loved your brother, at the end only you were able to provide that balm of Gilead his soul required.

And for all of us who mourn along with her, and with Paul and Marilyn, and David and Susan, and the nieces and nephews, there is this comforting awareness: how fortunate we were to have had Paul Robeson walk the earth among us! As artist and man he was a prophetic vision of how wondrously beautiful the human race may yet become. Now he belongs to the future.

By Robert S. Browne

My earliest recollection of Paul Robeson is from news stories about him in the *Chicago Defender,* which I read avidly as a child growing up on Chicago's South Side in the late thirties and the forties. The stories were full of Robeson's views on Africa—views which described a different Africa from the one the movies and the white press described.

I sent for literature from his organization, the Council on African Affairs, and I devoured it avidly, for Robeson wrote and talked about the Africa which I wanted to believe. Thanks to him, I discovered Africa a full two decades ahead of most of my contemporaries.

In 1942, I was privileged to meet Robeson when he came to Champaign-Urbana to sing at the University of Illinois. Few of the black students could afford to buy tickets to the university's cultural events. However, after his performance Robeson met with a number of us at the Alpha house and I recall how his presence electrified us as had no one else's. He sang a few songs for us— spirituals, work songs, songs of other lands. He explained to us what some of the songs meant, what their origin was, and in so doing he taught us a great deal about the world and its people. During this period he was especially concerned with the fortunes of the allied nations, which were locked in mortal combat with Nazi Germany. We questioned him a good bit about the Soviet Union, about which we knew very little, and his insights certainly whetted our thirst for more information on this far-off and highly controversial nation. To the best of my then limited knowledge, he was the only black man who had ever been there and the society which he described excited my imagination and opened new vistas of thought for me.

I was to meet him on a couple of later occasions when he visited Chicago, for he usually stopped with the Hansberrys and Lorraine would invite a group of us over to see him. By this time he was being overtly persecuted by the federal government and his stirring bass voice had been banished from America's major concert halls. His admiration for the Soviet Union, which had been acceptable (grudgingly) to Washington during the brief wartime interlude, was clearly unacceptable in the cold-war climate of the fifties, but for us the validity of his anti-imperialist message was merely enhanced by the consternation he caused in Washington.

It must have been around 1951 when he came to Chicago and could find no auditorium in which he was permitted to perform. Undaunted by this, he scheduled the concert for Washington Park and a tremendous crowd turned out to hear him. In those days he had developed the habit of cupping one hand around his ear when he sang, and he often joined in the applause the audience gave him. His political message at that period was one exposing U.S. aggressiveness in the Korean War, and he predicted that if the U.S. were to attack the Soviet Union, black Americans would refuse to fight.

We should all be grateful that this giant, who like so many other great men found his thinking to be too far ahead of his people's, has lived to see his life's work vindicated and his name publicly restored to the position of eminence from which it never slipped in the minds of some of us. Thank you, Paul, for bringing me insights and perspectives that have meant so much to me in later life.

By Margaret Burroughs

I am thinking of Paul Robeson now and I am thinking of myself.
I am thinking that had it not been for Paul Robeson, for what he
is, for what he believed, for what he stood and fought for, for what
he sacrificed for, that I, myself, might not be, to a great degree,
what I am, how I am, stand, fight for or hold the beliefs that I
hold today. Perhaps I might not be imbued with certain ideals
which are tremendously important to me. I am filled with gratitude as I think of how Paul Robeson, this so humane human, this
beautiful man, this splendid son of the African peoples, this great
American inspired me and certainly countless untold others like
me. For years, Paul Robeson has been my barometer, a system of
checks and balances to measure how much my life, our lives, have
been involved with concern for people and the liberation of our
own black people, of oppressed peoples all over the world.

I am thinking back to the time when I was seventeen. That is
when my love affair with Paul Robeson began. And now I am remembering appreciatively my favorite Uncle Louis who presented
me with a ticket to hear Paul Robeson in concert at Orchestra
Hall, Chicago, Illinois. As an impressionable teenager, whose ho-
rizons were circumscribed by the black belt, as it was called in
those days, I was magically entranced by the artistry, the dignity,
the lucidity and the genius of the man. On that occasion, Paul
Robeson meteorically ascended and became a star in my sky, a
position he occupies today, and ever will.

I remember how, after the concert, the audience was invited to
attend a reception in honor of the singer and his family. It was
to be at the Appomattox Club on Grand Boulevard, later South
Parkway Avenue, now Dr. Martin Luther King Drive. I took the
number three bus and got off at 35th Street. I wanted to get a
close look at this magnificent black artist. I remember how frightened and insignificant I felt surrounded by so many elegant and

prominent people, both black and white. I was jostled along in the receiving line where I got a chance not only to shake Paul's hand but also those of his wife, Eslanda, his son Pauli, about eight years of age at that time, and his mother-in-law, Mrs. Goode. Paul shook my hand, me, an insignificant, awed and frightened black daughter of a worker, with just as much warmth, sincerity and interest as he did the furred and sequined fancily dressed dowagers of the black bourgeoisie. Then Paul spoke of his travels in faraway lands and how much he learned from other peoples and their cultures. Throughout it all, he exuded love and respect for people, especially the common people.

From that moment on I was and am, until now, as I have said, transformed by the Robeson magic. As a high school student, I began to read everything I could find about my idol. I collected his records and made it my business to be present whenever he was scheduled to appear in Chicago. Via the news, I followed his travels to distant lands. In fact, my first knowledge of the existence of socialism was gleaned from reading reports of Paul Robeson's travels in the USSR.

Whenever faced by grave and serious decisions, I would ask myself: What would Paul Robeson do or decide in this case? What would Paul Robeson think of this? What side of this question would Paul Robeson take? Whatever I concluded Paul would do, is what I did. Indirectly, his guidance and direction sustained me through the thirties and forties and steeled me to come unscathed through the inquisitions of the fifties.

I am remembering how during the early fifties, those years of seeming incipient fascism, I was, as many others, questioned concerning my beliefs. I was called down before a Committee of the Chicago Schools and interrogated and pilloried concerning my views, especially political. A key question was, "What do you think of Paul Robeson?" I answered, "Mr. Robeson is a great artist. I am proud that I belong to the same race of people as he." The inquisitors continued, "Don't you know he is supposed to be a communist sympathizer? Why he even sent his son to school in Russia." "I don't know what Mr. Robeson's sympathies are," I said, "all I know is that he is a great man and a great artist and I guess he has the right to send his son to school wherever he wishes." The intimidation of that committee or their veiled threats of separating me from my means of livelihood did not cause me to repudiate Paul Robeson. Now, almost twenty years later, my appreciation of the contribution of this great man, not only to American life and culture, but to the life and culture of the world, has not diminished one iota.

I am remembering the humility and the humanity of the man. When Paul played Othello in Chicago, along with some other admirers I was invited to have dinner with him at his hotel. I remember how nervous and frightened I was as we went up in the elevator. I could hardly believe that I would be in the close presence of the great Paul Robeson. And to sit down and have dinner with him to boot! As soon as we stepped from the elevator, the great man put me at ease when he said, "Come right on in and make yourself at home."

Now, I am remembering that many people today date the fight against institutionalized racism from the early sixties. I am wondering if such militant protests and demonstrations would ever have surfaced, if it had not been for the groundwork previously laid at great personal sacrifice by a Paul Robeson. At a time when many of today's most militant militants were in swaddling clothes, Paul Robeson ripped the cover off and exposed the racist establishment for what it was, is. And that establishment wreaked its vengeance upon him, by pulling down a curtain of silence and vilification. That is why two generations of black and white youth too, are not aware of Paul Robeson, surely the tallest tree in the forest.

On Paul's last several visits to Chicago when he sang and spoke to predominantly working people, safe in the heart of the black communities, I had the honor of being a sort of Girl Friday to him. The last time I heard him sing before his retirement was at Mandel Hall. With me at this concert was a very special guest, my seventy-five-year-old Uncle Louis, who had gifted me with my first Paul Robeson concert ticket twenty years before, the one which transformed my life and that of so many others.

By Alice Childress

There are bits and pieces of scattered time, fragmented odds and ends of sight and sound which, fitted together, make a revelation. A large, gaping hole in the earth on 125th Street, in Harlem, is disturbing . . . far beyond the question of whether we do or do not need a New York State Building on that site. I feel troubled when I pass that place where an entire block was razed, a block of Afro-American businesses, boot-strappers all.

Paul Robeson's newspaper *Freedom,* was once located nearby at 53 West 125th Street. The year I'm remembering is 1951. The same address housed The Council On African Affairs, with offices occupied by Dr. Alphaeus Hunton and Dr. W. E. B. Du Bois. Louis Burnham was the editor of *Freedom* and served it with understanding dedication. John Gray frequently dropped in and contributed his services of organization and fund raising. Robeson was seldom able to enter the building without stopping outside to have a chat with some of the people who lived or worked on that block. Even Harlemites just passing by were not shy about talking to him. Attitudes, more than words, conveyed brotherly and sisterly feelings toward him.

"Hey there, excuse me, Mr. Robeson, I just wanta say I'm in agreement with you and would like to take this opportunity to shake your hand."

I see Paul taking visitors to the offices of Du Bois and Hunton, laughing and chatting, greeting and well-wishing . . . followed by deep and earnest conversation about Africa, and at a time when too many of us thought it strange that some of us found so much identification with that continent. Lorraine Hansberry typing a paper for Robeson. Actors and writers and musicians dropping in because . . . "I want to ask Paul something." If Paul was there . . . never a refusal.

Remembering Eslanda Robeson bringing in the works of young artists, introducing them to the editor, asking him to give

272

them an opportunity to present their talents in *Freedom*. Paul and Essie welcoming people from all over the country, from every part of the world, showing them through the narrow rooms of that small publishing house named *Freedom* . . . after the first black newspaper, *Freedom's Journal*.

Remembering the many times Paul told us how much he enjoyed going to the quiet of a closed room and playing his collection of foreign language tapes and records.

> Well, now, there is nothing more beautiful than the sounds and inflections, the musical scales and tones found in the many languages spoken by the human race. I can spend hour after hour listening and comparing, for example, the Chinese and African tongues in which inflection changes the meaning of the word. Language is music, rich music. . . .

And then Paul demonstrating in Mandarin, Swahili and Krio.

Recently passing through 125th Street . . . I thought of Dr. Du Bois sitting in his office and making out his plan for writing a dream into a reality . . . *The Encyclopaedia Africana* . . . of Paul and Eslanda Robeson fighting the good fight for freedom.

All over New York City we see bronze tablets announcing who slept where and did what, etc. In Harlem bronze signs are scarcer . . . and landmarks are fast disappearing. We can find the Jumel Mansion, Audubon's former residence, the home of Alexander Hamilton, where George Washington fought the British, etc. But where did Du Bois live and work? Where is Garvey's former place of residence in Harlem? Where was the first office of Marcus Garvey's United Negro Improvement Association? Leadership is a unique quality, not to be found every day, and it should not be taken lightly, or taken away lightly. Perhaps when the New York State edifice is finished there will be room for dozens of bronze tablets to remind us of the varied and great examples of leadership which fought in many different ways against the evils of a white-supremacist society.

Happy Birthday, Paul Robeson! May you enjoy this April period of retirement and use many hours to study languages and music. You generously poured your time, artistry and political conviction into the liberation struggle. Your gift will remain with us.

By John Conyers *

Paul Robeson stands as a monument to the capacity of the human spirit to achieve excellence in the face of adversity. His talent and courage fused to manifest personal greatness despite the conditions under which he lived. Mr. Robeson gave of himself, whether on the concert stage or the picket line. He sang, struggled, suffered and died for the cause of human dignity. We could ask no more of him.

---

* From Tribute to Paul Robeson held in the U.S. House of Representatives on January 28, 1976.

By George W. Crockett *

We join to pay tribute tonight to the greatest American of us all: Paul Robeson.

His voice, his talent, his genius, all are part of the magnificent heritage left to us and to the world despite the brutal and desperate efforts to silence that voice, to stifle that talent and to bury that genius.

They would erase the legacy of Paul Robeson. They would forget his works, obliterate his gifts and expunge his thoughts. They would still his sounds and cloak his name and his greatness in a suffocating miasma of empty nothing. They would make of him, as they have tried to make of so many others, an invisible man.

But kings will not be dethroned by fools. Giants will not be toppled by pygmies. And the people's heroes will survive even the mightiest onslaughts of the mightiest imperialists. Along with Frederick Douglass and W. E. B. Du Bois, Paul Robeson is one of the greatest of these people's heroes.

His life is an inspiration—one without parallel today. He has confidence in the people. He is fully committed to the fight against the evils of war, poverty and racism. His loyalties and his friendships are inviolable. And he believes in America.

There would come to pass in the years following World War II that the forces of reaction would mount an ever increasing and brutally vicious attack upon the loyalty and the Americanism of Paul Robeson. And those forces would, for a cruel moment in history, prevail.

Those like Thomas E. Dewey, governor of New York, who tried to prosecute the victims of vicious stormtrooper assaults

* This speech was delivered at *Freedomways* Annual W.E.B. Du Bois Cultural Evening honoring Paul Robeson on February 16, 1973 at Carnegie Hall, New York City.

against the peaceful Robeson concert-goers at Peekskill. Like J. Parnell Thomas of the Un-American Committee who led the fight in 1950 to revoke Robeson's passport and who himself was later tried, convicted and imprisoned for fraud. Like the stage, radio, movie and TV magnates who effectively blacked out the vibrant image and the glorious music of Robeson in their senseless rush to censor into oblivion all that was good and decent in the culture of our country.

Paul Robeson's Americanism will long outlive the lies and slanders of those evil men who feared the people. Because Paul Robeson was of the people. He worked with them, performed for them and fought for them. All of them, all over the world. "Especially the people, especially the people," he sang, "that's America to me."

In Africa, long before the inevitable drive toward self-determination and national independence, Paul Robeson was there to awaken the long suppressed desires for freedom, to ignite the sparks of self-realization and active resistance. Long before their names were known, he had talked to and become fast friends with Nkrumah, Azikiwe and Kenyatta, names which would soon become synonyms for African liberation.

Spain in 1938 was a major turning point in his life. "There," said Robeson, "I saw that it was the working men and women of Spain who were heroically giving 'their last full measure of devotion' to the cause of democracy in that bloody conflict, and that it was the upper class—the landed gentry, the bankers and the industrialists—who had unleashed the fascist beast against their own people." In Spain he sang with his whole heart and soul for the gallant fighters of the International Brigades, for the brave antifascist heroes of the Abraham Lincoln Battalion.

In China, India, the Soviet Union, even in the pre-Nazi Germany of 1932 Robeson traveled, acted and sang and everywhere he met with the people.

When the protectors and defenders of Americanism revoked his passport, even this did not succeed in stilling the Robeson voice in other lands. By international telephone he performed in concert to the coal miners of Wales, to the textile workers of Manchester, England, and to many people in many other lands. Prohibited from fulfilling an invitation to attend the Canadian convention of Mine, Mill and Smelter Workers, he sang to 30,000 Canadians who came to the border between the State of Washington and the Province of British Columbia.

To tell of the achievements, the successes and the experiences of Paul Robeson would be to relate the history of most of the first half of this century, and for all of this there is too little time.

What I would like most to tell about Paul Robeson is about his humanity, his warmth and his love for people—especially little people.

I remember that day in 1948 when Paul came to Detroit to sing to the workers of the Rouge plant of the Ford Motor Company. Local 600 of the United Auto Workers had sent an honor guard to accompany me to the airport to pick up Paul. I was to bring him to our home for Sunday breakfast, which my wife had prepared for six people. But the honor guard consisted of thirty UAW members. And no sooner did the neighbors learn via an instant grapevine that Paul Robeson was our guest than the crowds began to swarm into our home. My wife did herself proud. She prepared breakfast for at least forty—until everything ran out, eggs, toast and all. At the height of the noise, the crowd and the confusion, I had lost track of our honored guest. I ran thru the house, then outside. There on the porch I found him, surrounded by at least a dozen kids, with Paul sitting on the floor, two on his lap and all of them wide-eyed, excited and enthralled with the man and his love.

Love for people, a passion for justice and a yearning for freedom. That is the Paul Robeson that no power on earth can conceal.

Without the punishing persecution to which he was subjected, I have a feeling Paul Robeson would be here with us tonight. With us he would share our hatred and our rejection of the values and the violence and the greed and the bitterness which have given support in our country to the wickedness of war, of racism and of poverty. He would be in the front ranks of the fighters for peace, for equality and for decency.

How tragic for this present generation of our youth to be denied his participation in their lives! Not only the magnificence of his art, but also the genius of his mind—and for black youth in particular. What a model for this and every generation to aspire to!

I have had the great good fortune to know that genius and to want to emulate that model. But of all the superlatives we can justifiably bestow, I would point first to his loyalty . . . loyalty to principle, to justice and to friends.

At the Foley Square Trial of 1949, eleven Communists were to be tried and jailed for their beliefs. To appear to be on the side of the defendants was to invite suspicion, calumny and often legal persecution. But one of those on trial was Ben Davis, and Paul Robeson was a friend of Ben Davis. So Paul Robeson put it all on the line—his economic security, his safety, his career. Without hesitation or equivocation, in those darkest days when the very right to think was itself on trial, Paul Robeson gave definition to the meaning of friendship. As his lawyer, I met frequently with Ben Davis to prepare our defense, and in several of those meetings Paul was there. His testimony, like the testimony of many other unimpeachable and courageous witnesses for the defense, was ruled out by the judge. But his help, his support and his loyalty were a rock of faith that we all leaned on throughout that terrible trial. Paul Robeson stood up tall and proud, not only for his friend, but for truth, for honor and for an end to McCarthyism in America.

But history does not apologize for its unspeakable crimes, nor does it make amends for its mindless cruelties. It is for us, the inheritors, to inscribe in the pages of history for all to see the full truth of the full meaning of Paul Robeson. Robeson—the inspiration for the now generation. Robeson—the extraordinary artist. Robeson—the revolutionary.

Yes, a revolutionary in the true sense of the word. He was appalled by the status quo. He exposed the sins of our times. He struggled for change. He gave his boundless energies and his superb gifts freely, but most of all to those who were fighting for change—to the unions, to the antifascists, to the youth and to the struggle for black power. May his revolutionary fervor live on!

Each of us, in our own life, in our own heart, in our own yearning has a special place and a special gratitude for the man we honor tonight. I know what the richness of his presence has meant to me. I know hundreds of people in the city in which I live who remember, who are grateful to him, and who love him.

"To be free," he said, "to walk the good American earth as equal citizens, to live without fear, to enjoy the fruits of our toil, to give our children every opportunity in life—that dream which we have held so long in our hearts is today the destiny that we hold in our hands."

Paul, that dream we share with you tonight. That destiny is our commitment.

By Tom Dent

I remember meeting Paul Robeson when I was very young. He had come to New Orleans to do a concert and was staying at Dillard. I remember him then as a massive, physically impressive man (from my vantage point), huge, dark and imposing, yet kindly and strangely reflective. At that time he was a world-famous singer, a great hero of our race, and we were deeply honored to have him visit our home. But at that age I was more impressed by the fact that Robeson had been a football star, the third great black All-American. Someone steered him out to the athletic field where the Dillard football team was practicing, and it wasn't long before Robeson was throwing and catching passes and drawing a large crowd of admiring students. Ah, that was an exciting day.

That was a time of undisputed racial heroes (everyone seems more controversial now), at the time of the "talented tenth," those few black folk whose accomplishments were accepted and acclaimed by white America, in fact the entire Western world. Joe Louis, Marian Anderson, Roland Hayes, Charles Drew, Jesse Owens, Percy Julian, Bill Hastie, Robeson. Later Jackie Robinson, Ralph Bunche and Leontyne Price would join this group.

Think what an *interesting* collection of heroes. (Calvin Hernton once asked, "Why is it we have only one Marian Anderson when I find singers just as talented in the Baptist church choirs all over the South?") Great people, but most or all were acclaimed for accomplishments in areas white Americans thought laudable, like performing European music, athletics, law, medicine. The theory of "overcoming" was current then, black people overcoming barriers and handicaps, as if we were afflicted with some sad and unfortunate disease that only the truly talented could transcend. And then too, wasn't it *wonderful* that America was such a great country that even the ("yes, the NEGRO in our melting pot too") black man could find success and happiness if he worked hard enough, if he was talented enough, and if he said the right things (or at any rate, didn't say the wrong things).

Others, like Du Bois, Richard Wright—well, we weren't so sure about them. We were told America was the "land of opportunity" and they weren't sure about that at all. Still others—Leadbelly, Count Basie, Langston Hughes, well really they weren't that important; they were "race" artists, and one had to be "universal" to be a Negro hero in white America.

And then Robeson opted out. To us in the South, to those of us becoming of age, attending the southern black college, being encouraged, exhorted to "make it," to make "successes" of ourselves, to "prepare for integration by being well-prepared," to us in those days Robeson became a figure who made us think (some of us) about what we were doing like no one else of that time. The charge "Communist" was bandied around; we didn't know what it meant; we knew it sounded terrible. Our teachers were dumbfounded. Why would a man turn his back on all that hero worship to say America was *not* a land of opportunity but rampant with racism and economic exploitation, why would a man say that America would never achieve its promise unless it treated the black man fairly, why would a man say that the black man, so busily striving to belong, should not lay his life down any longer in foreign wars for a country that considered his life worthless at home? He was upsetting the apple-cart. And just when our teachers thought we were in.

We, in our youth, did not know if Robeson was a Communist, but we knew that he didn't have to be a Communist to know, certainly as a black man, that there was something sick about America that any honest man, black or white, ought to speak out against. Not necessarily brave, brilliant, militant, Marxist: just honest. Like, babe, ride the bus. And if you can't do that look out the window.

And we knew that *any* black man, particularly in the South, who spoke out against racism and oppression was branded a "Communist" by southern politicians. That's how they stayed in office. To be an outspoken opponent of racism in the South was to accept that you would be labeled a Communist. Which was the final insult on top of the lynching: the black man didn't have sense enough to protest being beat in the head and murdered on his own, he had to be *seduced* into protest by "foreign commies" from Russia.

Robeson returned once more to New Orleans in the years after Peekskill for a concert which I believe was his last in this city. I was away at that time but my mother attended. When I asked her about the concert she said, "Well, he didn't sing much. He spoke most of the time. He talked about America, about the way our people are treated, about the need for peace with Russia, about American imperialism." She thought it was an unusual concert, but beautiful. "He talked very informally," she said.

The change in American public opinion toward Paul Robeson once he began to speak out for freedom and equality gave us an unforgettable insight into how black heroes of that time were made, and who controlled them. If Robeson said that black boys would not fight for a racist America Jackie Robinson was hauled before Congress to assure white America we were "all right." Suddenly Robeson wasn't a great singer, a great actor, a football star any longer. His concerts were boycotted, he couldn't get work. No more southern tours to sing for the black people who had so recently loved him, exalted him, flocked around him as a source of black strength, talent and wisdom.

Yet in his decision to become more than an artist by enlisting his body and mind in the fight for freedom of our people against oppression, Robeson became a prophet of the Black Arts Movement of the sixties and seventies. A prophet because it is this very concept of the black artist as community mover-builder in a *political as well as cultural sense* that dominates our movement today.

John O'Neal once wrote that he was surprised how many people in the southern civil rights movement considered themselves poets. Out of this potential could come something like the Free Southern Theater, a conscious effort to merge the black cultural with the fight for political freedom.

In New York black actors, musicians, painters, dancers can pursue their careers as "careers," but in the South we have learned that this sort of isolated ambition makes no sense. We must work toward the building of the community; the artist has as much obligation to join the fight against racism as anyone else. Both are sides of the same coin.

And this is the legacy of Robeson's lesson. That any success achieved at the expense of our people or at the cost of ignoring our condition in America is worthless. That the black artist cannot isolate himself in an Ellisonian cocoon, no matter how important he thinks his work is. That it is senseless to talk about black artistic development unless we have a concomitant community development (and vice versa).

To the furtherance of these ideas and images Paul Robeson gave us the commitment of his life. He was far, far ahead of his time. For those of us working in the South today, we see him, in our mature vision, as an indelible source of black strength, black talent, black wisdom.

By Shirley Graham Du Bois

Paul Robeson—Tallest tree in the forest—"High as the Mountains," they said of him in Europe. And BIG! That big smile embracing everybody in sight—and beyond; the big Voice speaking or singing. All-American, unexcelled at a people's rally, on stage, or in the concert hall.

OUR PAUL!

I took a picture of Paul and W. E. B. at Stratford-on-Avon where we went to see him in *Othello*. He towers like a giant over my husband, but both of them stand so straight and gratified that their pride and joy in each other are caught by the camera.

I think of him leaning on the mantel of our sitting room in Grace Court, looking up at the painting of Frederick Douglass; W. E. B. stretched out on his lounging chair before the fire and both of them talking. They loved to talk, to exchange ideas and experiences, to swap stories. And how they laughed together!

I remember that Sunday evening when he sang in London's famous St. Paul's Cathedral—his magnificent voice rising to the vaulted dome, reflected in the stained glass windows and resting upon the hushed crowd like a benediction.

I never heard Paul say that black is beautiful—he simply *lives* beautifully.

Paul Robeson—Symbol of Manhood, of Courage, of Loyalty to the Best, the Unbowed and Undefeated:

Paul Robeson—Beautiful!

                    With sincere gratitude for his being.

By Dick Gregory

Paul Robeson is a man so far ahead of his time. He personifies so well what I often say in college lectures across America—that the so-called "generation gap" is not based upon age but rather upon pure moral values and commitment. Those who find themselves at odds with the spirit of young people today are the older folks who try to trick the nation's young by repeating the same old lies and expecting youth to believe them. But Paul Robeson could walk onto any college campus in America and be the youngest person around because his morality and commitment would shine.

Paul Robeson is both a prototype and an inspiration to the new black attitude which is shared by the pure spirits in America today of all ages and colors. His life tells us all that a man does not have to buckle under and give in to an oppressive, racist, insane social and political system. Paul Robeson is truly a man and the system has never been able to alter, change or subdue his manhood.

Those who share the vision of a liberated society owe a great debt to Paul Robeson; for his life has embodied the reminder of Tom Paine, "what we obtain too cheap, we esteem too lightly." To stand up for the right demands courage and commitment and Paul Robeson has shown us that one man who truly possesses such qualities can expose evil and oppression for what they are.

What can I say to or about Paul Robeson? Only "Thanks, baby, for showing the rest of us how to be men and women." The system of oppression in America seems less invincible because of Brother Paul.

By J. Clinton Hoggard

Paul Robeson, singer, actor, peacemaker, human rights activist and minority peoples' friend, has joined the immortals.

Born in a parsonage, reared in a Christian family home, surrounded by culture and courage inherited from his mother and his father, Paul Robeson was fitted for the battle of life both physically and mentally.

Our family associations go back to 1904. In 1912 my father, now of sainted memory, was assigned to the pulpit in Westfield, N.J., where the late Reverend W. D. Robeson, father of Paul and four other children, had built the new edifice for the St. Luke A.M.E. Zion congregation. My father carried his bride, my mother, to the Westfield congregation while the Robeson family moved to Somerville, N.J., for the Reverend W. D. Robeson to pastor the St. Thomas A.M.E. Zion church.

It was here that Paul began to discover his singing ability as he sang with the church choir on Sundays. He also would be called upon to fill the pulpit from time to time as the health of his father began to deteriorate. While in high school at Somerville, N.J., he competed in an oratorical contest with professors from Rutgers University serving as judges. His forensic skill won him a scholarship to Rutgers which resulted from the persuasion of the late Dr. Charles S. Whitman, prominent head of the English Department at Rutgers. The hard road of life began. Encountering racial slurs, gridiron attacks, social ostracism and some campus exclusions, Paul tightened his belt and determined to achieve what his father had taught all of his children, to wit: excellence is the only rating a Robeson should have in scholarship, competition of athletic powers or cultural performances. This was evidenced by his election to the highest academic honor society in America, Phi Beta Kappa, in his junior year at a college where he could not live on campus in a dormitory.

Living in a residence on Morrell Street in New Brunswick, N.J., with Mrs. Cummings and family, Paul used his strong body in athletic engagement which led him to become a fifteen-letter man in four major sports—football, baseball, basketball and track.

Part of the social exclusion led him from "white" fraternities at Rutgers to initiation into the grand old original Greek letter fraternity among American Blacks at the Lincoln University chapter of Alpha Phi Alpha.

Paul Robeson, at the time of graduating from college, could rightfully say that he bore on his body marks of vengeance placed there because he tried to live as a person who was created by God with dignity and a potential for fulfilling life's dream. These battle scars did not deter him from pursuing studies of law at Columbia University.

After marriage to Eslanda Cardozo Goode in 1923, he launched into a career of drama. His acclaim was nationwide, then worldwide. Finding a climate for "being a person" in Europe sooner than he experienced being a free man in America, he began to use his platform of dramatic performances as a launching pad for crying out against the oppressors of race in the economic and political arenas of life.

As Paul saw more of the world and compared life in countries other than the United States, he invoked hostility, governmental vindictiveness which led to the lifting of his passport, and personal harassment during the McCarthy years which subjected him to inquisition and interrogations. But the course of his ex-slave father, who ran to freedom, spurred Paul on to no compromise with any man on the matter of conscience, human rights, civil rights or personal dignity. Ultimately, he was vindicated by the U.S. Passport Office which returned his passport under mandate from a ruling of the Supreme Court. This case set the precedent for the rights of citizens to travel at home or abroad without penalty being inflicted due to political persuasions contrary to the majority opinion.

Paul was denied the opportunity to sing in the Rutgers University Glee Club, the prestigious organization on Queens' campus. When I became the first black member of the Glee Club in the fall of 1934, Paul returned from Europe and gave a concert in Princeton, N.J. Several of the Rutgers' men attended the concert. When it was over, we went backstage to talk with Paul. He greeted us, remembered my family and asked how I was getting along "on the banks of the old Raritan." I told him of my activities, including membership in the university choir and Glee Club. He offered his massive hand to shake my puny hand which was almost lost in search of his and said, "Congratulations, Clinton, I never was able to make the Glee Club." I said, "Well, you can make a good living at concert singing now, but I had not better try." This reflected some change in the climate of Rutgers University from 1915 to 1934. Today, students have a center on campus named for Paul, and the President, Dr. Edward Bloustein, is active with Alpha men and college presidents seeking to have Paul enshrined in the Football Hall of Fame.

It seems right that this service of celebration of a great personality should be enacted within these consecrated walls of Mother A.M.E. Zion Church. His brother, Benjamin Congleton Robeson, pastored here from 1936 to 1963. For twenty-seven years the Robeson tradition of character, individualism and stalwart determination was manifest on Manhattan Island. I served as a student minister in this church in 1939 and 1940 while pursuing theological studies at Union Theological Seminary. This caused me to have even closer contact with the family. When Paul was in the U.S. he worshiped regularly in this sanctuary as a modest, humble, unobtrusive member. He did not enjoy being a celebrated personality when he came to worship. His brother carried the pastoral leadership of the congregation which was under a heavy mortgage responsibility. Many times, Paul gave his service to this church in the form of concerts which packed this building, and all proceeds went to the liquidation of the debt of $160,000 on the church and $40,000 on the organ, which occurred in 1945.

A freedom fighter belongs to rest in freedom's palace. This church, now in its eightieth year of continuous history, is the oldest black organization on Manhattan Island. It was the cradle for freedom's cause in the late eighteenth and nineteenth centuries when it broke from the John Street Methodist Church because of the indignities perpetrated against people of color in the name of Jesus. Harriet Tubman, Frederick Douglass and a host of bishops of the church have passed through these portals of Mother Zion Church as members of the local congregation and as members of the national church. Paul sang gloriously within these walls, "Freedom, freedom, freedom over me," and "Before I'd be a slave, I'd be buried in my grave and go home to my God and be free."

Since in one's patience, one possesses one's own soul, it can be truly said that Paul learned how to be patient in adversity. He lived a long active life until harassment began to take its toll on his physical frame; even so, he was comforted by words of long ago from his all-famous performance of *Othello:*

> Good name in man and woman, dear my lord,
> Is the immediate jewel of their souls:
> Who steals my purse steals trash; 'tis something, nothing;
> 'Twas mine, 'tis his, and has been slave to thousands;
> But he that filches from me my good name
> Robs me of that which not enriches him,
> And makes me poor indeed.

The legacy of a good name is bequeathed Paul, Jr. and his family; his sister, Mrs. Marion Forsythe, her daughter, the nieces, the nephews, the grandnieces, the grandnephews—keep it good for justice and freedom, for character and culture, for racial pride and religious commitment.

When Paul would close a concert before labor unions singing "Joe Hill," a song about a union organizer executed for an alleged murder, he would sing the final line as a challenge—"Don't mourn for me—organize!" Let me paraphrase it: "Don't mourn for me but live for freedom's cause during this Bicentennial of America and say to any and all who may urge you to leave America that 'Because our ancestors were slaves, and our people died to build this country, we are going to stay right here and have a part of it, just like you. And no fascist-minded people will drive us from it. Is that clear?' "

By Lena Horne *

In the last years of my father's life, I would often listen while his grandson, tape recorder spinning, would say, "Hey Granddad, talk about what it was like." It was thrilling as they argued and debated, and young Ted would say to me, "You know, Mama, Granddad really lays down some heavy stuff." And when young Ted would show up with some new "cultural crush" Big Ted would say, "The times may have changed, son, but it is still the same old hustle." And so late in my life I was learning about two beautiful black men's life experience, and I felt so blessed to belong to them.

You are honoring tonight the third great black hero of my life, Paul Robeson. I came to know him as a young woman, alone, trying to find myself, trying to know why I reacted to the outside world as I did, why my pride was so fierce and so bleak, and what had created this pride. Paul Robeson told me about my heritage, my grandmother, my forebears, about black people everywhere. He told me about my black self. He seemed to me to become the repository of the information that dictated my life style.

You, the Academy, say that you will keep and nourish all these things for the coming generation of young Blacks who will need this strength more than ever. I pray that this will be so. I therefore ask you to dedicate your honor to me as my salute to the greatness of Paul Robeson and the two other beautiful men in my life.

---

* Excerpts from speech by Lena Horne to the Black Academy of Arts and Letters in New York City, September 20, 1970.

By Mbiyu Koinange

Office of the President
Nairobi, Kenya

Dear Brother Paul Robeson,

His excellency Mzee Jomo Kenyatta and I often think of you, your worldwide contributions to humanity, to Africa, and to both of us in particular during our dark years of national struggle for independence.

You and your name will never be forgotten by us in Africa, let alone in the world.

With warmest regards, peace and brotherly love.

By John Lewis *

Ladies and gentlemen, I should say my fellow freedom fighters, let me begin by congratulating *Freedomways* and all of you tonight for having this affair to honor Paul Robeson at such a fitting moment in our history and its critical juncture in the Civil Rights Movement. For two generations of Americans, Paul Robeson represented the entire Negro people of this country. He was a spectacular hero who seemed to have been born lucky: first, an All-American football star, a Phi Beta Kappa scholar, and, in the twenties and thirties, an internationally famous actor and singer.

Paul Robeson was a tall, suave, handsome, rich man who was actually chosen to represent all America in a CBS production of "A Ballad for Americans." But then he began to emerge as not just America's favorite Negro artist. During his years of life and travel in London, he met African leaders in exile, such as Kenyatta and Nkrumah. He went to the Soviet Union. He began to speak for Negro rights—for human rights. He talked and listened to the representatives of the Communist party. He called for direct action to solve our problems at a time when it was not popular, even extremely "unfashionable." Some white people seemed to think that Paul Robeson betrayed them. Some began to say, "Now look, he's being ungrateful, look what we've done for you, and you've turned against us."

He also scared away the so-called responsible Negro leadership. Robeson was ostracized, unable to sing or travel. This man, who had made people happy throughout the world, and was everybody's favorite Negro, was soon a hated man. And then began years of persecution by Senator Eastland, and the House Un-American Activities Committee. Yet, Robeson didn't waver. For him, being a Negro meant no compromising of important prin-

---

* Speech at the *Freedomways* salute to Robeson, April 22, 1965.

ciples. It meant taking unpopular stands despite the opposition of the responsible Negro leadership and "white liberal" friends. He might have kept quiet as so many other Negro celebrities have done; he might have taken it easier, and kept his friends happy, but he couldn't. *Tonight, as we salute Paul Robeson, we salute more than a man, we salute a cause. We salute the dreams and aspirations and the hopes of an oppressed people whether they be in Selma, Alabama, in Jackson, Mississippi, or in Vietnam.*

In many ways, we of SNCC are Paul Robeson's spiritual children. We, too, have rejected gradualism and moderation. We, too, have called for nationwide protests and massive organizing of ordinary people. We, too, have met African leaders, and we, too, have made enemies of some of our erstwhile supporters. We, too, have been told to wait, "be patient," go slow, and be a little more moderate. We, too, have been accused of being radicals, and of "Communist influence" and for the same reasons as Robeson. Such accusations are inevitable when you speak out independently and radically. Such accusations are an attempt to discredit an organization by those who fear they can no longer control that group or pocket the revolution. They are part of a program to isolate one element in this great struggle, in this great revolution (in this case the Student Non-Violent Coordinating Committee), from the other respectable groups of our society. We recognize this program as such, and reject it as such. We will maintain our independence of any political party or influence, but this includes The Establishment also. Why and what was so dangerous about Paul Robeson? What is so dangerous about SNCC? It is our faith in the numberless poor and uneducated black people in the South, our belief they must be free and decide their own political destiny. This belief was manifested when we of SNCC helped to establish the Mississippi Freedom Democratic Party, which has now challenged the right of the five segregationist congressmen from Mississippi who were "elected" last fall, not by all of the people of Mississippi, but by a relatively *few* people. You will remember that sixty-eight delegates of the Mississippi Freedom Democratic Party came to Atlantic City last August to challenge the regular Democratic delegation. You may remember last January 4 when the right of the five Mississippi congressmen to be seated was challenged. And 149 other congressmen cast votes which indicated their support of that challenge. But many people do not know that the challenge has continued. Hundreds of sworn depositions have been taken in Mississippi supporting the Mississippi Freedom Democratic Party, and showing that Negroes are prevented from registering to vote in Mississippi by varied forms of intimidation, harassment, and discriminatory testing devices. These depositions are now being reviewed and soon they will go to a congressional subcommittee for consideration. That committee is scheduled to make a report to Congress this summer and a decision taken on whether or not to recommend that Congress aid the fight for representative government for all the people of that state. In the struggle for justice, freedom, fair play and human dignity, nothing is more important than this Mississippi challenge. And I urge all you people to support it in every way possible. I can think of no more fitting way to pay homage to Paul Robeson than by supporting the Mississippi Freedom Democratic Party and its challenge.

Meanwhile, we are continuing our program in the deep South —in Arkansas, in southwest Georgia, in Mississippi and Alabama. These are the programs organizing the people, the black oppressed people in the South, around the vote, freedom schools, community centers and public school boycotts for equal education. In Alabama we are now working in several new counties— all of them rural, all of them areas of great intimidation and harassment. In Lowndes County, for example, not a single Negro was registered to vote as of last month, but there are 12,000 Negroes and 3,000 whites living there. It was in Lowndes County that Mrs. Viola Liuzzo was shotgunned to death. And we know that the Klan is increasing its supply of arms there and elsewhere in the South. Alabama students are still being arrested by the hundreds. Whatever kind of voting bill is passed (and we hope it will be strong), whatever kind it is, we know that life ahead for the Negroes who seek to vote in Mississippi, Alabama, in southwest Georgia, and in Louisiana will be hard. We need a bill, a strong voting bill that will provide guarantees for "free elections" in the South. If our government can demand "free elections" in

Saigon, *we* can demand free elections in Selma, Alabama; Jackson, Mississippi and throughout this country! They tell us to be afraid of "Communist infiltration," that we are too radical, that we are irresponsible and "destructive." I think I know what Paul Robeson would have said to them—"No," he would say. And I would like to quote some of his words, from his book, *Here I Stand*. These words seem prophetic, when he said:

> We have the power to achieve our goal; what we, ourselves, do will be decisive. It is easy for the folks on the top to take a calm, philosophical view, to tell those who bear the burden to restrain themselves and wait for justice to come. And Lord knows, my people have been patient and long-suffering, but patience can wear out. The plain fact is that a great many Negroes are thinking in terms of *now,* and I maintain that the goal of "Equal Rights Now" can be achieved. I say that the Negro action can be decisive. I said that we ourselves have the power to end the terror and to win for ourselves peace and security throughout this land. We ask for nothing that is not ours by right, and here lies the great moral power of our demand. It is the admitted rightness of our claim which has earned for us the moral support of the majority of white America. We have the right, and above all, we have the duty to bring the strength and suppport of our entire community to defend our lives and property of each individual. Indeed, the war, itself, will move a hundred times quicker whenever it is apparent that the power of our numbers has been called forth. The time for pussyfooting is long gone. Positive direct action will develop in the grass roots and spread from community to community, and the building of that unity is a task which each of us can undertake wherever we are.

Mr. Robeson, we hope to honor you best by performing that task. Tonight we honor a man. Tonight we salute and honor a great cause which is personified in the person of Paul Robeson.

By George B. Murphy, Jr.

Great art ministers to the deepest, noblest feelings of love, beauty and the oneness of humanity.

In the ceaseless struggle of nations and peoples to develop everlastingly self-fulfilling lives, great art harmonizes, in diversity, the rich cultures of working people flowing from their struggles to harness and appropriate for themselves, the bountiful, life-giving resources of mother earth. The practitioners of great art in every age of world history have come to know and understand this through their immersion of themselves and their art in the struggles of the people.

That is why Paul Robeson is a great artist, who stands on the stage of world history, the greatest American artist of this century.

Robeson began his world travels back in 1922. Employing his brilliant mind and his linguistic talents in a diligent study of languages, he quickly learned the folk songs of many countries, songs that expressed the backbreaking toil of the workers, their love of life, their determination to have liberty, to enjoy the pursuit of happiness.

Wherever he traveled to sing, to act, to speak, to write, he continued to perfect and deepen his knowledge of languages, eagerly alert, with his marvelous ear, to catch the accent, the nuance, the tone, the rhythm, the beauty of speech patterns, as he talked with the peoples of many lands.

With these peoples he shared our spirituals, coming out of the hell of our slavery, our work songs, our love songs and our songs of struggle for freedom in these United States.

And these peoples, men, women and children; what riches they showered upon him; what strength they let flow into that huge frame, that mellifluous voice, just as his own black people here in America did for him, going back into his childhood as far as he could remember, and would continue to do for him throughout his long artistic career.

The universal appeal of folk music, sung in his magnificent baritone, became for him a universal language for unlocking the door to a world view of peoples, working peoples, and the history of their struggles for justice, freedom, dignity and peace.

He began to appreciate more fully the indivisibility of the centuries-long struggles of his black people in the United States, against death-dealing, racist tyranny and the freedom struggles of the peoples of Europe, Asia, Africa, Latin America and the Caribbean.

And with this new understanding came a deepened awareness and appreciation of the vital role of the artist in the struggle of workers, especially black workers, against American capitalist exploitation; in the struggles of the black people of South Africa and throughout that vast continent, to reclaim for themselves from the bloody hands of world imperialism the immense treasures of their earth.

Now he understood that we black people, Indian people, other minorities, and the poor whites living in the United States, the most powerful imperialist power on earth, are not alone in our struggle for freedom.

Now, it became clear that more than a billion and a half peoples living in socialist countries; and three quarters of the peoples on the planet Earth, black, brown, yellow and red, all engaged in a fight to the death to break the chains of imperialist greed, are indeed our brothers and sisters in the fight for a better life.

The American government utilized every weapon in its racial arsenal, under the banner of McCarthy anti-Communist hysteria, to silence the great Paul Robeson's voice, to keep him from speaking, singing, acting, here and abroad. Stripping him of his passport, the government of the United States denied him his right to practice his art abroad while closing every concert hall and theatre to him in this country.

Indeed, the government permitted his very life to be at stake at the hands of dehumanized white mobs, but for the strong, protective arms of black and white men and women, progressive trade unionists. The American Communist Party, then in the midst of its seventeen-year-long struggle for survival, against a government bent on its total destruction and with it the destruction of our nation's Bill of Rights, helped organize and participate in a mass people's movement in defense of the great artist.

The movement, involving labor, black people and other minorities, black and white youth, artists, writers and actors, found powerful support from peoples throughout the world, Europe, Asia, Africa, Latin America, and the island nations of the Caribbean area.

Now, once again, the reactionary racist forces, in and out of government, operating behind the backs of the American people, are attempting to erase the name of Paul Robeson, even while he lives, from music, the performing arts, theatre, film and sports; indeed, from every repository of America's cultural and literary history.

This must not be allowed to happen, nor will it. For the matchless integrity, courage and strength of this great artist, which defined his oneness with the struggles of his people and world humanity, and illumined his art, live on today. They live on in the national consciousness of black youth, expressed in their daily battles against racism, as a policy of government in every facet of American life.

The heritage of Robeson's strength and courage lives on in the national and world struggle now mounted, to free from prison the young, brilliant, black communist, Angela Davis, leaders of the Black Panther Party, and hundreds of black and white youth struggling against murder and repression at home, and the genocidal policy of our government against the heroic people of Indo-China, South Africa, North Korean and the Arab countries of the Middle East.

The black people of the deep South expressed their love in defense of Paul Robeson, in a stirring poem written and dedicated to the artist, in 1950, by the distinguished, Mississippi-born black actress, Beah Richards. These words from that poem speak loud and clear for us today:

> But, most of all your songs have
> taught me how to fight

To speak out, stand up for what
is right.
So now I say NO to those who
clasp unseemly silence
on your golden tongue,
who dare obscure the light
of life. . . .
Paul Robeson must speak
for Dan
for me
for us
Even yet. Today.

By Jawaharlal Nehru

I am happy to know that an All-India Committee has been formed under the distinguished chairmanship of Chief Justice Chagla, to celebrate the sixtieth birthday of Paul Robeson. This is an occasion which deserves celebration not only because Paul Robeson is one of the greatest artists of our generation, but also because he has represented and suffered for a cause which should be dear to all of us—the cause of human dignity.

The celebration of his birthday is, therefore, something more than a tribute to a great individual. It is also a tribute to that cause for which he has stood and suffered.

I send all my good wishes to Paul Robeson on this occasion and I trust that he will have many long years before him to enrich the world with his great art.

By William L. Patterson

We Charge Genocide, the Crime of Government Against the Negro People has never been surpassed as an indictment of those who control the reins of power save perhaps, that indictment against Nazi war criminals after their defeat in the Second World War. On that occasion, the murderous leaders of Hitler's Third Reich were condemned, tried, convicted and shot for the monstrous crimes committed, not only against the Jewish people, but against all humanity. Progressive mankind approved that historic step.

It was after the Nuremberg trial, the formulation of the Charter of the United Nations and the founding of that international forum that the monstrous crimes of the racists who rule affairs in the United States were spelt out at length. They were crimes against black nationals. But the racists of the USA remained in power after the fall of the Nazi murderers. They did not change the racist preachment and practices from which the Nazi butchers had learned so much. Both remained features of the "American-way-of-life."

The racists had split a multinational state along the color line, making for the easy exploitation of the white working and middle classes and all "colored" people. The dehumanizing effects of racist ideology and its practices of force and violence upon the masses of exploited whites are even more damaging than the degrading conditions of black ghetto life. The former failed to recognize that the masses of this country have a mutual enemy who is also the relentless foe of progressive mankind. It failed to understand that racism was a threat to the security of our national interests and the peace of the world. Many "left" intellectuals failed as well to recognize this fact. The myths of white superiority have blinded the eyes of millions of white Americans to the realities of the system under which they live.

We Charge Genocide was written to awaken its exploited and oppressed white masses and all those unconscious of the menace of racism. Racism had become a formidable weapon of war at home and abroad. The domestic victim is a "nigger," "greaser" and/or "spic." The foreign victim is a "kook"—"gook" and/or "chink." There was no court of jurisdiction to listen to the cries of the anguished victims of America's ruling class.

With the founding of the U.N. in San Francisco in 1945 the leadership of the Civil Rights Congress began an intensive study of its charter, covenants and conventions. It sought to determine what, if any, use might be made of the charter and its provisions in the national liberation struggles of Americans of color.

Paul Robeson was consulted. He was the most outstanding artist-revolutionary this country had produced. We sat down to analyze the charter. There were no illusions. No rulers of the USA had ever kept a commitment to mankind that included respect for progressive humanity or the dignity of man. It had made mockery of the Declaration of Independence and flouted those amendments to the Constitution which declared equality of rights and opportunities for all. The charter was signed by Edward Stettinius, a noted imperialist, and Senator Tom Connally of Texas, a well-known lynch advocate. Neither reflected the needs of the people or represented the people's interests. The spirit and the letter of the charter of the U.N. had been breached by American rulers when *We Charge Genocide* was written. Imperialism believed that it had been breached with impunity. But of the propaganda value of that indictment we had no doubt. The charter's "Convention for the Prevention and Punishment of Genocide" was a scathing indictment of the USA's rulers' attitude toward their "colored" nationals.

Paul Robeson was one of the first to sign the indictment. He gave thought and study to its contents. He led the delegation which carried this historic document to the secretariat of the U.N. while the general secretary of the CRC presented an identical petition to the delegates to the General Assembly in Paris, France.

Paul Robeson's action was unique. He was already a celebrated internationally known concert artist, a noted actor of stage and screen. His future was secure if he but stuck to his own affairs. But his concern was for the poor and oppressed of the world. He believed that there was security for none if not for all. Life had taught this lesson. Paul's experiences with segregation in the ghetto, his knowledge of the trials and tribulations of other citizens of color were lessons he could not forget. He made of his art a weapon for the people. He was ready to charge genocide against those who had butchered Filipinos in the Philippines, Cubans in Cuba and nationals of color in the USA.

He charged genocide. So too did the world of progressive mankind. The crime remains a policy of government. Vietnam reveals racism as an exportable crime; a people's court will one day try the guilty. It is even now in process of being created as more and more people take the cry into the streets. Those who charge genocide against the rulers of the USA will bring the criminals to book. Paul Robeson's name will be among them. It holds a special place among those who give priority to human freedom.

By Thelma Dale Perkins

I shall always remember and be most grateful to Paul and Eslanda Robeson for the joy and beauty they brought to our lives and for their enormous contributions to the fight for peace and human rights. Their unselfish devotion and tireless efforts were inspirational and decisive in helping to mobilize millions of people to fight against repression at home and for colonial liberation in Africa and throughout the world.

These two extraordinary people helped to build bridges of understanding among many divergent groups. These alliances led to unity and commitment in the fight against reaction in the form of an incipient but growing fascism in the United States, which was, at least for a moment in history, turned back.

I knew the Robesons best during the McCarthy years when Paul, denied the use of his passport, was literally a prisoner in the land of his birth and yet was barred from making a living on the concert stage and in the theatre. But they were also the years when the talents of both the Robesons were in great demand and were freely given by them to further the causes of peace, civil rights, African independence, American-Soviet friendship and many others too numerous to list. These were the years when the Robesons lived on Jumel Terrace in upper Manhattan where family and friends old and new were free to drop by for a chat—nor was an impromptu music session with Paul unusual. Although they were years of great frustration and often anger for Paul, I sensed that for Essie they were years of personal fulfillment. She was needed to make a home for Paul and to take care of him and support him in every way. In many ways they seemed closer than their independently busy lives had ever permitted them to be before. Despite her recurring illness and the serious medical treatments she was undergoing she seemed very happy in this all-encompassing responsibility of caring for Paul. In one of her columns in *Freedom,* Essie said that Paul had become a symbol and a challenge of freedom and peace in the world. She freely accepted the challenge to work with Paul, while at the same time carrying on her own pursuits as correspondent at the United Nations, fulfilling speaking engagements and maintaining a voluminous correspondence.

The day in August, 1953 that Essie appeared before the McCarthy Committee, my admiration for her soared even higher than ever and my understanding of her deepened immeasurably. Everyone including Essie knew that McCarthy was really after Paul. Even the mob violence such as had occurred at Peekskill in August, 1949 had not stopped hundreds of thousands of people from turning out to hear Robeson in churches, public parks and auditoriums in Negro areas.

Most people called before McCarthy's Committee were expected to be coerced into being informers or, if they did not "cooperate," then there was the threat of a contempt of Congress citation and usually a jail sentence or fine or both. For many this meant ruined reputations, loss of livelihood, dissolution of families and in some instances worse. Needless to say, while Essie was her usual jolly self, she did indeed take her appearance before the committee very seriously. I went to the hearing with considerable apprehension. Essie had competent legal assistance, but we knew that she was quite capable of becoming "independent" of her counsel and striking out on her own. Such action, of course, could mean legal entrapment and perhaps a contempt citation and all that could entail in time, expense and, perhaps, jail.

Well, it was a beautiful day. Essie did strike out on her own. In her exuberant way she had the committee counsel and McCarthy running to try to catch up with her. The more they pressed her about communism and Communists the more she pressed them about the Negro question and the enforcement of the Fifteenth Amendment and her second-class citizenship. Finally, in a burst of male-chauvinist pique, McCarthy dismissed her from the witness stand, saying if she had been a man and performed like that she would have been held in contempt!

In writing about her appearance in her husband's column in *Freedom* (September, 1953) she said, in part:

They kept on trying to change the subject, but I kept sticking to it and it soon became crystal clear that before any Committee starts yelling for first class loyalty and cooperation from me, they'd better get busy and put me and my Negro people in the First Class Department by making us First Class Citizens.

Some of our friends, Negro and white, wonder why we Paul Robesons don't just sit down and be quiet, make the big money and enjoy Paul's fabulous success, instead of raising so much sand about our constitutional rights as American citizens.

Well, it's all a question of what you mean by ENJOY. Personally, I wouldn't enjoy being dressed up in Paris gowns, mink coats and diamonds, and presiding over a gorgeous mansion, if any old un-American could come along and lynch or rape or kill me—as they tried to kill Paul at Peekskill—could bomb or dynamite me and my mansions, as they did to the Harry Moores in Florida and other Negroes in Alabama, Chicago, and other points North, East, South and West in these United States.

No, indeed, I'd rather be all dressed up and living in my Civil Rights. I would feel safe and very well dressed if I wore my first class citizenship; that would be much more stylish and becoming and comfortable than anything else any American could wear.

Because no other arrangements had been made, I was delighted to invite Essie to have dinner at my parents' home in Anacostia. On this day of triumph, I could not conceive of her going back home without some kind of celebration. That afternoon, Essie relaxed and enjoyed the visit with my parents and their neighbors as though she had known them all her life. And in reality she had, in a way. For they were like so many, many others who did support the Robesons and felt them to be symbols of courage in the fight for our rights, and were eager to have them know about that support.

The day was concluded as we stood on the front porch of the Frederick Douglass Home looking across the river to the Capitol where Essie had begun this eventful day. We talked of the comparisons between these two great sons of the Negro people: Frederick Douglass, who had experienced more than his share of hardships including the tyranny of slavery, and Paul Robeson, present-day symbol of his people's fight for equal rights. Douglass too had joined the fight against slavery with the fight to save the Union and for women's rights. As was true of Robeson and civil rights, Douglass took the cause of the abolition of slavery to England and Europe and made it an international question.

To know and understand the roles of Paul and Eslanda Robeson in this period should be instructive to our present younger generation in their search for identity. The Robesons, like Douglass and W. E. B. Du Bois and many others, are part of a long and proud heritage of Blacks who have lent their talents, their energies and sometimes their lives to the struggles for freedom. The social studies and history books touch only lightly if at all on what role the Robesons and other Blacks have played in the freedom struggles of this country and the world. Black and white children are led to believe, as a well-meaning friend said recently, that "Blacks have *finally* taken the initiative for their own freedom." That is not the fact. Not only have Blacks fought for their own freedom throughout history, but consistently they have been responsible in no small part for enabling our society now as in the past to enjoy human freedom to the relative measure it exists today.

By Paul Robeson, Jr.*

I cannot speak today of the full measure of the family's personal grief and overwhelming sense of loss. There are no words for that. My father's immense power and great gentleness, his intense spiritual force and great intellect, his unbending courage and his deep compassion have left each one of us with special memories that will always sustain us, for each was touched by him in a special way.

To me, his son, he gave not only his love but also the freedom and encouragement to think my own thoughts, to follow my own inner convictions, to be my own man. To all of us he gave, by example, a set of standards to guide our own lives, each of us in our own way.

But I speak today not only because I loved him as a father. I loved him as a friend and as a great and gentle warrior with whom I worked and fought side-by-side.

And so I come to speak of both the disappointments and the triumphs of Paul Robeson's last years—disappointment because illness forced him into complete retirement; triumph because he retired undefeated and unrepentant. He never regretted the stands he took, because almost forty years ago, in 1937, he made his basic choice. He said then:

> The artist must elect to fight for freedom or for slavery. I have made my choice. I had no alternative.

He knew the price he would have to pay and he paid it, unbowed and unflinching. He knew that he might have to give his life, so he was not surprised that he lost his professional career.

---

* The above speech was delivered at Paul Robeson's funeral on January 27, 1976, at the Mother A.M.E. Zion Church in Harlem. Despite a heavy rainfall, mourners filled the sanctuary and auditorium to capacity to pay respects to the great freedom fighter.

He was often called a Communist, but he always considered that name to be an honorable one.

Paul Robeson felt a deep responsibility to the people who loved him and to all those to whom he was a symbol. When *he* felt that he could no longer live up to their expectations, he chose to retire completely. When he could no longer raise his voice in song to inspire and to comfort, he chose silence; because Paul Robeson's views, his work, his artistry, his life, were all of one piece.

But there was also gratification in retirement. In my father's last public message in June 1974 he said:

> It has been most gratifying to me in retirement to observe that the new generation that has come along is vigorously outspoken for peace and liberation. . . . To all the young people, black and white, who are so passionately concerned with making a better world, and to all the old-timers who have been involved in that struggle, I say: Right on!

And there was the secure knowledge that his own people, who had protected him and nourished him during the days of the fiercest oppression against him, appreciated his sacrifice and respected his privacy.

The one person who did most to give my father some joy in his last years is my Aunt Marion. It is she who created a haven for him in Philadelphia and surrounded him with those close old friends who made him feel loved and at ease. And I will always remember what my father said about Aunt Marion: "The thought of Sis always brings an inner smile."

Many other Philadelphians, black and white, expressed their respect and admiration for my father. During my father's last illness, his personal doctor and the entire hospital staff cared for him as if he had been their own loved one. And the people from all walks of life wrote him letters of encouragement.

It is fitting that my father now comes home to Harlem and Mother Zion Church. Eighteen years ago he wrote:

> Not far away is the house where my Brother Ben lives: the parsonage of Mother A.M.E. Zion Church of which Ben—Reverend Benjamin C. Robeson—has been pastor for many years. My brother's love which enfolds me is a precious, living bond with

the man, now forty years dead, who more than anyone else influenced my life—my father, Reverend William Drew Robeson. It is not just that Ben is my older brother, but he reminds me so much of Pop that his house seems to glow with the pervading spirit of that other Reverend Robeson, my wonderful, beloved father.

Next door to the parsonage is the church where on Sunday mornings I am united with the fellowship of thousands of my people, singing with them their songs, feeling the warmth of their handshakes and smiles. . . .

Yes, I've got a home in that rock!

There are others here today, and some who have passed on, who were as close to my father as anyone in his family. There are people whose lives he enriched and who enriched his life in return. I reach out to them today to share with them the family's grief, for they will always be part of us.

My father's legacy belongs also to all those who decide to follow the principles by which he lived. It belongs to his own people and to other oppressed peoples everywhere. It belongs to those of us who knew him best and to the younger generation that will experience the joy of discovering him.

Yesterday, someone very dear to me was reading some poetry and was moved to write the following lines. They say a great deal about my father's legacy:

> He is not mine,
> I may give to him my love,
> But not my thoughts
> He passes by me,
> But he does not pass from me
> For although he was with me in some ways
>   and will stay with me in others,
> He does not belong to me.
>
> I may keep memories of him
>   but not his essence,
> For that will pour forth tomorrow.

By Pete Seeger

It was in the late 1930s: 20,000 crowded Madison Square Garden to protest the growing world menace of fascism. I was one more teenager in the upper tiers. There had been many speeches that evening, mostly by white people, some lecturing, some shouting and declaiming at ever higher pitch. Then this tall, broad-shouldered black man stepped up to the microphone.

"Good evening, friends." The voice was so low, so deep and resonant, it seemed to represent the whole vast mass of rank-and-file humanity. The entire auditorium responded with one big, warm and loving exhalation. This man represented us, all of us.

In subsequent years, hearing Robeson speak and sing at rallies, in concerts, I never failed to be amazed at the combination in one person of great strength, great tenderness and great intellectuality. In an individual any one of these qualities might be highly developed, but here were all three, kept in beautiful balance in one man.

He was the hero of my youth. Several million other young whites must have also felt so. When I was in the U.S. Army in World War II my wife wrote me a long description of the huge birthday party given him in New York City. After the encomiums, the ceremony, he sang, and some would have wanted him to sing all night, but others knew he had a hard schedule, playing six nights a week in *Othello,* and their admonition was picked up by thousands, "Save your voice, Paul!"

After the war I met him in person. I waited in line after a concert, knocked on his dressing-room door, and asked if he would be one of the sponsors of our fledgling organization, People's Songs. "Why, of course," he said with that broad smile. With all the other things on his mind he took time to help us, to advise us.

During the Henry Wallace campaign of 1948 I heard him speak many times, and saw how that combination of physical

311

strength with delicate tenderness was driven by extraordinary courage and honesty.

In Peekskill, September, 1949, ultra-rightists tried to kill him. I was a relatively unknown performer at the time, but was honored to be asked to sing a few songs on the first half of the program. After the great concert was over, the audience of thousands got into cars to drive home. The police (secretly in league with the KKK) stood at the gate, ordering all cars to turn right. Along that road were stationed men with waist-high piles of stones which they heaved at every car. Ten thousand car windows must have been smashed that day. When my wife and I got home we rinsed the broken glass out of the heads of our babies. Inside the car we found two rocks which had actually come through the glass. I later cemented them into our fireplace.

The rulers of America never dared put Robeson in jail—I'm sure because they feared international repercussions. But in the early fifties, every single concert hall was closed to him. Every "respectable" person and organization were running for cover. As Martin Luther King later said, "The ultimate tragedy is not the brutality of the bad people, but the silence of the good people." In 1954 the Oberlin College chapter of the NAACP told me, "We wanted Robeson to come and sing for us last year, but we were told by the National Office that they would revoke our charter if we did so."

If, if, if! If we had only fought harder for him. If Americans had seen through the Cold War lies quicker. If his health had only held out for another twenty years. No use. We only know that one of this country's greatest Cold War Crimes was the stopping of his voice, so it could not be heard by hundreds of millions.

Well, for me, Paul Robeson will live forever. His strength made us stronger; his artistry inspired us to be better artists. The day will come when the hard-working people of the world will put an end to class exploitation, an end to racism, and militarism, and poverty, and I am glad that this book will remind our sons and daughters how another step on Jacob's Ladder was brought closer and sooner by this tender giant of the twentieth century, Paul Robeson.

By Hope R. Stevens [*]

The assassins of Freedom have been trying for many years to erase the personality of one whose broad shoulders were squared to confront them. Your presence here in this vast assemblage gives evidence to the totality of their failure.

Man's history is literally a sequence of voices calling upon the masses of the people to provoke or to accept change in the way of human life. There have been calls to aggression and calls to defense; calls to battle and calls for peace; in one way or another the power of the voice has been used to inspire, influence, arouse, inflame or debase the spirit of man from before the dawn of history.

There are examples of many whose voices were raised in the cause of freedom of mind and body at the price of life itself—*Socrates, Jesus, Luther, L'Ouverture, John Brown, Robert Emmett, Gandhi*, to mention but a few.

The purpose of our presence here tonight is to pay tribute to one who has long since been called to his proper place in the Hall of Fame by the lovers of freedom and the fighters for peace and justice all over the world. His has been appropriately called democracy's most powerful voice. Nature endowed him with a magnificent talent, housed it in a massive, robust, rugged and most attractive frame; provided a winsome and congenial personality to go along with it; instilled in him a quality of courage in direct ratio to his enormous physique; and topped it off by saturating this extraordinary man with boundless love for his fellows and an uncompromising hatred of injustice and oppression in all their ugly forms. He, on his part, accepted these gifts as tools with which to work. He invested them, developed them,

---

[*] Speech at the *Freedomways* salute to Robeson, April 22, 1965.

applied them and continues to exhaust them. He has probably personally addressed, in speech and in song, without the aid of television, more people on the earth, than any other living human being. I am, of course, referring to Paul Robeson.

In the decade of the 1930s, the name and voice of Paul Robeson became synonymous with protest—for the working people it condemned injustice, long hours, low wages; for the black man it demanded equality, dignity and the end of segregated living and discrimination. Paul sang the songs of freedom, of love, of gaiety, of hope, with a new meaning for all oppressed and dispossessed people—but particularly for black people. The songs of protest and solace that the black people of America had composed and sung to noteless music for over three centuries, he dignified and glorified by presenting them with pride and confidence everywhere he went.

Trained as a lawyer, he decided early that the forum which the bar provided would be too narrow for his work. He wisely chose the stage instead. In the United States, he attempted to come to his own—his own received him not. So he went abroad. There he was accorded that measure of acceptance which made it possible for him to return to America to perform his most important task. And strive he did. All across our country, in the North and in the South—in the little churches and the large—in the field, stadium and concert hall—his message was boomed, "Go down Moses into Egypt land, tell old Pharaoh to let my people go." The ferment was already there—the leaven of revolt was swelling—he stirred it up wherever he went. The challenge was clear—his call was clarion.

Paul linked the struggle of black America with the struggles of black Africa, brown India, yellow Asia and the Blacks of Brazil and Haiti and the peons of Mexico and South America—all seeking justice and freedom from oppression, exploitation and degradation. This made him dangerous. He moved back and forth across the continents and oceans—a ubiquitous voice of freedom everywhere he passed. Then, against the oppressors of the Afro-American, he laid the charge of genocide of his people before the United Nations.

So there came a time when he had to be stopped—the political economic bosses of our society decided that he had gone too far—the name of Paul Robeson had come to be synonymous with exposure of harsh and embarrassing truths. First it was sought to put him behind bars. He refused to share his conscience and the privacy of his political convictions with the agents of the zealots. Then it was sought to immobilize him—this time with more success—without a passport he could not travel—indeed, he would not choose to do so. Lastly came the greatest and most effective blow of all, the consortium between government, industry, organized labor, the cultural media and the press, to destroy him as an artist—to cut the ground from under his feet—to deny him the stage and the forum in the hope that he would be silenced. A venial theatre, an opportunistic clergy and the jealous, insecure and cowardly leadership of the organizations of the black people, made it possible to curb through circumscription, the artistic, cultural and political work of Robeson, the freedom fighter.

The ever-rolling stream of time—that factor which evil men so often forget and ignore—has seen many of the changes come about for which Paul labored. Younger men and women have arisen to seize the torch of freedom and carry it many steps forward. The songs that Paul used as the vehicles for protest and incitement—that heritage of musical resources given to us by the myriad of those anonymous geniuses of our bondage, the poets, lyricists, composers, musicians and balladeers, known as the spirituals and gospel songs, have now become recognized as the spiritual weapons of struggle in America and have even been adopted as political slogans by the president of the United States.

How could all this have come about without Paul's work? To this question, of course, there is no answer. However, we have come here tonight to honor ourselves by reaffirming our limitless respect, deep affection, warm admiration and grateful homage for and to one who has indeed laid down his artistic and professional life for a cause to which he himself elected to dedicate it. For if ever a man placed himself on the altar of sacrifice for his people, that man was Paul Robeson. In the climate in which he refused to bend the knee to the tyrants of thought-control and paid the price therefore, others less rigid and less strong—in conformity or by compromise—went on to riches and approval.

It is to this man, this Robeson, that we extend our acclaim tonight, confident that history will set the record right—that after the names and the deeds of the pygmies who in their pomp and circumstance attempted to detract and to defame him, have long been forgotten—this moral giant of our time will live in the hearts of his people and of the fighters for freedom yet unborn and his voice can never be stilled.

His use of music as a bond of understanding with and between people led him to research that revealed the firm cultural ties existing between the Blacks of Brazil, those of the Caribbean in Trinidad, Martinique, Jamaica and Haiti, and the creators of rhythm and jazz in our own southland.

The peoples of the great rivers, the Mississippi, the Danube, the Don, the Niger, the Ganges and the Yangtse, all know our hero and his voice, now permanently preserved on disk and tape, will continue to evoke the emotions which are freedom's guardians wherever men struggle against wrong and terror.

May he be spared to spend many long years with us—and may the same patience which enabled him to curb his temper when his fingernails were stomped from his hands by racists on the football field continue to be extended to our faltering efforts as we try to play our parts in the continuing drama of the freedom struggle here in this country that was built with the blood and sweat and tears of our forefathers torn from ancestral Africa.

By *Afro-American* (Newspaper)

With a great deal of pomp and publicity the Thirteenth Annual National Football Foundation Hall of Fame awards banquet was held at the Waldorf-Astoria Hotel in New York last week.

And for the thirteenth time one of college football's all-time greats was not honored.

Paul Robeson, who was elected All-American two years in a row—one of the few in the history of the game so chosen—was bypassed for this great honor.

It did not go unnoticed by his alma mater, Rutgers University, New Brunswick, N.J., where the Hall of Fame is located, though. Not only did the head football coach, Dr. John Bateman, send an angry letter to the chairman, Vincent Draddy, but he resubmitted Paul Robeson's name for nomination in 1971. Nominees usually are not submitted until March.

Backing the coach in his staunch stand is the president of Rutgers, Dr. Mason W. Gross. Both agreed they would submit only Robeson's name until he is admitted, although they can send in three selections. This will be the third straight year the great athlete, singer and civil rights leader has been submitted by his alma mater.

We agree with Coach Bateman in his stand that Paul Robeson is a great man and should be recognized.

We must also admire and applaud Dr. Bateman and Dr. Gross for not being afraid to do what they believe is right, and for standing behind their belief that "One day this man [Paul Robeson] will be admitted to the Football Hall of Fame."

December 15, 1970

Paul Robeson
Chronology *

(handwritten:) Pauls important dates from birth to death

1898	April 9, born in Princeton, N.J., to William Drew Robeson and Maria Louisa Bustill.
1915-1918	Wins scholarship to Rutgers University. Receives 15 varsity letters: football, basketball, baseball, track. Phi Beta Kappa, debating champion, valedictorian of his graduating class.
1919	Enters Columbia Law School.
1921	Marries Eslanda Cardozo Goode (1896–1965), the first Black analytical chemist at Columbia Medical Center.
1923	Graduates from Columbia Law School. Has brief law practice.
1924	Stars in O'Neill's **Emperor Jones** and **All God's Chillun Got Wings.** In Oscar Micheaux's film **Body and Soul.**
1925	Lawrence Brown and Robeson give their first concert on April 19 at the Greenwich Village Theatre.
1926	Stars as prize fighter in the film **Black Boy.**
1928	Plays role of Joe in Jerome Kern's **Showboat,** London production.
1930	Famous Savoy production of **Othello** in London. Robesons appear together in film **Borderline.**
1932	Receives Honorary Degree, Master of Arts, Rutgers University.
1933	Appears in New York production of **Emperor Jones.**
1934	Stars in film **Sanders of the River.** Travels to the Soviet Union.

---

* From *DuBois—Robeson: Two Giants of the 20th Century: The Story of an Exhibit and a Bibliography* by Erwin A. Salk (Chicago: Columbia College Press, 1977). 20 pp. (paper).

1935   Appears in film version of **Showboat** made in Hollywood; Herbert Marshall's play **Stevedore** in London.

1936   Has leading role in film **Song of Freedom**, produced in London.

1937   Visits Spain to support and entertain the Spanish Loyalist Government. Sings for the International Brigade. Appears with Lawrence Brown in film **Jericho,** produced in Egypt and London. Appears with Eslanda Robeson in film **Big Fella**. Appears in film **King Solomon's Mines,** British production.

1938   The Robesons travel to Spain. Robeson appears in play **Plant in the Sun** for benefit of workers theatre, London.

1939   Performs in world premiere of Earl Robinson's **Ballad for Americans** at CBS Radio Studios in New York City, Nov. 5. Appears in film **Proud Valley,** British production. Awarded Badge of Veterans of Abraham Lincoln Brigade (Spanish Civil War).

1940-1943   Many concert appearances.

1940   Receives Honorary Degree, Doctor of Humane Letters, Hamilton College.

1943   Receives Honorary Degree, Doctor of Humane Letters, Morehouse College, June 1.

1944   Receives Donaldson Award, Best Acting Performance, **Othello.** Awarded gold medal, National Institute of Arts and Letters.

1945   Presented with 30th Spingarn Medal of the NAACP by Marshall Field. Gives concert tour for USO. Makes over 30 appearances in Germany, Czechoslovakia, and France.

1946   Performs **Ballad for Americans** with CIO chorus, June 6. Awarded Honorary Degree, Howard University.

1947   Famous concert at University of Utah in Salt Lake City. Announces he will no longer give concerts for entertainment; will perform benefits instead.

1949   European concert tour, including Soviet Union. Attends Paris Peace Conference, makes statement ". . . It is unthinkable that American Negroes could go to war on behalf of those who have oppressed us for generations against the Soviet Union, which in one generation has raised our people to full human dignity." Gives concert

at Peekskill, N.Y.; violent mob attacks Robeson supporters.

1949-1950	85 concerts cancelled by music promoters attempting to silence Robeson.
1950	Recives "Champion of African Freedom" Award from National Church of Nigeria.
	Passport revoked by State Department ". . . in view of his frank admission that he has been for years politically active in behalf of the colonial people of Africa." Edits monthly journal **Freedom**. Receives Afro-American Newspapers Award.
1952	Awarded Lenin Peace Prize.
1955	Speaks at meeting of the Council on African Affairs.
1956	Appears before House Committee on Un-American Activities, June 12. "My father was a slave and my people died to build this country, and I am going to stay here and have a piece of it just like you. And no fascist-minded people will drive me from it. Is that clear?" Paul Robeson.
1957	Concert ban lifted. Robeson performs first concert in seven years, Oakland, California.
1958	Passport returned under worldwide pressure and protest. Robesons leave for London. European concert tour, including the Soviet Union. Famous concert at Carnegie Hall, New York City. Book **Here I Stand** published. Guest of Honor at Ersteddfod Cultural Festival, Wales.
1959	Performs in **Othello** at Stratford-on-Avon, England. Honorary Degree, Professor of Music, Moscow State Conservatory.
1960	Last concert tour, Australia and New Zealand. Speaks on behalf of the Aborigine Civil Rights Movement. Awarded German Peace Medal, German Democratic Republic. Receives Honorary Degree of Doctor of Philosophy, Humboldt University, Berlin.
1961	Retires from singing and acting due to illness.
1963	Returns to U.S.
1965	Appears at "Freedomways Salute to Paul Robeson," April 22, New York City. Eslanda Goode Robeson dies.

1969 Celebrates Nigerian Independence with Nnamdi Azikiwe.

1970 Receives Ira Aldridge Award from Association for the Study of Afro-American Life and History; Civil Liberties Award from American Civil Liberties Union.

1972 Dedication of the Paul Robeson Campus Center, Rutgers University. Receives Whitney M. Young, Jr., National Memorial Award from the New York Urban League. Elected to Theatre Hall of Fame.

1973 Lawrence Brown Memorial Concert. Seventy-Fifth Birthday Celebration at Carnegie Hall, New York City, April 15. "Warmest thanks to the many friends here and throughout the world who have sent me greetings on my 75th birthday. Though I have not been able to be active for several years, I want you to know that I am the same Paul, dedicated as ever to the worldwide cause of humanity for freedom, peace and brotherhood. Here at home, my heart is with the continuing struggles of my own people to achieve complete liberation from the racist domination, and to gain for all Black Americans and the other minority groups not only equal rights but an equal share. . . ." Receives Honorary Doctor of Humane Letters degree, Rutgers University, May 17, on his 75th birthday anniversary.

1976 Paul Robeson dies, January 23. Funeral services at A.M.E. Zion Church, New York City, January 27.

Notes

Paul Robeson: Black Warrior

1. Walter Camp's full remarks appear in his summaries of the 1917 and 1918 college football seasons in the January 5, 1918, and January 4, 1919, issues of *Collier's Magazine*.
2. Details of my father's performances on the football field can be found in published newspaper accounts of Rutgers football games in 1916, 1917 and 1918.

Paul Robeson in Film: An Iconoclast's Quest for a Role

1. *The New York News*, April 3, 1926.
2. *The Daily Film Renter* (London), Vol. IV, no. 964, March 7, 1930.
3. *Evening Standard* (London), June 12, 1930.
4. *Bioscope* (London), October 25, 1930.
5. Agreement between John Krimsky and Gifford Cochran, Inc., and Paul Robeson, February 24, 1933.
6. Letter from Eugene O'Neill to Eslanda Robeson, April 10, 1930.
7. Mortimer Franklin, "Art in Astoria," *Screenland*, Vol. 27, October, 1933, p. 84.
8. Wanda Hale, *The New York Daily News*, September 20, 1933. This opinion was seconded by Rose Pelswick, *New York Journal*, September 20, 1933.
9. T.R. Poston, *New York Amsterdam News*, September 27, 1933.
10. Editorial, *The Philadelphia Tribune*, November 2, 1933.
11. *Reynold's Illustrated News* (London), September 20, 1925.
12. Doris Mackie, Interview with Paul Robeson, "Negro Films I Want to Make," *Film Weekly*, September 1, 1933.
13. Glyn Roberts, "He Has Never Failed," *Film Pictorial*, May 13, 1933.
14. Mackie, op. cit.
15. *The Afro-American*, July 6, 1935.
16. Leslie Banks, "Britain Puts Her Empire on the Screen at Last," *Film Pictorial*, April 16, 1935, p. 43.
17. *Daily Herald* (London), April 3, 1935.
18. *The Observer* (London), July 2, 1934.
19. *Evening News* (London), April 2, 1935.
20. T.R. Poston, *New York Amsterdam News*, October 5, 1935.
21. Ben Davis, Jr., Interview with Paul Robeson, *Sunday Worker* (New York), May 10, 1936.

22. Ric Roberts, Interview with Paul Robeson, *Pittsburgh Courier*, August 13, 1949.
23. Ibid.
24. Marie Seton, *Paul Robeson* (London: Dennis Dobson, 1958), pp. 94-95.
25. Paul Robeson, *The Negro People and the Soviet Union* (New York: New Century Publishers, 1950), p. 5.
26. *The Era* (London), May 13, 1936.
27. *California News*, May 8, 1936.
28. *Daily Express* (London), February 3, 1936.
29. Paul Robeson, "Primitives," *The New Statesman and Nation*, Vol. XII, no. 285, August 8, 1936, p. 191.
30. *The Song of Freedom*, typed script, sequence 374, p. 128.
31. Peter Noble, *The Negro in Films* (London: British Yearbooks, Ltd., 1948), p. 117.
32. "Paul Robeson Introduces 'The Song of Freedom,'" *Film Weekly*, May 23, 1936, p. 17.
33. *The Era* (London), September 16, 1936.
34. *Evening News* (London), September 19, 1936.
35. Margaret Burrows, "Paul Robeson—The Man," *Film Pictorial*, March 6, 1937.
36. George Campbell, "What Paul Robeson Could Do," *The Bystander*, September 30, 1936, p. 566.
37. Ibid.
38. *King Solomon's Mines*, screen treatment by Michael Hogan, sequence E, p. 44.
39. *Picture Show*, December 12, 1936.
40. Frank S. Nugent, *The New York Times*, July 3, 1937.
41. *Pittsburgh Courier*, August 14, 1937.
42. *Kinematograph*, June 10, 1937.
43. *Sundown Gazette*, January 27, 1938.
44. *Daily Express* (Glasgow), December 3, 1936.
45. Letter from Fenn Sherie to James Elder Wills, Esq., October 14, 1936.
46. Ibid.
47. *Film Weekly*, October 29, 1937.
48. *The Daily Mail* (London), October 29, 1937.
49. *Film Pictorial*, November 13, 1937.
50. *Daily News-Chronicle* (London), April 2, 1937.
51. Ralph Matthews, *The Washington Afro-American*, August 20, 1938.
52. *Truth*, October 27, 1937.
53. *New York Amsterdam News*, June 2, 1938.
54. Philip Bolsover, *Daily Worker* (London), November 22, 1937.
55. Louise Morgan, *Daily News-Chronicle* (London), November 8, 1937.
56. *Manchester Guardian*, October 14, 1938.
57. Eugene Gordon, *Sunday Worker* (New York), June 4, 1939.
58. *Manchester Dispatch*, November 1, 1938.
59. *Blackthorn Telegraph*, May 27, 1939.

60. *Glasgow Record*, November 1, 1938.
61. Ollie Stewart, *The Afro-American*, May 24, 1941.
62. Elspeth Grant, *Daily Sketch* (London), March 8, 1940.
63. *Cue*, Vol. 10, no. 2, January 11, 1941, p. 16.
64. Archer Winston, *New York Post*, September 25, 1942.
65. Dan Burley, *New York Amsterdam News*, October 3, 1942.
66. *PM*, September 22, 1942.
67. Archer Winston, op. cit.
68. Tom O'Connor, *PM*, September 22, 1942.
69. Ibid. In a telegram to Robert Rockmore, Robeson wrote: "Script much (too) naive, childish general pattern can be returned. But my character must not believe all came from heaven, etc. Perhaps can see bit of wreckage and get what he wished for not prayed for etc. At this point cannot wholly approve. Paul." November 20, 1941.
70. *The Hartford Daily Courant*, September 23, 1942.
71. *The New York Times*, September 23, 1942.
72. Bosley Crowther, *The New York Times*, May 12, 1942.
73. Marie Seton, *Paul Robeson*, op. cit., p. 133ff.
74. James Weldon Johnson, *Black Manhattan* (New York: Atheneum, 1968), pp. 229-230.
75. Quote from Paul Robeson in *The Detroit Tribune*, May 22, 1937.
76. Herb Golden, *Variety*, January 3, 1940.
77. Claude McKay, *The New Leader*, January 20, 1940.

Paul Robeson's Mission in Music

1. Paul Robeson, quoted in the *Boston Evening Globe*, March 13, 1926.
2. *The Star* (London), September 11, 1925.
3. Julia Dorn, "Paul Robeson Told Me," *TAC*, Vol. 1, no. 12, July, 1939, p. 23.
4. W.R. Titterton, *Sunday Graphic and Sunday News* (London), January 19, 1939.
5. *The New York Times*, September 12, 1925.
6. Paul Robeson quoted in *Detroit Evening Times*, January 20, 1926.
7. Ibid.
8. Paul Robeson quoted in the *Sheffield Daily Telegraph*, March 14, 1930.
9. Mortimer Franklin, "Art in Astoria," *Screenland*, Vol. 27. October, 1933, p. 84.
10. *Edinburgh Dispatch*, March 8, 1930.
11. Paul Robeson quoted by Jerome Beatty, "America's No. 1 Negro," *The American*, Vol. CXXXVII, no. 5, May, 1944, p. 42.
12. Paul Robeson quoted in the *Daily Gleaner* (Jamaica), January 9, 1932.
13. Marie Seton. *Paul Robeson* (London: Dennis Dobson, 1958), p. 84.
14. Paul Robeson quoted in the *Daily Gleaner* (Jamaica), December 17, 1932.
15. *Cambridge Daily News*, March 31, 1934.

16. *Daily Express* (London), November 27, 1937.
17. *The New York Times*, December 20, 1937.
18. *Daily News-Chronicle* (London), December 20, 1937.
19. *Aberdeen Express*, January 18, 1939.
20. Ibid.
21. Letter to Paul Robeson from Harold Holt, June 10, 1938.
22. Russell McLauchlin, *The Detroit News*, December 7, 1940.
23. Kraft Radio Program, Correspondence of Columbia Management Bureau, 1941.
24. Merril Osenbough, *The Sacramento Union*, March 8, 1943.
25. *The Chicago Defender*, July 31, 1943.
26. Letter from Lawrence Brown to Robert Rockmore, sent from Ausburg, Germany, August 21, 1945.
27. Excerpt included in letter from L.E. Behumer Concert Bureau on West Coast, to Fred Schang, March 22, 1946.
28. Jack Goodman, *Philadelphia Inquirer*, March 16, 1947.
29. *The New York Times*, April 21, 1949.
30. Will Parry, *People's World*, May 21, 1952.
31. *The Afro-American*, July 18, 1953.
32. *People's World*, August 10, 1957.
33. Arthur Bloomfield, *San Francisco Call Bulletin*, February 10, 1958.
34. *Pittsburgh Courier*, April 26, 1958.
35. Harold Schonberg, *The New York Times*, May 10, 1958.
36. Samuel Haynes, *The Afro-American*, May 17, 1958.
37. Ibid.
38. *The Courier-Mail* (Brisbane), October 14, 1960.

A Rock in a Weary Lan'

1. For a comprehensive account of the activities of this early youth organization in the South, see Augusta Strong's article, "Southern Youth's Proud Heritage," *Freedomways* (Winter, 1964).
2. North Atlantic Treaty Organization.

Paul Robeson at Peekskill

1. *New York Times*, April 21, 1949.

Paul Robeson's Impact on History

1. In his biography Robeson himself notes, "The main charge against me has centered upon my remarks at the World Peace Conference held in Paris in 1949, and what I said on that occasion has been distorted and misquoted in such a way as to impugn my character as a loyal American citizen." Paul Robeson, *Here I Stand* (Boston: Beacon Press, 1971), p. 41.

Marie Seton, *Paul Robeson* (London: Dennis Dobson, 1958), p. 196. Edwin P. Hoyt, *Paul Robeson: The American Othello* (New York: World Publishing Co., 1967), p. 173.

2. Lamont Yeakey, "Robeson's Contribution to Domestic Politics and International Affairs." Paper delivered at the National Conference on Paul Robeson at Purdue University on April 22, 1976, West Lafayette, Indiana.

3. Hope R. Stevens, "Paul Robeson—Democracy's Most Powerful Voice," *Freedomways*, vol. 5, no. 3 (1965), p. 366.

4. Sterling Stuckey, "Cultural Philosophy of Paul Robeson." Paper delivered at the National Conference on Paul Robeson at Purdue University on April 21, 1976. For further information on his cultural philosophy and talents as a linguist, see Sterling Stuckey, "The Cultural Philosophy of Paul Robeson," *Freedomways*, vol. 11, no. 1 (1971), pp. 78-90.

5. Richard M. Dalfiume, "The 'Forgotten Years' of the Negro Revolution," *Journal of American History*, vol. 55 (June, 1968), pp. 90-106.

6. Robeson, *Here I Stand*, p. 83.

7. Dalfiume, "The 'Forgotten Years,' " pp. 90-106.

8. Article in *Freedom*, March, 1954: excerpts in *Freedomways*, vol. 11, no. 1 (1971), p. 121. J. H. O'Dell, "A Rock in a Weary Lan': Paul Robeson's Leadership and 'The Movement' in the Decade Before Montgomery," *Freedomways*, vol. 11, no. 1 (1971), pp. 34-36.

9. J. H. O'Dell, "A Rock," pp. 34-36.

10. Excerpts from address to the National Labor Conference for Negro Rights, Chicago, June 10, 1950, in *Freedomways*, vol. 11, no. 1 (1971), p. 112.

11. Excerpts from *Freedom*, March, 1954. "Ho Chi Minh Is Toussaint L'Ouverture of Indo-China," in *Freedomways*, vol. 11, no. 1 (1971), p. 121.

12. Excerpts of a speech given in 1953, reprinted in *Freedom*. See *Freedomways*, vol. 11, no. 1 (1971), p. 119.

13. Jack Anderson, "U.S. Supports Latin Dictators," October 11, 1976. Lafayette *Journal and Courier*.

14. Excerpts from address to National Labor Conference for Negro Rights, Chicago, June 10, 1950. Reprinted in *Freedomways*, vol. 11, no. 1 (1971). Seton, *Paul Robeson*, pp. 161-70. Recent figures on African resources:
    Diamonds—almost all the world's reserves
    Chromium—nearly all of the free world's reserves
    Cobalt—90 per cent
    Cocoa—65 per cent of world production
    Gold—half of world reserves
    Platinum—40 per cent of reserves
    Uranium—nearly a third of free-world reserves
    Bauxite—more than a fourth
    Coffee—25 per cent of output
    Natural Gas—12 per cent
    Petroleum—8 per cent of world reserves
    See *U.S. News and World Report*, May 3, 1976.

15. Seton, *Paul Robeson,* pp. 169-70. Taken from speech delivered at a Madison Square Garden Rally in New York sponsored by the Council on African Affairs, June 6, 1946. Henry A. Kissinger in a speech before the Opportunities Industrialization Centers, "The Challenges of Africa" (Philadelphia, August 31, 1976), said, "Nearly a third of the world's some 150 sovereign nations are on the continent of Africa. Africa's independence has transformed the character and scope of international institutions; their importance to the world economy is growing; the interdependence of Africa and the industrialized world is obvious." But he concluded his remarks with words that are at best ominous. "We are determined to avoid unnecessary arms races. But when friendly and moderate nations like Kenya or Zaire make modest and responsible requests for assistance to protect themselves against belligerent neighbors possessing substantial quantities of modern Soviet weapons, we owe them our serious considerations." Robeson, *Here I Stand,* p. 87.

16. Speech of Ako Adjei, Minister of Justice of Ghana, quoted in Robeson, *Here I Stand,* p. 87.

17. Virginia Hamilton, *Paul Robeson: The Life and Times of a Free Black Man* (New York: Harper and Row, 1971), p. 164. Hoyt, *Paul Robeson,* p. 205. Seton, *Paul Robeson,* p. 230.

18. Robeson, *Here I Stand,* p. 68.

19. Ibid., pp. 66–67.

20. Hoyt, *Paul Robeson,* pp. 205-12. Hamilton, *Paul Robeson,* p. 164.

21. Hoyt, *Paul Robeson,* p. 212.

22. *Rockwell Kent v. John Foster Dulles,* Secretary of State 357 U.S. 116, 2 L ed. 1204.

23. Hamilton, *Paul Robeson,* p. 181.

A Bibliography by and About Paul Robeson

Ernest Kaiser

Introduction

Paul Robeson, a towering giant and genius of Black political protest and Black culture in the twentieth century, had a fantastic, many-sided career which ran from 1916 into the 1960s. Athlete, lawyer, actor, singer, scholar, linguist, and political and cultural leader, he was truly a Renaissance man who did it all. Robeson was also an international peace and cultural figure and a world citizen.

A comprehensive, thorough bibliography covering Robeson's almost fifty-year span of activities is a tremendous undertaking. Anatol Schlosser's doctoral dissertation on Robeson's artistic career alone, done at New York University in 1970, has a seventy-page bibliography which I haven't seen. I have not tried to do anything so exhaustive but rather an overall, lengthy listing of as much material on various aspects of Robeson's life and activities as I could find. Some of the more virulent attacks on Robeson are omitted. Also left out are his regular columns in his newspaper *Freedom*, published monthly in Harlem from 1951 to 1955, and his weekly columns in the *People's Voice*, a Black New York City newspaper published in the 1940s.

The Schomburg Center has very good holdings on Robeson including books, pamphlets, programs, magazine articles, and newspaper clippings on microfiche and in folders, albums of phonograph records, and some of his papers which are restricted for some years after his death. The Robeson papers, held by the Robeson family, were placed in the Paul Robeson Archives established in New York City in March 1973, with Paul Robeson, Jr. as president and treasurer, Lloyd L. Brown, vice-president and Martin Popper, secretary. The purpose of the Archives was "to collect, preserve and catalog the life works of Robeson including his writings, recordings, films, tapes and correspondence" and to "conduct and encourage study and research of these materials and make them available to the interested public." The Robeson Archives holdings are going to Howard University and the Archives will close. The Robeson papers will be put on film by Howard University. The articles, speeches, and interviews are being published independently of the Archives as *Paul Robeson Speaks*, edited by Philip S. Foner. But the Robeson correspondence should also be published.

The University of Pennsylvania, Philadelphia, has recently set up a Paul Robeson Library—prompted and assisted by the great Black collector of Black materials in the Philadelphia area, Charles L. Blockson, whose Robeson collection is one of the best in the United States. The Rutgers University Library and Alumni Association holdings or collections on Robeson are very good, even unique, especially on the early part of Robeson's career. The Alexander Gumby Collection of valuable scrapbooks compiled by Gumby, a New York Black, over many decades and now at Columbia University Library, also has newspaper clippings on Robeson. The James Weldon Johnson Memorial Collection of Negro Arts and Letters in the Yale University Library has Robeson material. Samuel Woldin, a white Somerville, New Jersey resident who went to Somerville High School with Robeson, has spent years collecting materials about Robeson. There are the Herbert Marshall Collection on Ira Aldridge and Paul Robeson at Southern Illinois University at Carbondale; the Russell Malone Collection on Ira Aldridge and Robeson at Northwestern University; material on Robeson at Tuskegee Institute, Alabama; and photographs and programs of Robeson held by George Norman of Detroit. John Southard of Madison, Wisconsin has many rare old phonograph records made by Paul Robeson, many imported from Europe. Many people have some material on Paul Robeson. There is also a Paul Robeson Archive set up in April 1965 at the Academy of Arts in Berlin in the German Democratic Republic "to collect and preserve the many documents, records, tape recordings, photos, newspaper cuttings, etc., connected with his life and work." (*Information* from the Peace Movement of the German Democratic Republic, May 1965.)

There is a tremendous Robeson revival underway at this time. It started several years ago, but his death in January 1976 gave it great impetus. It was the special issue of *Freedomways* (1st quarter 1971) on "Paul Robeson: The Great Forerunner" that launched this Robeson revival. This resurgence of interest can be seen in the latter part of the chronological listings in this bibliography. This revival is also reflected in the reissuing of many of Robeson's albums listed below, in the many celebrations of his birthday, programs in tribute to him, and in many awards given recently to him or to others in his name; in the coming publication of a biography by Robeson's friend and collaborator, Lloyd L. Brown; in the republication by Beacon Press of Robeson's autobiography *Here I Stand* in 1971, and in this book publication of the expanded special issue of *Freedomways* on Robeson. There are also other things: the several theses and dissertations on Robeson and many recent books about Robeson for adults and children; the many radio programs in New York City, Philadelphia, Detroit, etc., on Robeson; the Paul Robeson film festivals; Mary Cygar's honors thesis in history at Northwestern University, "Paul Robeson and the Press" (1973); Professor Frank Greenwood's play *The Decision*, about Robeson's struggle with the un-Americans which was produced, I think, in Los Angeles in 1974; Charles Fuller's 1972 play on the Peekskill, New York incidents in Paul Robeson's life; the naming of the library at the State University of New York, Cobleskill, for Robeson; the naming at Rutgers University of the Paul Robeson Lounge on the New Brunswick, New Jersey campus and the Paul Robeson Campus Center on the Newark campus; the Storefront Museum's Robeson Theatre in Jamaica, Queens, New York City; the Paul Robeson Players of the Compton, California community; the Paul Robeson Black Arts Ensemble student group at Rutgers University and the Afrikan History Club's program "We Remember, Paul," a tribute to a forgotten freedom fighter, and Robeson exhibit at the McFarlane Elementary School, Detroit, Michigan, April 23, 1974, with research materials on Robeson and his recordings listed in the back of the printed program.

Andrew Buni, author of *Robert L. Vann of the Pittsburgh Courier* (1974), has written a book about Paul Robeson to be published soon. Herbert Marshall is writing a book on Robeson but, judging from his extremely anti-Soviet Union article on Robeson at his death early in 1976, the book will be a distortion of Robeson's life insofar as his relations with the Soviet Union are concerned.

The six sections in this bibliography are books, pamphlets, theses, and dissertations; chapters or parts of books and dissertations; magazine and newspaper articles, book reviews and radio and TV programs; old, reissued, and other phonograph recordings and tapes by and about Paul Robeson; films and portable exhibits; and poetry inspired by Paul Robeson. The books are listed alphabetically by the authors' last names or by the articles in the books; the magazine and newspaper articles, book reviews, radio and TV programs, and poetry are listed chronologically. The phonograph recordings are listed alphabetically. There are some comments or annotations. The introduction and the listings have been filled out and brought up to date since the publication of the special issue of *Freedomways* (1st quarter 1971) devoted to Robeson. And thanks to Lloyd L. Brown, the late great Black New York collector, Glenn Carrington, Lamont H. Yeakey, Charles L. Blockson, Dr. Charles H. Wright, Paul Robeson, Jr., and the listings of Erwin A. Salk, Patricia Turner, and John Southard, I have been able to add many important articles and news stories about Paul Robeson from the *Daily Worker* newspaper during the 1940s and 1950s; from the *National Guardian* newspaper during the 1950s and 1960s, and from other newspapers and magazines as well as many record albums. This bibliography plus the extensive footnotes in the several theses and dissertations listed here cover Robeson's life and diverse career quite well.

Books, Pamphlets, Theses, and Dissertations

Brown, Lloyd L. *Lift Every Voice for Paul Robeson.* New York: Freedom Associates, 1951. 14 pp. (pamphlet).

———. *Paul Robeson Rediscovered.* Occasional Paper No. 19, American Institute for Marxist Studies, New York. 1976. 23 pp. (paper). This paper was presented at the National Conference on Paul Robeson under the auspices of the Africana Studies and Research Center, Purdue University, Ind., Apr. 21–23, 1976.

Fast, Howard. *Peekskill: U.S.A.; A Personal Experience.* New York: Civil Rights Congress, 1951. 124 pp. (photographs). A book about the mobs of whites who attacked those who attended two Paul Robeson outdoor concerts in Peekskill, N.Y., on Aug. 27 and Sept. 3, 1949, while police ignored the mob or protected it. New York State accused and tried to indict the victims of the mob. See review of book by Doxey A. Wilkerson in *Masses and Mainstream*, vol. 4, no. 5 (May 1951), pp. 87–89.

Foner, Philip S., ed. *Paul Robeson Speaks.* Brunner/Mazel, Inc., 64 University Place, New York City 10003, 1978. 640 pp. (cloth and paper). Virtually all of Robeson's writings, speeches and interviews from his school days to his death in January 1976.

Freedomways Annual W.E.B. Du Bois Cultural Evening Honoring the 75th Birthday Year of Paul Robeson. At Carnegie Hall, New York City, Feb. 16, 1973. (Dancers, singers, Ruby Dee and Ossie Davis, Judge George W. Crockett, Rev. Jesse L. Jackson, and Judge Bruce McM. Wright). See Carnegie Hall program.

Georgiady, Nicholas P., Louis G. Romano, and Robert L. Green. *Paul Robeson: American Negro Actor.* Franklin Publishers, Inc., 4145 N. Green Bay Ave., Milwaukee, Wisc. 53209, 1969. 16 pp. (pamphlet). A biographical sketch of Robeson. One of a series of 60 pamphlets about outstanding Blacks in history, living and dead.

Gilliam, Dorothy Butler. *Paul Robeson: All-American.* Washington, D.C.: New Republic Book Co., 1976, x, 216 pp. (cloth and paper). Here a Black woman journalist writes a politically inept and amateurish biography of Robeson. She accepts all of the premises and lies of the anti-Communist Cold War period. So Robeson, not his persecutors, is condemned as the cold warrior in error. This book is almost a rewrite of Edwin P. Hoyt's Red-baiting book.

Gorochov, Viktor. *Ich Singe Amerika: Ein Lebensbild Paul Robesons.* Berlin: Verlag Neues Leben, 1955. 190 pp. Biography with many photographs.

Graham, Shirley. *Paul Robeson, Citizen of the World.* New York: Julian Messner, 1946, 264 pp.; 1971. 280 pp. This is a biography of Robeson for young people. Reissued in 1971. Was out-of-print for many years.

Greenfield, Eloise. *Paul Robeson.* New York: Thomas Y. Crowell, 1975. 33 pp. A book for children by the outstanding Black woman writer.

Hamilton, Virginia. *Paul Robeson: The Life and Times of a Free Black Man.* New York: Harper & Row, 1974. 217 pp. A book for young people and adults by the well-known Black woman author.

Hoyt, Edwin P. *Paul Robeson: The American Othello.* Cleveland: World Publishing Co., 1967. 228 pp. This is a vicious, Red-baiting, anti-Robeson book from beginning to end and should be listed and labeled as such here.

The Job To Be Done. New York: Council on African Affairs, 1946 or 1947. 6 pp. Pamphlet on the Council's democratic action for African freedom. Paul Robeson, chairman, W. Alphaeus Hunton, educational director of the Council.

Mercadel, Kevin. Senior thesis on Paul Robeson at Harvard University written in 1976.

Miers, Earl Schenck. *Big Ben,* a novel. Philadelphia: Westminster Press, 1942. 238 pp. A novel about Robeson's life.

Myerson, Michael. Master's thesis on Paul Robeson at the University of California, Berkeley.

Paul Robeson in Film. A 1973 booklet by the Paul Robeson Film Retrospective, Rutgers University, New Brunswick, N.J.

Paul Robeson Souvenir Program. (Hotel Americana, New York City, Apr. 22, 1965; photographs, listing of awards.) Freedomways Associates, Inc., 799 Broadway, New York City 10003.

Paul Robeson Speaks to Youth. Challenge (magazine), 799 Broadway, New York City 10003, 1951. 21 pp. Pamphlet contains Robeson's address to the public session of the First National Convention of the Labor Youth League, Nov. 24, 1950.

Paul Robeson: Tributes and Selected Writings. Compiled and edited for the Paul Robeson Archives, Inc., by Roberta Yancy Dent assisted by Marilyn Robeson and Paul Robeson, Jr. New York: Paul Robeson Archives, Inc., 1976. 112 pp. The first five tributes here were delivered at the funeral service for Paul Robeson at the Mother A.M.E. Zion Church, New York City, Jan. 27, 1976. The innumerable other tributes excerpted came from around the world. They are from individuals and from newspapers and magazines. Robeson's selected writings, speeches, and interviews before committees are under culture and heritage, civil rights, and politics and labor.

Robeson, Eslanda (Goode). *Paul Robeson Goes to Washington.* Salford, Lancashire, England: National Paul Robeson Committee, 1956? 12 pp. Pamphlet of Robeson's confrontation with the House Un-American Activities Committee.

———. *Paul Robeson, Negro.* New York: Harper and Bros., 1930. 178 pp.

Robeson, Paul. *For Freedom and Peace.* New York: Council on African Affairs, 1949. 16 pp. Pamphlet of his address June 19, 1949, in New York on his return from European tour.

———. *Forge Negro-Labor Unity for Peace and Jobs.* New York: Harlem Trade Union Council, 1950. 15 pp. (pamphlet).

———. *Here I Stand.* New York: Othello Associates, 1958. 128 pp.; London: Dennis Dobson, 1958. 128 pp.; Boston: Beacon Press, 1971, xx, 121 pp. Two of the five appendices in the first edition have been dropped in the 1971 edition published by Beacon Press, including Alphaeus Hunton's note on the Council on African Affairs. This edition has Lloyd Brown's preface and Robeson's 1964 statement to the Black press. First edition also published in Hungarian, Czechoslovakian, Yugoslavian, German, etc.

———. *The Negro People and the Soviet Union.* New York: New Century Publishers,

1950. 15 pp. A pamphlet of his speech at the banquet sponsored by the National Council of American–Soviet Friendship in New York City, Nov. 10, 1949, celebrating the 32nd anniversary of the USSR.

Salk, Erwin A. *Du Bois—Robeson: Two Giants of the 20th Century. The Story of an Exhibit and a Bibliography.* Chicago: Columbia College Press, 1977. 20 pp. (booklet). The exhibit described here was prepared by professor and author Salk and his assistant Richard Cooper for the Chicago meeting of the Association for the Study of Afro-American Life and History in 1976. There are a profile, a chronology, and a bibliography of Paul Robeson that includes books about him, recordings and tapes, and films and videotapes. All songs on each record album are listed and distributors of each film are also given. All of this is repeated with variations for Du Bois. A valuable source book.

Salute to Paul Robeson: A Cultural Celebration of His 75th Birthday. At Carnegie Hall, New York City, Apr. 15, 1973. A beautiful 44-page brochure telling the story of Robeson's life with text and many pictures. Has birthday greetings, Pablo Neruda's "Ode to Paul Robeson" (translated into English from the Spanish by Jill Booty), etc.

Schlosser, Anatol. *Paul Robeson: His Career in the Theatre, in Motion Pictures and on the Concert Stage.* Unpublished Ph.D. dissertation, New York University, 1970.

Seton, Marie. *Paul Robeson.* London: Dennis Dobson, 1958. 254 pp. (photographs).

Symposium: Paul Robeson and the Struggle of the Working Class and the Afro-American People of the USA Against Imperialism. Held at the German Academy of Art, Berlin, GDR, April 13–14, 1971. 1972. 69 pp. (35 photographs). Participants: William L. Patterson, Albert Norden, Brigette Boegelsack, Mrs. Martin Luther King, Jr., Paul Robeson, Jr., Angela Davis, Claude Lightfoot, Hilde Eisler, Horst Ihde, Diana Loeser, Sigrid Jahn, Alex La Guma, Lloyd L. Brown, John Henrik Clarke, Sydney Gordon, etc.

To Live Like Paul Robeson. Young Workers Liberation League, 235 W. 23rd St., 5th floor, New York City 10011. 1977. 24 pp. (pamphlet). Introduction by William L. Patterson; "Scaling the Heights of Mount Paul Robeson for Peace, Jobs, Equality" (speech) by James Steele; Paul Robeson pledge, and "A Home in This Rock" (poem) by Anne Sadowski.

Wright, Charles H. *Robeson: Labor's Forgotten Champion.* Detroit: Balamp Publishing Co., 1975, vii. 171 pp. The author is a Black medical doctor who has written for the stage and TV.

Yeakey, Lamont H. *The Early Years of Paul Robeson: Prelude to the Making of a Revolutionary, 1898–1930.* Unpublished Master's thesis, Columbia University, 1971.

Yergan, Max, and Paul Robeson. *The Negro and Justice: A Plea for Earl Browder.* New York: The Citizens' Committee to Free Earl Browder, Nov. 1941. 12 pp. (pamphlet). Browder, then general secretary of the Communist Party, USA, was in prison.

Chapters or Parts of Books and Dissertations

Adams, Julius J. *The Challenge: A Study in Negro Leadership.* New York: Wendell Malliet, 1949. 154 pp.

Adams, Russell L. *Great Negroes: Past and Present.* Chicago: Afro-American Publishing Co., 1964, pp. 148–49; 1969, pp. 182–83.

Anderson, Jervis. *A. Philip Randolph: A Biographical Portrait.* New York: Harcourt Brace Jovanovich, 1972, xiv, 398 pp.

Aptheker, Herbert, ed. *A Documentary History of the Negro People in the United*

States, 1933–1945. Vol. 3. Secaucus, N.J.: Citadel Press, 1974. Contains "I Breathe Freely" by Paul Robeson, pp. 133–35. Reprinted from *New Theatre*, vol. 11, no. 7 (July 1935), p. 5. About Robeson's visit to the USSR.

Baker's Biographical Dictionary of Musicians. Revised by Nicholas Slonimsky. New York: G. Schirmer, 1958; supplements in 1965 and 1971, p. 1353.

The Biographical Encyclopaedia & Who's Who of the American Theatre, 1966. Edited by Walter Rigdon. New York: James H. Heineman, Inc., p. 779.

Black Titan: W.E.B. Du Bois. An anthology by the editors of *Freedomways*: John Henrik Clarke, Esther Jackson, Ernest Kaiser, J. H. O'Dell. Boston: Beacon Press, 1970. "Tribute to W.E.B. Du Bois" by Paul Robeson, pp. 34–38.

Bogle, Donald. "Paul Robeson: The Black Colossus." In *Toms, Coons, Mulattoes, Mammies and Bucks: An Interpretive History of Blacks in American Films*. New York: Viking Press, 1973, pp. 94–100 plus 20 other references.

Bracey, Jr., John H. August Meier, and Elliott Rudwick, eds. *Black Nationalism in America*. Indianapolis: Bobbs-Merrill, 1970. (cloth and paper). Contains "Negro Spirituals Are 'the Soul of the Race Made Manifest'" by Paul Robeson, pp. 331–33. It is a reprint of "The Culture of the Negro," *The Spectator* (June 15, 1934), pp. 916–17.

Brawley, Benjamin. *The Negro Genius*. New York: Dodd, Mead, 1937, xiii. 366 pp. Now available in paperback.

Buck, Pearl. *American Argument*. With Eslanda Goode Robeson. New York: John Day Co., 1949. 206 pp.

Buckle, Richard. *Jacob Epstein, Sculptor*. Cleveland and New York: World Publishing Co., 1963, plate 243. Epstein's bust of Paul Robeson, 1928.

Butterfield, Stephen. *Black Autobiography in America*. Amherst: University of Massachusetts Press, 1974, pp. 5, 103–6, 225–26. Discusses Robeson's autobiography *Here I Stand*; how it was ignored by the white press, reviewed by some of the Black press.

Cripps, Thomas R. *Slow Fade to Black: The Negro in American Film, 1900–1942*. New York: Oxford University Press, 1976. 447 pp.

Cruse, Harold. *The Crisis of the Negro Intellectual*. New York: William Morrow, 1967. 595 pp. (cloth and paper). Cruse's chapter "Paul Robeson" (pp. 285–301) is just one long, bitter, Red-baiting attack on Robeson, his newspaper *Freedom*, and his book *Here I Stand* for being left-wing and not nationalist enough and separatist. Cruse is a gnat picking at a giant. Paul Robeson, Jr.'s piece in this book on his father deals effectively with some of Cruse's lies and twisted statements about Robeson.

Dalin, Ebba (Dahlin), ed. *The Voice of America: An Anthology of American Ideas*. Uppsala, Sweden: Dryer, 1950. 365 pp. Contains "Paul Robeson and the Provincetown Players" (pp. 139–45) from *Paul Robeson, Negro* by Eslanda G. Robeson. Also has other material about Robeson.

Davis, John P., ed. *The American Negro Reference Book*. Englewood Cliffs, N.J.: Prentice-Hall, 1966. 969 pp. Has many references to Paul Robeson as football and basketball player, actor, singer, etc. Robeson was on the All-America football team in 1917 and 1918 while playing at Rutgers University. Harvard University football player William H. Lewis was the first Black All-American in 1892 and 1893; Brown University's Fritz Pollard in 1916 and then Robeson.

Dobrin, Arnold. *Voices of Joy, Voices of Freedom*. New York: Coward McCann & Geoghegan, 1972. 127 pp. A book for children about the lives of Ethel Waters, Sammy Davis, Jr., Marian Anderson, Paul Robeson, and Lena Horne.

Douglas, William O. *Go East Young Man: The Early Years*. New York: Random

House, 1974, xv. 493 pp. Book has references to Paul Robeson and to the Cardozo family of Eslanda Robeson. Robeson was a 1920s Columbia Law School classmate of U.S. Supreme Court Justice Douglas who retired from the Court in 1975.

Douglass, William. *Annals of the First African Church, in the United States of America, Now Styled The African Episcopal Church of St. Thomas.* Philadelphia: King and Baird Printers, 1862. pp. 35–57. About Cyrus Bustill, the great-great-grandfather of Paul Robeson and a founder of the Free African Society of Philadelphia in 1787. He was an upright, religious man and leader respected for his sound judgment. Bustill also baked bread for George Washington's troops.

Du Bois, Shirley Graham. *His Day Is Marching On: A Memoir of W.E.B. Du Bois.* Philadelphia and New York: J. B. Lippincott Co., 1971. 384 pp. There are many references here to Robeson and Du Bois together; their activities. They were old friends.

Du Bois, W.E.B. *The Autobiography of W.E.B. Du Bois.* New York: International Publishers, 1968. 448 pp. There are many references to Robeson here: their work in the Council on African Affairs, excerpts from Du Bois's speech on the persecution of Robeson at Robeson's 60th birthday celebration in 1958, etc.

Ebony Pictorial History of Black America by the editors of *Ebony.* Vols. 2 and 3. Chicago: Johnson Publishing Co., 1971. Volumes have six references to Paul Robeson.

Embree, Edwin R. "Paul Robeson, Voice of Freedom." In *13 Against the Odds.* New York: Viking Press, 1944, pp. 243–61. Reprinted in Arnold Herrick's *This Way to Unity,* 1945.

Favorite Songs of the Red Army. Foreword, "Soviet Culture," by Paul Robeson. New York: Russian-American Music, 1941.

Fax, Elton C. *Through Black Eyes: Journeys of a Black Artist to East Africa and Russia.* New York: Dodd, Mead, 1974, pp. 128–30. Section on Paul Robeson.

Ferguson, Blanche E. *Countee Cullen and the Negro Renaissance.* New York: Dodd, Mead, 1966. 213 pp. Book has material on Robeson's activities.

Fisher, Dorothea F. *American Portraits.* New York: Henry Holt, 1946, pp. 294–297.

Fitzhugh, H. L., and P. K. Fitzhugh. *The Concise Biographical Dictionary of Famous Men and Women.* New York: Grosset and Dunlap, 1949, pp. 811–12.

Foner, Philip S., ed. *The Voice of Black America: Major Speeches by Negroes in the United States, 1797–1971.* New York: Simon and Schuster, 1972, xv. 1216 pp. There are two speeches here by Paul Robeson: "Anti-Imperialists Must Defend Africa," pp. 833–36, and "The Negro Artist Looks Ahead," pp. 849–57.

Foster, William Z. *The Negro People in American History.* New York: International Publishers, 1954, 1970. 608 pp. Has several references to Robeson and his many political activities.

Gelb, Barbara, and Arthur Gelb. *O'Neill: A Biography.* New York: Harper & Row, 1962, pp. 547–57. About the opening of O'Neill's play *All God's Chillun Got Wings* with Robeson as the star.

Grove's Dictionary of Music and Musicians, 5th edition. 9 Vols. Edited by Eric Blom. New York: St. Martin's Press, 1954. Vol. 7, pp. 190–91, has Robeson's biography.

Guzman, Jessie P., ed. *Negro Year Book, 1947.* Dept. of Records and Research, Tuskegee Institute, Ala. 708 pp. Biography of singer, actor in *Othello,* received the NAACP's Spingarn Medal in 1945. Got honorary Doctor of Humane Letters degrees from Hamilton College in 1940, Morehouse College in 1943, and Howard University in 1945.

Hare, Maud Cuney. *Negro Musicians and Their Music.* Washington, D.C.: Associated Publishers, 1936, xii, 439 pp. New York: Da Capo Press, 1974, xii, 439 pp.

Henderson, Edwin B., and the editors of *Sport* magazine. *The Black Athlete: Emergence and Arrival.* Washington, D.C.: United Publishing Corp. and the Association for the Study of Negro Life and History, 1968, xiv, 306 pp. A volume in the International Library of Negro Life and History encyclopedia set.

Henderson, Edwin B. *The Negro in Sports.* Washington, D.C.: Associated Publishers, 1949, xvi, 507 pp.

Hill, Adelaide C., and Martin Kilson, eds. *Apropos of Africa: Afro-American Leaders and the Romance of Africa.* London: Frank Cass & Co., Ltd., 1969, 396 pp.; New York: Humanities Press, 1969; New York: Anchor Books/Doubleday, 1971 (paper). Has short biography of Robeson plus his essay on African culture.

Himber, Charlotte. "Let My People Go, Paul Robeson." In *Famous in Their Twenties.* New York: Association Press, 1942, pp. 91–101.

Hughes, Langston, and Milton Meltzer. *Black Magic: A Pictorial History of the Negro in American Entertainment.* Englewood Cliffs, N.J.: Prentice-Hall, 1967. 375 pp.

Isaacs, Edith J. R. *The Negro in the American Theatre.* New York: Theatre Arts, 1947. 143 pp. Reprint College Park, Md.: McGrath Publishing Co., 1970. 143 pp.

Jewish Life Anthology, 1946–1956. New York: Jewish Life, 1956. Contains "Bonds of Brotherhood," pp. 196–199, by Paul Robeson.

Johnson, Hewlett. *The Soviet Power: The Socialist Sixth of the World.* New York: International Publishers, 1940, pp. 255–57. Section on Robeson and his small son in the Soviet Union.

Johnson, James Weldon. *Black Manhattan.* New York: Alfred A. Knopf, 1930, 1940, xxxiv, 284 pp. Reprint New York: Atheneum Publishers, 1968. New York: Arno Press, 1968. Has quite a bit about Robeson in the theatre.

Jones, Wally, and Jim Washington. *Black Champions Challenge American Sports.* New York: David McKay Co., 1972, pp. 41–43, 44, 45, 50, 60. One-hundred-year history of the rise of Black athletes including Robeson.

Karsh, Yousuf. *Faces of Destiny: Portraits.* New York: Ziff-Davis, 1946, pp. 122–23.

Kaufman, Helen Loeb, and Eva vB. Hansl. *Artists in Music of Today.* New York: Grosset and Dunlap, 1933, p. 87. Paul Robeson and Roland Hayes are included.

Kempton, Murray. *Part of Our Time: Some Ruins and Monuments of the Thirties.* New York: Simon and Schuster, 1955, pp. 236–60.

Kutsch, K. J., and Leo Riemens. *A Concise Biographical Dictionary of Singers.* Translated by Harry Earl Jones. Philadelphia: Chilton Book Co., 1969, pp. 362–63.

Lamparski, Richard. *Whatever Became of . . . ?,* second series. New York: Crown Publishers, 1968, pp. 80–89.

Landay, Eileen. *Black Film Stars.* Drake Publishers, 381 Park Ave. S., New York City 10016, 1974. 192 pp. (photos).

Leab, Daniel J. *From Sambo to Superspade: The Black Experience in Motion Pictures.* Boston: Houghton Mifflin, 1975, viii, 301 pp. (photos).

Locke, Alain. *The Negro and His Music.* Washington, DC: Associates in Negro Folk Education, 1936. 142 pp. (paper). Reprint New York: Arno Press, 1969. 143 pp. (cloth and paper) combined with Locke's *Negro Art: Past and Present.* Was in the Bronze Booklet Series. Discusses Robeson as a singer of Black folk songs.

Lovell, Jr., John. *Black Song: The Forge and the Flame.* New York: Macmillan, 1972. pp. 432, 441–42. Has material on Paul Robeson's life and as an internationally known interpreter of Negro spirituals. Photos, etc.

Lukac, George J., ed. "Review of the 1917 Football Season" by Paul Robeson in *Aloud to Alma Mater.* New Brunswick, N.J.: Rutgers University Press, 1966, pp.

121–27. Modest article by and about Robeson as an All-American and others on the Rutgers University football team. It was reprinted from the *Rutgers Alumni Quarterly*, vol. 4, no. 2 (Jan. 1918), pp. 69–75.

McKean, Else. *Up Hill.* New York: Shady Hill Press, 1947, pp. 16–23. Robeson's is one of six Black biographies in this book for children.

Mannin, Ethel. *Confessions and Impressions.* New York: Doubleday Doran and Co., 1930, pp. 157–61. Chapter 8 is "Paul Robeson: Portrait of a Great Artist."

Mapp, Edward. *Blacks in American Films: Today and Yesterday.* Metuchen, N.J.: Scarecrow Press, 1972, iv, 278 pp.

Miers, Earl Schenck. *The Trouble Bush.* Chicago: Rand McNally & Co., 1966. Miers, a white who graduated from Rutgers University years after Robeson, wrote about Robeson and defended him when he was attacked.

Mitchell, Loften. *Black Drama: The Story of the American Negro in the Theatre.* New York: Hawthorn Books, 1967. 248 pp.

———. *Voices of the Black Theatre.* Clifton, N.J.: James T. White & Co., 1975, ix, 238 pp. A book of interviews. Mitchell's "Time to Break the Silence Surrounding Paul Robeson," *The New York Times*, Arts and Leisure, Section 2 (Aug. 6, 1972), pp. 1, 7 is reprinted here. Also references to Robeson's inspiration to black actors and to Actors Equity to try to have a Broadway theatre named for Robeson, etc.

Murray, James P. *To Find an Image: Black Films from Uncle Tom to Super Fly.* Indianapolis: Bobbs-Merrill, 1974.

New York Herald Tribune. *Report of the New York Herald Tribune 12th Forum on Current Problems*, Waldorf-Astoria Hotel, New York City, Nov. 16–17, 1943, pp. 42–47. Paul Robeson is introduced; his speech on the problems of U.S. Blacks and Africans is included.

Noble, Peter. *The Negro in Films.* London: Skelton Robinson, 1948. 288 pp. Reprint Port Washington, N.Y.: Kennikat Press, 1969. New York: Arno Press, 1970. This book has a lot of material on Robeson's life, his American films, his European films, etc.

Null, Gary. *Black Hollywood: The Negro in Motion Pictures.* Secaucus, N.J.: Citadel Press, 1975. 254 pp. (mostly photos).

Ovington, Mary White. *Portraits in Color.* New York: Viking Press, 1927, pp. 205–17.

Patterson, Lindsay, ed. *Anthology of the American Negro in the Theatre: A Critical Approach.* Washington, D.C.: United Publishing Corp. and the Association for the Study of Negro Life and History, 1968, xiv, 306 pp.; 1976 revised edition. A volume in the International Library of Negro Life and History encyclopedia set.

Patterson, William L. *The Man Who Cried Genocide. An Autobiography.* New York: International Publishers, 1971. 223 pp. (cloth and paper). Patterson, a long-time friend of Robeson's, has many references to Robeson and devotes pages to his early development, his fight against discrimination that barred Black players in organized baseball, and his work with Patterson on the *We Charge Genocide* petition presented to the U.N. in 1951. There are also photographs of Robeson alone and in groups.

"Paul Robeson and Negro Music" (interview). In Thomas O. Fuller's *Pictorial History of the American Negro.* Memphis, Tenn.: Pictorial History, Inc., 1933. pp. 225–26. Reprinted from *Southern Musical Journal*, Memphis, Tenn.

Paul Robeson sings and talks to white and black U.S. soldiers at Berchtesgarten, Austria, 1945. In *The Invisible Soldier: The Experience of the Black Soldier, World War II.* Edited by Mary Penick Motley. Detroit, Mich.: Wayne State University Press, 1975, pp. 158–59. (photo).

"The Pennsylvania Abolition Society & The Pennsylvania Black." The Catalog of the Two Hundredth Anniversary Exhibition at the Historical Society of Pennsylvania, Apr. 17–July 17, 1974. This exhibition was prepared from the collections of the Historical Society of Pennsylvania, the collections of the Black collector Charles L. Blockson of Norristown and others. The large, 24-page catalog has an introduction by Blockson and Maxwell Whiteman and a full-page photograph of Paul Robeson plus a brief biography of him.

Ploski, Harry A., et al., eds. *The Negro Almanac.* New York: Bellwether Publishing Co., 1967, pp. 724–26; 1971, pp. 783–84; 1976, pp. 838–39. Has a biography of Robeson; he is also listed as 1945 NAACP Spingarn Medal winner, etc. The 1971 edition was also published as *Reference Library of Black America* (5 vols.).

Proceedings of the Conference on Africa—New Perspectives. New York: Council on African Affairs, 1944. 52 pp. Opening statement by Paul Robeson, pp. 10–12.

Redding, J. Saunders. *The Lonesome Road.* New York: Doubleday, 1958, pp. 275–88. Section on Robeson.

Robeson, Eslanda. *African Journey.* New York: John Day Co., 1945. 154 pp.

Robinson, Wilhelmena S. *Historical Negro Biographies.* Washington, D.C.: United Publishing Corp. and the Association for the Study of Negro Life and History, 1968, pp. 242–43; 1976 revised edition. A volume in the International Library of Negro Life and History encyclopedia set.

Rogers, Joel A. "Paul Robeson, Intellectual, Musical and Histrionic Prodigy." In *World's Great Men of Color.* Vol. II. Published by the author, 1947, pp. 672–78. Reprint New York: Macmillan, 1972, pp. 512–20.

Rust, Brian, with Allen G. Debus. *The Complete Entertainment Discography from the Mid-1890s to 1942.* New Rochelle, N.Y.: Arlington House, 1949?, pp. 551–59. Has a biographical sketch plus a listing of every Robeson recording with every song on each record up to 1942.

Sargeant, Elizabeth. *Fire Under the Andes: A Group of Literary Portraits.* New York: A. A. Knopf, 1927. Reprint Port Washington, N.Y.: Kennikat Press, 1966, pp. 193–209.

Silber, Irwin, ed. *Lift Every Voice!* With an introduction by Paul Robeson. New York: A People's Artists Publication, 1953. 96 pp. The second People's songbook.

Smythe, Mabel M., ed. *The Black American Reference Book.* Englewood Cliffs, N.J.: Prentice-Hall, 1976, xxviii, 1026 pp. Has material on Robeson as an actor, an athlete, and a concert singer.

Southern, Eileen. *The Music of Black Americans: A History.* New York: W. W. Norton, 1971, xviii, 552 pp. Has a biography of Robeson and other musical references to him.

Stuckey, Sterling. *The Spell of Africa: The Development of Black Nationalist Theory, 1829–1945.* Unpublished Ph.D. dissertation, Northwestern University, 1973. Dissertation has a chapter on Robeson published as " 'I Want To Be African': Paul Robeson and the Ends of Nationalist Theory and Practice, 1914–1945," *The Massachusetts Review,* vol. 17, no. 1 (Spring 1976), pp. 81–138.

Taruc, Luis. *Born of the People.* Foreword by Paul Robeson. Bombay, India: People's Publishing House, Ltd., 1953. Taruc was a leader in the Philippines.

Thompson, Oscar, ed. *The International Cyclopedia of Music and Musicians,* 10th edition. Edited by Bruce Bohle. New York: Dodd, Mead, 1975, p. 1852.

Turner, Patricia. *Afro-American Singers: An Index and Preliminary Discography of Opera, Choral Music and Song.* Challenge Productions, Inc., P.O. Box 9624, Minneapolis, Minn. 55440. 1977, xvi, 255 pp. Published privately in typewritten form in 1976 by the author at the University of Minnesota. Has several pages of excerpts from reviews of Robeson's records; a listing of his record albums; and a biographical bibliography of books, magazine and newspaper articles about Robeson including obituaries.

U.S. Congress. House Committee on Un-American Activities. *Thirty Years of Treason: Excerpts from Hearings before the House Committee on Un-American Activities, 1938–1968.* Edited by Eric Bentley. New York: Viking Press, 1971. Has Paul Robeson's hearing, pp. 768–89, and a statement by Paul Robeson, pp. 977–80.

Vaughn, Robert. *Only Victims: A Study of Show Business Blacklisting.* New York: G. P. Putnam's Sons, 1972. 355 pp. Has a chapter: "The Paul Robeson–Arthur Miller Passport Investigations, 1956." Vaughn's comments are all against Robeson and in favor of the House Committee on Un-American Activities.

What I Want from Life by Fifteen Actors and Actresses. London: George Allen & Unwin, 1934? Robeson has an essay here. Reprinted in *Royal Screen Pictorial*, Apr. 1935.

Who's Who Among Black Americans, 1975–1976. Edited by William C. Matney. 3202 Doolittle Drive, Northbrook, Ill. 60062. 1976. 772 pp.

Who's Who in America, 1932–1933. Chicago: A. N. Marquis Co., 1932, p. 1958. Robeson remained in this *Who's Who* until his death in 1976, when he went into *Who Was Who in America.*

Who's Who in Colored America, 1950. Yonkers on Hudson, N.Y.: Christian E. Burckel and Associates, 648 + 34 pp. Robeson is in this volume and in all earlier editions of this *Who's Who* going back into the 1920s.

Woollcott, Alexander. "Colossal Bronze." In *While Rome Burns.* New York: Grosset and Dunlap, 1934.

The World Book Encyclopedia. Vol. 14. Chicago: Field Enterprises, Inc., 1957, 1973.

Wright, Richard. *Uncle Tom's Children: Four Novellas.* With a foreword by Paul Robeson. London: V. Gollancz Ltd., 1939. 286 pp. This edition with the Robeson foreword was translated into French and published in 1946.

Wynn, Daniel W. *The Black Protest Movement.* New York: Philosophical Library, 1974. 258 pp. Like Black minister Wynn's earlier book, *The NAACP Versus Negro Revolutionary Protest* (1955), this one is full of errors, misinterpretations, superficialities, and acceptance of all vicious, anti-Communist, lying books as gospel truth. Chapter 3 on Revolutionary Protest Action has a lot about Robeson, but almost all of it is false and libelous. Robeson's independent newspaper *Freedom* is called the organ of the Communist Party.

Young, A. S. "Doc." *Negro Firsts in Sports.* Chicago: Johnson Publishing Co., 1963. 301 pp.

Magazine and Newspaper Articles, Book Reviews, and Radio and TV Programs

"Review of the 1917 Football Season" by Paul Robeson. *Rutgers Alumni Quarterly*, vol. 4, no. 2 (Jan. 1918), pp. 69–75.

"Review of the 1918 Football Season" by Clifford N. Baker. *Rutgers Alumni Quarterly*, vol. 5, no. 2 (Jan. 1919), p. 153.

"The New Idealism" by Paul LeRoy Robeson. *Rutgers Daily Targum*, vol. 50, no. 30 (June 1919), pp. 570–71. Also p. 566 about Robeson's career.

"Theatre Review of Paul Robeson in O'Neill's 'All God's Chillun'" by George Jean Nathan. *The American Mercury*, vol. II, no. 7 (July 1924), pp. 371–73.

Review of Oscar Micheaux's movie *Body and Soul* with Paul Robeson in his first movie role. *Variety* (Nov. 26, 1924), p. 1.

"Reflections on O'Neill's Plays" by Paul Robeson. *Opportunity*, vol. 2, no. 24 (Dec. 1924), pp. 368–70.

"An Actor's Wanderings and Hopes" by Paul Robeson. *The Messenger*, vol. 7, no. 1 (Jan. 1925), p. 32.

"The Bustill Family" by Anne Bustill Smith. *The Journal of Negro History*, vol. 10, no. 4 (Oct. 1925), pp. 638–47. "Documents," vol. 11 (1926), pp. 82–87. This is Paul Robeson's mother's family.

"Paul Robeson, Son of Slave Parents, Reaches Pinnacle." *Pittsburgh Courier* (Nov. 7, 1925), p. 10.

"The Man with His Home in a Rock: Paul Robeson" by Elizabeth S. Sargeant. *The New Republic*, vol. 46, no. 587 (Mar. 3, 1926), pp. 40–41.

"When Robeson Sings" by Frank Lenz. *Association Men* (July 1927), pp. 495–96.

"King of Harlem" by Mildred Gilman. *New Yorker*, vol. 4 (Sept. 29, 1928), pp. 26–29.

Article on Paul Robeson's nude statue. *Opportunity*, vol. 8, no. 6 (June 1930), pp. 168–69.

"Ambassador to the World" by Langston Hughes. *New York Herald Tribune* (June 29, 1930), sec. 11, p. 2.

"*Paul Robeson, Negro* by Eslanda Goode Robeson." Book review by Stark Young. *New Republic* (Aug. 6, 1930), pp. 345–46. A condescending review.

"A Great Personality, Paul Robeson Speaks About Art and the Negro" by T. Thompson. *The Millgate*, vol. 26, part 1, no. 303 (Dec. 1930), p. 158.

"Robeson's Advice to His Race." *New York Herald Tribune* (Jan. 11, 1931), sec. 8, p. 2.

Article about Paul Robeson. *Opportunity*, vol. 9 (Jan. 1931), pp. 14–15.

"Robey Comes Home" by Edward Lawson. *The Anthologist* (Rutgers University) (Jan. 1932), pp. 7–23.

"Riches of the Black Man's Culture" by Paul Robeson. *African Observer* (June 1933).

"Ol' Man River—in Person" by Alexander Woollcott. *Cosmopolitan* (July 1933), pp. 54–55, 101–3.

Article on Paul Robeson. *British Musician* (July 1933), pp. 156–68.

Paul Robeson comments on Hollywood's two Negro films *Hallelujah* and *Hearts in Dixie*. *Film Weekly* (Sept. 1, 1933).

Photograph of Paul Robeson as Emperor Jones. *Theatre Arts Monthly* (Oct. 1933).

"The Emperor Jones" by Herman G. Weinberg. *Close Up*, vol. 10 (Dec. 1933), pp. 351–52.

"The Culture of the Negro" by Paul Robeson. *The Spectator*, vol. 152 (June 15, 1934), pp. 916–17. A very important, pioneering essay on African culture in Africa and throughout the world.

"African Culture" by Paul Robeson. *The African Observer*, vol. 2, no. 5 (Mar. 1935), pp. 19–21.

"I Breathe Freely" (interview in Moscow with Paul Robeson) by Julia Dorn. *New Theatre*, vol. 11, no. 7 (July 1935), p. 5. In the special issue on the Negro in the theatre.

"Paul Robeson" (interview) by Rev. Father J. C. O'Flaherty. *West African Review* (Aug. 1936), pp. 16–17.

"Primitives: On African Languages" by Paul Robeson. *New Statesman and Nation*, vol. 12 (Aug. 8, 1936), pp. 190–92.

Paul Robeson comments on his European film *Song of Freedom*. *Film Weekly* (Sept. 19, 1936).

"Paul Robeson—The Man and His Art" (interview) by K. A. Harvey. *The Millgate*, vol. 33, part 2, no. 396 (Sept. 1938), pp. 706–12.

"Paul Robeson Told Me" (an interview) by Julia Dorn. *TAC* (July 1939), p. 23.

Robeson Sings *Ballad for Americans* by John Latouche (words) and Earl Robinson (music) on "Pursuit of Happiness" radio program, CBS, Nov. 9, 1939. See New York City Lewisohn *Stadium Concerts Review* (June 23, 24, 25, 1941), pp. 7–8. Robeson as soloist with mixed chorus and orchestra.

"Bravos," *Time* (Nov. 20, 1939).

"Paul Robeson Is John Henry" by Roark Bradford. *Collier's*, vol. 105, no. 2 (Jan. 13, 1940), pp. 15, 45.

Photograph of Paul Robeson as John Henry. *Theatre Arts* (Feb. 1940).

Robeson speaks out. *New Masses*, vol. 34, no. 8 (Feb. 13, 1940), p. 21.

"Robeson, Man of His People" by John Pittman. *Daily Worker* (Nov. 25, 1940).

Paul Robeson's concert at Lewisohn Stadium, New York City, June 23, 1941. *Stadium Concerts Review* (June 23, 24, 25, 1941).

"Paul Robeson," *Current Biography* (1941), pp. 716–18.

"Born Lucky" by Avery Strakosch. *Look* (Mar. 10, 1942), pp. 64–67.

Photograph of Paul Robeson as Othello. *Theatre Arts* (Aug. 1942). Entire issue on the Negro in the American theatre.

"Tragic Handkerchief: First U.S. Appearance in Othello," *Time* (Aug. 24, 1942).

"For I Am Black" by Alvah Bessie. *New Masses* (Sept. 8, 1942). Review of Robeson in *Othello* at Princeton, N.J.

Paul Robeson as Othello. *New York Times Magazine* (Oct. 3, 1943), p. 15. (photographs).

"Saga of a Nonpareil" by Ed Sullivan in his Little Old New York column. *New York Daily News* (Oct. 5?, 1943).

"Paul Robeson's Othello" by Samuel Sillen. *New Masses* (Nov. 3, 1943), pp. 24–26.

"'Othello': Paul Robeson Gives a Magnificent Performance as the Moor of Venice," *Life* (Nov. 22, 1943), pp. 87–89.

Paul Robeson in "Othello." *The Worker*, sec. 1 (Nov. 28, 1943), p. 7.

"These Words Let All Americans Remember" by Paul Robeson. *The Worker Magazine Section* (Nov. 28, 1943), p. 4.

"Robeson Remembers, 'An Interview with the Star of Othello,' Partly About His Past" by Robert Van Gelder. *The New York Times* (Jan. 16, 1944), sec. 2. p. 1.

"Two Strikes on Jim Crow" by Paul Robeson. *Spotlight* (Jan. 1944), pp. 3–4. Here Robeson discusses the question of Blacks in professional baseball as he did when he spoke before the baseball managers, magnates, and the baseball commissioner, Kenesaw Mountain Landis.

Speech by Paul Robeson at Sun Yat-sen Memorial Meeting. *Daily Worker* (Mar. 17, 1944), p. 6.

"America's No. 1 Negro" by Jerome Beatty. *The American Magazine* (May 1944), pp. 28–29, 142–43, 148.

"Robeson of Rutgers." Condensed from the book *Paul Robeson: Negro* by Eslanda Goode Robeson. *Negro Digest*, vol. 2, no. 7 (May 1944), pp. 76–80.

Paul Robeson received a special gold medal on May 19, 1944, from the National Institute of Arts and Letters at the annual ceremony in the Academy Auditorium, New York City. At this meeting Dr. W.E.B. Du Bois was inducted into the National Institute of Arts and Letters. From National Institute program.

"Shakespeare's American Play" by Cpl. John Lovell, Jr. *Theatre Arts* (June 1944), pp. 363–70.

"On Soviet Culture" by Paul Robeson. *Daily Worker* (July 24, 1944), p. 11.

"Paul Robeson" by John K. Hutchens. *Theatre Arts* (Oct. 1944), pp. 579–85.

"Paul Robeson Sings First Time Since *Othello* Started Its Tour" (in Los Angeles). *New York Amsterdam News* (Mar. 31, 1945).

"Some Reflections on Othello and the Nature of Our Time" by Paul Robeson. *American Scholar* (Oct. 1945).

"No Real Minorities in U.S.S.R." by Paul Robeson. *Daily Worker* (Nov. 22, 1945), p. 7.

"Important American Artists" (on Robert Gwathmey) by Paul Robeson. *Daily Worker* (Feb. 4, 1946), p. 11.

Paul Robeson Defies Un-American Committee. *Daily Worker* (Oct. 11, 1946), p. 11.

Unseat (Sen. Theodore) Bilbo Dinner (given by Civil Rights Congress in New York City). Robeson one of the speakers. *New York Amsterdam News* (Oct. 26, 1946).

Pioneers in the Struggle Against Segregation. *Survey Graphic* (Jan. 1947), pp. 90–91. Photograph of Robeson. This is a special issue on segregation.

Robeson quits formal concert field. Says he will sing only where and what he pleases. *The New York Times* (Mar. 16, 1947).

Portraits of Outstanding Americans of Negro Origin. A set of 24 reproductions of paintings by the late Laura Wheeler Waring (black) and Betsy Graves Reyneau (white) prepared by the Harmon Foundation, New York City, in the 1940s; one of these is a reproduction of a painting of Paul Robeson as Othello by Betsy Graves Reyneau.

Robeson raps ban on Peoria concert. *Daily Worker* (Apr. 19, 1947), p. 12. Follow-up stories: *Daily Worker* (Apr. 21, 1947), p. 1; (Apr. 26, 1947), p. 12.

Albany schools barred to Robeson concert. *Daily Worker* (Apr. 25, 1947), p. 12.

I'll keep fighting, Robeson vows. *Daily Worker* (Apr. 28, 1947), p. 4

Robeson lashes witch-hunters. *Daily Worker* (Apr. 30, 1947), p. 11.

Robeson sings to 6,000 in Toronto despite talk gag. *Daily Worker* (May 22, 1947), p. 11.

Robeson triumphs at Stadium. *Daily Worker* (July 12, 1947), p. 11

Paul Robeson scores big Lewisohn [Stadium, New York City] music triumph. *New York Amsterdam News* (July 26, 1947).

"Patterson Papers Try to Frighten Robeson" by R. F. Hall. *Daily Worker* (June 8, 1948), p. 9.

Pastors support Robeson's rights. *New Republic*, vol. 119 (July 26, 1948), pp. 17–18.

"Paul Robeson, Campaigner" by A. W. Berry. *The Worker Magazine Section* (Oct. 17, 1948), p. 1.

"Freedom in Their Own Land" by Paul Robeson. *National Guardian* (Dec. 20, 1948). About Robeson's concert tour through Jamaica and Trinidad in the West Indies.

Robeson Addresses Negro Youth Group at YMCA in Harlem. *The New York Times* (Jan. 29, 1949). Negro Youth Builders Institute, Inc., New York City, protest meeting after lynching of Robert Mallard in Lyons, Ga.

Paul Robeson's speech at Peace Conference in Paris. *New York Amsterdam News* (Apr. 30, 1949), p. 1. *Afro-American* (Apr. 30, 1949), p. 1.

"Robeson Challenges the Warmongers and Jimcrow" by Benjamin J. Davis, Jr. *The Worker* sec. 1 (May 8, 1949), p. 5.

British *Worker* interviews Robeson. *Daily Worker* (May 25, 1949), p. 12.

Robeson speaks for Robeson. (NAACP separates itself from Robeson.) *Crisis*, vol. 56, no. 5 (May 1949), p. 137.

"People's Welcome for Paul Robeson" by Benjamin J. Davis, Jr. *The Worker* sec. 1 (June 5, 1949), p. 8.

How Prague welcomed Paul Robeson. *Daily Worker* (June 8, 1949), p. 12.

Robeson leaves U.S.S.R after celebration of 150th anniversary of Pushkin's birth for New York City to testify in the trial of the 13 Communist Party leaders. (He considers their defense important.) *New York Herald Tribune* (June 16, 1949).

"Robeson Blasts *Old Man River.*" (Oscar Hammerstein, the lyricist, objects to Robeson's changing his racist words of the song.) *New York Age* (June 18, 1949).

5,000 jam Harlem rally to welcome Robeson home. *Daily Worker* (June 20, 1949), p. 1.

Paul Robeson in Moscow. *New Times,* no. 26 (June 22, 1949), p. 20.

"I'm Looking for Full Freedom" by Paul Robeson. *The Worker Magazine Section* (July 3, 1949), p. 6.

Robeson weighs equal rights practice of U.S. and the Soviet Union. *USSR Information Bulletin* (Washington, D.C.), vol. 9, no. 13 (July 15, 1949), p. 425.

Robeson rips House Un-Americans. *Daily Worker* (July 21, 1949).

1,500 hail Robeson in Newark; demand Trenton Six be freed. *Daily Worker* (July 22, 1949), p. 3.

"Paul Robeson's Soviet Journey" by Amy Schechter. *Soviet Russia Today,* vol. 17, no. 16 (Aug. 1949), pp. 9–11, 24. Robeson's picture on cover.

"My Answer" by Paul Robeson. A series of five articles. *New York Age* (Aug. and Sept. 1949).

"Police Commended in Peekskill Fray" by Warren Moscow. *The New York Times* (Sept. 8, 1949), pp. 1, 34. Includes report on the Peekskill rioting sent to the governor of New York State, Thomas Dewey.

"Robeson Concert Slated Sunday in Bigger Park near Peekskill." *New York Herald Tribune* (Sept. 9, 1949).

Robeson sings to 12,000 in Los Angeles. *Daily Worker* (Oct. 4, 1949), p. 4.

Russian mountain named for Paul Robeson. *New York Amsterdam News* (tabloid edition) (Oct. 8, 1949), p. 2.

"What Russia Does for Negroes" by Paul Robeson. *The Worker Magazine Section* (Dec. 18, 1949), p. 6.

Robeson blasts Africa slaughter (Singer tells of Liberian-South African riot acts). *New York Age* (Feb. 25, 1950).

"Paul Robeson: Right" by W.E.B. Du Bois—"Wrong" by Walter White. *Negro Digest* (Mar. 1950), pp. 8–18.

NBC refuses to reveal who got Robeson banned from TV. *Daily Worker* (Mar. 15, 1950), p. 1.

"Wall Street Fears Robeson" by John Pittman. *Daily Worker* (Mar. 16, 1950), p. 6.

Pickets blast NBC on gagging of Robeson. *Daily Worker* (Mar. 17, 1950), p. 3.

TV ban on Robeson hit by Negro press. *Daily Worker* (Mar. 30, 1950), p. 11.

"U.S. Cancels Robeson's Passport After He Refuses to Surrender It" by A. J. Gordon. *The New York Times* (Apr. 4, 1950).

Robeson Urges Action for 25 Facing Prison (Cold-war suppression of free thought and speech then sweeping America). *The Worker* (Apr. 16, 1950).

"Paul Robeson—Made in America" by Earl Schenck Miers. *Nation* (May 27, 1950), pp. 523–24.

"Paul Robeson Speaks to You" (exclusive interview) by Charles Morgan. In *In Defense of Peace* (about the Stockholm Appeal, Great Britain), no. 12 (July 1950), pp. 32–37.

"To Whom Should Paul Be Grateful?" by Eslanda Robeson. *The Worker Magazine Section* (Aug. 20, 1950), p. 3.

Ask Robeson's silence on oppression of Negroes as price of passport. *Daily Worker* (Aug. 25, 1950), p. 4.

Boston museum official hits ban on Robeson portrait. *Daily Worker* (Oct. 18, 1950), p. 4.

"Paul Robeson" by Earl Schenck Miers. *Negro Digest* (Oct. 1950), pp. 21–24.

"The Lessons of the Peekskill Riots" by James Rorty and Winifred Raushenbush. *Commentary*, vol. 10 (Oct. 1950), pp. 309–23. A long attack on Paul Robeson.

Langston Hughes's poem "Freedom Train" read by Paul Robeson (phonograph record). Southern Conference for Human Welfare, New Orleans, La. 1950?

"Paul Robeson: Messiah of Color" by Winifred Raushenbush. *Freeman*, vol. 1 (Nov. 13, 1950), pp. 111–14. A vicious, anti-Robeson article.

Personalities—Paul Robeson among guests at the Soviet Embassy's reception in Washington, D.C., celebrating the 33rd anniversary of the Revolution in Russsia. *The New York Times* (Nov. 19, 1950). (photograph).

Hotel Cancels Robeson Meet. *Daily News* (Dec. 18, 1950). American Labor Party meeting in Bronx cancelled by Concourse Plaza Hotel management. Robeson was to receive an international peace prize given by the 2nd World Peace Congress at Warsaw, Poland, to share with Pablo Picasso, a $14,300 prize.

"Our People Demand Freedom" by Paul Robeson. *Masses & Mainstream*, vol. 4, no. 1 (Jan. 1951), pp. 65–67.

"The Strange Case of Paul Robeson" by Walter White. *Ebony*, vol. 6, no. 4 (Feb. 1951), pp. 78–84.

State Department rebuffs crusade for peace; tells Robeson and group U.S. won't quit Korea now. *New York Herald Tribune* (Mar. 16, 1951).

"Mr. Freedom, Himself" by John Pittman. *The Worker Magazine Section* (Apr. 15, 1951), p. 1.

"Unity for Peace" by Paul Robeson. *Masses and Mainstream*, vol. 4, no. 8 (Aug. 1951), pp. 21–24.

Scots Seek to Free, Honor Robeson (Scotland). *National Guardian* (Sept. 19, 1951).

"Free Paul Robeson!" by Elizabeth Moos. *Masses and Mainstream*, vol. 4, no. 10 (Oct. 1951), pp. 8–10. (About Robeson's imprisonment in the U.S. through the State Department's denial of his passport.)

"Paul Robeson—The Lost Shepherd" by R. Alan. *Crisis*, vol. 58, no. 9 (Nov. 1951), pp. 569–73. This article and the Walter White piece in *Ebony* listed above were U.S. State Dept. inspired. See Oct. 1977 listing below.

"The Negro Artist Looks Ahead" by Paul Robeson. *Masses and Mainstream*, vol. 5, no. 1 (Jan. 1952), pp. 7–14. His speech at the National Council of the Arts, Sciences and Professions Conference for Equal Rights for Negroes.

Salem Bars Appearance by Robeson. (Salem Methodist Church in Harlem bars sacred concert by Robeson as not in the best interest of the church, Rev. Dr. Charles Y. Trigg, pastor.)

"But Robeson's Voice Got Through" by Abner W. Berry. *The Worker Magazine Section* (Feb. 24, 1952), p. 2.

Robeson urges support for Africans' fight on Jimcrow (text). *Daily Worker* (Mar. 12, 1952), p. 5.

Heads of 11 million Africans thank Robeson for U.S. aid. *Daily Worker* (Mar. 31, 1952), p. 1.

"Washington Exposes Its Own Hand in Robeson Passport Case" by John H. Jones. *The Worker*, sec. 1 (Apr. 6, 1952), p. 4.

"Government Confesses in Answering Paul Robeson" by Abner W. Berry. *The Worker Magazine Section* (Apr. 13, 1952), p. 2.

"Why Robeson Is Known as Greatest Baritone" by Abner W. Berry. *Daily Worker* (May 1, 1952), p. 4.

"He Spoke when I had No Tongue" by Abner W. Berry. *The Worker*, sec. 1 (May 11, 1952), p. 1.

AME Zion church conference hits State Department ban on Robeson's travel. *Daily Worker* (May 22, 1952), p. 3.

People Rally to Robeson on Tour (coast-to-coast tour on behalf of *Freedom* news-paper). *Freedom* (June 19, 1952).

"Open Letter to Robeson from a Soviet Actor" by M. Nasvanov. *The Worker Magazine Section* (July 6, 1952), p. 7.

Robeson tells Progressive Party delegates of Negroes' stake in '52 vote. *Daily Worker* (July 8, 1952), p. 4.

"Voting for Peace" by Paul Robeson. *Masses and Mainstream*, vol. 5, no. 8 (Aug. 1952), pp. 9–14. His address at the National Convention of the Progressive Party in Chicago in 1952.

Robeson says fight for civil rights now; don't wait for November elections. *Daily Worker* (Aug. 7, 1952), p. 1.

"Land of Love and Happiness" by Paul Robeson. *New World Review* (Dec. 1952), pp. 3–4. His speech on Nov. 13, 1952, about the Soviet Union at the National Council of American-Soviet Friendship meeting on the 35th anniversary of the U.S.S.R.

"Noose of Silence Around Paul Robeson" by Milton Howard. *The Worker Magazine Section* (Dec. 7, 1952), p. 7.

"Denounce Scheme to Circulate Unauthorized Robeson Records" by Abner W. Berry. *Daily Worker* (Dec. 16, 1952), p. 7.

Robeson wins Stalin peace prize. *Daily Worker* (Dec. 22, 1952), p. 3.

Robeson accepts Stalin prize on behalf of U.S. peace fighters. *Daily Worker* (Dec. 24, 1952), p. 3.

"Robeson's Stalin Peace Prize Shows World-Wide Prestige" by William Z. Foster. *Daily Worker* (Dec. 29, 1952), p. 5.

"Paul Robeson, the Voice of the People" by I. Yermashov. *Soviet Literature*, no. 3 (1953), pp. 186–88.

"Conspiracy Can't Silence Robeson's Great Voice" by E. S. Hicks. *The Worker* (May 24, 1953), p. 9.

25,000 on Canadian border hear Robeson. *Daily Worker* (Aug. 20, 1953), p. 2.

Paul Robeson wins Stalin Peace Prize ($25,000). *New York Amsterdam News* (Oct. 3, 1953), p. 13 (photograph).

"Robeson Receives 'Highest Award Humanity Can Bestow' " by Joseph North. *The Worker*, sec. 1 (Oct. 11, 1953), p. 7.

"Signal Event" by M. Nasvanov. *News* (Moscow), no. 20 (Oct. 15, 1953), p. 17.

From the Soviet actor who portrayed Robeson. *The Worker* (Jan. 10, 1954), p. 8.

Seek passport for envoy of the people (Paul Robeson). *The Worker* (May 16, 1954), p. 6.

"No Borders for Art" by Samuel Sillen. *Masses and Mainstream*, vol. 7, no. 6 (June 1954), pp. 4–5. About Robeson's passport denial. His photograph on cover of magazine.

"They Tried to Scandalize His Name—and Failed" by Abner W. Berry. *The Worker* (June 20, 1954), p. 10.

"Letter to Charles Chaplin" by Paul Robeson. *The Worker* (July 11, 1954), p. 8.

"Letter to France" by Paul Robeson. *National Guardian*, vol. 6, no. 39 (July 19, 1954), p. 12.

Renews bid for right to passport (Paul Robeson). *Daily Worker* (July 24, 1954), p. 2.

"My Brother—Paul Robeson—An Appraisal" by Rev. B. C. Robeson. *Quarterly Review of Higher Education Among Negroes* (Oct. 1954), pp. 159-64.

"Floodtide of Peace" by Paul Robeson. *Masses and Mainstream*, vol. 7, no. 10 (Oct. 1954), pp. 6–10.

Magazine sponsors cultural tribute to the Robesons. *Daily Worker* (Oct. 20, 1954), p. 7.

"Bonds of Brotherhood" by Paul Robeson. *Jewish Life*, vol. 9, no. 1 (Nov. 1954), pp. 13–14.

State Department bans Robeson visit to Soviet writers. *Daily Worker* (Nov. 30, 1954), p. 8.

"A Word About African Languages" by Paul Robeson. *Spotlight on Africa* (Feb. 1955), pp. 3–5. Article printed in the Council on African Affairs' publication.

"My Dad" by Paul Robeson, Jr. *New Challenge* (Feb. 1955), pp. 16–18. Photo.

Robeson urges struggle to defeat "double jeopardy" effort. *Daily Worker* (Mar. 10, 1955), p. 6.

"How I Discovered Africa" by Paul Robeson. *Fighting Talk* (April 1955).

Robeson sang and spoke to 1,000 students at Swarthmore. *Daily Worker* (May 15, 1955), p. 6.

Robeson offered Othello role in Soviet film; again applies for passport. *Daily Worker* (May 16, 1955), p. 3.

Robeson asks passport both as a "natural" and "equal" right. *Daily Worker* (July 19, 1955).

Robeson may travel, but not in Europe. *Daily Worker* (July 20, 1955), p. 1.

Robeson visits campuses; tells what he found. *Daily Worker* (July 20, 1955), p. 6.

Robeson wins limited right to travel; seeks full right without signing oath. *National Guardian* (Aug. 1, 1955).

"Once There Was a Man" by Abner W. Berry. *Daily Worker* (Aug. 4, 1955), p. 5.

"Canadian View of Robeson's Great Peace Arch Concert" by T. McEwen. *Daily Worker* (Aug. 16, 1955), p. 8.

Court rules Robeson's passport suit is premature. *Daily Worker* (Aug. 17, 1955), p. 3.

"Robeson's Popularity Greater than Ever, Concert Tour Shows" by E. Keeler. *Daily Worker* (Sept. 6, 1955), p. 6.

"They Want the Cadillac Curtain Lowered for Paul Robeson" by Cedric Belfrage. *National Guardian*, vol. 7, no. 49 (Sept. 26, 1955), p. 3.

"Song to Sing" by Paul Robeson. *Masses and Mainstream*, vol. 8, no. 10 (Oct. 1955), pp. 12–14.

Real issues behind the denial of (Paul Robeson's) passport. *Daily Worker* (Oct. 17, 1955), p. 6.

"Britain—Right to Left—Cries 'Let Robeson Come!'" by John Williamson. *The Worker* (Oct. 23, 1955), p. 8.

"My New Year Hopes" by Paul Robeson. (Short messages reprinted from *Pravda*.) *New Times*, no. 2 (Jan. 5, 1956), p. 20.

Robeson greeted by 2,700 in Toronto. *Daily Worker* (Feb. 17, 1956), p. 1.

Canadians acclaim Robeson on concert stage, TV, radio. *The Worker* (Feb. 26, 1956), p. 10.

Court hears Robeson passport plea. *Daily Worker* (Mar. 9, 1956), p. 3.

"Big Rally in England Demands Robeson Get Right to Travel" by Cedric Belfrage. *National Guardian* (Mar. 26, 1956).

"Robeson Denounces 'Un-Americans,' Faces Contempt" (before House Committe on Un-American Activities). *National Guardian* (June 25, 1956).

High court denies hearing to Robeson. *Daily Worker* (Nov. 6, 1956), p. 2.

"Some Aspects of Afro-American Music" by Paul Robeson. *Afro-American* (newspaper) (Dec. 21?, 1956).

British actors' union votes support for Paul Robeson. *Daily Worker* (May 3, 1957), p. 7.

"Robeson Sings to London by Telephone" by Cedric Belfrage. *National Guardian*, vol. 9, no. 32 (May 27, 1957), p. 1.

"Robeson's Phone Concert [to London] a Smash Success" by Cedric Belfrage. *National Guardian*, vol. 9, no. 34 (June 10, 1957), p. 6.

"Paul Robeson Sings to 10,000 on the West Coast" by D. Ordway. *Daily Worker* (Aug. 15, 1957), p. 6.

"The Related Sounds of Music" by Paul Robeson. Written in Sept. 1957 for a musical journal in Czechoslovakia. (An abridged retranslation from the German made available by the Robeson Archive in Berlin. First publication in the U.S.) *Daily World Magazine Section* (Apr. 7, 1973), pp. 6–7.

Robeson urges government defend constitution against racists. *Daily Worker* (Sept. 23, 1957), p. 5.

"Has Paul Robeson Betrayed the Negro?" by Carl T. Rowan (interview). *Ebony*, vol. 12, no. 12 (Oct. 1957), pp. 31–42.

Life of Paul Robeson, Soviet Documentary Film, Nears Completion. *Jet* (Mar. 13, 1958), p. 65; (Feb. 19, 1959), p. 62.

"India Plans to Honor Robeson at 60; Nehru Cites 'Cause of Human Dignity.'" *The New York Times* (Mar. 21, 1958). Photograph.

"The Feeling About Paul at Home" by Louis E. Burnham. *National Guardian*, vol. 10, no. 25 (Apr. 7, 1958), p. 6.

"Robeson Birthday Parties Set in 27 Countries" by Cedric Belfrage. *National Guardian*, vol. 10, no. 25 (Apr. 7, 1958), p. 7.

"The Real Reason Behind Robeson's Persecution" by W.E.B. Du Bois. *National Guardian*, vol. 10, no. 25 (Apr. 7, 1958), p. 6.

"His Voice Is Better Now Than Ever" by Eslanda Goode Robeson. *National Guardian* (Apr. 7, 1958).

"Paul Robeson Makes a New Album" by Nat Hentoff. *Reporter*, vol. 18 (Apr. 17, 1958), pp. 34–35.

Paul Robeson's sixtieth birthday. *New Times*, no. 15 (Apr. 1958), p. 16.

Triumph of Paul Robeson. *New Times*, no. 16 (Apr. 1958), p. 2.

"Paul Robeson: The Man and His Meaning" by Benjamin J. Davis, Jr. *Political Affairs*, vol. 37, no. 4 (Apr. 1958), pp. 1–8.

"Robeson at Ross" (Calif.) by Albert E. Kahn. *National Guardian* (Apr. 14, 1958). Celebration of Robeson's 60th birthday.

Travel ban on Robeson eased; U.S. allows hemisphere trips. *The New York Times* (Apr. 20, 1958), p. 1.

Robeson at Stratford (in *Othello*). *National Guardian* (Apr. 20, 1958).

1,000 greet Robeson in Chicago. *National Guardian* (Apr. 21, 1958).

Here I Stand by Paul Robeson. Book review by Phillip Bonosky. *The Worker* (May 4, 1958).

"Paul Robeson Sings, Lectures in First City Recital in 11 Years" by Harold C. Schonberg. *The New York Times* (May 10, 1958). Photograph.

"Robeson Returns to Carnegie Hall" by Harriett Johnson. *New York Post* (May 11, 1958).

Paul Comes Home (report to readers). *National Guardian* (May 19, 1958).

"Paul Robeson in Carnegie Hall" by Irving Kolodin. *Saturday Review*, vol. 41 (May 24, 1958), p. 35.

Honors for Paul Robeson in India. *Christian Century* (June 4, 1958).

Didn't My Lord Deliver Daniel, and Why Not Every Man? Review of Paul Robeson's *Here I Stand*. *The Comet*, vol. 1, no. 4 (June 1958), p. 3.

Robeson, (Corliss) Lamont Given Passports. *National Guardian* (July 7, 1958).

U.S. State Department issues Paul Robeson a passport after refusing for eight years. *Jet* (July 10, 1958), p. 5.

"Paul Robeson Gets a Roaring Welcome in Britain" by Cedric Belfrage. *National Guardian* (July 21, 1958), Concerts, TV shows, *Othello*—and lots more.

"Ochen Rad! Polrobson" (from Moscow). *National Guardian* (Sept. 8, 1958).

Robeson Intends to Live in London. *The New York Times* (Sept. 22, 1958).

Article probably about Robeson's upcoming Oct. 12, 1958, concert in St. Paul's Cathedral. *London Musical Events*, vol 13 (Sept. 29, 1958).

"Go Down, Moses, Tell Old Pharaoh, Let My People Go!" by Peggy Middleton. *National Guardian* (Oct. 20, 1958). Paul Robeson sings in St. Paul's Cathedral (London, England) on Sun., Oct. 12, 1958.

"2 U.S. Actors Star on British Stage. Robeson and [Sam] Wanamaker in *Othello* as Stratford Fete Opens 100th Season" by W. A. Darlington. *The New York Times* (Apr. 8, 1959).

"Paul Robeson's Latest Success" (letter) by William L. Patterson. *New Times*, no. 20 (May 1959), p. 31.

New Triumph for Robeson in *Othello* in England. *Hue* (June 1959) pp. 38–41.

Robeson and (Yehudi) Menuhin (violinist). *National Guardian* (Feb. 15, 1960).

Robeson in East Berlin. *National Guardian* (July 18, 1960).

Paul Robeson Receives Two Awards and Honorary Doctorate from Humboldt University, East Germany. *Jet*, vol. 18 (Oct. 20, 1960), p. 15. *Daily World Magazine Section* (Apr. 7, 1973), p. 6.

"Mount Paul" by John Pittman. *New World Review* (Feb. 1962), pp. 24–28. About a Soviet mountain peak that bears Robeson's name

"Paul Robeson" by Martha Dodd. *Mainstream*, vol. 16, no. 5 (May 1963), pp. 53–56.

"Robeson Greets Soviet Efforts for World Peace" by Art Shields. *The Worker* (May 19, 1963), p. 6.

"Exposes Slanders Concerning Robeson" by Eslanda Goode Robeson. *The Worker* (June 2, 1963), p. 2.

"About Paul Robeson" by Eslanda Goode Robeson. (Letter from Mrs. Robeson in London, England.) *National Guardian* (June 6, 1963).

"A Voice Is Silenced" (Paul Robeson) by Robert G. Spivack. *New York Herald Tribune* (Sept. 15, 1963).

"Why He 'Sneaked' to East Germany" (Paul Robeson) by Eslanda Goode Robeson. *Afro-American* (Nov. 2, 1963), p. 20.

"Disillusioned Native Son—Paul Robeson." *The New York Times* (Dec. 23, 1963). Photograph.

"Welcome Home, Paul Robeson" (editorial). *Freedomways*, vol. 4, no. 1 (1st quarter 1964), pp. 6–7.

(National) Guardian luncheon Apr. 14 (Eslanda Robeson will speak). *National Guardian* (Mar. 28, 1964).

"Voice of Paul Robeson" by Elizabeth Gurley Flynn. *The Worker*, vol. 29, no. 236 (Apr. 19, 1964), p. 7.

"Turning Point" by Paul Robeson. *American Dialog*, vol. 1, no. 2 (Oct.–Nov. 1964), p. 6.

"The Legacy of W.E.B. Du Bois" by Paul Robeson. *Freedomways*, vol. 5, no. 1 (1st quarter 1965), pp. 36–40.

Speech in honor of Alexander Trachtenberg by Paul Robeson. *The Worker*, vol. 30, no. 8 (Jan. 31, 1965), p. 6.

"2,000 Hail Robeson at Freedomways Tribute" by D. Archer. *The Worker*, vol. 30, no. 33 (May 2, 1965), p. 3.

"We Shall Overcome" by Paul Robeson. *American Dialog*, vol. 2, no. 2 (May–June 1965), p. 18.

"Salute to Robeson" (editorial). *Freedomways*, vol. 5, no. 3 (3rd quarter 1965), pp. 363–64.

"Paul Robeson—Democracy's Most Powerful Voice" by Hope R. Stevens. *Freedomways*, vol. 5, no. 3 (3rd quarter 1965), pp. 365–68. Speech at "Salute to Paul Robeson," Hotel Americana, New York City, Apr. 22, 1965.

"Paul Robeson—Inspirer of Youth" by John Lewis. *Freedomways*, vol. 5, no. 3 (3rd quarter 1965), pp. 369–72. Speech at "Salute to Paul Robeson."

"It's Good To Be Back" (excerpts from the speech by Paul Robeson at "Salute to Paul Robeson"). *Freedomways*, vol. 5, no. 3 (3rd quarter 1965), pp. 373–77.

"Eslanda Goode Robeson Is Dead; Writer and Wife of Singer, 68." *The New York Times* (Dec. 14, 1965).

Mrs. Paul Robeson, wife of singer, 68, dies. *The New York World Telegram* (Dec. 14, 1965).

Eslanda Robeson dies (on Dec. 13, 1965) in New York. (Singer's wife was anthropologist, writer.) *National Guardian* (Dec. 18, 1965).

"Eslanda Robeson—1897–1965" by Jessica Smith. *New World Review* (Jan. 1966), pp. 8–13. Mrs. Robeson was roving correspondent and editorial consultant on Negro and colonial questions for *New World Review* magazine.

Tribute to Eslanda Robeson. (Remembrances of her from friends and associates and selections from her writings.) *Freedomways*, vol. 6, no. 4 (4th quarter 1966), pp. 327–57.

"To Eslanda Robeson" by Janet Jagan. *Freedomways*, vol. 7, no. 2 (2nd quarter 1967), pp. 175–76.

Paul Robeson's 69th birthday celebrated in East Germany. *New York Courier* (June 17, 1967), p. 1. Photograph.

"The Power of Negro Action" by Paul Robeson. *Political Affairs*, vol. 46, no. 8 (Aug. 1967), pp. 33–46. This is Chapter 5 of *Here I Stand*. A powerful, clear-headed statement.

"British Hail Robeson on His 70th Birthday." *New York Amsterdam News* (Apr. 20, 1968), p. 47.

Paul Robeson—70th Birthday. *Political Affairs*, vol. 47, no. 5 (May 1968), p. 17.

"Paul Robeson: A Giant Among Men" by William L. Patterson. *Political Affairs*, vol. 47, no. 5 (May 1968), pp. 17–21. Photo.

"Movies in the Ghetto Before [Sidney] Poitier" by Thomas R. Cripps. *Negro Digest*, vol. 17, no. 4 (Feb. 1969), pp. 21–27, 45–48.

"Recognize Robeson" Is Demand at Rutgers (University), *Daily World* (March 14, 1969), p. 9. Photo.

Paul Robeson celebrates 71st birthday on April 9. (His alma mater, Rutgers University in New Brunswick, N.J., dedicated a music and arts lounge honoring him.) *New York Amsterdam News* (Apr. 12, 1969), p. 2. Photograph.

"In Honor of Paul Robeson" by William L. Patterson. *Political Affairs*, vol. 48, no. 5 (May 1969), pp. 17–22. An address at a meeting in tribute to Paul Robeson's 71st birthday in Chicago, Apr. 13, 1969.

"Paul Robeson's Student Days and the Fight Against Racism at Rutgers" by George Fishman. *Freedomways*, vol. 9, no. 3 (3rd quarter 1969), pp. 221–29.

"Robeson Gets Tribute from Alpha at Rutgers." *New York Amsterdam News* (Apr. 18, 1970), p. 42.

Robeson, Jr., Sets Record Straight. (Speech Apr. 5, 1970, at Alpha Phi Alpha Fraternity Eastern Region's "Tribute to Robeson" at Rutgers University.) *Daily World* (Apr. 24, 1970), p. 8.

Rutgers University, New Brunswick, N.J., dedicates the Paul Robeson Arts and Music Lounge in the school's student center. *Jet* (Apr. 30, 1970), p. 60. Photographs.

Paul Robeson receives the Ira Aldridge Award at the 33rd annual Negro History Week meeting of the New York Chapter of the Association for the Study of Negro Life and History in New York City in February 1970. *Negro History Bulletin*, vol. 33, no. 5 (May 1970), p. 128.

"Paul Robeson: World Renowned Actor, Singer and Scholar" by Gertrude P. Mc-
Brown. *Negro History Bulletin*, vol. 33, no. 5 (May 1970), pp. 128–29. Photograph.
"Ahead of His Time: Paul Robeson" by Leonard Karp. *The Churchman*, vol. 184,
no. 6 (June–July 1970), pp. 10–13.
"Paul Robeson and Black Identity in American Movies" by Thomas Cripps. *The
Massachusetts Review*, vol. 11, no. 3 (summer 1970), pp. 468–85.
"Rutgers Salutes Paul Robeson" by Paul Robeson, Jr. *Freedomways*, vol. 10, no. 3
(3rd quarter 1970), pp. 237–41. Speech given at Rutgers University in April 1970
at an affair sponsored by the Eastern Region of Alpha Phi Alpha Fraternity and
the Rutgers Student Center.
Portrait of Paul Robeson by Alvin C. Hollingsworth presented to Rutgers Univer-
sity, New Brunswick, N.J., by the Alpha Phi Alpha Fraternity Eastern Region.
The Sphinx, vol. 56, no. 3 (Oct. 1970), pp. 25–28.
"Paul Robeson: Black Star" by C.L.R. James. *Black World*, vol. 20, no. 1 (Nov.
1970), pp. 106–15. James, who knew Robeson in London in the 1930s, reminisces,
but he is still the Trotskyist who is one up on Robeson and second-guesses what
Robeson should have done politically in the U.S.
On Sept. 20, 1970, the Black Academy of Arts and Letters, at its meeting in New
York City, gave a special award to Paul Robeson "for his inestimable contribu-
tion to the understanding of the Black Experience." Paul Robeson, Jr., accepted
the award for his father. *Black World*, vol. 20, no. 2 (Dec. 1970), pp. 70, 125.
Local 1199, Drug and Hospital Employees' Union, opens its new headquarters in
New York City with a tribute to Paul Robeson on Nov. 29, 1970, directed by
Ossie Davis. *Jet*, vol. 39, no. 14 (Dec. 31, 1970), pp. 48–49. *1199 News* (Nov. 1970),
pp. 8–9. Photographs.
(Local) 1199 gets it all together at tribute to Paul Robeson (on Nov. 29, 1970). *1199
News* (Jan. 1971), pp. 14–15. Photographs.
"To Paul Robeson" by Ossie Davis. *Freedomways*, vol. 11, no. 1 (1st quarter 1971),
pp. 99–102; vol. 11, no. 2 (2nd quarter 1971), pp. 192–97.
Cover portrait of Paul Robeson and note on him in annual theatre number. *Black
World*, vol. 20, no. 6 (Apr. 1971), p. 49.
"A Giant of a Man Who Told It on the Mountain" (a review of *Paul Robeson, the
Great Forerunner*, a special issue of *Freedomways*, vol. 11, no. 1, 1971) by Phillip
Bonosky. *Daily World* (Apr. 30, 1971), p. 8. Photographs.
TV Channel 13 in New York City carried a three-part, one-half-hour each, pro-
gram of filmclips and discussion on Paul Robeson, May 17, 18, 19, 1971, on its
"New Jersey Speaks" program. Radio station WBAI in New York also carried a
2½-hour program on Robeson around this time and repeated it later.
Paul Robeson did most to herald black plight, says black sociologist Dr. Joyce Lad-
ner. *Jet* (June 3, 1971), p. 49.
Display exhibit on Robeson at Detroit's International Afro-American Museum—
"The Life and Times of Paul Robeson." *Jet* (June 17, 1971), p. 20. Photograph.
Paul Robeson's 73rd birthday celebrated in the German Democratic Republic with
a two-day international symposium and a large solidarity meeting. *Muhammad
Speaks* (July 16, 1971), pp. 9–10. Photograph.
Letters commenting on the Paul Robeson number of *Freedomways* (1st quarter
1971). *Freedomways*, vol. 11, no. 3 (3rd quarter 1971), pp. 292–97.
"A German Tribute to Paul Robeson" by William L. Patterson. *American Dialog*,
vol. 6, no. 1 (Autumn 1971), pp. 15–16. About a two-day international symposium
in Apr. 1971 in Berlin, GDR, honoring Robeson on his 73rd birthday.
"Paul Robeson and Africa" by Alex La Guma. *The African Communist*, no. 46 (3rd
quarter 1971), pp. 113–19. Alex La Guma, the South African writer, read the

paper printed here at a symposium on "Paul Robeson and the Afro-American Struggle," Apr. 13–14, 1971, held at the Academy of Arts, Berlin, GDR. William L. Patterson's piece is also about this symposium.

Here I Stand by Paul Robeson. Review of new edition of book. *Negro History Bulletin*, vol. 34, no. 7 (Nov. 1971), p. 167.

Local 1199 Drug and Hospital Workers Union's second annual tribute to Paul Robeson at its union auditorium in New York City on Oct. 31, 1971. *Muhammad Speaks* (Nov. 26, 1971), p. 4.

Paul Robeson to be honored by concert by Dizzy Gillespie at Princeton University, Princeton, N.J. *New York Amsterdam News* (Dec. 4, 1971), p. C–1.

"Cyrus Bustill Addresses the Blacks of Philadelphia" by Melvin H. Buxbaum. *William and Mary Quarterly*, vol. 5 (Jan. 1972), pp. 99–108. Bustill, the great-great-grandfather of Paul Robeson, was a founder of the Free African Society of Philadelphia in 1787.

Radio station WRVR in New York City carried a half-hour program of tapes of songs and speeches by Paul Robeson in the afternoon of Jan. 28, 1972. Paul Robeson, Jr., conducted the program and introduced the songs and speeches.

"History Does Move Ahead" by George M. Fishman. *American Dialog*, vol. 7, no. 1 (Winter 1972), pp. 32–35. Mentions a letter in an exhibit revealing Rutgers University racism toward Robeson when he was an undergraduate; the naming of the Paul Robeson Lounge on the New Brunswick campus of Rutgers University and the Paul Robeson commemorations in 1969–1970.

New student center at the Rutgers University Newark campus named for Paul Robeson; action voted by Board of Governors of Rutgers University in time for Robeson's 74th birthday, Apr. 9, 1972. *Freedomways*, vol. 12, no. 1 (1st quarter 1972), p. 67.

Portrait of Brother Paul Robeson Presented to Rutgers University (reprinted from *New York Amsterdam News*). *The Sphinx*, vol. 58, no. 1 (Feb.–Mar. 1972), pp. 1, 14–16. Cover photo. Robeson was a member of the Alpha Phi Alpha Fraternity whose official organ is *The Sphinx* magazine.

"Paul Robeson: The Forgotten Man" (He Pioneered for Human Rights) by Gledhill Cameron. *This Week*, magazine of the *Times Advertiser*, Trenton, N.J. (Feb. 13, 1972), pp. 1–5. Photos and illustrations. This is a long article on Robeson carried appropriately in a New Jersey newspaper to mark the 1972 national Black history week celebration.

Fame Vote Slights Robeson. (12 judges who decide who gets into the National Football Foundation's College Hall of Fame at Rutgers University have again bypassed selecting Robeson, one of the greatest college gridders of all time.) In Mike Jay's column "The View from Left Field." *Daily World* (Feb. 22, 1972).

Rutgers Honors Robeson—At Last. Student center on the Newark campus of Rutgers University recently named the Paul Robeson Campus Center. *New York Amsterdam News* (Mar. 4, 1972), p. D–1. Photo.

"The Robeson Confusion" (Do you really know what's happened to Paul Robeson?) by William J. Slattery. *Encore*, vol. 1, no. 1 (Spring 1972), pp. 70–74; vol. 1, no. 2 (Summer 1972), pp. 72–75. Says: "At least three people are at work on Robeson biographies now, his recordings are being reissued, his films are enjoying a vogue in museums and among film historians and a massive bibliography of Robesoniana running more than seven pages in small type has been compiled by a young Black historian at Columbia University; television, radio and academic symposia on various aspects of the career, the talent and the impact of Robeson are being broadcast and conducted with increasing frequency. A Robeson revival waits in the wings, a revival that many hope will bring back to prominence a major American athlete, actor and singer blacklisted and blacked out in the hysterical political night of the American 1950's."

Robeson Center Dedication Ceremonies Held (Rutgers-Newark Student Center on Robeson's 74th birthday, Apr. 9, 1972). *The Rutgers Newsletter* (Apr. 10, 1972), p. 2. Photograph.

Garland about Robeson's noble head, in the twilight of his days. Board of Governors of Rutgers University votes to name new student center at the Newark campus for Paul Robeson. *Muhammad Speaks* (June 30, 1972), p. 4. Photograph.

(Paul) Robeson's *Here I Stand* (new edition published in 1971) reviewed by Harold D. Weaver. *Black World*, vol. 21, no. 9 (July 1972), pp. 85–87.

Paul Robeson given the Solomon Carter Fuller award of the Black Psychiatrists of America for "demonstrating the qualities of community leadership, compassion and selflessness so emphasized by America's first Black psychiatrist, and for the forthright furtherance of the mental health of Black people." The award was given at the American Psychiatric Association meeting in Dallas, Tex. *Black World*, vol. 21, no. 9 (July 1972), p. 80.

Paul Robeson's 74th birthday celebrated by the Du Sable Museum of African American History, Chicago, Ill. Lloyd L. Brown was the speaker. April 9 is Robeson's birthday. This celebration will be held every year. *Black World*, vol. 21, no. 10 (Aug. 1972), pp. 80–81.

"Time to Break the Silence Surrounding Paul Robeson" by Loften Mitchell. (A Black playwright reminisces about Robeson and what happened to him.) *The New York Times*, Arts and Leisure, section 2 (Aug. 6, 1972), pp. 1, 7. Photo of Robeson as Othello. Article is reprinted from *Equity* magazine. "They Recall Robeson." (Three letters in the "Drama Mailbag" replying to Loften Mitchell's article.) *New York Times*, Arts and Leisure Section, Sept. 10, 1972. pp. 12, 16.

"Ten Greats of Black History." (Paul Robeson is one of the ten who include Frederick Douglass, W.E.B. Du Bois, Martin Luther King, Jr., Marcus Garvey, Carter G. Woodson, etc.) *Ebony*, vol. 27, no. 10 (Aug. 1972), pp. 35–42. Photographs.

"The Vindication of Paul Robeson" (part 1). *The New York Final* (newspaper) (111–05 128th St., South Ozone Park, N.Y. 11420), vol. 2, no. 32 (Aug. 1972), p. 16. "The Destruction of Paul Robeson" (part 2). *The New York Final* (Sept. 1972).

Paul Robeson, 74-year-old former actor, singer and pioneer activist in the civil rights movement, named as the recipient of the second annual Whitney M. Young, Jr. National Memorial Award by the directors of the New York Urban League. The award, along with others, to be presented at Yankee Stadium in New York City, Saturday, Sept. 9, during the halftime of the Whitney M. Young, Jr. Memorial Football Classic featuring Grambling College against Morgan State College. *The New York Times* (Sept. 7, 1972).

"30 Black Musicians Get Ellington Medal at Yale" by John S. Wilson. *The New York Times* (Oct. 9, 1972), p. 36. Paul Robeson was one of the eight singers to receive the medal in honor of Duke Ellington as part of Yale University's Ellington Fellowship Program.

Robeson dedication speech (by Dr. Edward J. Bloustein, president of Rutgers University, at the dedication of the Paul Robeson Campus Center at Newark-Rutgers, Apr. 9, 1972). *Negro History Bulletin*, vol. 35, no. 6 (Oct. 1972), p. 141.

"The Real Forerunner in Civil Rights" (Paul Robeson) by James Audrey. *National Scene Magazine Supplement*, vol. 1, no. 13 (Nov.–Dec. 1972), pp. 3–4. Photos and front cover drawing of Robeson by Black artist Robert S. Pious.

Paul Robeson gets a special Image Award of the NAACP Hollywood chapter for his "eminence as an artist and a fighter for human justice." *Jet*, vol. 43, no. 12 (Dec. 14, 1972), p. 56.

"Transcending Racist Trash: A Legacy of the First Black Movie Stars" by Donald Bogle. *Saturday Review of the Arts*, vol. 1, no. 2 (Feb. 3, 1973), pp. 25–29. Photographs. About Stepin Fetchit, Bill Robinson, Hattie McDaniel, and Paul Robeson.

Freedomways Annual W.E.B. Du Bois Cultural Evening honoring the 75th birthday year of Paul Robeson, Feb. 16, 1973, at Carnegie Hall, New York City. Speakers: Judge George W. Crockett, Jr., Rev. Jesse L. Jackson, Judge Bruce McM. Wright, Angie Dickerson; artists: Ossie Davis, Ruby Dee, Loretta Abbott and Al Perryman Dance Duo, Brother John Sellers, Zarefah Storey, Elly Stone. Carnegie Hall Program; *The New York Times*, Arts and Leisure, section 2 (Feb. 11, 1973), p. 36.

Lincoln Vets Honor Robeson. (Veterans of the Abraham Lincoln Brigade who fought in Spain against Franco, celebrated their 36th anniversary at a dinner where they presented a plaque to Paul Robeson on his 75th birthday for his contributions to the anti-Franco cause and to the freedom of all peoples. Lloyd Brown, Robeson's biographer and friend, accepted the plaque for Robeson.) *Daily World* (Feb. 13, 1973), p. 11.

Freedomways Annual W.E.B. Du Bois Cultural Evening will honor Paul Robeson and other outstanding Black Americans. Carnegie Hall, New York City, Feb. 16, 1973. *Jewish Currents*, vol. 27, no. 2 (Feb. 1973), p. 42.

For Paul Robeson's 75th Birthday, Apr. 9, 1973 (address by Dr. Edward J. Bloustein, president of Rutgers University, delivered at the Newark campus, Apr. 9, 1972). *Jewish Currents*, vol. 27, no. 2 (Feb. 1973), p. 13.

Paul Robeson's *Here I Stand* (1971 edition) reviewed by Morris U. Schappes in "The Editor's Diary." *Jewish Currents*, vol. 27, no. 2 (Feb. 1973), pp. 22–23.

"Paul Robeson, Singing" (sculpture) by Herb Rosenberg of Brooklyn, N.Y. (30" x 24") reproduced on front cover of *Jewish Currents*, vol. 27, no. 2 (Feb. 1973).

Birthday: Paul Robeson's 75th birthday year celebration tonight at Carnegie Hall sponsored by *Freedomways* magazine. Speakers and artists participating listed plus address, telephone numbers, and ticket prices. In Richard F. Shepard's "Going Out Guide" column. *The New York Times* (Feb. 16, 1973), p. 20. Photograph.

Article on Paul Robeson in *Emergency Civil Liberties Committee Bulletin* (Mar.? 1973).

"Remembering Larry Brown" by Lloyd L. Brown. Speech delivered at the Memorial Concert for Lawrence Brown, Feb. 11, 1973, at St. Martin's Episcopal Church, New York City. Lawrence Brown died on Dec. 25, 1972, at the age of 79. He was a composer and arranger of Afro-American folk songs and was for 40 years the accompanist of Paul Robeson. The Memorial Concert was sponsored by the Committee for the Preservation of the Lawrence Brown Collection. *Daily World* magazine section (Mar. 3, 1973), p. M11. Photos of Brown and Robeson.

"Paul Robeson: True Revolutionary" by George W. Crockett. Speech made by Judge Crockett at Carnegie Hall, New York City, Feb. 16, 1973, at the *Freedomways* Cultural Evening honoring the 75th birthday year of Paul Robeson. Also "Paul Robeson," a statement by the editors of *Freedomways* read at Carnegie Hall by Ossie Davis, and the reproduction on the front cover of *Freedomways* of a painting of Paul Robeson by Leopoldo Mendez. *Freedomways*, vol. 13, no. 1 (1st quarter 1973), pp. 10–13, 5–7.

"Slate Paul Robeson Birthday Tribute" by Joe Walker (at Carnegie Hall, New York City, Apr. 15, 1973; Robeson will be 75 years old on Apr. 9, 1973). *Muhammad Speaks* (Mar. 23, 1973), p. 6. Photo of Paul Robeson, Jr.

"The Propaganda Machine of White America" (Part I) by Minister Louis Farrakhan. Has section: Black people made to hate Paul Robeson. *Black Nation Information Bulletin*, vol. 1, No. 5, Mar. 1973, p. 2.

"A Tribute to Paul Robeson" produced by Kay Farmer and Charles Hobson on radio station WBAI-FM in New York City on Sunday, Apr. 8, 1973, from 1 to 3:30 P.M. A magnificent program covering with tapes and recordings many of the highlights of Robeson's career and struggle: his many work songs and spirituals, speeches, *Ballad For Americans, Othello,* his politicking in the South for Henry Wallace for president in 1948, his Peekskill, N.Y. concerts, his singing at the Canadian border and by wire to the miners of Wales when his passport was lifted denying him the right to travel. Some of the participants on this program were Lawrence Brown, Lloyd L. Brown, Alan Booth, Pete Seeger, Douglass Turner Ward, Alice Childress, Ted Poston, Hope Stevens, William Patterson, and Howard Fast.

"A Collector's Easter." Host Francis Robinson, assistant manager of the Metropolitan Opera of New York, celebrates the 75th birthday of Paul Robeson with selections of his recorded art. A 54-minute program on radio station WQXR, New York City, Apr. 16, 1973. *The New York Times* (Apr. 16, 1973), p. 75.

Paul Robeson's 75th Birthday (editorial comment). *Political Affairs,* vol. 52, no. 4 (Apr. 1973), pp. 1–3, 52.

"The Time Is Now" (Chapter 4 from *Here I Stand* by Paul Robeson). *Political Affairs,* vol. 52, no. 4 (Apr. 1973), pp. 41–52.

Salute to Paul Robeson: An Exhibition on His 75th Birthday, Apr. 16–June 8, 1973. Gallery 1199, 310 W. 43 St., New York 10036. Inside front cover and back outside cover of *1199 News* (Apr. 1973). Photo.

"Robeson Will Miss Rutgers Week of Honor" by Ann Ledesma. *The Home News Today* (New Brunswick, N.J.) (Apr. 4, 1973), pp. 1–2. Photo.

Belafonte, Others Plan Apr. 15 Robeson Tribute. (Also Local 1199, Drug and Hospital Union, plan a portrait and sculpture exhibition of Paul Robeson at the same time.) *Jet,* vol. 44, no. 2 (Apr. 5, 1973), p. 54. Photos of Harry Belafonte and Paul Robeson.

"A Giant of Our Age." A commemoration of Paul Robeson's 75th birthday Apr. 9, 1973: articles, photos, poem, chronology on his life and career. *Daily World* magazine section (Apr. 7, 1973), pp. 5–8 and front cover.

The Paul Robeson Week—A 75th Birthday Tribute, Apr. 8–14, 1973, Dept. of Africana Studies, Rutgers College, Rutgers University, New Brunswick and Newark, N.J. Included showing of Robeson's films, concert of his records, exhibits, symposia on Robeson on stage and screen; the making of the man; concerts, political ideology and Mrs. Robeson; Robeson: labor and the U.S. government; and Robeson and politics. From Paul Robeson Week Program and earlier private news release on the Week.

"Salute to a Man They Couldn't Put Down" (Like It Is column) by Claude Lewis. *Philadelphia Sunday Bulletin* (Apr. 15, 1973), pp. 1, 7. Photo. For Robeson's 75th birthday.

For Paul Robeson on His 75th Birthday. *New World Review,* vol. 41, no. 2 (2nd quarter 1973), pp. 44–46, 50–52. Editorial comment on Robeson and reports on the *Freedomways* Carnegie Hall Cultural Evening honoring Robeson, Feb. 16, 1973, and the Salute to Paul Robeson, Apr. 15, 1973, also at Carnegie Hall.

Afro-American Delegation (led by George B. Murphy, Jr.) Visit USSR Aug. 1–15, 1973 (as part of worldwide celebrations in honor of Robeson's 75th birthday and to pay tribute to the strong bonds of friendship between Afro-Americans and the Soviet people fashioned by Robeson and his wife Eslanda, writer and anthropologist, over many years). *New World Review,* vol. 41, no. 2 (2nd quarter 1973), p. 51.

"The Voice of the Century," a one-hour documentary written and narrated by Dr. Charles H. Wright. A radio documentary produced on a station in Detroit, Mich.

Available on cassette or reel for $10.00 from Detroit Afro-American Museum, 1553 West Grand Blvd., Detroit, MI 48208.

A one-half-hour TV program on a Detroit station. It showed the large Paul Robeson exhibit at the International Afro-American Museum, Detroit, with narration by Sheldon Tappes of the UAW-CIO, Judge George W. Crockett, Mrs. Harold Bledsoe, a long-time friend of the Robeson family, and Dr. Charles H. Wright. A kinescope of this program is available from the Detroit Afro-American Museum.

"All American" (I and II) Pete Hamill's two columns on Paul Robeson in the *New York Post* (Apr. 9 and 11, 1973).

Rutgers University will confer on Paul Robeson on May 17, 1973, the honorary Doctor of Humane Letters degree on his 75th birthday anniversary, Apr. 9. Paul Robeson, Jr. received the diploma, hood, and citation for his ailing father. There was a week-long Robeson celebration at the University. Robeson received the Bachelor of Arts degree from Rutgers in 1919 and an honorary Master of Arts degree in 1932. *Rutgers News Release* (Apr. 9 and May 17, 1973), pp. 1–2; *Jet*, vol. 44, no. 5 (Apr. 26, 1973), p. 16. (photograph); *The Sphinx*, vol. 59, no. 2 (May–June 1973), p. 34 (photograph); *Daily World* (May 19, 1973), p. 7 (photograph).

Special issue of the *Rutgers Daily Targum* (Apr. 10, 1973), 12 pp. devoted to Paul Robeson. This is a very good issue of the *Targum* finally, as it says, giving tribute to Robeson including all phases of his career.

"A Son's Stirring Tribute to His Father" (two parts) by Paul Robeson, Jr. Reprint of "Paul Robeson: Black Warrior" *Freedomways*, vol. 11, no. 1, (1st quarter 1971). *New York Amsterdam News* (Apr. 14 and 21, 1973), pp. D–1, D–1.

Salute to Paul Robeson: A Cultural Celebration of His 75th Birthday, Apr. 15, 1973, at Carnegie Hall, New York City. Artists and speakers: Harry Belafonte, Angela Davis, Mayor Richard G. Hatcher, Mrs. Coretta King, Leon Bibb, James Earl Jones, Ruby Dee, Odetta, Sidney Poitier, Pete Seeger, etc. Beautiful program covering Robeson's life with pictures and text. Also in Leonard Lyons's column "The Lyons Den," *New York Post* (Mar. 29, 1973), p. 29; *The New York Times*, Arts and Leisure, section 2 (Apr. 15, 1973), p. 16; (April 16, 1973), p. 48. Photographs.

"Somerville Alma Mater Plans Hometown Tribute to Robeson" by Muriel Freeman. *Somerset Messenger Gazette* (Apr. 19, 1973), p. 49. One of the six photographs of this full-page story shows four of Robeson's white Somerville High School friends, one holding the picture of the school's 1915 football team that includes Robeson. Samuel Woldin, in the photograph with Robeson's friends but not a classmate, has spent years collecting material on Robeson.

"A 'Paul Robeson Public School' in the GDR" by Victor Grossman. *Panorama* DDR (Mar. 3, 1973). *Jet*, vol. 44, no. 4 (Apr. 19, 1973), p. 15. School in eastern borough of Berlin, capital of the German Democratic Republic, to be named for Paul Robeson on his 75th birthday, Apr. 9, 1973, with a big program. His birthday will be celebrated in the GDR with radio and TV programs and with meetings featuring films of Robeson's visit there in 1960 when tens of thousands heard him sing.

"Robeson Revisited." About an exhibition of nearly 60 photographs, posters, drawings, paintings, and sculptures in honor of Robeson's 75th birthday tracing his life from a 1917 Rutgers football photo onward. In the main-floor gallery of the 1199 Union's Martin Luther King, Jr. Labor Center headquarters, 310 W. 43 St., New York City. In Richard F. Shepard's "Going Out Guide" column, *The New York Times* Apr. 19, 1973, p. 50. (Photograph).

"Paul Robeson's Not Forgotten" by Ed Jardim. The *Courier-News* (N.J.) (Apr. 20, 1973), p. A–11. Robeson's white childhood friends in Westfield, Somerville, New

Brunswick, and Princeton, N.J., remember him. Photograph of Somerville High School baseball team of 1914 includes Robeson.

"Tribute to Robeson" (text of speech at Carnegie Hall on Apr. 15, 1973, by Mayor Richard G. Hatcher of Gary, Ind., on Robeson's 75th birthday). *New York Amsterdam News* (Apr. 21, 1973), pp. A4–A5.

"Lest We Forget." (Leading editorial denouncing the Cold War treatment of Paul Robeson in the 1950s, calling him our living Nat Turner and urging the establishment in Harlem of a Paul Robeson Center for the Arts and the setting up of a Paul Robeson archive either at the Center or at the Schomburg Center. The Paul Robeson Archives, set up in March 1973 in New York City, was announced in the Apr. 15, 1973, Carnegie Hall program.) *New York Amsterdam News* (Apr. 21, 1973), p. A-4.

Special issue of *Black Voice* (Apr. 24, 1973), the Black students' newspaper at Rutgers University, New Brunswick, N.J., devoted in great part to Paul Robeson. Included are a long review by Harold D. Weaver, Jr., of the second edition of *Here I Stand* and an article on the Paul Robeson Black Arts Ensemble, a student group at Rutgers, and its performance there of Broadway music.

"The People of the World Salute Paul Robeson" (Robeson's message and excerpts from greetings from the world community at the Apr. 15, 1973, Salute to Paul Robeson at Carnegie Hall, New York City.) *Daily World* (Apr. 26, 1973), p. 12.

"Salute Paul Robeson" by Alex Murray. *Antillean Caribbean Echo*, vol. 4, no. 174 (Apr. 28, 1973), p. 16. Photograph. (The *Echo* was a weekly newspaper published in New York City by West Indians.)

Establish Paul Robeson Scholarship Fund (NU Chapter of Alpha Phi Alpha Fraternity at Lincoln University, Pa.). *The Sphinx*, vol. 59, no. 2 (May–June 1973), p. 34.

"Paul Robeson: A Misunderstood Giant" by Talib Abdur-Rashid. *The Western Sunrise* (May–June 1973), pp. 1, 12–13. Photograph. Article in a Muslim newspaper then published in New York City by Blacks.

New York Public Library Exhibition Celebrates Paul Robeson's 75th Birthday. The Lincoln Center's Theatre Collection exhibit covers the New York and London productions of *Othello*, the many films with Robeson, and the Eugene O'Neill plays, etc. The exhibit runs through May and June 1973. *New York Public Library News* (May 2, 1973), pp. 1–2.

Actors' Equity Association will present a special citation to Paul Robeson in June 1973. *New York Public Library News* (May 2, 1973), p. 2.

3,000 Honor Robeson in Carnegie Hall Tribute. *Jet*, vol. 44, no. 6 (May 3, 1973), p. 63. Photograph.

"Hugo Gellert—Style and Tenacity" by Hugo Gellert. *Daily World*, magazine section (May 19, 1973), pp. 5–7. About Gellert's successful struggle to get Robeson into his mural for Hillcrest High School in Queens, New York City. Also about Gellert's print of Robeson exhibited at the New York World's Fair of 1939–40 and later given to the library of Birmingham, Ala.

"Paul Robeson Honored": Twin Salutes at Carnegie Hall on 75th Birthday of Famed Scholar by Joe Walker. *Muhammad Speaks* (May 25, 1973), p. 28. Photograph.

Robeson Given Honorary Doctorate by Rutgers University (Doctor of Humane Letters degree [full citation in *Black World*] received by Paul Robeson, Jr., for his father in May 1973). *Jet*, vol. 44, no. 11 (June 7, 1973), p. 16. (photograph); *Black World*, vol. 22, no. 9 (July 1973), p. 89.

Rutgers Honors Paul Robeson. (He gets honorary Doctor of Humane Letters degree from Rutgers University.) *Black Panther* (June 9, 1973), p. 5.

Tribute to a Black Man (to Paul Robeson at Carnegie Hall on Apr. 15, 1973, near his 75th birthday on Apr. 9th). *Black World*, vol. 22, no. 9 (July 1973), pp. 88–89. Photograph.

Eric Bentley's *Are You Now or Have You Ever Been?* WBAI-FM radio station, New York City (July 6, 1973), 8–10:30 P.M. A repeat of a great program of stoolpigeons and heroes presented in March 1973 based on the published testimony of Ring Lardner, Jr., Larry Parks, Elia Kazan, Lillian Hellman, Lionel Stander, Arthur Miller, Abe Burrows, and others before the House Committee on Un-American Activities. Robeson's heroic testimony before this committee ends the program on a great note of defiance and struggle.

Afro-American Delegation Honors Robeson in USSR. (The delegation, led by George B. Murphy, Jr., will visit the USSR during Aug. 1–15, 1973. An oil portrait of Robeson done by Bertrand Phillips, professor of art at Northwestern University and a member of the delegation, will be presented to the Kirghis friendship society in the Soviet Republic of Kirghizia. In 1949, the Soviet citizens of Kirghizia expressed their love for Robeson by naming one of the highest peaks of the Tien Shan mountains Mount Paul Robeson.) *Daily World* (July 25, 1973), p. 11.

Report on Carnegie Hall Apr. 15, 1973, Program (honoring Paul Robeson). *Crisis*, vol. 80, no. 7 (Aug.–Sept. 1973), p. 250.

"A Student Without Peer: The Undergraduate College Years of Paul Robeson" by Lamont H. Yeakey (paper read at the Association for the Study of African-American Life and History's 56th annual meeting in Philadelphia, Pa., Oct. 1971). *Journal of Negro Education*, vol. 42, no. 4 (Fall 1973), pp. 489–503.

"A Letter to Paul Robeson on Our Visit to Mt. Robeson" by Thelma Dale Perkins. George B. Murphy, Jr., led an Afro-American delegation to Mt. Paul Robeson in the Soviet Union. The delegation carried a painting of Robeson to the Kirghiz people who named the highest peak in the Ala-Tau mountains for Robeson. *New World Review*, vol. 41, no. 4 (Fall 1973), pp. 52–58.

William Marshall Named to the Paul Robeson Annual Awards Committee of Actors Equity. Richmond Barthe commissioned to create bust of Robeson to be on permanent display at Equity's New York City headquarters. A replica of bust and $4,000 grant to be awarded annually to outstanding person in the arts and humanities. *Jet*, vol. 45, no. 2 (Oct. 4, 1973), p. 86.

"Paul Robeson Revisited" by Sterling Stuckey. *New York Times Book Review* (Oct. 21, 1973), pp. 40–41. Photograph.

The Paul Robeson Lecture Series at the University of Massachusetts, Amherst, for 1973–74. Lecturers on Robeson or readers of their poetry were C.L.R. James, Lamont H. Yeakey, Sterling Brown, Mari Evans, and Gwendolyn Brooks.

Professor Paints Portrait of Paul Robeson for U.S.S.R. (Bertrand Phillips, a Black assistant professor of art at Northwestern University, Evanston, Ill., paints Robeson portrait for the Soviet Union's rededication ceremony of Mt. Paul Robeson there in Aug. 1973 for his 75th birthday.) *Jet*, vol. 45, no. 8 (Nov. 15, 1973), p. 36. *Daily World* (June 13, 1975), p. 2. Photograph.

"Chicago Rally Salutes U.S.-Soviet Detente" (and pays tribute to Paul Robeson, 75 years old, in a celebration of the 56th Anniversary of the Great October Bolshevik Revolution) by Ted Pearson. *Daily World* (Nov. 16, 1973), p. 9. Photograph.

"The Cold War: Its Impact on the Black Liberation Struggle Within the United States" (part 2) by Charles W. Cheng. *Freedomways*, vol. 13, no. 4 (4th quarter 1973), pp. 281–93. The first four pages deal with Paul Robeson's struggle against the U.S. Cold War of the late 1940s and 1950s.

"Paul Robeson: Beleaguered Leader" by Harold D. Weaver, Jr. *The Black Scholar*, vol. 5, no. 4 (Dec. 1973–Jan. 1974), pp. 24–32. Photograph. Paper read Oct. 19,

1973, at the 58th annual meeting of the Association for the Study of Afro-American Life and History, New York City.

"A Bibliographic, Discographic and Filmographic Note" (on Paul Robeson) by Harold D. Weaver, Jr. *The Black Scholar*, vol. 5, no. 4 (Dec. 1973–Jan. 1974), p. 32. Discusses Robeson holdings in several libraries including the Tuskegee Library's clippings of articles by Robeson from the *Afro-American*, the *Pittsburgh Courier*, and the *New York Amsterdam News*, Black weekly newspapers. One correction: The Council on African Affairs published a monthly bulletin or newsletter, *Spotlight on Africa*. The monthly newspaper *Freedom* was not a Council publication as is stated here. It was published independently of the Council and dealt with the Blacks in the U.S. as well as with Africa.

"Paul Robeson and Film: Racism" by Harold D. Weaver, Jr. *Negro History Bulletin*, vol. 37, no. 1 (Jan. 1974), pp. 204–6. Photo.

"Witch Hunters Haunted Paul Robeson . . . And They Robbed America of a Great Talent" by James G. Crowley. The *Philadelphia Inquirer* (Jan. 27, 1974), pp. 81, 121. Photograph.

"Paul Robeson, the Athlete." In Mike Jay's column The View from Left Field. *Daily World* (Feb. 14, 1974), p. 12. Photo. Reprinted at his death in *Daily World* (Jan. 27, 1976), p. 12.

"The Resurrection of Paul Robeson" by Steven Neal. *Today Magazine* (The *Philadelphia Inquirer*) (Mar. 10, 1974), pp. 10–12, 14, 16, 18. Photographs. (Subtitled: Behind the drawn curtains of a dingy West Philadelphia rowhouse lives a great black man—a victim of anti-Communist hysteria.)

A panel radio program on the life of Paul Robeson (2½ hours). The Don Henderson Show, WCAU, Philadelphia, Pa. (Mar. 25, 1974). Panelists were Charles H. Blockson, William Griffin, long-time friend and basketball teammate of Robeson during the 1920s, Alfred Newschafer, Robeson's football teammate at Rutgers University, and Robert Smith, a sports writer and collector of Robeson material, on the staff of the athletics department at Rutgers University.

"Paul Robeson, 76, a Titan." The Black journalist and writer Chuck Stone's column in the *Philadelphia Daily News* (Apr. 9, 1974).

"Ailing, Lonely Paul Robeson Observes His 76th Birthday" by Robert E. Johnson. *Jet*, vol. 46, no. 3 (Apr. 11, 1974), pp. 10–17.

"Paul Robeson: A Tribute to a Mighty American" by James Jackson. (For his 76th birthday Apr. 9, 1974.) *Daily World Magazine* (Apr. 13, 1974), p. M–2.

Robeson Ideal Honored. Actors Equity Association, AFL-CIO, honored Paul Robeson at the union's June 1974 meeting in New York City by naming Robeson the first recipient of an annual award named for Robeson. Also Robeson's letter of appreciation to the Actors Equity on this occasion. Paul Robeson, Jr., accepted the award for his ailing father. *Daily World* (July 13, 1974), p. 8. Photo.

John Henry Memorial Jubilee for Paul Robeson. Second Annual John Henry Memorial Authentic Blues and Gospel Jubilee on Labor Day weekend 1974, near Beckley, W. Va., dedicated to Paul Robeson because he has the same qualities as John Henry who died at Talcott, W. Va., while working and competing with the steam drill on the Big Bend tunnel for the C & O Railroad. *Daily World* (Aug. 15, 1974), p. 8. Photo.

From the USSR to Howard University: A Gift in Friendship. Letters to Paul Robeson from 200 Soviet citizens were delivered to Howard University, Washington, D.C., by a 14-member Soviet delegation. Also exhibit at Howard University on the Black Presence in the Soviet Union, a large part devoted to Robeson in the Soviet Union. *Daily World* (Oct. 15, 1974), p. 8. Photo.

Infection Hospitalizes Paul Robeson. *Philadelphia Tribune* (Mar. 22, 1975), p. 1.

Photo. (In University of Pennsylvania Medical Center from Mar. 12–20, 1975, with infection caused by his pacemaker in his chest to regulate heartbeats.)

"A Very Special Honor to Paul Robeson" by Margrit Pittman. (About the activities at Paul Robeson High School named in 1974 in the German Democratic Republic. Also the work of the Paul Robeson Archive there founded in 1965.) *Daily World Magazine* (Apr. 12, 1975), pp. M–6, 7. Photos.

Salute to Paul Robeson: A Tribute to a Forgotten Freedom Fighter. Presented by the Afrikan History Clubs, No. 2 and No. 3, Mackenzie High School, Detroit, Mich., Apr. 25, 1975. (From large 16-page program.)

"Paul Robeson at Peekskill" by Charles H. Wright. *Freedomways*, vol. 15, no. 2 (1975), pp. 101–11. (Part of Wright's book *Robeson: Labor's Forgotten Champion*.)

Who Is Paul Robeson? Tribute to an American Hero. All-day program at Emerson College, Boston, Mass. (May 6, 1975). Produced by the Student Union to raise money for the Paul Robeson Archives, New York City. (From program and flyer.)

A Profile of Paul Robeson. Interface with Tony Batten. Public Broadcasting System, Channel 13 TV, New York City, June 3, 1975. *The New York Times* (June 3, 1975), p. 67; *New York Amsterdam News* (May 31, 1975), p. B–11. (One-quarter-page ad in *The New York Times*.)

Robeson Citation Award to Ossie Davis and Ruby Dee. Actors Equity's second annual Paul Robeson Citation given at June 6, 1975, meeting in New York City "in grateful recognition of distinguished contributions to the performing arts and for commitment to the struggle for a decent world in which all men can live in dignity and peace." *Daily World* (June 12, 1975), p. 8. Photos. Program broadcast on radio station WNYC on June 28, 1975, from 11–11:35 A.M.

Robeson Benefit Sunday. Concert at the Mother A.M.E. Zion Church in Harlem, New York City, June 8, 1975, to aid the work of the Paul Robeson Archives in New York City and the James Varick Community Center. The Archives were established by the Apr. 9, 1973 Salute to Paul Robeson Committee in June 1973; it processed 12,000 or more items; tape recordings, films, photographs, news articles, documents and writings went to Howard University, Washington, D.C., in 1977 and the Archives are slated to close. *New York Amsterdam News*, Arts and Entertainment section (June 11, 1975), p. D–13; *Daily World* (June 12, 1975), p. 8.

Hugo Gellert's lithograph of Paul Robeson, produced on the WPA Fine Arts Project, was purchased and presented to the Birmingham, Ala., Public Library in the late 1930s. Gellert hopes it is still in existence. In " 'American Art Today' a High Point of Artistic Activity" (part 3) by Johnny Woods. *Daily World* (Sept. 4, 1975), p. 8. Photo.

"Rutgers [University] Seeks to Get Paul Robeson in [National Football Foundation] Hall of Fame" by Gordon S. White, Jr. *The New York Times* (Sept. 23, 1975), p. 44. Also letter by David Sehres about Robeson and the Rutgers team beating the Great Lakes Naval Training Station team, the all-American team, 14 to 0 at Ebbets Field, Brooklyn, N.Y., in Nov. 1918. *The New York Times*, Sports, section 5 (Oct. 5, 1975), p. 2.

Article about Paul Robeson. *Newsweek*, vol. 86 (Oct. 6, 1975), pp. 58–59.

Korvettes' Weekly Classical Music Program on WQXR, New York City, Sun., Oct. 26, 1975, 12 to 1 P.M., devoted wholly to *The Essential Paul Robeson*, a new 2-record album with 31 selections which Korvettes stores were featuring for one week.

Effort Launched to Put Versatile Robeson in Hall [of Fame for college football stars]. *Jet*, vol. 49, no. 6 (Oct. 30, 1975), p. 48.

The Africana Studies and Research Center of Purdue University, West Lafayette, Ind., will be host to a national conference on Paul Robeson, Apr. 21–23, 1976. A listing of topics and speakers; showings of some of his films. *New York Daily Challenge* (Nov. 14, 1975), p. 4; *Black World* (Mar. 1976), p. 77.

Paul Robeson was a Columbia Law School classmate of U.S. Supreme Court Justice William O. Douglas. There are references to Paul Robeson and the Cardozo family (Eslanda Robeson's family) in Douglas's book *Go East Young Man*, published in 1974. *Jet* (Nov. 20, 1975), p. 9.

The Paul Robeson Humanitarian Award, to be presented annually by the Alpha Phi Alpha national fraternity, will be presented to Robeson at Rutgers University, New Brunswick, N.J., in Dec. 1975. (Taken from Rutgers University Press release, Dec. 1975.)

TV Channel 13 repeated its Interface program on Paul Robeson with Tony Batten as narrator, Jan. 23, 1976, the night after Robeson died.

"Paul Robeson Is Dead at 77" by Laura Murray. *Philadelphia Daily News* (Jan. 24, 1976), pp. 1, 3. Photos.

"Paul Robeson Dead at 77; Singer, Actor and Activist" by Alden Whitman. Also "Paul Robeson" editorial. *The New York Times* (Jan. 24, 1976), pp. 1, 26, 30. Photos. "Paul Robeson Is Dead at 77" by Fern Marja Eckman. *New York Post* (Jan. 23, 1976), pp. 5, 59. Photo. *Daily World* (Jan. 24, 1976), p. 1. Photo. *Long Island Press* (Jan. 24, 1976).

"The Death of Paul Robeson" by Gary Hoenig. *The New York Times* (The Week in Review) (Jan. 25, 1976), p. 7. "Mourners at the Chapel 'Go Tell It' to Robeson" and "Robeson Funeral 'Back in Harlem'" by Charlayne Hunter. *The New York Times* (Jan. 27 and 28, 1976), pp. 34, 36. Photo.

Radio station WBAI-FM, New York City, repeated its 3-hour show on Paul Robeson (done originally months earlier) on Jan. 25, 1976, after Robeson's death.

Robert Sherman's *Listening Room* radio program, WQXR, New York City, Jan. 26, 1976, devoted the first hour to playing recordings by Paul Robeson. This hour was repeated on Sherman's *Woody's Children* radio program, WQXR, Apr. 3, 1976. Another program of Robeson's music, played on the *Listening Room* program Feb. 2, 1976, based on the letters in response to the Jan. 26 program, was repeated on Sherman's *Woody's Children* program on Apr. 10, 1976.

The World Mourns Robeson's Death; Tribute to Paul Robeson (editorial); Robeson Memorials, *Mirror* (Jan. 25 and 28, Feb. 3, 1976). (*Mirror* is the newspaper of the People's Progressive Party of Guyana, South America, Cheddi Jagan, General Secretary.)

Paul Robeson—Humanitarian, Actor, Athlete; Paul Robeson Rites to be held in New York City Tonight. Also "Robeson" on WHYY-TV, Channel 12, on Jan. 28, 1976, in Philadelphia, Pa., 8–9 P.M. *Philadelphia Tribune* (Jan. 27, 1976), pp. 1, 6. Photos.

Tribute to Paul Robeson held in the U.S. House of Representatives, Jan. 28, 1976. Representative John Conyers of Michigan spoke. See *Congressional Record* (Jan. 28, 1976); *Freedomways*, vol. 16, no. 1 (1976), p. 18.

"Robeson Legacy" by Ted Bassett; Robeson, People's Champion . . . for World Peace (editorial). For Paul Robeson (tributes); Mourned Throughout USSR. *Daily World* (Jan. 27, 1976), pp. 1, 7–9, 12. Photos.

Paul Robeson's funeral services of Jan. 27, 1976, at Mother A.M.E. Zion Church in Harlem, New York City, were taped and broadcast on Delores Costello's TCB program on radio station WBAI-FM, New York City, on Jan. 28, 1976, from 12 to 3 or 4 A.M. including two hours of a Robeson concert plus the Haydn *Mass*. Program repeated on Apr. 6, 1976.

5,000 Pay Final Respects to Robeson; Robeson and the [College Football] Hall of Fame. *Daily World* (Jan. 29, 1976), pp. 1, 9, 12. Photo.

"Paul Robeson Comes Home" by Stan Isaacs. (Obituary article.) *Newsday* (Jan. 29, 1976), p. 3A. Photo.

Goodbye Paul! (11 articles plus editorial on Robeson). *New York Amsterdam News* (Jan. 31, 1976), pp. A–1–2, D–1, D–10–11. Photos.

On the Death of Paul Robeson: An Immortal Legacy. *Freedomways*, vol. 15, no. 4 (1975), pp. 304–5. Photo. Published just after Robeson died on Jan. 23, 1976.

"A Tribute to Robeson" by Byron Belt. *Long Island Press* (Feb. 1, 1976), pp. 1, 16. Photo.

James A. Wechsler's column on Paul Robeson. *New York Post* magazine section. (Feb. 4, 1976), p. 5.

Paul Robeson left three-fourths of his $150,000 estate to his son Paul Robeson, Jr., of Brooklyn, N.Y., and the rest to a sister Marion Forsythe, with whom he lived in Philadelphia, Pa. In "Notes on People" by Laurie Johnston. *The New York Times* (Feb. 4, 1976), p. 65.

Rutgers Memorial Service Pays Homage to Robeson. *The New York Times* (Feb. 6, 1976), p. 32.

Tribute to Robeson. By the Academy of Arts of the German Democratic Republic and the Paul Robeson Committee of the GDR, Berlin. *Daily World* (Feb. 6, 1976), p. 8.

"Harlem Bids Farewell to Paul Robeson" by Vivian Gornick. *Village Voice* (Feb. 9, 1976), pp. 73, 75. Photo.

Delores Costello's regular Tuesday night programs on WBAI-FM, New York City, 12 to 4 or 5 A.M., just after Robeson's death in Jan. 1976 devoted to reading of Robeson's testimony before the U.S. House Committee on Un-American Activities and chapters from Robeson's *Here I Stand*.

Harlem Bids Robeson Goodbye in the Rain; Paul Robeson: Fearless Foe of White Racism. *Jet*, vol. 49, no. 20 (Feb. 12, 1976), pp. 14–20. Photos.

Obituary article on Paul Robeson. *The Guardian* (Feb. 4, 1976). "Paul Robeson: The Real Tragedy" by Frank Lovell. *Militant* (Feb. 13, 1976), p. 23. A bitter obituary attack on Robeson.

"Remembering Paul Robeson; All-American, Scholar, Singer, Fighter for Freedom" by Bart Cohen. *Public Employee Press* (Feb. 13, 1976), p. 17. Photo.

Two Tributes to Paul Robeson at his funeral in New York City on Jan. 27, 1976, by Paul Robeson, Jr., and Lloyd L. Brown; two statements by Robeson and a poem *Tribute* by Susan Kling dedicated to him. *Daily World Magazine*, Black History Issue (Feb. 14, 1976), pp. M–1, M–5–8. Photos.

Dr. Donald Harrington, pastor of the Community Church, New York City, preached a sermon about Paul Robeson at his church on Sunday, Feb. 15, 1976, from 11 to 12 noon. The service was broadcast on radio station WQXR, New York City.

"Hometown, Ill., Holds Memorial for Paul Robeson" by Larry McGurty. *Daily World* (Feb. 17, 1976), p. 3.

Paul Robeson's Estate Valued at $150,000. This does not include his library of books, speeches and tapes. *Jet*, vol. 49, no. 21 (Feb. 19, 1976), p. 57. Photo.

John Henrik Clarke on a 15-minute special on Paul Robeson on the TV program *Today* (Feb. 20, 1976).

"Paul Robeson: A Giant Among Men" by Kasisi Jitu Weusi. (Also a listing of research materials.) *Black News*, vol. 3, nos. 6 and 7 (Jan. and Feb. 1976), pp. 22, 7–8.

Tributes to Paul Robeson: "Paul Robeson: A Home in That Rock" by Paul Robeson, Jr.; "Paul Robeson: Now He Belongs to the Future" by Lloyd L. Brown; "Don't Mourn for Me—But Live for Freedom's Cause" by J. Clinton Hoggard:

"Ode to Paul Robeson" by Pablo Neruda. *Freedomways*, vol. 16, no. 1 (1976), pp. 8–24. First three given at Robeson's funeral.

Another Hero Passes (editorial about Paul Robeson's death). *The Western Sunrise* vol. 5, no. 1 (Dec. 1975–Mar. 1976), p. 2. It asked "How many Paul Robesons lie wasted by the roadsides of American bi-centennial 'progress'?"

Robeson Memorial Held at the University of Michigan. *Daily World* (Feb. 24, 1976), p. 2.

"*Here I Stand* [by Paul Robeson]. Portrait of a Man and His Epoch" by Sumner Jones. *Daily World* (Feb. 25, 1976), p. 8.

Robeson's Burial Place to be Secret—For Now. *Jet*, vol. 49, no. 22 (Feb. 26, 1976), p. 6. Photo.

In Memoriam: Paul Robeson, 1898–1976. *Black Scholar*, vol. 7, no. 5 (Jan.–Feb. 1976), Front cover drawing of Robeson.

Paul Robeson (Apr. 9, 1898–Jan. 23, 1976): brief biography; excerpts from three of Robeson's statements; letter from Paul Robeson Archives asking for funds and Afram Associates' Preston Wilcox's reply with $25.00 gift. *National Afrikan Kalendar* (Jan.–Mar. 1976), pp. 13–16. Photo.

Article on Paul Robeson. *The Paper* (Feb. or Mar. 1976). Photo. (College of the City of New York newspaper of Black and Puerto Rican students.)

"Paul Robeson—Obituary" by John Henrik Clarke. *Africa: International Business, Economic and Political Magazine*, no. 55 (Mar. 1976), pp. 68–69. Photo.

In Memoriam: Paul Robeson (Apr. 9, 1898–Jan. 23, 1976). *Phylon*, vol. 37, no. 1 (Mar. 1976), pp. v, vi.

Guest Editorials: Paul Robeson (Apr. 9, 1898–Jan. 23, 1976)–from *Washington Post* (Jan. 28, 1976); *New York Amsterdam News* (Jan. 31, 1976); and *The New York Times* (Jan 24, 1976). Article from Reuters (News Service) on life of Paul Robeson.

"Paul Robeson: A Remembrance" (excerpts from eulogy by Bishop J. Clinton Hoggard at funeral service for Robeson at Mother A.M.E. Zion Church, New York City, Jan. 27, 1976). *Crisis*, vol. 83, no. 3 (Mar. 1976), pp. 77–83. Front cover photo.

In Memory of Paul Robeson. "Anti-Imperialists Must Defend Africa" by Paul Robeson (abridged speech at Council on African Affairs meeting in Madison Square Garden, New York City, June 6, 1946). *Black Liberation Journal*, vol. 1, no. 1 (Winter 1976), pp. 1–4. Photo.

Paul Robeson: Fallen Warrior (obituary). *CORE Magazine* (Mar. 1976), p. 25.

The Publisher's Page: "The Issue of Energy" by Earl G. Graves. (About half of the page is devoted to Paul Robeson's career and why he will be remembered.) *Black Enterprise*, vol. 6, no. 8 (Mar. 1976), p. 5.

Two paragraphs from Paul Robeson's book *Here I Stand*. *Black-World-View*, vol 1, no. 1 (Mar. 1976), p. 1. Photo. (Published by the Institute of the Black World, Atlanta, Ga.)

Paul Robeson was inducted into the Black Filmmakers Hall of Fame at its first ceremonies in 1974. At the third annual ceremonies held in Oakland, Calif., there were tributes to the late Paul Robeson and silence was observed in memory of the singer-actor. *Jet*, vol. 49, no. 24 (Mar. 11, 1976), pp. 60–61.

"Robeson Remembered" by Waldemar Hille. (One of the tributes to Robeson given at a program at the First Unitarian Church of Los Angeles, Calif., Feb. 15, 1976.) *Daily World Magazine* (March 20, 1976), p. M–12. Photos.

"Paul Robeson" by Jessica Smith. *New World Review*, vol. 44, no. 2 (Mar.–Apr. 1976), pp. 3–4. Photo.

Robeson's Son Won't Cooperate on Film. (Paul Robeson, Jr., says he will not cooperate with Universal-TV and NBC-TV in their plans to make a 3-hour special of Paul Robeson's life since they denied Robeson access to TV during his active career.) *Jet*, vol. 49, no. 27 (Apr. 1, 1976), p. 51.

A Tribute to Paul Robeson Exhibit at the Museum of the City of New York (after Robeson's death) in Apr. 1976. (Taken from Museum brochure.)

"Toward a Democratic Earth We Helped Build" by Paul Robeson. (Speech at the founding convention of the National Negro Labor Council, Cincinnati, Ohio, 1951.) *Daily World* (Apr. 8, 1976), p. 8. Photo.

"Paul Robeson: Farewell to a Fighter" by Carlyle Douglas; "Paul Robeson" (letter on his death) by Lorenz Graham. *Ebony*, vol. 31, no. 6 (Apr. 1976), pp. 33–42, 17. Photos.

"Paul Robeson: A Giant Among Giants" by Ted Bassett; "Forge Negro-Labor Unity for Peace and Jobs" by Paul Robeson. *Political Affairs*, vol. 55, no. 4 (Apr. 1976), pp. 1, 26–43. Photo. Bassett's "Robeson Legacy" (*Daily World*, Jan. 27, 1976) has been rewritten here.

A Paul Robeson Picture Profile. *Negro Heritage*, vol. 16, no. 2 (1976), pp. 41–44.

" 'I Want To Be African': Paul Robeson and the Ends of Nationalist Theory and Practice, 1914–1945" by Sterling Stuckey. *The Massachusetts Review*, vol. 17, no. 1 (Spring 1976), pp. 81–138. Photo of Jacob Epstein's bronze bust of Paul Robeson. (A chapter of Stuckey's doctoral dissertation [listed elsewhere] read at the national conference on Paul Robeson, Purdue University, Indiana, Apr. 21–23, 1976.)

The Paul Robeson Players founded in 1971 in Compton, Calif., Robert Browning, director. Group has shifted from adult to youth theatre and now gets some financial support from the Compton city government. It will produce some plays of local writers. *Black World*, vol. 25, no. 6 (Apr. 1976), p. 80.

Black Athletes' Hall of Fame inducts Paul Robeson and twenty others on Mar. 31, 1976. *Jet*, vol. 49, no. 28 (Apr. 8, 1976), p. 54; *Daily World* (Apr. 7, 1976), p. 12. Photo.

Symposium on Paul Robeson in Countee Cullen Library, Harlem, New York City, Apr. 10, 1976, 2 P.M. Leonard Jeffries, Barbara Wheeler, Edward Scobie from College of the City of New York, participants.

Paul Robeson: The Tallest Tree in Our Forest, Special *Like It Is* program, ABC-TV, Apr. 11, 1976, 12:30–2 P.M., Gil Noble, Narrator. *New York Amsterdam News*, Arts and Entertainment Section (Apr. 10, 1976), pp. D–15, D–20. Program repeated on Paul Robeson's birthday, Apr. 9, 1977, 1:30–3 P.M.

Paul Robeson Citation Committee of Actors Equity Association unveils the sculpture of Paul Robeson by Richmond Barthe in the auditorium of the Library & Museum of the Performing Arts, Lincoln Center, New York City, Apr. 23, 1976, from 6 to 7:30 P.M.

Friends of the Paul Robeson Archives to have a reception to mark the publication of *Paul Robeson: Tributes and Selected Writings*, a commemorative book published by the Paul Robeson Archives. At Automation House, New York City, Apr. 24, 1976, 2 to 7 P.M.

Paul Robeson (obituaries). *Opera News*, vol. 40 (May 1976), p. 46; *Time*, vol. 107 (Feb. 2, 1976), p. 55.

Concert Tribute to Robeson. Beatrice Rippy, soprano; Carroll Hollister, accompanist; Antar S. K. Mberi, poet. McMillan Auditorium, Columbia University, New York City, May 16, 1976. *Daily World* (May 14, 1976), p. 8; (May 20, 1976), p. 8. Photos.

"World Homage to the Great Paul Robeson" by Tim Wheeler. Tribute to Robeson program at Shiloh Baptist Church, Washington, D.C., Apr. 30, 1976, with representatives from Ghana, Nigeria, India, USSR, Jamaica, German Democratic Republic, World Federation of Trade Unions, Panama, black women restaurant workers' local in Washington, D.C., the Paul Robeson Multimedia Center, Washington, D.C., plus other U.S. Blacks. *Daily World* (May 14, 1976), p. 8. Photo.

"Paul Robeson: A Career Dedicated to the Human Spirit" by D. Wilmeth. *Intellect Magazine* (May-June 1976), pp. 104–9.

Be Like Robeson, Trudeau Urges. (Canadian Prime Minister, in a message on the occasion of the fourth annual nation Black awards presentation, called on Blacks in Canada "to follow in the tradition of Paul Robeson who . . . is best known for his dedication to the improvement of society and his loyalty to his convictions.") *Canadian Tribune* (June 7, 1976).

The Day They Named the School for Paul Robeson. Public School 191, an elementary school in Brownsville-East New York, Brooklyn, N.Y., named Paul Robeson Public School in June 1976. *New York Amsterdam News* (June 19, 1976), p. B–1. Photo.

Guillen and Robeson Meet in Spain, 1938. (Interview [translated by Katheryn Silver] with Robeson conducted by Nicolas Guillen in 1938 in Spain during the Spanish Civil War.) *Mediodia* (1938); *Bohemia* (May 7, 1976) (both in Spanish in Cuba); *Daily World Magazine* (July 24, 1976), p. m–7. Photo.

"Paul Robeson: His Dreams Know No Frontiers" by Acklyn Lynch. *Journal of Negro Education*, vol. 45, no. 3 (Summer 1976), pp. 225–34.

Late Paul Robeson Honored at Congressional Black Caucus Dinner (in 1976). *Delegate 76*, p. 326. Photo.

Delegate Salutes Paul Robeson and Langston Hughes. *Delegate 76*, pp. 344–45. Photos.

Friends of the Paul Robeson Archives sponsor an Artists' Tribute to the Life of Paul Robeson at Carnegie Hall, New York City, Oct. 18, 1976. *Daily World* (Oct. 5, 1976), p. 9; (Oct. 27, 1976), p. 8. Photo.

Paul Robeson, Jr., on the Delores Costello show on WBAI-FM, New York City, Oct. 14, 1976, 12 to 3 or 4 A.M., talking about Robeson and playing songs and speeches by him.

Four Robeson tapes of songs played on Robert Sherman's program *Woody's Children* on WQXR, New York, Oct. 16, 1976, between 7 and 8 P.M.

Honoring Robeson. (Article about the renaming of Avalon Place and a part of Walnut Street as Paul Robeson Place in the town of Princeton, N.J.) *Princeton Packet* (newspaper) (Oct. 16, 1976).

"Paul Robeson, 1898–1976" by Gloster B. Current. *The Black Perspective in Music*, vol. 4, no. 3 (Fall 1976), pp. 302–6. Photo.

The 1976 Jane Addams Children's Book Award won by Eloise Greenfield's *Paul Robeson* with illustrations by George Ford. Presented in Washington, D.C., on Oct. 28, 1976, by the Jane Addams Peace Association for book's "literary merit and themes that stress peace, social justice and the dignity and equality of all people." *Daily World* (Nov. 11, 1976), p. 8. Photo.

"Paul Robeson, the Giant" by Sharon Odessa Biggs. *The Black American* (newspaper) (Nov. 18–24, 1976), p. 13. Photo.

"Paul Robeson: There He Stood" by William L. Patterson. *New World Review*, vol. 44, no. 6 (Nov.–Dec. 1976), pp. 10–13. Photos.

"Paul Robeson" by Marcella Pope. (Excerpt from speech at Robeson Memorial meeting, Washington, D.C., Apr. 30, 1976; how Robeson gave a concert and contributed $5,000 himself to help Black women restaurant workers on strike in Washington, D.C., in the winter of 1948.) *New World Review*, vol. 44, no. 6 (Nov.–Dec. 1976), p. 12.

1976 Exhibit in the Schomburg Center, New York City, on Paul Robeson's life (playbills, sheet music, programs, photographs, etc.). *Bulletin of the New York Public Library* (Winter 1977), p. 305.

A Paul Robeson scholarship fund for minority and legal studies is being established by Black students at the Columbia University Law School, New York City. *Jet* (Feb. 17, 1977), p. 29.

Tribute of dance, songs and words to the late Paul Robeson at the fourth annual Oscar Micheaux Awards ceremony Feb. 20, 1977, in Oakland, Calif., of the Black Filmmakers Hall of Fame (shown on educational TV in the spring of 1977). Also presentation of the first Paul Robeson Medal of Distinction to Alice Childress. *The New York Times* (Feb. 22, 1977), p. 38.

Paul Robeson's sister, Marion Forsythe, with whom he lived in Philadelphia, Pa., until his death, died in Philadelphia Feb. 17, 1977, at the age of 82. *Philadelphia Tribune* (Feb. 22, 1977), pp. 1, 21. Photo.

History Brought to Life—"You're the Un-Americans!" (Review of play *Point of Order: An Inside Look at the Backside of the Front* in which Paul Robeson's testimony before the U.S. House Committee on Un-American Activities in 1956 is the climax of the play. Produced at the Dudley Riggs' ETC Theater, Minneapolis, Minn., in Mar. and Apr. 1977. *Daily World* (Mar. 17, 1977), p. 8. Photo.

Black International Communication Association has Paul Robeson Memorial Program, Apr. 4, 1977, 6–10 P.M., at the New York City Community College, Brooklyn. (Taken from flyer.)

Paul Robeson and the State Department. *Crisis* (May 1977). pp. 184–89.

The Paul Robeson Cultural Center at Pennsylvania State University, University Park, will publish a magazine *Minority Voices* three times a year. *First World* (May–June 1977), p. 38.

Proclamations or resolutions were passed by the City Council and the Board of Education of Washington, D.C., in Apr. 1976 memorializing Paul Robeson. *New World Review*, vol. 44, no. 6 (Nov.–Dec. 1976), p. 13; vol. 45, no. 4 (July–Aug. 1977), p. 23.

Report on the Hands Around the World—Paul Robeson Friendship Society of Washington, D.C. *New World Review*, vol. 44, no. 6 (Nov.–Dec. 1976), p. 13; vol. 45, no. 4 (July–Aug. 1977), p. 23. Photos. After the Ad Hoc Committee to Memorialize Paul Robeson held a public meeting on Apr. 30, 1976, the Committee decided in July 1976 to become a permanent organization—Hands Around the World. This group has helped Paul Robeson, Jr., and his wife in setting up and maintaining the Paul Robeson exhibit at the annual meeting in Washington, D.C., of the Congressional Black Caucus; raised funds for the Paul Robeson International Multimedia Center, Washington, D.C.; secured signatures for the New Stockholm Peace Appeal; distributed information in all Washington schools about the youth program of the National Council of American-Soviet Friendship among other activities. George B. Murphy, Jr., is an officer of this organization.

James Earl Jones Is in Rehearsal in Los Angeles, Calif., for One-Character (play) *Paul Robeson* by Phillip Hayes Dean. Play will open on Broadway, New York City, in 1978. *The New York Times* (Aug. 13, 1977), p. 12. Photo.

"James Jones Gives Robeson Part Life" by Robert Lindsey. (Jones calls Robeson's life a tragedy.) *The New York Times* (Aug. 31, 1977), p. C20. Photo.

University of Pennsylvania's annual Paul Robeson International Film Festival in Philadelphia shows old Black films. *Encore* (Sept. 12, 1977), p. 36.

"Truth Dishonored in Play About Robeson" by Anne Braden. (Issues of our time reduced to trivia; the giant Robeson reduced to a dwarf.) *Daily World* (Sept. 22, 1977).

"What They 'Forgot' in the Play About Robeson" (shown in Louisville, Ky.) by Anne Braden. Calls play a shallow treatment of Robeson, devoid of politics and real issues and therefore of drama. *Daily World* (Oct. 7, 1977).

"The Paul Robeson Archives/Legacy of Courage" by Harriet Jackson Scarupa. *Essence*, vol. 8, no. 6 (Oct. 1977), pp. 60–61, 84, 86, 88, 91. Photos.

"Slander with a State Department Label" ("The Robeson Story" by Vice Consul Roger P. Ross in Ghana) by Terry Cannon. *Daily World* (Oct. 13, 1977), p. 8. Paul Robeson, Jr.'s freedom of information suit released a Ross memorandum to the U.S. State Department calling for a slanderous article about Paul Robeson to be written and placed in a U.S. magazine, then later reprinted and distributed in Africa. The requested article was written and placed in the NAACP's the *Crisis* magazine (Nov. 1951) titled "Paul Robeson—The Lost Shepherd" and written under the pseudonym Robert Alan. Cannon says the editorial in *The New York Times* in 1951 and the Walter White article attacking Robeson in *Ebony* magazine (Feb. 1951) were likewise a part of the U.S. government's inspired or planted pieces designed to discredit Robeson.

Protest False Play About Robeson. (The play *Paul Robeson* starring James Earl Jones and written by Phillip Hayes Dean, being tried out in Boston, Mass.) *Daily World* (Nov. 4, 1977), p. 8.

"Why Robeson Was Loved and Revered by Millions" (review of Lloyd L. Brown's pamphlet *Paul Robeson Rediscovered*) by John Kailin. *Daily World* (Dec. 6, 1977), p. 8. Photo. Brown says that Robeson unified his art with his militant, consistent, and profound anti-imperialism. So the naive humanitarianism attributed to Robeson by the play *Paul Robeson* is false and reduces the great understanding of this giant figure.

Central State (University, Wilberforce, Ohio) Art Center Named After Paul Robeson. (Paul Robeson Cultural and Performing Arts Center; new $6 million building.) *Jet*, vol. 53, no. 12 (Dec. 8, 1977), p. 15. Photo.

Detroit (Mich.) Prepares for "Paul Robeson Day" (and Robeson week), Apr. 9–15, 1978. Apr. 9, 1978, is the 80th anniversary of Paul Robeson's birth. Dr. Charles Wright is coordinator of the Program. *Bilalian News* (Dec. 9, 1977), p. 29. Photo.

Open Letter to the Citizens of Washington: A Statement of Conscience Concerning the Theatrical Production *Paul Robeson*. (The play opened in Washington, D.C., on Dec. 5, 1977. This statement, signed by many prominent Black leaders, writers, and actors, condemns the play as a pernicious perversion of the essence of Paul Robeson.) *Daily World* (Dec. 9, 1977), p. 8. Photo.

Robeson Award Goes to Pete Seeger. (Fourth annual Paul Robeson Award of Actors Equity Association for 1977 to be presented Jan. 6, 1978, at meeting in New York City. Previous winners are Paul Robeson in 1974; Ossie Davis and Ruby Dee in 1975; and Lillian Hellman in 1976.) *New York Amsterdam News*, Arts and Entertainment Section (Jan. 7, 1978), p. D–7.

"What is 'Paul Robeson' All About?" by George B. Murphy, Jr. (About the play *Paul Robeson*.) *Afro-American* (newspaper) (Jan. 10–14, 1978), p. 5. Photo; *Daily World Magazine* (Jan. 28, 1978), p. 16. Photos.

Open Letter to the Entertainment Industry: A Statement of Conscience. *Variety* (Jan. 11, 1978). About the play *Paul Robeson* that opened for a limited run on Broadway, New York City, on Jan. 19, 1978. The statement is the same as that printed in the *Daily World* (Dec. 9, 1977), but there are 56 signatures of prominent Black Americans here.

Wide Protests to Greet New York Debut of *Robeson*. (Play *Paul Robeson* opening on Broadway, Jan. 19, 1978.) *Daily World* (Jan. 17, 1978), p. 3.

"Stage: James Earl Jones as Robeson" by Richard Eder. *The New York Times* (Jan. 20, 1978), p. C3. Photo.

Paul Robeson's Legacy (editorial on statement in *Variety* by Blacks protesting the play *Paul Robeson*). Also "A Correlary to Robeson." *New York Amsterdam News* (Jan. 21, 1978).

David Lampell's Black Ethics radio program. WBLS-FM, New York City, Jan. 22, 1978, 10–11 A.M. Program on Paul Robeson. Paul Robeson, Jr., on program. He played tapes of Robeson speaking and singing.

Some Facts About Paul Robeson, the Man, Vis-à-Vis the Stage Play. Prepared for distribution by the National Ad Hoc Committee to End the Crimes Against Paul Robeson. c/o Black Theology Project, Interchurch Center, Rm. 349, 475 Riverside Dr., New York City 10027. 13 pp. plus 9-page appendix.

"Robeson Play Is a Mixed Bag" by Townsend Brewster. Also "Sadness in Dark Old Men" (about Robeson's death) by Juanita R. Howard. New York Amsterdam News, Arts and Entertainment Section (Jan. 28, 1978), p. D–11. Photo.

USSR Named 40,000-Ton Tanker for Paul Robeson. Jet, vol. 53, no. 20 (Feb. 2, 1978), p. 26.

"Robeson Commemorative Week Set in Detroit, Apr. 9–16" by William Allan. Daily World (Feb. 8, 1978), p. 6. Photos. His 80th birthday celebrated.

"Paul Robeson and the Play that Masks His Greatness" (Part 1) by Ted Bassett. Daily World (Feb. 22, 1978), p. 8. (To be in three parts.)

Interface: Biography of Paul Robeson. TV Channel 13, New York City, Sun., Feb. 26, 1978, 6–7 P.M. The New York Times, Arts and Leisure, section 2 (Feb. 26, 1978), p. 28–A. A repeat of the earlier Interface program.

The Paul Robeson Lecture Series at Medgar Evers College, City University of New York, Brooklyn, Feb. 28, Mar. 28, Apr. 25, May 23, 1978. Guest lecturers: Acklyn Lynch, Gil Noble, Charles Wright, John Killens, on Robeson and politics, Robeson and media, champion of labor and as artist, respectively. New York Daily Challenge (Feb. 26, 1978), p. 4.

"Robeson to Reopen on Colored Girls Bill" by Thomas Lask, The New York Times (Mar. 2, 1978), p. C17. Photo. Paul Robeson will have four performances a week beginning Mar. 9, 1978, at the Booth Theater, New York City; For Colored Girls will have five performances a week there.

Special Committee Against Apartheid to Observe Anniversary of Paul Robeson. U.N. Centre Against Apartheid Information Note 28 (Mar. 10, 1978). United Nations Committee announced that it would hold a special meeting on Apr. 10, 1978, to pay tribute to Paul Robeson on the 80th anniversary of his birthday in recognition of his efforts for freedom of African countries and his support to the liberation struggle in South Africa. The Committee notes Robeson's work as chairman of the International Committee on African Affairs formed in 1937, his leadership of the Council on African Affairs, and the National Church of Nigeria's award of Champion of African Freedom to Robeson, Kwame Nkrumah, and Nnamdi Azikiwe in Lagos, Nigeria, in 1950.

"Carl Stokes Takes on Paul Robeson" by John J. O'Connor. The New York Times, Arts and Leisure, section 2 (Mar. 12, 1978), p. 29. About Stokes's six Urban Journal segments on NBC-TV mostly in defense of the play and attacking the integrity of the 56 signers of "a statement of conscience" in Variety against the play. O'Connor praises Stokes and agrees with him.

"For Colored Folks Who Have Considered Censhorship" by Richard Goldstein. Village Voice (Mar. 13, 1978), p. 44. Photo.

"Paul Robeson: Another View" by Jewell Handy Gresham. New York Amsterdam News (Mar. 18, 1978). Also editorial on the Paul Robeson play controversy. (Ms. Gresham was Executive Director of the Coalition of Concerned Black Americans.)

Old, Reissued and Other Phonograph Recordings and Tapes by and About Paul Robeson

American Balladeer (Paul Robeson). Everest, Los Angeles. 1977.
The Best of Paul Robeson. Vol. 1. EMI. 1970.
The Best of Paul Robeson. Vol. 2. Capitol/EMI.
The Best of Paul Robeson. Vol. 3. Starline.
Chorus: Robeson with chorus and orchestra, Harriet Wingreen, piano. (Records, *Daily World*, 205 W. 19 St., New York 10011.)
Encore, Robeson! Paul Robeson: Favorite Songs, Vol. 2. Monitor.
The Essential Paul Robeson. Vanguard. 1975. (Two records).
An Evening with Paul Robeson. 1971. (Record made from tapes of Robeson concerts in the early 1950s. Robeson also speaks. Available at Detroit Afro-American Museum, 1553 W. Grand Blvd., Detroit, MI 48208.)
The Famous Recordings of Paul Robeson. Pathe. 1969.
Incomparable Voice. Odeon. 196?.
Lift Every Voice and Sing. Album by Max Roach, et al. (The "Troubled Waters" section is dedicated to Paul Robeson.)
The Mighty Voice of Paul Robeson. British import.
Othello/Shakespeare. Columbia Records. Paul Robeson, Jose Ferrer, Uta Hagen and Edith King. (The Broadway play was recorded in 1943. There were later reissues of this play.)
Paul Robeson. Pathe. Marconi-EMI. 197?.
Paul Robeson. Verve. 1960.
Paul Robeson. Empire Records.
Paul Robeson. Supraphon. 1961.
Paul Robeson at Carnegie Hall: May 9, 1958. Vol. 1. Vanguard. 1959. (Many favorite song plus monologue from *Othello*. Sold by Records, *Daily World*.)
Paul Robeson at Peace Arch Park, Blaine, Washington, 1953 (from tape of Robeson concert and speech for the Canadian miners in 1953. Afro-American Museum, Detroit, Mich.).
Paul Robeson: Ballad for Americans and Carnegie Hall Concert. Vol. 2. Vanguard. 1965. Originally *Ballad for Americans*. A two-record, 78 r.p.m. album brought out by RCA Victor in 1939 with Robeson as soloist, mixed chorus and orchestra. Sold by Records, *Daily World*, 205 W. 19 St., New York 10011.
Paul Robeson: Favorite Songs. Vol. 1. Monitor.
Paul Robeson: In Live Performance. At Harlem's AME Zion Church, June 1, 1958, and in London's Royal Albert Hall, Aug. 10, 1948. Columbia Masterworks. 1971. (Sold by Records, *Daily World*, 205 W. 19 St., New York 10011.)
Paul Robeson—A Man and His Beliefs. Everest, Los Angeles. 1971.
Paul Robeson: Old Folks at Home and Other Classics. (Recording on sale in 1971 at Marlboro Books, 131 Varick St., New York City 10013, and by Publishers Central Bureau, Dept. 299, 30–20 Hunters Point Ave., Long Island City, NY 11101.)
Paul Robeson Recital. Vanguard. 1958.
Paul Robeson: Scandalize My Name. The Classics Record Library. Book of the Month Club. 1976. (Three records or 8-track tape.) Booklet written by Nat Hentoff.
A Robeson Recital of Popular Favorites. Columbia Records. 1954?
Robeson Sings. Othello Records. 1953?
Salute to Paul Robeson. Paul Robeson Archives. Cassette tapes.
Solid Rock: Favorite Hymns of My People. Othello Records. 1954?
Song of Free China. 78 r.p.m. album.
Songs of Free Men. Columbia Records. 1942.
Songs of Free Men/Spirituals. Columbia. 1945; Odyssey. 1968.

Songs of My People. An RCA 1972 reissue collection of about two dozen Black spirituals and work songs recorded by Paul Robeson with piano accompaniment by Lawrence Brown between 1925 and 1929, half of these songs from Robeson's first recital. Album reviewed in Douglas Watt's column "Record Review," *New York Sunday News* (July 16, 1972), Leisure section, p. 9. Photo. "From Swing Low to Super Fly to Simone" by Clayton Riley (article begins with a review of the early, 1925–29 Robeson-recorded spirituals as the album *Songs of My People* along with comment on Robeson as a great cultural and political figure). *The New York Times,* Recordings, section 16 (Nov. 26, 1972), p. 1. Photo.

The Special Magic of Paul Robeson. Verve (import).

Spirituals and Popular Favorites. Columbia Records. 1949.

Swing Low Sweet Chariot. Columbia Records. 1949.

When I Have Sung My Songs: The American Art Song, 1900–1940 (Paul Robeson). New World Records. 1976.

Films and Portable Exhibits

Paul Robeson—A Celebration. A 25-minute film made by Barbara Jamison (27 Constantine Pl., Summit, NJ 07901). This is a compendium of live film and still photographs, with an accompanying taped commentary and a "cast of thousands" including Pete Seeger, Nikita S. Khrushchev, Prof. Harold D. Weaver, and Eugene O'Neill. It is, in essence, a folk mass on film, a new documentary form combining news, music, history, nostalgia, social comment, and politics, some in color, other parts in black-and-white. Available from Barbara Jamison in both super-8 and 16 mm.

"Black Series." (Three rare black films—*The Emperor Jones* with Paul Robeson and Dudley Diggs, *St. Louis Blues* with Bessie Smith, and *Jazz at the Apollo*—shown Sunday, Dec. 12, 1971, at 3 P.M. at the New York Shakespeare Festival's Public Theatre, Martinson Hall, 425 Lafayette St. The film program was the second event in a new series of Sunday afternoon black events.) *The Village Voice* (Dec. 9, 1971), p. 28. (*The Emperor Jones* and other old Black films produced by Blacks were shown several times in New York City in 1971.)

Two Robeson Films Off Festival List. *The New York Times* (Apr. 7, 1973), p. 38. (Paul Robeson, Jr., withdraws *The Emperor Jones* and *Song of Freedom* from the American Film Institute Festival in protest of the Festival's cancellation of Constantin Costa-Gavras's film *State of Siege.* The Robeson films were to be shown at the Kennedy Center, Washington, D.C., on Apr. 9, 1973, as a tribute to the actor and singer on his 75th birthday.)

A six-panel, portable Robeson exhibit entitled *The Making of a Militant.* Available from Detroit Afro-American Museum, Inc., 1553 West Grand Blvd., Detroit, MI 48208, for $50.00 a day plus shipping costs.

"Paul Robeson, Beleaguered Leader." A panel, Oct. 19, 1973, at the 58th annual meeting of the Association for the Study of Afro-American Life and History, Commodore Hotel, New York City, Oct. 18–21, 1973. Participants: Herman Brown, C.L.R. James, Harold D. Weaver, Jr., and John Henrik Clarke. Two of Robeson's films were shown in the evening at the Association meeting. See Association program.

Rutgers University's film retrospective of Paul Robeson at the New Brunswick, N.J. campus under the supervision of Harold D. Weaver, Jr. *Sanders of the River* and *Proud Valley* were shown on the night of Nov. 12, 1973. *The New York Times,* section 2, Arts and Leisure (Nov. 11, 1973), p. 38. Photo.

The Paul Robeson Film Retrospective, sponsored by the Rutgers College Department of Africana Studies, New Brunswick, N.J., Nov. 5–19, 1973. Harold D. Weaver, Jr., chairman. Screenings and discussions of Robeson's eleven feature films, three documentaries in which he was a narrator or a subject, and several biographical documentaries. The American Film Institute, Washington, D.C., helped in locating and supplying films in which Robeson appeared. The Film Study Center of the Museum of Modern Art, New York City, has some films. A pictorial booklet, *Paul Robeson in Film* (1974), containing a complete filmography with commentary, could be obtained by writing The Paul Robeson Film Retrospective. Some of the film titles are *Body and Soul* (1924), *The Emperor Jones* (1933), *Song of Freedom* (1937), *Proud Valley* (1939), and *Native Land* (1942). *Daily World* (Nov. 13, 1973), p. 8; *The Black Scholar*, vol. 5, no. 4 (Dec. 1973–Jan. 1974), p. 32.

Paul Robeson: A Film Retrospective. Central Library, Lecture Hall, Logan Square, The Free Library of Philadelphia, Pa. A series of four showings on May 7, 14, 21, 28, 1974, of *Song of Freedom* (documentary on Robeson), *The Emperor Jones, Sanders of the River*, and *Proud Valley*, respectively. Dr. Harold D. Weaver, Jr., former chairman of the Africana Studies Department, Rutgers University, introduced *Song of Freedom*.

Native Land. Directed by Paul Strand and Leo Hurwitz. Songs and narrative by Paul Robeson. Music by Marc Blitzstein. Review in *The New York Times* by Bosley Crowther in 1942 when first shown and in the *Daily Worker*, etc. Shown for five days at the Whitney Museum of American Art's New American Filmmakers Series, Jan. 31–Feb. 4, 1975. Shown on TV Channel 13, New York City, on July 22, 1975, at night. Reviewed by Richard F. Shepard. *The New York Times* (Feb. 1, 1975), p. 19.

Films and Video Tapes (of Paul Robeson). In Erwin A. Salk's *Du Bois-Robeson: Two Giants of the 20th Century*, 1977. (A list of Robeson's films and the names and addresses of the distributors of these films. Very useful information.)

Paul Robeson's Legendary Triumph! Cinema Thirteen's showing of *The Emperor Jones* on Sat., Feb. 18, 1978, at 8 P.M. and *King Solomon's Mines* on Sat., Feb. 25, 1978, at 8 P.M. On TV Channel 13, New York City. *The New York Times* (Feb. 18, 1978), p. 47. (Advertisement with photo of Robeson.)

Sanders of the River (Paul Robeson) on TV Channel 9 (WOR) in New York City, Mar. 7, 1978, at 8 P.M. *The New York Times* (Mar. 7, 1978), p. 71.

Poetry Inspired by Paul Robeson

"To Paul Robeson" by Jean F. Brierre. Translated from the French by Frances Waldman. *The Negro Quarterly*, vol. 1, no. 4 (Winter-Spring 1943), pp. 363–64.

"Paul Robeson; Poem" by D. Littlewort. In *Opportunity* (Apr. 1946).

"To Paul Robeson" by Nazim Hikmet (written in October 1949 by the late Turkish poet while in prison). In *Poems by Nazim Hikmet* (1954), p. 55.

"Paul Robeson: A Poem" by David Gordon. In *The Daily Worker* around 1950.

"Paul Robeson" by Beah Richards. In *Freedom* (June 1951). Also in Paul Robeson Souvenir Program (Apr. 22, 1965).

"Zog Nisht Kaynmol . . ." To Paul Robeson by Binem Heller (a leading Yiddish poet of Poland). In *Jewish Life*, vol. 6, no. 7 (July 1952).

"To Robeson" by D. Titelbom. Translated from the Yiddish by Martha Millet. *The Worker* (May 31, 1953), p. 8.

"To Paul Robeson" (author?). *Daily Worker* (Sept. 12, 1955), p. 7.

"Paul Robeson (1960)" by Fred Field. In *The Forerunners and Other Selected Poems 1914–1970* (1970), p. 38.

"Until They Have Stopped" (dedicated to Paul Robeson, Sr.) by Sarah E. Wright. In *Freedomways*, vol. 5, no. 3 (3rd quarter 1965), pp. 378–79. A poem by the well-known Black woman poet and novelist.

"For Paul Robeson" by Henri Percikow. In *Freedomways*, vol. 5, no. 3 (3rd quarter 1965), p. 411.

"For Paul Robeson" by Edith Segal. In *Take My Hand* (1969), p. 96.

"Brother Paul" (To Paul Robeson) by Sarah Fell Yellin. In *Flower Children and Other Poems* (1969), pp. 28–29.

"To Paul Robeson, opus no. 3" by Percy Edward Johnston. From the magazine *Dasein: A Journal of Aesthetics, Literature and Philosophy*, edited by Johnston. Reprinted in *Cavalcade: Negro Writing from 1760 to the Present*, 1971, edited by Arthur P. Davis and Saunders Redding, pp. 771–72. Also in *To Paul Robeson* at the Library of Congress.

"Paul Robeson" by Gwendolyn Brooks. In *Family Pictures* (1971).

"Paul Robeson—The Sequoia" by Vernon-Turner Kitabu. In *Freedomways*, vol. 11, no. 4 (4th quarter 1971), pp. 370–71.

"Ode to Paul Robeson" by Pablo Neruda. Translated from the Spanish by Jill Booty. In *Salute to Paul Robeson: A Cultural Celebration of His 75th Birthday*, Apr. 15, 1973, Carnegie Hall, New York City, program. Also in *Freedomways*, vol. 16, no. 1 (1976), pp. 19–24.

"When Robeson Sings!" by Edith Segal. In *Poems & Songs for Dreamers Who Dare* (1975).

"Paul Robeson: We Are Now His Home" by David Cumberland. *Daily World* (Feb. 11, 1976), p. 8.

"Declaration" (the North or Polar Star Shall Be Called Paul's Star after Jan. 23, 1976) by Evelyn O. Chisley. *Daily World* (Feb. 11, 1976), p. 8.

"Tribute" (to Paul Robeson) by Susan Kling. *Daily World Magazine* (Feb. 14, 1976), p. M–7.

"Suite of the Singing Mountain," a blues/jazz cantata for Paul Robeson, written by Antar Sudan Katara Mberi. A long poem with subtitles such as "Deep within us a volcano burns," "We are gathering in your light, Big Paul," and "Erect as the sun at high noon, you rise like a mountain." *Daily World* (May 14, 1976), p. 8; (May 20, 1976), p. 8.

"Paul Robeson" by James Brown. *Freedomways*, vol. 16, no. 3 (1976), p. 178.

"Too Tall, Paul; Too Tall, That's All" by Willie J. Magruder, Jr. *Freedomways*, vol. 17, no. 1 (1977), p. 19.

"Paul Robeson" by Michael S. Harper. *Black Scholar*, vol. 8, no. 8 (Apr. 1977), p. 34.

"A Home in This Rock" by Anne Sadowski. On back cover of *To Live Like Paul Robeson* (Sept. 1977), p. 24.

Also poems to Paul Robeson by Nikki Giovanni, Edward Royce, and Richard Davidson included in this book.

Notes on Contributors

Edward J. Bloustein is president of Rutgers University.

Brigitte Bogelsack is manager of The Paul Robeson Archive in Berlin, Germany (The German Democratic Republic).

Gwendolyn Brooks is internationally recognized as one of America's greatest living poets.

Lloyd L. Brown is presently writing a comprehensive biography of Robeson, with whom he was associated for many years as a friend and collaborator. Mr. Brown is author of the novel, *Iron City*.

Robert S. Browne is founder of the Black Economic Research Center and is now with the Twenty-First Century Fund.

Margaret Burroughs, artist and teacher, is founder and executive director of the Du Sable Museum of African American History, Inc., Chicago, Illinois.

Alice Childress is playwright, novelist, and actress. Her most recent book, *A Hero Ain't Nothin' but a Sandwich*, has been adapted as a Hollywood film.

John Henrik Clarke is an associate editor of *Freedomways* and an associate professor in the Department of Black and Puerto Rican Studies of Hunter College in New York City. He is editor of *American Negro Short Stories, William Styron's Nat Turner— Ten Black Writers Respond*, and author of other books.

John Conyers, Jr., is U.S. congressman from Michigan and a member of the House Judiciary Committee. He has published many articles on foreign policy and on Blacks in the U.S. economy.

George W. Crockett is Judge, Recorders' Court, Detroit, Michigan, and is widely known and respected for his leadership in civil rights and civil liberties. He was a long-time friend of Paul Robeson.

Richard Davidson is a native of Chicago whose first poem was published when he was 15. His works include a collection of poetry, *Glass Roads*, and a play, *Nobody's Child*.

Tom Dent has written poetry, drama, and essays. He coedited *The*

373

Free Southern Theatre by the Free Southern Theatre. His collection of poetry is entitled *Magnolia Street*.

Shirley Graham Du Bois was the founding editor of *Freedomways* and wife of W.E.B. Du Bois. She was author of books of fiction, essays, historical novels; composer of music and opera. She died on March 27, 1977, in the People's Republic of China.

Harry Edwards is assistant professor of sociology, University of California at Berkeley. A scholar and athlete, he is author of *The Revolt of the Black Athlete*, *Black Students*, and *Sports: Its Myths and Realities*.

Nikki Giovanni is a prolific poet and lecturer whose works include *A Poetic Equation: Conversations Between Nikki Giovanni and Margaret Walker*, *Ego Tripping and Other Poems for Young People*, *Spin a Soft Black Song*, and others.

Dick Gregory, social satirist, comedian, and activist, is author of *Dick Gregory's Political Primer*, *No More Lies: The Myth and the Reality of American History*, and other books.

Ollie Harrington is one of the world's greatest living political cartoonists. He is currently cartoonist for the *Daily World*.

Nazim Hikmet, the late Turkish people's poet, wrote the poem "To Paul Robeson" while serving a 13-year prison sentence.

Darlene Clark Hine, an assistant professor of history at Purdue University, Indianapolis, Indiana, is active in the Association for the Study of Afro-American Life and History.

Bishop J. Clinton Hoggard is the Presiding Prelate, Sixth Episcopal District of the A.M.E. Zion Church. He was a childhood friend of Paul Robeson.

Lena Horne is singer and actress of stage, screen, and television.

Ernest Kaiser is a founding associate editor of *Freedomways*. He is on the staff of the Schomburg Center for Research in Black Culture and the editor of *A Freedomways Reader*, a collection of articles from *Freedomways*. He has contributed essays to many books and magazines.

Mbiyu Koinange is an author, educator, and leader with Jomo Kenyatta of the Kenyan people's struggle for independence and after in the 1950s and 1960s.

John Lewis is associate director for the antipoverty, community service domestic volunteers operations of ACTION, Washington, D.C.

Antar Sudan Katara Mberi is author of *Bandages and Bullets—In Praise of the African Revolution* and coauthor of an anthology of poetry, *Speak Easy, Speak Free,* with South African poet Cosmo Pieterse.

Loften Mitchell, playwright and lecturer at State University of New York, Binghamton, is author of *Black Drama, A Land Beyond the River, The Stubborn Old Lady Who Resisted Change, Voices of the Black Theatre,* and other works. He wrote the book for the long-running Broadway musical *Bubbling Brown Sugar.*

George B. Murphy, Jr., a contributing editor of *Freedomways,* has been long associated with the *Afro-American* newspaper chain. He is a friend of the Robeson family.

Jawaharlal Nehru is the late statesman and first prime minister of India.

Pablo Neruda was awarded the coveted Nobel Prize for Literature in 1971. The Chilean poet was universally acknowledged as the greatest poet of the century writing in Spanish and one of the greatest poets of all time. His death followed shortly after the bloody coup in Chile against the democratically elected government of Salvador Allende.

J. H. O'Dell is an associate editor of *Freedomways,* who frequently contributes articles to the magazine. He was associated with Dr. Martin Luther King, Jr., in the Southern Christian Leadership Conference.

William L. Patterson, an internationally known lawyer and American communist, was a lawyer in the famous Scottsboro case, a leader of the Civil Rights Congress, and editor of *We Charge Genocide: The Crime of Government Against the Negro People,* a petition to the United Nations on behalf of Black Americans.

Thelma Dale Perkins, a friend of Paul and Eslanda Robeson, was on the staff of the newspaper *Freedom* published by Robeson.

Paul Robeson, Jr., son of Paul and Eslanda Robeson, is an engineer, translator, and lecturer.

Eugene H. Robinson graduated from Rutgers University in 1969. He is an instructor in "Black History in the Twentieth Century" at Rutgers.

Edward Royce, a New York civil rights activist, lived in the German Democratic Republic during the last years of his life.

Erwin A. Salk is professor of history, Columbia College of Chicago, and author of *A Layman's Guide to Negro History* (1966, 1967).

Harriet Jackson Scarupa is a contributing editor of *Essence* magazine. She has been published in *Ebony, Ms., Glamour,* the *Baltimore Sun,* and other publications.

Anatol Schlosser is an associate professor in the Theatre Department of York University, Downsview, Ontario.

Pete Seeger, the internationally known folk singer and activist, received the 1977 Paul Robeson Award given by Actor's Equity, the performers' union, to that individual whose concern for and service to others are in the tradition of Paul Robeson.

Marie Seton is the author of the book *Paul Robeson*, published in London in 1958.

Hope R. Stevens is a New York lawyer who has been active in the Harlem community for many years.

Sterling Stuckey was one of the founders of the Emergency Relief Committee for Fayette and Haywood Counties, Tennessee, in 1960–61. A former regional director of CORE, he has taught history on the elementary, high school, and university levels.

Slava Tynes is on the staff of Novisti Press Agency, Moscow. This young Russian journalist is the son of an Afro-American agricultural specialist who migrated to the USSR in the 1930s.

Charles Wright, M.D., Chairman of the Board of Trustees of the Afro-American Museum in Detroit, is author of *Robeson: Labor's Forgotten Champion.*

Sarah E. Wright is a poet and novelist whose best known work is *This Child's Gonna Live.*

INDEX